100 Years of Soviet and Russian Military Parades 1917-2017 ★ Volume 2

The Soviet Army On Parade
1946 ★ 1991

To Elsie and Lena, with the wish that they had but once met.

The Soviet Army On Parade 1946-1991
©Canfora Publishing/Grafisk Form&Förlag, 2019
ISBN 978-91-984775-2-8
Print: Printall, Estonia

Canfora Publishing/Grafisk Form&Förlag, 2019
Upplandsgatan 96A
113 44 Stockholm, Sweden
info@canfora.se, www.canfora.se

Contents

Introduction	5
1. Soviet Military Parades in the late 1940s	14
2. Soviet Military Parades in the 1950s	56
3. Soviet Military Parades in the 1960s	110
4. Soviet Military Parades in the 1970s	180
5. Soviet Military Parades in the 1980s	218
6. Soviet Military Parades in 1990	264
7. Red Army "Tekhnika" Displayed on Red Square 1946-1991	282
Bibliography and Glossary	333

> *"The next war will not start with a naval action... nor by aircraft flown by human beings. It might very well start with missiles being dropped on the capital of a country, say Washington."*

General Henry H. Arnold. Commander US Army Air Force, 1945.[*]

---

[*] Henry Arnold (1886-1950) was taught to fly by the Wright Brothers at the turn of the 20th Century, subsequent to which he had a long aviation career with the United States Air Force. At the time of his statement at the end of the Second World War, he was Commander General of the US Army Air Force. His matter-of-fact assessment was borne out only a decade after his death, with the deployment of Soviet nuclear armed missiles on the island of Cuba, bringing most major cities of the United States within range of such weapons. The Soviet placement of missiles on Cuba was however in response to an earlier American and NATO decision to deploy ballistic missiles in Italy and Turkey as part of the Soviet-American "arms race" of the Cold War era.

Introduction

As the Red Army closed on Berlin in the final weeks of the Second World War in Europe, and Allied forces were closing on the remnants of the Third Reich in other regions of Germany, the Soviet Union and the Allies were already making their respective plans for post-victory Europe. With the war in Europe over by early May 1945, the Allied focus immediately turned to concluding the war against Japan. The Soviet Union declared war on Japan exactly three months after the declared end of war in Europe, as Stalin had promised the Allies at the Yalta Conference in February 1945. The Soviet land based invasion of Japanese territory in the Far East and the American dropping of atomic bombs on Hiroshima and Nagasaki brought a rapid end to the war with Japan, and closed the final chapter of World War Two. But with the end of the war in Europe and the Far East, the relationship between the wartime Allies began to rapidly change.

Whereas in the immediate post-war era the Red Army had the decisive advantage in terms of armoured might and conventional firepower, it was the attainment of nuclear supremacy that would drive the "arms race" in the second half of the 20th Century. The Soviet Union was in early 1945 well aware of the American nuclear advantage, and in the closing days of the war in Europe the Red Army took steps to attain German long-range rocket technology to complement the Soviet Union's indigenous and not entirely inconsequential experience in the subject. The Soviet "Katyusha" multiple rocket launchers had been one of the Red Army's great artillery (and indeed psychological) weapons of World War Two. But the late-war German development of the V-2 (A-4) rocket, and the American use of atomic bombs dropped from B-29 bombers in August 1945 led to the inevitable technical combination of these weapon types as the strategic nuclear-armed rocket that rapidly became the ultimate deterrent projected by both sides of the new political divide. Post-war weapon development by the new world superpowers led to a new and globally frightening era with the very real prospect of a nuclear holocaust.

As the war in Europe drew to a close, the Soviet Union was particularly cognisant of what technical and human assets Germany had in the way of rocket technology. As the Red Army closed on Berlin in the spring of 1945, a team of Soviet specialists including the rocket engineer Sergei Pavlovich Korolev was dispatched to Germany on a secret mission which included the capture of the German Peenemunde V-2 rocket facility. This mission would result in a significant number of rocket engineers being captured and taken to the Soviet Union, together with the early stage production facilities and enough parts to build 29 V-2 rockets (also known in the Soviet Union by the original German A-4 designation) from components obtained in Germany. The V-2 would soon be modified in the Soviet Union as the R-1, the first Soviet ballistic rocket. During the Cold War the rocket would ultimately replace the tank as the primary symbol of projected Soviet military might. The Soviet Red Square military parades of the Cold War era would meantime continue the Soviet tradition of demonstrating new military technology on Moscow's central square. In addition to the tanks, armoured cars and artillery of the pre-war era, the post-war mix would include the "tekhnika" or military equipment of the newly emerging Soviet airborne forces, which would be provided with significantly heavier firepower than their adversaries. From 1957 a long heralded new form of weapon also began to appear regularly on Red Square, the strategic ballistic rocket. The Red Square parades of the Cold War era were however rather more sophisticated than a direct show of the latest military strength. Some of the systems displayed on Red Square never actually entered service, and in some cases had been cancelled even before their initial parade appearances, but nevertheless served their deterrent purpose from the cobbles of Red Square. The display of long-range nuclear weapons in the second half of the 20th Century also directly tracked the prevailing political winds. The mass displays of such fearsome weapons in the 1960s were replaced in the mid 1970s by relatively benign displays of primarily defensive or tactical level weapons, mirroring compliance with agreements on reduced weapons deployment following the Soviet Union having by 1970 reached nuclear parity with the United States. With mutual destruction guaranteed, there was no need to display the deterrent that was acknowledged as in place on both sides of the political divide. Nearly two decades later, as the Soviet Union was in its swansong months, long-range offensive capability was unexpectedly reintroduced to Red Square, with the last vehicle paraded through the square on the last ever Soviet era parade held on Red Square on 7th November 1990 being the RT-2 PM (RS-12M) "Topol" (NATO: SS-25 Sickle) intercontinental ballistic missile (ICBM), the first public appearance of such a long-range strategic weapon since 1974. At the time of writing, with the benefit of almost three decades of hindsight, and with superpower relations at their lowest ebb since the 1960s, the appearance of such a weapon system as the finale of the last Soviet era Red Square parade seems particularly prophetic.

In 2018, the Russian Federation, minus the Soviet Union, is again the main perceived threat to Western civilisation according to some politicians and much of the world's mainstream press, particularly in Great Britain, including the once highly regarded broadsheet newspapers. When the Soviet Union was the centre of President Reagan's communist "Evil Empire" all was clear, the anti-Soviet rhetoric was related to a clash between "capitalist" systems led by the United States and "communist" or "socialist" systems led by the Soviet Union with their respective power bases and expansionist ideals. Today, the Russians are themselves a specific form of "capitalist", the "nomenclatura" live in London, New York and Miami, their children attend private schools in Europe and many less wealthy Russians also live and work abroad, seamlessly integrated into other countries and societies. But the Russians still remain the threat to the West in the minds of many who are influenced by what they have read in the mainstream media rather than what they actually know from first hand experience. Many people, particularly in government service, NATO and the Military Industrial Complex (MIC) maintain this position, in part because the primary role of government and any military is to plan for defence and the potential for war, and this is replicated by all governments worldwide, the former Soviet and current Russian

The Lenin Mausoluem on Moscow's Red Square, from which Red Square parades have been reviewed by the Soviet, and now Russian, leadership for more than 100 years. The concrete and polished stone finish building as it stands today was completed in the very early 1930s replacing an earlier wooden structure.

The Eternal Flame burns at the Tomb of the Unknown Soldier in Alexandrovsky Gardens outside the Kremlin walls, commemorating the currently estimated 27 million Soviet Russian souls that lost their lives in World War Two.

government included. But the constant threat of war, or proxy-wars that do not affect the protagonist's domestic population, has also financed the working lives and pension plans of many establishment decision makers. The sea change in the 21st Century is that the majority of educated and well-travelled people in all countries today are able to judge the world based on what they have personally experienced or can now individually research if so disposed. Governments no longer hold the monopoly on the established truth as dissipated to their increasingly disenfranchised electorates. Religion, and in recent history communism and fascism have all been forms of collective information dissemination and thereby control, and today the internet has become the new frontier both for the distribution and dissemination of information and increasing State efforts to control that information flow. In this context the Cold War era was actually a rather benign period of world history, with two primary superpowers competing on the world stage but not ultimately engaging in any direct conflict, conventional or nuclear. Meantime, a third superpower, China, gained economic and military strength almost by stealth as the two primary superpowers and their allies contested their respective ideologies for collective world governance in the second half of the 20th Century. Today, three decades after the end of the original Cold War, the alignment of Russia and China in the second decade of the 21st Century almost directly parallels that which prevailed within a few years of the end of the Second Word War. With the benefit of 21st Century halogen lighting reaching into the shadows, the indistinct elephant in the Cold War debriefing room may yet turn out to be not a bear but rather a dragon.

This volume covers the period of Soviet military parades on Red Square during the Cold War, from 1946 until the last Soviet military parade in November 1990. In retrospect, the period of Cold War superpower dominance and aligned "armed camps" was rather more controlled and stable than today's reality. The fundamental difference between Soviet, and indeed modern Russian mentality as compared with their potential adversaries during the Cold War and in the present time, is however that the Russians, and the citizens of the former Soviet Union, have experience of war on their own territory. Some older people still vividly remember the horrors of World War Two in an occupied country. The majority of former Soviet nationals do remember the inter-ethnic clashes and civil wars in Armenia, Azerbaijan, Chechnya, Dagestan, Georgia, Tajikistan and most recently in Ukraine. The Russians, in the wider sense of the term for what were previously nationals of the former Soviet Union, have experienced war on home territory and the tragic losses of innocent lives that war brings. While living and working in the Russian Federation and several former Soviet states, the author had the privilege of working with highly educated, well-travelled and exceptionally bright people some of whom had lost their immediate families and relatives during these civil wars. The majority of the populations in the countries that today still form NATO have no such benchmark of personal experience, and hence have a more abstract view of conflict. The Russians, and indeed the nationals of what were the former republics of the Soviet Union, know very well what war on home territory means, which reflects in their more reasoned approach to avoiding conflict at all costs. As Russians will point out, they throughout history have generally not started wars, but have excelled at finishing them. The Napoleonic war "started" in Russian terms as Moscow was burning in 1812 and this was repeated almost exactly in World War Two when the Wehrmacht was stopped before Moscow in November 1941 as German advance panzer units were within a few kilometres of the Kremlin. By contrast, the other Cold War superpower, the United States, has since the American Civil War of the mid 19th Century always fought on foreign territory, such that the civil population has never known or endured the reality of war on home soil. That is the critical difference between the Soviet, and now Russian, and American and NATO viewpoint on potential threats of war.

With recent politics having recreated the "Russian threat", Russians have, not unexpectedly, united behind what is perceived as a common threat to their country and nationhood. Real and ever present political grievances in the Russian Federation have been largely shelved at a personal level, and the world is today back where it was in the years immediately before World War One, immediately after the Russian Revolution of 1917, or in mid 1930s Europe, far from what was a new dawn with the potential for genuine world peace as it existed in 1991.

The Russian Federation, indeed the entire former Soviet Union, remains today a family based society. People around the world defend their own family first and foremost, particularly their children. And combat units fight first and foremost for their comrades in arms on whom they rely for their own survival, not the politicians who are happy to construct conflicts in which they themselves would never expect to participate. Somewhat ominously, the majority of Western "leadership" today by contrast have no children, and thereby no stake in the future of their own countries or societies. They are at odds with the majority of their own populations. Today, such a lack of national leadership is a greater threat to humanity than the Soviet Union ever was, but the Russians are again popular as the enemy of choice, as without such distractions many politicians would have to concede the negative reality of their own countries to their legitimate paymasters, the "ordinary" citizens, and take responsibility for their own direct roles in developing that situation.

Only days after the first volume of this work was published, a series of events beginning in Great Britain, linked to on-cue further events in Syria almost led to a direct 21st Century clash between the former Cold War superpowers, and plunged relationships between the Russian Federation and Great Britain in particular to lows not seen even at the height of the original Cold War. Meantime, as European trade with the Russian Federation dropped significantly as blowback from American driven and European backed sanctions placed on the Russian Federation, American exports to the Russian Federation were significantly increased in 2018 compared with the immediate pre-sanction era, while Europe lost a significant former export market as a result of its politician's compliance with American directed sanctions. The Russian Federation meantime continues to export rocket engines to the United States for launching satellites into space and continues to provide essential metallurgy for the American aviation industry. Western countries also remain heavily invested

Red Square was originally built as a market and showground long before the invention of the internal combustion engine, the tank or world revolution. These trophy guns are being displayed during the Russian Civil War that followed the Russian Revolution.

A Soviet era book, "Military Parades on Red Square", one of very few Soviet and Russian original sources on the subject.

in the Russian Federation, in the automobile, banking, energy and service sectors, with significant foreign ownership in Russian enterprises. The Russian Federation has also become a major exporter of wheat, which in the final years of the Soviet Union it was forced to import.

In 2018, the US government is as expected by its population looking after American interests, the Russian government is looking after Russian interests, and European governments with the noble exception of some former Warsaw Pact countries not so much. By 2018, the same Western countries that had invaded the newly emerged Russian State (the RSFSR) immediately after the revolution of 1917 were again pushing for conflict with a country which had since the break-up of the Soviet Union in 1991 normalised relations, and become a viable and reliable trading partner with the West. Meantime, Western countries with astounding unfunded financial debts, energy reliance issues and increasing breakdown of internal law and order are again gathering together against Russia as the new old enemy of choice in the 21st Century. Relations between Russia and China are again strengthening, while other countries such as Iran and Turkey are again influential beyond their economic status in world politics. The historical "Great Game" regarding influence in the Middle East, Central Asia and the Silk Roads connecting these areas with China was in 1991, when the Soviet Union was dissolved, to Western countries a historical study of a seemingly long-past era in world history. By 2018, the next chapter of the "Great Game" was rapidly unfolding. And for the first time in living memory for much of the population of the participating nations, the fear of direct military conflict and potential nuclear Armageddon became a reality which had troubled the thoughts of relatively few people for several decades, even during the majority of the years of what has now become historically the "First" Cold War.

A T-34-85 tank enters Red Square leading the mechanised section of the 9th May 2017 Victory Parade. (Russian Ministry of Defence)

The Cold War

The Cold War, the definition of the rivalry between the Soviet Union and its socialist Warsaw Pact allies on one side and the United States and the "Western" or NATO powers on the other, lasted in its broadest sense from immediately after the end of the Second World War until the collapse of the Soviet Union in 1991. There is no actual agreed and confirmed date denoting the start of the Cold War, though Churchill's "Iron Curtain" speech of March 1946 is sometimes taken as a starting point. Nor is there an exact date or definition as to when the Cold War formally ended, although the collapse of the Soviet Union in 1991 is usually taken as the default date. There are agreed years however when the Cold War might have turned hot within those decades.

The phrase "Cold War" was originally coined in 1945 by George Orwell in his essay "You and the Atom Bomb" published in the London Tribune in October 1945*, only weeks after the dropping of the atomic bombs on Hiroshima and Nagasaki. In his article, Orwell referred to the future partition of the world into "superpower" armed camps with nuclear weapons that would act as a deterrent to any one power using them against a similarly armed superpower. Such a situation would lead to the nuclear-armed superpowers being protected by the principles of what would later become known as "mutually assured destruction" while also allowing them to attack with impunity smaller countries without such protection. Orwell pondered the: *"kind of world-view, the kind of beliefs, and the social structure that would probably prevail in a state which was at once unconquerable and in a permanent state of "cold war" with its neighbours"*. Four years later, Orwell would publish his famous work "1984", the sinister predictions of which were in 1949 considered as a fictional warning, but would in later years become regarded as a highly prescient prediction of the future, today's present.

As to the actual reasons for the Cold War, the inevitable restructuring of wartime alliances and the emergence of the post-war Soviet Union as a world rather than a regional military power were a primary factor. Communism in its broadest sense gained ground in Eastern Europe under Soviet control in the immediate post-war years, and also in Asia Pacific, with China becoming an emerging communist led superpower in 1949, altering the balance of power in that region of the world. It could be argued that the Soviet Union itself emerged in the post-war order as a regional colonial power in Eastern Europe at a time when the former European colonial powers of the 19th Century continued to lose their more widely spread colonies in the second half of the 20th Century. In the case of Great Britain this included the immediate post-war loss of India, and for France the loss of its former colonies in Indo-China. The Soviet Union, as with all national participants, was greatly weakened by World War Two, but had emerged stronger on the world stage than some European colonial powers that had found themselves occupied during the war and were thereby not as politically arrogant as in previous decades. World War Two had devastated Europe, and the emergent superpowers of the post-war era were the United States and the Soviet Union, followed in later years by the rise of China. Today, with the benefit of decades of hindsight, and with the Russian Federation more capitalist and swathes of Europe becoming more communist, or even national-socialist, any viewpoint on the merits of the Cold War might vary considerably depending on the individual concerned, their nationality, age, personal life and travel experience in the big world, and inherent political bias. In essence, the Cold War was due to the mutual suspicions of two post-war rival superpowers, the United States and the Soviet Union, and their respective NATO and Warsaw Pact power blocs. But the Cold War was also a rivalry based on nominal-

---

* "You and the Atom Bomb". George Orwell. London Tribune. 19th October 1945.

ly political concerns, particularly with regard to the expansion of "communism", the definition of which has never been an exact science, with even Marx and Engels having difficulty defining the precise difference between socialism and communism. Irrespective of the motivations, the Cold War was a period of intense superpower rivalry, with protective alliances formed in what was in retrospect a period of relative peace and stability in Western Europe. The Cold War would be played out more directly in the potential front line states of Eastern Europe, and by proxy in Asia Pacific, the Middle East and Africa, a strategic game of chess played on the world stage.

The two superpowers began to formalise their respective power blocs in the immediate post-war years, with NATO being formed in April 1949, and the countries of the Warsaw Pact forming a respective alliance together with the Soviet Union in May 1955. While Europe was at peace, China meantime endured a period of civil war that resulted in a communist government coming to power in 1949. The spread of communism in post war Europe was a concern for the United States and its allies, tied with existing concerns over the future military intent of the Soviet Union. But the rise of communist China in addition to the Soviet Union greatly increased the communist threat from an American perspective, particularly as it began to spread into other countries in the Asia Pacific region. While NATO planned for a potential conflict in Europe, which never materialised, the first major clash between post-war superpowers would involve US and UN sponsored forces in direct combat with a different Red Army from that envisaged in 1945. The location would be Korea, and the army would be the Chinese Red Army.

The Cold War would from the late 1950s be predominated by the nuclear "arms race", with rockets supplementing long-range bombers as the preferred nuclear delivery mechanism of choice for the respective superpowers. While the headlines of the 1950s and 1960s would highlight the flash points in Germany, Hungary, Cuba and Czechoslovakia, it was the battlegrounds of Korea, Vietnam, and latterly Afghanistan where the respective adversaries of the Cold War would clash via proxy forces and the provision of direct military support. The frequent Middle East Wars, and those in Africa were also supported by opposing superpowers, financially, with military aid, and also in some cases with direct military or proxy intervention.

Both superpowers fought impossible and unpopular wars in the later years of the Cold War, the United States misadventure in Vietnam being followed by the Soviet Union repeating the same national experience in Afghanistan. In both cases the countries concerned had in part been dragged into those wars by external circumstances rather than exclusively an internally generated wish to directly intervene. Both wars would prove extremely unpopular with the combat troops and the civilian populations at home, and both would take a significant political toll on their respective governments. Afghanistan was to the Soviet Union of the 1980s essentially what Vietnam had been to the United States of the 1960s and early 1970s. The national outcome of both these wars was that the governments on either side of the political divide became acutely aware that their respective populations had seen enough of war and its consequences for no apparent tangible gain.

The Cold War began to be "won" by the United States and its NATO allies after the introduction of the Strategic Defence Initiative (SDI) under President Ronald Reagan in 1983, a programme better known colloquially as "Star Wars". After 18 years of steady and relatively benign leadership under Leonid Brezhnev the Soviet Union had, after his death, meantime entered a period of slow stagnation and decline, with a succession of short-term elderly premiers, and general economic stagnation. The American ramping up of rhetoric under Reagan threatened to return the superpowers to the competitive levels of the 1960s. But during the 1980s the Soviet Union was involved in the war in Afghanistan and was suffering economic stagnation domestically; and was otherwise engaged. By the mid 1980s it was clear to the Soviet leadership, particularly the up and coming reformer Mikhail Gorbachov, that the Soviet Union could not afford to compete further in what had become a financial and technology race as much as a political or purely military one. The 1980s would be the swansong decade of the Soviet Union, and the attempted coup of 1991 would be the final death-knell for the Soviet State that had survived revolution, civil war, invasion, World War Two and four decades of Cold War. It is a tremendous credit to the fortitude of the Soviet people, Russians and indigenous nationals from the former republics alike, that the countries of the Soviet Union were for the most part able to move to a more capitalist system of market economies and adjust from the often-painful changes involved in a matter of only a few years. After the fall of the Soviet Union, the Russian Federation with the exception of the short war with Georgia in Southern Ossetia in 2008, lived in peace with its external neighbours for two decades while it managed a series of internal conflicts within the southern regions of the country. That would end when political manoeuvring from an increasingly expansionist but internally unstable European Union caused clashes in 2014 that set the relationships between the Russian Federation and the "Western" NATO countries back to Cold War levels, with scenes of devastation in Eastern Ukraine paralleling those of "Operation Barbarossa" in 1941. Having "won" the Cold War, the original NATO and new acquisition EU and NATO countries by default moved the borders of Europe closer to the borders of the former Soviet Union, negating the Eastern Europe "buffer zone" that had existed throughout the Cold War. The European Union in collaboration with NATO then tried to expand into Ukraine. The events that followed will be argued by politicians and historians (the great majority of whom have no direct experience of either Russia or Ukraine) for decades to come, but had the however imperfect democratically elected government of Ukraine not been overthrown with the complicity of external sources, then the events of 2014 would not have occurred, just as they had not occurred in 1991, or 2001 or at any time when the Russian Federation and Ukraine had peacefully co-existed despite the historical tensions since long before the break-up of the Soviet Union in 1991. Since 2014 nearly 10 million people have emigrated from Ukraine as the country continues to collapse economically, of which as many as 4.5 million today live and work in the Russian Federation, suggesting that the pre-2014 order before the overthrow of a legitimate if imperfect government, was for the average Ukrainian citizen somewhat better than the new one.

When the first volume of this book was published, the Cold War was a chapter in history. By the time this second volume was published only a few months later, the Cold War had been relegated to the status of the "First Cold War" and the world had come close to a direct conflict between the

A Russian veteran receives a flower from a young woman during the 9th May 2014 Victory celebration. The sacrifices of previous generations are sincerely acknowledged, and the gestures such as giving flowers are entirely at a personal level.

The 9th May Victory Day parades of the 21st Century continue a 100 year tradition of military parades on Red Square. The modern day parades are however only the formal part of a day of remembrance, and respect for those that participated in or lived through the Great Patriotic War.

United States, Great Britain and France, with the Russian Federation over Syria, with relations declining to a level considered perhaps worse than the earlier Cold War era. Russia and China were again aligning, repeating a situation that had developed a decade after the end of World War Two, and "Old Europe" as it bickered internally, was slowly dying as the economic powerhouse of the east, China, became the new expansionist colonial power with financial, industrial and human capital investments on every continent and the prior hegemony of the United States now less assured. The position of the Russian Federation in 2018 from a politically neutral perspective meantime looks not unlike that of 1812 or immediately after 1917. The current world situation also has remarkable financial and political parallels with the immediate lead up to World War One, and the financial and political difficulties of Europe are at the time of writing not significantly different to those that led to the rise of fascism in Germany and Italy and the road to war in mid 1930s Europe. As in those previous global events, the Russian Bear patiently watches events from its home ground.

The future of the Russian Federation is in 2018 meantime assured not only by the Russian armed forces, but also by those in the general population that would fight to protect the shared common sense of citizenship and belonging, what is usually described as "society".

On 26th June 1945, Marshal of the Soviet Union Georgy Zhukov took the first Soviet Victory Parade on Red Square mounted on a white stallion. A monument to Marshal Zhukov was erected at the entrance to Red Square only in the 21st Century.

While NATO remains belligerent, it should be remembered that NATO was not correspondingly disbanded after the break-up of the Warsaw Pact and the fall of the Soviet Union, the enemies it was formed to defend against having effectively disappeared by 1991. NATO was formed to defend the borders of NATO member countries from the Soviet threat, but until post-Soviet NATO expansion into former Warsaw Pact and former Soviet Bloc countries, NATO at no point ever had to directly defend NATO territory involving a direct clash with invading Soviet troops. Today, there are limited contingents of NATO troops in a non-NATO country directly facing Russian troops on their own border. NATO and the later Warsaw Pact were both formed as defensive alliances, but the former "buffer countries" that separated the two power blocs are now largely absorbed into NATO, also resulting in NATO forces being today located directly on the Russian border. As such the current situation is more dangerous than during the original Cold War, in that "limited contingents" started both World Wars and many since that time, whereas even Korea and Vietnam had demilitarised zones as part of a solution rather than an escalation. The Russian Army is meantime a unified force under a single command, while NATO is a collection of armies with different languages, protocols, politics and military equipment, much of it as old as some Soviet era Russian inventory. Several key NATO countries were overrun and occupied within weeks of the beginning of World War Two and have lived under the protective umbrella of NATO since 1949. If a war was to happen between the post-Soviet "superpowers" it would inevitably involve Europe, and the question is which countries in Europe might be expected to shoulder the likely result of starting a conventional war with a determined and united enemy, real or perceived. And the NATO Cold War standard nuclear option would result in the majority of humanity being obliterated for no sane purpose or reason whatsoever. On reflection, the Cold War was by comparison with the present time perhaps a more benign period in world history.

T-44 tanks on parade after manoeuvres in the Urals Military District in the late 1940s. The lead tank is marked "Znamensky", the surname of a Russian revolutionary leader and also a wartime Hero of the Soviet Union.

The Late 1940s

On the world stage, the second half of the 1940s was a time of post-war recovery, and of constructing post-war allegiances and alliances. As the dust was settling after the 1945 "VE" Victory Parades in Berlin and Moscow and the later "VJ" parades in the Soviet Far East, the United Nations (UN) set about establishing a security organization that in the post-war world might prove less ineffective than the pre-war League of Nations which had proven an abject failure at all levels. On 24th October 1945, the United Nations Security Council was formed, consisting of the five primary "victors" in World War Two - China, France, Great Britain, the Soviet Union and the United States. Other countries would subsequently join, but the five "Permanent Members" of the UN Security Council with their veto authority would remain the principals. Considering the post-war situation as it would soon develop in Europe and the Far East in the years ahead, in which all the members were either directly involved or had strategic interests, the Security Council would throughout the Cold War be compromised by the frequently hostile relations between its core states.

Post-war, the former European colonial powers continued to lose their overseas territories in the same manner as had begun after World War One. India, the jewel in the crown of the British Empire became independent in 1947, while the Dutch and the French would soon lose control over countries in Asia Pacific including Indonesia and Vietnam. China was in the late 1940s fighting a civil war that would result in a communist government coming to power in that country, while the conflicts in Korea and later in Vietnam would become international in terms of political and military backing for the direct adversaries. While the Soviet Union was perceived as the primary threat in the late 1940s, particularly from a European perspective, the greatest area of instability and conflict in the post-war years was in Asia Pacific. The violence that began in Korea starting in the autumn of 1946 would lead to an international war at the end of the decade, involving the very core nations that had formed the United Nations Security Council only a few years prior.

With regard to the Soviet Union, the former British Prime Minister Churchill in March 1946 used the term "Iron Curtain" during a lecture tour of the United States, and that definition of Soviet bloc relations with what became defined as "The West" would become embedded in the Cold War lexicon. The United States would in May 1946 introduce the concept of the Marshall Plan, an American financed plan to promote economic recovery in devastated Europe, with the predicted main political benefit being that of stalling communist expansion. By the end of the decade the first political clashes had begun between the former Allied occupying powers in Germany, culminating in the Berlin Blockade. But the conflicts in Europe during the late 1940s were largely political rather than military. It was the beginning of a

Cold War of manoeuvring with a military aspect, rather than a hot war with direct military involvement. Compared with much of the world in the late 1940s, the situation in Europe was by comparison relatively benign.

One of the post-scripts of the Second World War was the ongoing resettlement of Jewish people within Europe, and from Europe towards a new homeland in the Middle East. The movement was not universally met with enthusiasm, not least by Great Britain, which had interests to protect in Palestine. From 1946, British police and military forces were involved in stemming the flow of what would today be called refugees or asylum seekers across the Mediterranean, travelling east in the 1940s rather than west as today. As Jewish people from various European countries gained numbers in Palestine looking to establish their own state, fighting inevitably broke out with the British authorities. The British government launched "Operation Agatha" in Palestine against what was referred to as "militant Jews", or "Zionist groups", involved in terrorism against British authorities. The fighting would ultimately result in the establishment of the new State of Israel in 1948, with the Israeli armed forces also subsequently becoming a formidable military power.

In the Soviet Union, the adjustment to a civilian economy and post-war rebuilding was protracted, as literally millions of troops returned to their home country decimated by war, slowly taking up civil employment and replacing those who had gone to war never to return. The early post-war years were blighted in the Soviet Union by a famine in 1946-47, again largely suffered by Ukraine and southern regions of the Soviet Union as in the previous decade. But in the 1940s the famine was the result of fields having not been worked during occupation, and a lack of serviceable machinery and manpower due to the war rather than a situation such as in the 1930s, that has been argued by some as having been deliberately engineered by the Soviet State.

1946

With the war in Europe over by the early summer of 1945, and the war against Japan over by the early autumn, the world returned to peace in the final months of 1945, and the slow process of rebuilding lives, families and infrastructure began across the world. There was no instant return to normality, with shortages of foodstuffs and raw materials even in the victorious Allied countries. In Europe, American, British and French troops took up positions in their respective zones of Germany, and the Red Army entrenched in its positions gained in the final weeks of the war. Politics inevitably turned to the post-war restructuring of Europe and the perceived threat that the Soviet Union and the powerful tank forces of the Red Army might cause to Western Europe. The change of mood might be best summed up in the aforementioned speech made by the former British wartime Prime Minister Winston Churchill, who now as the leader of the opposition made his famous "Iron Curtain" speech on 5th March 1946 while visiting Westminster College in Fulton, Missouri together with the American President Harry S. Truman. Reflecting on concern over the potential Soviet expansion in Europe in the immediate post-war era, Churchill summarised the cooling relations with the Soviet Union with the statement that: *"From Stettin in the Baltic to Trieste in the Adriatic, an iron curtain has descended across the continent."* The speech by Churchill is considered as one of the opening volleys announcing the beginning of the Cold War, and the term "Iron Curtain" became symbolic of the approaching Cold War era. Other parts of his speech are however less frequently quoted. Churchill also advised that: *"We understand the Russian need to be secure on her western frontiers by the removal of all possibility of German aggression."* and indicatively that: *"From what I have seen of our Russian friends and allies during the war, I am convinced that there is nothing they admire so much as strength, and there is nothing for which they have less respect than weakness, especially military weakness."* That perceptive statement holds as true today as much as it did in 1946, but it was Churchill's "Iron Curtain" statement that remained in the collective memory during the Cold War. Stalin responded the following week, advising the Soviet people that Churchill's position was that of: *"A firebrand of war."*

On 5th April 1946, exactly one month after Churchill's famous "Iron Curtain" speech, the Soviet Union agreed to remove Red Army (since February, Soviet Army) units from occupied Iranian territory (known as Iranian Azerbaijan - in the north west of Iran) in compliance with Resolution №1 of the newly formed UN Security Council. The Allies (specifically the Red Army, working together with Indian and other British Commonwealth troops) had effectively occupied Iran in the autumn of 1941, the aim of "Operation Countenance" having been to secure British controlled Iranian oilfields in the west of the country and also ensure "The Persian Corridor" as an overland conduit for Lend-Lease supplies to the Soviet Union for the duration of the war. The last Soviet Army units left Iran on 9th May 1946, exactly one year after Victory in Europe, and six months later than scheduled. Two weeks later, and also in accordance with a UN Security Council resolution, British and French forces departed from Lebanon and Syria.

A few weeks later, on 1st June 1946, Ho Chi Minh, the President and Prime Minister of the newly formed Democratic Republic of Vietnam (North Vietnam), visited Paris in an attempt to persuade Vietnam's French colonial overlords to give the country full independence. The meetings were unsuccessful, and the respective parties moved down a path that would lead to France becoming involved in a major war in Vietnam, which would in turn later embroil the United States in its defining military engagement of the second half of the 20th Century.

While events unfolded in the Middle East and Asia Pacific that would greatly affect some of the former wartime Allies in those regions, and

T-34-85 tanks and SU-76M self-propelled guns assemble for a parade rehearsal, Moscow Military District (MVO), 1946.

the term "Iron Curtain" was becoming commonplace in Europe, the Soviet Union in 1946 had its own difficulties to contend with. A war that had been fought on Soviet territory and had taken the lives of an estimated 27 million souls was not something from which there would or could be an instant recovery under any political system, and the Soviet Union was in 1946 largely preoccupied with internal matters related to post-war recovery and restructuring. The political situation in Ukraine was from a Soviet perspective particularly problematic during the immediate post-war years, and this was exacerbated by the famine of 1946-47. The war and consequent lack of farming equipment and manual labour caused further suffering when a severe drought in the spring and summer of 1946 led to harvest failures, and a return of the famine experienced in the "Golodomor" years of the 1930s. The famine would reach its height in the spring and summer of 1947. As with the famine of the 1930s, the brunt of the crisis was endured by the grain growing regions of Ukraine - where Nikita Khrushchev was head of the CP(b)U - the Communist Party (Bolshevik) of Ukraine. As with the earlier famine, the area affected was wider than Ukraine, including Moldova and regions of southern Russia including Kursk, Orel and Voronezh that had suffered major fighting during the war. The Soviet Union was able to distribute emergency grain supplies to most areas, but though Khrushchev advised Stalin of the issue, Stalin would not give the problem - that affected western Ukraine disproportionally - any official recognition or remedy. While the famine was endured in Ukraine, Moldova and southern Russia, the Soviet State continued to export reserve grain to Soviet occupied Germany, and also to Czechoslovakia, Hungary and Poland. The immediate post-war famine in the Soviet Union resulted in the death of another 1 to 1.5 million souls.

During the years of wartime German occupation, a small percentage of the Ukrainian population had actively supported Axis forces while under occupation, and had also served with some German SS legions against the Red Army. The Ukrainian Insurgent Army (UPA), the military wing of the Organization of Ukrainian Nationalists (OUN) formed of Bandera's ultra-nation-

SU-76M self-propelled guns of the Riga Garrison parade past a temporary parade review stand, Riga, Latvia, 1st May 1946. Photographer - Fedoseev (TsGAFF)

alists, still had approximately 90,000 men under arms as the war ended in Europe, largely concentrated in the west of Ukraine that had until 1939 been mostly Polish territory. The Soviet Union set about suppressing these forces as soon as hostilities in Europe were over, with significant numbers of NKVD and Red Army troops involved in the process. The suppression of these Ukrainian OUN forces was not without significant casualties, with local officials and Soviet forces being killed on a regular basis by what only months earlier would have been described as partisans. In order to gain control, the Soviet State deployed the Soviet Army, carried out a number of executions of specific individuals, and organised mass deportations in the immediate post-war years, all of which coincided with the aforementioned major famine in the same region. The current difficulties in Russian-Ukrainian relationships can be traced back via centuries of troubled history, and constantly changing borders and allegiances in the region, and the situation which developed in 2014 was yet another chapter in that ever-evolving relationship.

The Soviet Union from 1946 politically consolidated its position in regions of western Ukraine, which led to tensions with local inhabitants due to a combination of past wartime allegiances and much of the territory concerned having been ceded from Poland. There were political repressions in Western Ukraine from 1945 until Stalin's death in 1953, the origins of which were partially blamed on the hoarding of foodstuffs in a return to the "Kulak" collectivisation days of post-revolutionary Russia, and partly related to the aforementioned cooperation of a small percentage of Ukrainians with occupying Axis forces during World War Two. The political repressions carried out in the peak years of 1946-49 included mass arrests and the deportation into exile of up to 500,000 Soviet nationals from Western Ukraine. These underlying tensions would continue for years, and again erupt into war two decades after the dissolution of the Soviet Union.

The first months of 1946 witnessed the gradual consolidation of what would later become defined as "Eastern Europe" and later the Warsaw Pact under Soviet control. The year began with

T-34-85 tanks during final parade practice, Khodynskoye Pole (Khodynka Field), Moscow, 1946.

the establishment of the Hungarian Republic on 2nd February, with a communist president, and other countries in Eastern Europe would follow in the months ahead. Churchill, who had been personally involved in three major wars, had perhaps a more pragmatic view of the Soviet Union and its armed forces than many European politicians in the immediate post-war years. He clearly considered Soviet expansionism as a real concern in post-war Europe. But he also knew that the Soviet position of military strength was an inevitable factor in negotiations, and that a direct clash with Soviet military forces would bring little if any benefit for a war weary Europe. Despite the potential for a flash point and war, the sabre-rattling was thereby always kept at a politically safe level in Europe.

The Soviet Union had suffered huge losses during the war, and the difficult conditions encountered in the immediate post-war era were exacerbated by the lack of male population. One consequence of this ongoing austerity was that the Soviet Union did not witness the "baby boom" of population growth that occurred in much of Europe and the United States in the immediate post-war years, and the significant imbalance between the male and female population in the Soviet Union would last for decades.

While the Soviet Union dealt with its internal issues in 1946 in typical Soviet style, events were unfolding far from the public gaze which would have a profound effect on the forthcoming Cold War "arms race" between the de-facto post-war superpowers. One of the major events of 1946 from a future Cold War perspective was the Soviet relocation of captured V-2 rocket production facilities, component and German rocket engineers captured at the end of the war from the Soviet occupied sector of Germany where they had been located back to the Soviet Union. In the closing days of the war in Europe, the United States had inherited the chief German rocket engineer Wernher von Braun and more than 100 of his

SU-100 self-propelled guns during parade practice, Moscow Military District (MVO), 1946. From 1st June 1945, a stowage box for crew personal effects was added to new production SU-100s built at UZTM. The early design proved flimsy, and was replaced by a redesigned box, which became standard fitment from November 1945. How many SU-100s were fitted with the early box is not known.

scientific team, who had surrendered to American forces in the last days of World War Two, together with enough components to produce eighty V-2 rockets, which would jump-start the postwar American rocket programme. The Red Army had meantime captured the original Peenemunde assembly facilities, together with the rocket designer Helmut Gröttrup and 250 of his engineers. From 1946 these rocket engineers were gradually relocated to the Soviet Union to work within the NII-88 institute, indirectly supervised by Sergei Korolov who had been sent on the special mission to Germany in 1945 as the Red Army closed on Berlin, with the specific purpose of capturing German rocket technology for use in the immediate post-war era.

The Soviet Union would ultimately assemble a number of V-2 rockets from German sourced components, which were test launched at the Kapustin Yar test range near Stalingrad, and would be used to develop the first Soviet ballistic rocket, the R-1. Authorization to develop the R-1 was given in accordance with a Resolution of the Central Committee of the Communist Party and Council of Ministers (TsK VKP (b) i SM SSSR) №1017-419ss dated 13th May 1946. The "FAU-2" or V-2 (A-4) was reverse engineered by Korolev and his team at the NII-88 rocket design institute, the original Soviet R-1 rocket being virtually a direct copy of the German original. The first Soviet rocket study unit was also formally established in June 1946, by re-designating the 92nd Guards Mortar Regiment at Bad Berka (Nordhausen) in the Soviet sector of Germany as the 22nd Brigade for Special Use of the Reserve of the Supreme High Command. The Soviet Union and the United States were now well established in their postwar "rocket race", with both countries using the wartime German V-2 rocket and the captive German engineers that had designed it as the basis for their respective rocket development programs.

While rocket developments were undertak-

T-34-85 tank crews take a minute for the camera during parade practice, Moscow Military District (MVO), 1946. Note the relatively rare "cruciform" gun mantlet.

en in utmost secrecy, the Soviet Union would at a more mundane level in the immediate post-war years begin to re-orientate a large percentage of its wartime production back to civilian output. In a small concession to the overall austerity measures of the immediate post-war era, Stalin in 1946 authorised the production of two new civilian cars, the GAZ M-20 "Pobeda" (Victory), to be built at GAZ in Gorky, and the "Moskvich" (the Muscovite) to be built in Moscow. Small numbers would be made, which could theoretically be sold to individuals. The hand built ZiS-110 limousine was meantime being built for the Soviet hierarchy. Production had started in late 1945, with 71 vehicles being built in 1946, with the convertible ZiS-110B later becoming a standard vehicle used during Red Square parades.*

At an administrative level, Stalin authorised the renaming of People's Commissariats (NKs) as Ministries, while the name of the Red Army was changed on 25th February 1946 to the Soviet Army. This apparent subtlety was done in order to emphasise the inclusiveness of the Soviet Union (and in particular its republics), and as a means of ensuring that the role of the Soviet armed forces was clear in some of said post war republics that might view the Soviet Union from a more independent perspective subsequent to the end of

T-34-85 tanks at halt during parade practice, Moscow Military District (MVO), 1946. These tanks have the enlarged commander's cupola with single piece hatch. The SU-76M self-propelled guns in the background are fitted with their weather protection tarpaulins.

A T-34-85 tank and its enthusiastic crew at a Soviet garrison in Germany, August 1946. The tank is enscribed "Pobeditel Berlina" (Victor of Berlin). Photographer - I. Kolly. (RGAKFD)

* The historic meeting of parade commanders on horseback continued on Red Square until 1953. The parade debut of the ZiS-110B was at a parade held in Vladivostok in 1950. The lesser status GAZ-M-20 "Pobeda" was used in some regional parades, the first being in Petrozavodsk in 1948.

hostilities. Red Army soldiers returning from the war in Europe to their various republics had seen many different countries, including Germany, and were thereby now aware of some of the creature comforts available in those Western European countries. Any disgruntlement at an organised level in the republics thereby needed to be curtailed by all means, subtle or otherwise. "The Day of the Red Army and Fleet", established as an annual professional holiday in 1922, was in 1946 also renamed as the "Day of the Soviet Army and Navy", and has since, albeit in modified form been celebrated annually on 23rd February through to the present day.

A T-34-85 and its wartime journey being dedicated at a Soviet base in Germany, August 1946.
Photographer - I. Kolly. (RGAKFD)

The same T-34-85 tank as above. The tactical marking 321 is overwritten by the tank's wartime journey through Ukraine to Berlin and finally Prague, a total journey of 3.572km.
Photographer - I. Kolly. (RGAKFD)

1st May 1946

With the Red Army having been re-designated as the Soviet Army in February 1946, a definition that would remain in place until the dissolution of the Soviet Union in December 1991, the first Soviet Army military parade was duly held on Red Square on 1st May 1946. Stalin presided over the parade as People's Commissar for the Armed Forces, a position he held personally from 15th March 1946 until 3rd March 1947. The parade was attended by Marshal of the Soviet Union Georgy Zhukov, who after taking the parade from horseback then stood on the review stand of the Lenin Mausoleum together with Stalin and other members of the Party and the armed forces. It would be Marshal Zhukov's last such public appearance during Stalin's reign before being moved to a new regional position. With the obvious popularity of Zhukov and the Soviet armed forces now perhaps considered an unnecessary threat within the leadership of the post-war Soviet Union, Stalin relieved Zhukov from his post the following month and continued to assume personal control of the armed forces. Zhukov was given a regional posting such that he might fade from view, but even Stalin would not risk any other action, as Stalin's power was not as absolute in the post-war 1940s as before and during the terror years of 1936-38.

The 1946 May Day parade was commanded by the MVO commander Colonel - General P. A. Artemev.* The marching elements included participants from the "M.V. Frunze" Military Academy, VAMM, the VVS (Soviet Air Force) Academy, the Tula "Suvorov" Academy and units representing all of the Soviet armed forces.

The 1st May parade included all the typical trappings of such parades, but was unusual in starting with massed columns of cavalry led by three military commanders mounted on white horses, followed by revolutionary era "tachanki" machine gun carts pulled by teams of four white horses and mounting twin 7.62mm M-1910 "Maxim" machine guns, with all the troops in historic rather

ISU-152 self-propelled assault howitzers during parade training, MVO, 1946.

* The rank General-Polkovnik (General-Colonel) is usually translated in English as Colonel-General.

than modern uniforms. The parade line up generally resembled that of May and November 1945, with Soviet wartime built GAZ-67 light vehicles leading columns of trucks, followed by towed artillery, self-propelled guns and tanks.

The famous wartime "Katyusha" multiple rocket launcher (MRS) systems were represented, with there being as in November 1945 large numbers of BM-8-48, BM-13N and BM-31 multiple rocket launchers all mounted on Lend-Lease supplied Studebaker US6 chassis, and more Studebaker trucks with seated infantry. The BM-8-48 was a late wartime production model of the original BM-8 MRS. Soviet built Ya-12 tracked tractors towed 122mm M-1931/37 and 152mm M-1937 "Corps Duplex" artillery pieces and the always impressive 203mm B-4 tracked howitzer. There were GAZ-MM trucks, followed by heavier three tonne payload ZiS-5V trucks, still with their distinctive wartime era production wooden cabs, transporting infantry and 12.7mm DShK anti-aircraft machine guns. ZiS-5V trucks were also displayed in airborne forces markings with sixteen "desantniki" VDV (airborne forces) paratroopers in the rear cargo areas as the Soviet airborne forces came of age in the immediate post-war era.

Tank forces were in May 1946 represented by the 4th Guards Kantemirovskaya Tank Division displaying sixteen IS-3 heavy tanks, with motorised rifle troops being represented by the 2nd Guards Tamanskaya Motor-Rifle Division; with the respective divisions continuing to provide the majority of armoured vehicles displayed on Red Square to the present day. The first tank contingent on 1st May 1946 consisted of columns of T-34-85 medium tanks of the 2nd Guards Tamanskaya Motorised Rifle Division. Various military vehicles followed, including the aforementioned GAZ and ZiS vehicles. Pre-War ZiS-12 trucks with the distinctive lowered rear cargo area were displayed mounting the 25mm M-1940 (94KM) anti-aircraft gun system, joined by standard wartime ZiS-5V trucks towing 85mm M-1939 anti-aircraft guns, and Ya-12 tractors towing 122mm M-1931/37 (A-19), 152mm M-1937 (ML-20) and 203mm B-4 heavy artillery pieces. Lend-Lease Allis-Chalmers HD-10W tracked tractors towed 203mm B-4 tracked howitzers and other

IS-3 tanks cross Manezhnaya Square before entering Red Square, 1st May 1946. The photograph was taken from the then current American Embassy, which had a grandstand view of early post-war parades. Note the T-34T armoured recovery vehicle.
Tank Museum TM 2948/B1

heavy artillery pieces across the square. The same American origin HD-10W tractors also towed the even larger 210mm M-1939 (Br-17) and 305mm M-1939 (Br-18) artillery pieces of Škoda origin broken down into gun carriage and barrel sections.

The main tank contingent also consisted of columns of the now world famous T-34-85 tank that had served the Red Army from late 1943 through to the end of the Second World War. Before the outbreak of war the Soviet Union had built a total of only 1,225 T-34 tanks. After the inevitable chaos of plant evacuation to Siberia, the production output of tanks and self-propelled guns (SAUs) on tank chassis during the war had risen exponentially, with 24,000 tanks and SAUs manufactured in 1943, rising to approximately 30,000 units built during the last twelve months of the war.

Red Square was in May 1946 also traversed by massed columns of SU-76M self-propelled guns; the most numerically significant Soviet wartime AFV in production terms after the T-34 medium tank, joined later in the parade by the heavy ISU-152 self-propelled close support weapon. The SU-76Ms were followed by the highlight of the military contingent of the 1st May 1946 parade, namely the Red Square public debut of the IS-3 heavy tanks of the 4th Guards Kantemirovskaya Tank Division. The IS-2 heavy tank had made its public debut in combat in Berlin before it was seen for the first time on Red Square on 1st May 1945, and the IS-3 had in turn also had its public debut at the Allied Victory Parade in Berlin in September 1945 before being seen in Moscow. By May 1946 the IS-3 heavy tank had been in service for almost a year, the first production batch having been sent to Germany to participate in the Allied Victory Parade in Berlin in September 1945. The lead tank and twenty IS-3s of the now famous 4th Guards Kantemirovskaya Tank Division paraded in May 1946 are believed to be the same tanks displayed in Berlin in September 1945.

Several new military transport vehicles were introduced into Soviet Army service and also appeared on Red Square immediately post-war, including the 4x2 ZiS-150. Some Soviet sources including archive records indicate that the new ZiS-150 was demonstrated for the first time on 1st May 1946, including standard cargo vehicles and versions mounting the BM-13 "Katyusha" and BM-31 MRS. The first pre-series production

IS-3 tanks during their Red Square parade debut on 1st May 1946. The IS-3 was by 1946 a well-known design, having had its public debut the previous September during the Allied Victory Parade in Berlin.

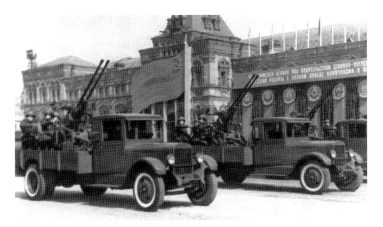

The pre-war ZiS-12 was still displayed in the immediate post-war Red Square parades, here mounting the 25mm M-1940 (94KM) anti-aircraft system. Photographer - Dorensky (TsGAFF)

Wartime production ZiS-5V trucks with infantry and towing 85mm M-1939 anti-aircraft guns, Red Square, 1st May 1946. Photographer - Kinelovsky

Establishment Lot was however completed at ZiS only on 30th October 1947, suggesting the earliest parade debut of any version could have been not earlier than November of that year. The ZiS-150 had been developed towards the end of the war, but its introduction had been delayed so as not to disrupt the flow of other wartime production. The ZiS-150 would appear from the limited records available to have been regularly paraded slightly later, in the period 1947-50, with the standard version in VDV markings first shown in 1948. Some sources claim that the first Soviet jet fighter designs were also flown over Red Square in May 1946. There was however a separate air display in 1946, which would repeat annually, described as "Dien Vozhdushnogo Flota SSSR" (Day of the Soviet Air Force) or as "Dien Aviatsiya" (Aviation Day) held at Tushino airfield in northwest Moscow on 18th August 1946. The newly developed Mikoyan-Gurevich MiG-9 and Yakovlev YaK-15 jet fighters were displayed during this closed air show, both having made their first test flights on 24th April 1946.

Lend-Lease tractors such as these Allis-Chalmers HD-10Ws were used to tow Soviet heavy artillery pieces including the 152mm Br-2, 203mm B-4 and 280mm Br-5 tracked heavy artillery systems across Red Square.

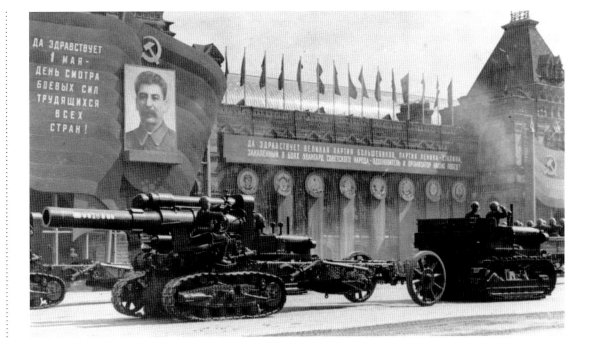

8th September 1946 - Tankman's Day

In 1946, yet another military parade was instigated to add to the May and November parades, celebrating a new national professional holiday - "Dien Tankista" (Tankman's Day), a national day for tank forces, designers, manufacturing plants and all those professions and plants associated with armoured warfare. The new professional holiday was decreed by Order of the Presidium of the Verkhny Soviet (the Upper Council) of the USSR on 11th July 1946, signed by N. Shvernik and enacted in accordance with Order №27 of the Soviet Defence Ministry, duly signed by the Deputy Minister of the Soviet Armed Forces, General Bulganin. The new holiday was to be celebrated on the second Sunday of September in 1946, and on the same Sunday annually thereafter in the capital cities of all republics of the Soviet Union. Furthermore, the day would involve official celebrations in the Soviet cities of Chelyabinsk, Gorky, Khabarovsk, Kharkov, Leningrad, Nizhny Tagil, Omsk, Stalingrad and Sverdlovsk - and for good measure Vladivostok in the Soviet Far East. The holiday has remained on the calendar to the present day, held by tradition on the second Sunday of September, albeit celebrated at a local unit level rather than with parades on Red Square.

The choice of date for "Dien Tankista" was not incidental. It was the date in 1944 on which armoured spearheads of the 3rd Ukrainian Front had entered Bulgaria and units of the 1st and 4th Ukrainian Fronts had crashed across the border of what is modern day Slovakia and engaged in combat with the German and Axis invaders of 1941 on their "home" territory. The date thereby in part pays homage to the Red Army tank forces direct involvement in the beginning of the end of the Third Reich on former German and Axis forces territory.

In accordance with Ministry of Defence Order №43, "Dien Tankista" was celebrated in Moscow on 8th September 1946 with a parade held on Red Square led by the 4th Guards Kantemirovskaya Tank Division. Locations other than Red Square were originally considered for the parade, including the Kantemirovskaya Tank Division base at Naro-Fominsk, and the Tushino Airfield in northwest Moscow, but the final decision was to hold the parade in central Moscow for full public consumption.

Columns of ZSU-37 self-propelled anti-aircraft guns on Gorky Street await parade start-up instructions. The small Establishment Lot of ZSU-37s built for evaluation was demonstrated on Red Square only in 1946.

The first ever "Tankman's Day" military parade, as held on Red Square in Moscow in September 1946 was distinct from May and November parades in that it was a late afternoon parade. Moreover, the armoured contingent of the parade was assembled from the early morning and left parked up on Gorky Street (today Tverskaya) during the day allowing the general public to inspect the parked "tekhnika" awaiting the parade and converse with the tank crews. The actual parade on Red Square started at 17:00 in the late afternoon rather than the usual parade start time of 10:00 in the morning. Stalin personally presided over the 1946 "Tankman's Day" parade, which was on a huge scale, with 600 individual pieces of military "tekhnika" on display.

The late afternoon parade began with M-72 motorcycle combinations, and included Lend-Lease M3A1 "White" scout cars, T-34-85 medium tanks, SU-76M, SU-100 and ISU-152 self-propelled guns and as a parade finale, forty IS-3 heavy tanks, filing in mixed and particularly varied columns past the Lenin Mausoleum where Stalin stood in silence together with the party nomenclature, observing the display before him.

Also in contrast with standard Red Square parades, the tanks and vehicles were in combat drab paint rather than parade markings. The M-72

IS-3 heavy tanks move down Gorky Street towards Red Square for the Tankman's Parade, September 1946. (RGAKFD)

motorcycle columns that began the parade were immediately followed by T-34-85s (a mix of production types including the post-war Plant №183 split-turret ventilator production type), and the aforementioned Lend-Lease M3A1 "White" scout cars directly followed by SU-76M, SU-100 and ISU-152 self-propelled guns. There were also some unusual vehicles on display, such as the limited production ZSU-37 anti-aircraft gun system, which was at the time being considered for general service.

There were ZiS-5V trucks each with a 16-man infantry section on bench seats, and more ZiS-5Vs mounting tandem 25mm M-1940 (94KM) anti-aircraft guns in the rear cargo bed. ISU-152 self-propelled guns trundled past, the wartime "Zveroboi" (animal killer) so-named as during the war it had hunted "cats" such as Panthers and Tigers. Lend-Lease Studebaker US6 trucks towed 85mm M-1939 anti-aircraft guns followed by more columns of M3A1 "White" scout cars. ZiS-5Vs towed 122mm M-1938 (M-30) howitzers, followed by BM-13N "Katyusha" multiple rocket launchers also mounted on Studebaker US6 chassis.

SU-76M self-propelled guns then entered the square, followed by another regiment of post-war production T-34-85s (with split turret vent common to Plant №183 tanks) and then a regiment of SU-100s. A regiment of IS-3 heavy tanks, at the time still causing great consternation among the Soviet Union's former allies, culminated the parade, manoeuvring across Red Square in columns of three. The majority of other tanks and armoured vehicles passed the Lenin Mausoleum in single columns or columns of two, with much wider spacing between vehicles compared with typical parades, such that the parade was particularly long even by standards of some of the larger Soviet parades.

The 8th September parade was also unusual in that the tank types displayed were repeated at different stages of the parade, The M-72 motorcycle combinations which began the parade were later paraded followed by Lend-Lease M3A1 "White" scout cars, ZiS-5V trucks with infantry and ZiS-5V trucks mounting 25mm M-1940 (94KM) anti-aircraft guns. Columns of T-34-85 medium tanks and ISU-152 self-propelled howitzers followed, then it was back to more wheeled vehicles

A post-war production T-34-85 crosses Red Square, on Tankman's Day, 8th September 1946. Note the up-armoured turret, split turret ventilators and post-war tow cable mounting.
Photographer - Baranov

in the form of Lend-Lease Studebaker US6 trucks towing 85mm M-1939 anti-aircraft guns, more M3A1 "White" scout cars, ZiS-5V trucks towing 122mm M-1938 (M-30) howitzers and Studebaker US6 mounted BM-13N "Katyusha" and other calibre multiple rocket launchers. The new tracked ZSU-37 self-propelled anti-aircraft gun demonstrated at the parade represented almost all the vehicles at the time manufactured, with the anti-aircraft vehicles being followed by the SU-76 and then more columns (a third regiment) of T-34-85s. The final columns of T-34-85 tanks again featured the split turret ventilators specific to Plant №183. SU-100s and IS-3 heavy tanks then crossed Red Square, the latter in columns three tanks wide.

The inaugural "Tankman's Day" was the largest military parade ever staged on Red Square, larger even than the Victory Parade the previous year, and was accompanied by a large-scale flypast. The Soviet Union was still years away from developing its first nuclear bomb, and as such the ongoing displays of armoured might on Red Square were the default show of the Soviet Union's main weapon in its military arsenal - massed tank forces - to counter the American possession of nuclear weapons. "Tankman's Day" remains a professional holiday in the present day; however the huge public Gorky Street display and Red Square parade of September 1946 was never repeated in Moscow.

In the same month that the Soviet Union celebrated its inaugural ceremonial "Tankman's Day" parade on Moscow's Red Square, violence erupted on the other side of the world in what would become the first major test of post-war superpower military relationships. The post-war re-alignment of the Allied powers behind the United States and the Soviet Union respectively was a known quantity, but a new superpower began to emerge from the ruins of World War Two. The violence in September 1946 developed within the American controlled zone of occupied Korea, and was ostensibly due to staple food (i.e. rice) shortages and consequent rocketing prices. The violence would escalate over the months and years to come, leading to a major war at the end of the decade, with the direct participation of the new wild-card post-colonial and World War Two "superpower". This new military force on the world stage, which was at the end of the decade emerging from its own civil war that would introduce a brand of communism similar to that heralded by the Russia Revolution of 1917, was China.

IS-3 heavy tanks pass the hotel "Moskva" on Manezhnaya Square moving towards Red Square, 1st May 1946. (RGAKFD)

The tracked ZSU-37 was developed to provide air defence support for armoured units, but was not ultimately accepted for service, its only public viewing being on Red Square during 1946.

7th November 1946 – 29th Anniversary of the Great October Socialist Revolution

The 7th November 1946 parade was taken by Marshal of the Soviet Union Leonid A. Govorov, with the armoured elements of the parade being per tradition provided by tanks of the Kantemirovskaya Guards Tank Division and the Tamanskaya Motor-Rifle Division. During the parade, medium tanks were represented by the T-34-85, and heavy tanks were represented by the IS-3. Also present during the parade was the wartime T-34 №0460, an early production and widely travelled tank named "Kantemirovets" which had ended the war in Prague. The tank may have appeared at least twice on Red Square, in 1945 and 1946, before being subsequently mounted on a plinth as a memorial outside the "Dom Offitserov" - the Officers Club - at the Kantemirovskaya Tank Division headquarters located at Naro-Fominsk.

A large variety of artillery, infantry support weapons, self-propelled guns, and heavy mortars were displayed during the parade. The SU-76Ms paraded through Red Square were indigenous to the Tamanskaya Motor Rifle Division, with ISU-152 heavy self-propelled howitzers of the Kantemirovskaya Tank Division also being displayed, together with various calibres of "Katyusha" rocket

IS-3 heavy tanks cross Red Square, 7th November 1946. The triangulated welded glacis gave the tank its "Schuka" (Pike) nickname. The wartime practice of bolting spare track links onto the glacis for additional armour protection persisted with the IS-3.

launcher mounted on their Lend-Lease Studebaker US6 chassis. The 7th November parade was again accompanied by a flypast.

One of the more novel items of military equipment again displayed in November 1946 was the newly developed ZSU-37 self-propelled anti-aircraft gun mounting, based on the same chassis as the later SU-76M assault gun. The system which had been demonstrated on Red Square "Tankman's Day" on 8th September, had been developed to provide mobile all-terrain air defence support to armoured units, which had been an accepted failing during World War Two. Only a small batch of ZSU-37s was built for evaluation trials purposes, and the ZSU-37 did not subsequently enter series production, so the ZSU-37 was one of those weapon types that would only ever be seen during rare cameo appearances on Moscow's Red Square.

A flypast, which was to have included the new prototype Lavochkin "Izdeliye-150" jet fighter, unofficially designated La-13, was cancelled due to bad weather.

This ISU-152 heavy assault howitzer crossing Red Square is fitted with a 12.7mm DShKM anti-aircraft gun. The ISU-152 was armed with the 152mm ML-20S version of the towed 152mm M-1937 (ML-20) gun-howitzer that was concurrently towed through Red Square in the early post-war years.

Ya-12 tracked artillery tractors towing 122mm M-1931/37 (A-19) "Corps Duplex" heavy guns across Red Square, 7th November 1946.

Abroad meanwhile, Soviet backed communists began to assume greater control in some countries in Soviet dominated Eastern Europe, becoming powerful in coalition governments in Bulgaria and Romania, while there was also a purge of Hungarian politicians in December 1946, leading to a more communist orientated government. The Soviet grip on Eastern Europe was beginning to tighten and would tighten further in the following year. The lynchpin of the Allies in Europe, Great Britain, would in 1947 meantime be distracted by both the loss of India as a colony and by the situation in Palestine, where terrorist acts against British police and military continued unabated.

The emerging post-war Soviet VDV airborne forces began to be paraded in mechanised form from 1946. These ZiS-5V trucks with "desantniki" are being paraded in November 1946.

ZSU-37 self-propelled air defence systems crossing Manezhnaya Square, 7th November 1946.

ZSU-37 self-propelled air defence systems passing through Red Square, 7th November 1946.
Photographer - Sitnikov

1947

The year 1947 began with further gains for Soviet backed communism in Europe, with the Communist Party consolidating power in Romania on 19th January. A socialist government took power in Poland the same year, and communist political chiefs in Central and Eastern Europe met with Stalin's personal representative Andrey Zhdanov regarding plans to thwart what was described in Soviet terms as American imperialist expansion. The meetings resulted in the formation of the international Communist Information Bureau (Cominform), which also included representatives from France and Italy.

On what might be described as the "Superpower Front", 1947 was the year when the wartime alliances between the Allied powers began to irretrievably break down. The American President Harry Truman launched his doctrine of supporting "free peoples" and US Secretary of State George Marshall unveiled his plan announced in 1946 to rebuild Europe through American strategic loans, which was firmly rejected under Soviet pressure by the countries in Eastern Europe that it was primarily aimed at. The United States began to transmit radio broadcasts of the "Voice of America" into the Soviet Union from February 1947, and the Soviet Union in turn began blocking the broadcasts from February the following year.

The phrase "Cold War" which would be used throughout the second half of the 20th Century to describe the superpower tensions of the era was

Post-war production SU-100s crossing Red Square. These SU-100s are also fitted with the post-war stowage bin for crew personal kit as introduced at UZTM from 1st June 1945 and fitted to some new production SU-100s. The stowage box was reintroduced in a strengthened form on all SU-100s produced at UZTM from November 1945. (Nikolai Polikarpov)

further embellished in the United States in April 1947 by the American financier and presidential advisor Bernard Baruch. His statement was relatively vague political rhetoric at the time but nevertheless foretold the deteriorating future relations between the United States and the Soviet Union. Baruch stated: *"Let us not be deceived. We are today in the midst of a Cold War. Our enemies are to be found abroad and at home."* The US statement also reinforced the developing narrative of "Reds under the Bed" which would reach its height under Senator Joseph McCarthy after a speech made by him in 1950 that was directed towards suspected communists in the United States, particularly those in government service.

On 5th June 1947, the United States formally announced the "Marshall Plan", named after US Secretary of State George C. Marshall. The financial aid package was from an American perspective a tool by which the United States could assist the mainland European nations devastated by war and still suffering severe post-war deprivations to make a quick recovery. The unstated aim was as indicated to also ensure the same countries would resist the slide towards communism that was seen as an inevitable consequence of Soviet occupation and political influence. President Truman would finally sign the Economic Cooperation Act that became known in popular parlance as the Marshall Plan on 3rd April 1948. The Soviet Union was understandably unenthusiastic, and Stalin considered the Marshall Plan as a highly divisive American strategy, splitting Europe into two armed camps. Although intended for all of mainland Europe, with the aforementioned political aim as the main strategy driver, the rejection of the plan by the countries in Eastern Europe under Soviet domination had the (perhaps) unintended consequence of splitting Europe further, though the reasons for this were by 1948 numerous. Rationing, which had been ongoing in much of Europe, was finally abolished in the Soviet Union on 14th December 1947, though rationing would continue in Germany until January 1950, and in Great Britain until as late as July 1954.

As communist led governments began to consolidate power in Eastern Europe ahead of any potential mitigating effects of the newly announced Marshall Plan, the pre-war European colonial status quo was meanwhile being challenged in the Far East. Violence continued in Korea and had also begun in Vietnam after Ho Chi Minh's approach to Paris had been rejected, with the Viet Minh (the Vietnam Independence League) beginning guerrilla action against their French colonial masters in late 1946. The French had at the time expected to defeat the Viet Minh within a matter of days, but the troubles for France were only just beginning. In China meanwhile, Chian Kai-shek had in March taken military action in Yenan Province and created his own National Assembly, and by June his government was involved in combat against rival Chinese communist forces. China was now in a state of civil war that would last until the end of the decade, with the communists becoming ultimately victorious.

While events were underway in Europe and Asia Pacific, the main strategic military event of 1947 within the Soviet Union was far from Moscow and not to be found reported in the news. On 18th October 1947, the 22nd Brigade for Special Use of the Reserve of the Supreme High Command, established for deployment of the first generation of Soviet strategic rockets, conducted the first launch of the remanufactured former German V-2 (A-4) ballistic missile from the rocket range at Kapustin Yar on the steppe near Stalingrad to where 29 assembled rockets and parts for another 10 rockets had been shipped from the Soviet occupied sector of Germany. There were 11 test launches of these rockets in October 1947, with the first Soviet R-1 ballistic rocket built from domestic parts being test fired on 17th September 1948. Later, in the early 1950s, the 77th and 90th Brigades were also formed to operate the R-1 (NATO: SS-1 Scunner) strategic rocket. The 54th and 56th Brigades were formed to conduct test launches of the R-2 (NATO: SS-2 Sibling) at Kapustin Yar on 1st June 1952, and by 1957 the later R-5M strategic rocket had made its first appearance on Red Square.

1st May 1947

The 1st May 1947 parade, taken by the newly appointed Defence Minister, Marshal of the Soviet Union Nikolai Bulganin, included participants from the Leningrad "Nakhimovsky" school, columns of cavalry, and marching ranks from the Moscow based military academies in addition to all the assembled arms of the Soviet armed forces.

The tank contingent on Red Square in May 1947 again consisted of T-34-85 medium and IS-3 heavy tanks. The parade still included wartime Lend-Lease supplied Allis-Chalmers HD-7 and HD-10W tracked tractors, the latter as in the previous year towing 152mm M-1937 (ML-20) and 203mm B-4 and other tracked howitzers. The rapidly developing VDV airborne forces were paraded through Red Square in ZiS-5V 4x2 trucks in airborne forces markings, with post-war production GAZ-51 4x2 trucks towing 160mm mortars also being on parade according to conflated original sources, and with Lend-Lease Studebaker US6 6x6 trucks still on display. The 152mm M-1943 (D-1) howitzer was demonstrated on Red Square, being the post-war replacement for the 122mm M-1938 (M-30) howitzer, to which it was near identical in appearance but for the double baffle muzzle brake.

The highlight of the 1947 May Day parade was however in the air rather than on the ground. The first Soviet jet fighters, which had their own debut at the "Dien Aviatsiya" (Aviation Day) airshow at Tushino airfield in Moscow on 18th August 1946, overflew Red Square, with the new MiG-9 and YaK-15 fighters having taken off from the Monino airfield near Moscow, accompanied by Tu-2 and Pe-8 bombers, Il-12 transport aircraft and the prototype Tu-70 passenger aircraft. The new Tu-4, a Soviet copy of the American B-29 "Superfortress", would be demonstrated at an airshow at Tushino airfield in northwest Moscow on 3rd August, but would not overfly Red Square for another two years.

ISU-152 self-propelled assault howitzers parked up on Ulitsa Gorkogo (Gorky Street) in the summer sunshine, 1st May 1947. Photographer - M. Alpert.

IS-3 heavy tanks traverse Red Square, 1st May 1947. Note the now standard mounting of twin fuel tanks on each side of the hull rear, and the radio antenna mount on the turret denoting an early production tank.

The 1st May military parade in Leningrad included some unusual vehicles such as these Lend-Lease GMC-353 based DUKWs moving in front of the Zimny Dvorets (Winter Palace) on Dvortsovaya Ploschad (Palace Square) in the city. (Mikhail Baryatinsky)

BA-64B armoured cars passing the Zimny Dvorets on Dvortsovaya Ploschad in Leningrad during the same 1st May parade as the GMC DUKWs shown overleaf.

7th November 1947 – 30th Anniversary of the Great October Socialist Revolution

For the 30th Anniversary of the "Great October Socialist Revolution" November parade, taken by Defence Minister Marshal of the Soviet Union Bulganin, the venerable T-34-85 medium tank, the SU-100 tank destroyer and the ISU-152 self propelled assault howitzer were again the main wartime service armoured vehicles on display on what was a cold and wet day with melting snow on the glistening cobbles of Red Square. The parade began with M-72 motorcycle combinations, followed by T-34-85 medium and IS-3 heavy tanks, self-propelled assault artillery and the late wartime Ya-12 tracked artillery tractor which towed Soviet heavy artillery pieces including the 152mm M-1937 (ML-20) through Red Square. The ZiS-150 truck Establishment Lot was completed on 30th October 1947 and was according to Soviet sources duly displayed on Red Square in November 1947. Another new military transport vehicle displayed on Red Square on 7th November 1947 was the YaAZ-200.* During the war, the YaAZ (YAZ) plant in Yaroslavl had concentrated on the production of artillery tractors and engines, but as the war situation eased, the plant had begun work on wheeled military vehicles, with the first prototype of a new 4x2 general service truck being completed at the Yaroslavl Plant in the winter of 1944-45; the prototype being shown to

* Though sources are conflated, the official MAZ history states the parade debut of the YaAZ-200 series was 7th November 1947, for which purpose a pre-series production batch was specifically assembled.

The late 1940s witnessed a number of new military transport vehicles making their debut appearance on Red Square. A pre-production batch of YaAZ-200 vehicles was prepared especially at YaAZ in Yaroslavl for the November 1947 parade. Production was latterly transferred to Minsk, with the nomenclature thereafter changed accordingly to MAZ-200.

Stalin at the Kremlin on 19th June 1945. The new YaAZ-200, the first Soviet series produced truck fitted with a diesel engine, had a 5,000kg all-terrain load capacity, increasing to 7,000kg on roads. The YaAZ-200 series was produced at YaAZ in Yaroslavl from 1947 until 1951. The new military general service truck had its public debut on Red Square on 7th November 1947, before the vehicle underwent military trials in 1949-50, with production thereafter transferred to Minsk where assembly continued as the MAZ-200.

The Yaroslavl Plant had also meantime developed the 6x4 YaAZ-210G artillery tractor, which would also appear on Red Square. YaAZ 4x2 and 4x4 designs were subsequently series produced at MAZ in Minsk, the capital city of the Soviet Belorussian Republic, with the larger 6x6 designs being built at KrAZ located at Kremenchug in Ukraine. Some of these new vehicles would make cameo parade appearances on Red Square from 1947 until the mid 1950s.

Ya-12 tracked medium artillery tractors move towards Red Square, 7th November 1947. The Ya-12 tractor was replaced by the modernised Mytischi-2 (M-2) on Red Square from the following year.

Moscow was only the best known (certainly abroad) of many cities where regular military parades were held. These post-war production T-34-85s are on parade in Minsk, Belorussia, 7th November 1947 (Mikhail Baryatinsky)

T-34-85s parade through Tallinn, Estonia on 7th November 1947. Note the detail differences between the lead tanks, such as the early and late production type commander's cupolas and hatches. (Mikhail Baryatinsky)

SU-76Ms on parade in Riga, Latvia, 7th November 1947. (Mikhail Baryatinsky)

1948

Romania had fallen under communist control at the beginning of 1947, and 1948 in Europe began in a similar vein, with a Soviet backed coup in Czechoslovakia on 25th February 1948. Following on from the similar events in Poland and Yugoslavia, Europe was continuing to divide along lines of alignment to the former Western Allies or the Soviet Union.

In 1948, sixteen European countries, including France, Great Britain, Germany, Holland, Norway, and even wartime neutral Sweden and Switzerland signed up to the American Marshall Plan announced in June 1947. The Marshall Plan was effectively a trade agreement on production, raw materials and currency regimes that promised the countries concerned a return to economic self-sufficiency with American financial sponsorship. As alluded to earlier, the Marshall Plan also had as an unwritten primary American aim the intent to strengthen the war ravaged countries of Europe against leanings towards the Soviet cause. Less well broadcast in Europe, the plan and its terms were also extended to China and Korea. Those countries with allegiance to the Soviet Union, namely Albania, Bulgaria, Czechoslovakia, Finland, Hungary, Poland and Romania, all refused any involvement in the Marshall Plan. The European divide was already by 1948 beginning to formalise into what would later be termed Western and Eastern Europe.

The big event in Europe in 1948 was the Berlin Blockade and the ensuing Allied airlift of supplies into the besieged city. There had been tensions over Berlin and its location deep within the Soviet sector since the end of the war in Europe, but they ostensibly came to a head over an American and

IS-3 heavy tanks moving down Gorky Street towards Red Square. Unusually, these tanks have no external fuel tanks fitted. Note also the tow cable mounting, track guards and turret grab rails.

Allied attempt to introduce the Deutschemark as the base currency in Berlin, in retaliation for which the Soviet Union closed the access corridor to the city. The Berlin blockade began in June 1948 and would last for almost a year.

From a military perspective, the tensions in 1948 related to Berlin and Soviet intentions in Eastern Europe were not eased by the apparent spread of communist backed regimes in the region, but it was events in other parts of the world which were of more immediate concern to the European former colonial powers. In the Middle East, fighting was ongoing in Palestine, culminating in David Ben Gurion of what was known as the Jewish Agency declaring on 14th May 1948 the formation of the new State of Israel. In Asia Pacific, Holland had in January rejected Indonesian demands for independence, which would lead to war in the years ahead. On 8th February, North Korea announced it was activating its own army. Meantime in the United States, General McArthur was insisting that all foreign forces should pull out of occupied Korea, which was rapidly developing into another global trouble spot. General McArthur on 8th April announced that all US forces would be withdrawn from Korea during 1949. Ensuing elections in the US occupied zone were accompanied by violence, and the slide to war continued in a country that had already experienced much since the days of significant Japanese aggression during the 1930s. Ironically, it was the exit of Soviet and American forces from their respective zones of occupied Korea, that created the vacuum in which the future war would be conceived.

Meanwhile, far from the glare of highly public and highly publicised events in Europe, the Soviet Union on 17th September 1948 launched its first R-1 ballistic rocket, developed on the basis of the V-2 (A-4) rocket technology described earlier, at the Kapustin Yar polygon. Soviet ballistic rocket development had come of age.

1st May 1948

The military contingent of the 1st May 1948 parade, which was again taken by Soviet Defence Minister Marshal of the Soviet Union Nikolai Bulganin, began per tradition with marching columns of infantry from the Soviet armed forces and related defence institutions. Though not as dramatic or perhaps as interesting as the armoured vehicles displayed on Red Square in May 1948, marching infantry on 1st May 1948 were armed with the first post-war generation of self-loading and semi-automatic rifles. The 7.62mm Simonov SKS self-loading rifle was a replacement for the wartime Simonov SVT-1938 and SVT-1940 weapons. The 7.62mm AK-47 which debuted concurrently, designed by the then relatively unknown Mikhail Kalashnikov, was a revolutionary weapon which would become the definitive Soviet infantry weapon in the second half of the 20th Century.

There were no major surprises with regard to armoured vehicles at the 1st May 1948 parade. The tank contingent of the parade comprised the late 1940s parade standard of T-34-85 medium and IS-3 heavy tanks. Some Russian photographic archive sources claim that the BTR-152 was first paraded on 1st May 1948, but based on the small number of pre-series production BTR-152 vehicles built, it would appear that the parade debut was in fact 1951.

Several new secondary military vehicles were however paraded in 1948, demonstrating both the post-war industrial recovery and significant expansion of the Soviet military vehicle production industry. In May 1948, the wartime indigenous production GAZ-67 was joined by the 4x2

A T-34-85 crosses Red Square past portraits of both Lenin and Stalin, 1st May 1948

GAZ-51, the post-war production replacement for the venerable GAZ-AA and GAZ-MM general service trucks. The GAZ-51 made its debut appearance together with the larger and 6x6 ZiS-151, the first series production Soviet three-axle all-terrain military vehicle, based heavily on Red Army wartime experience with the Lend-Lease Studebaker US6 truck. Both vehicle designs as shown on Red Square were fitted with cabs of part wooden construction, reflecting the lack of machine tooling available to press form sheet steel in the immediate post-war years. Standard series production GAZ and ZiS vehicles would later have press formed and welded all steel cabs.

The Ya-12 tracked artillery tractor towed the 152mm M-1937 (ML-20) gun-howitzer through Red Square for the last time in May, as the wartime vehicle was replaced by the similar looking but more powerful post-war M-2 (Mytischi-2) which was produced at Mytischi near Moscow as the Yaroslavl plant re-orientated on military truck production. The 152mm M-1943 (D-1) howitzer, resembling the wartime 122mm M-1938 (M-30) howitzer but with a double baffle muzzle brake, and replacing earlier 122mm and 152mm weapons, was also again displayed. Lend-Lease Allis-Chalmers HD-10W tracked tractors were still in evidence, towing the tracked 203mm B-4 howitzer through Red Square.

The wartime 85mm M-1939 and M-1944 towed anti-aircraft guns were displayed as in previous years, but were now joined by the 100mm KS-19 anti-aircraft gun and its related off-carriage PUAZO control system. Though resembling

These SU-100s are also post-war production, denoted by minor features such as the absence of a grab rail behind the commander's cupola, deleted at UZTM from July 1945. Note also the later, widened commander's cupola with single piece hatch and the absence of a storage box for crew personal effects, which was standardised on SU-100s produced after November 1945.

the earlier 85mm weapons, the 100mm KS-19 could reportedly engage jet fighter aircraft flying at 1,200km/hour at a range of 15,000m at a time when the new MiG-9 jet fighter had a maximum airspeed of 910km/h and the YaK-15 a corresponding airspeed of 965km/h, in line with foreign first generation jet powered aircraft.

As the Soviet Union celebrated the 1st May 1948 holiday on Red Square, events on the other side of the world proved more newsworthy. In the north of Korea, Premier Kim Il Sung chose the same day to close the border with South Korea, claiming jurisdiction over all of Korea after elections with an officially declared 85% turnout. Two weeks later, and closer to home, the National Council of "Representatives of the Jewish People in Palestine and the Zionist Movement" on 14th May 1948 declared their new Jewish state - the State of Israel. The Middle East was undergoing massive changes, and the new state formed in 1948 would be central to those changes. The day following the declaration of the new State of Israel, the country was at war with Egypt, Iran, Lebanon, Saudi Arabia, Syria and Transjordan. The position of Israel in 1948 was also not so very different to that of the fledgling Bolshevik state founded in 1917, in that the country had many detractors, including countries in Europe, that also did not wish to see it survive as a separate and independent state. The Middle East would in the years ahead become the setting for Middle East proxy-wars between the post-war superpowers, and a testing ground for their respective military equipment designs, with the United States and Great Britain arming the Israelis and the Soviet Union arming the majority of their Arab adversaries.

Meanwhile in Europe, the post-war fractures between the former Allied powers were beginning to grow. On 24th June, the Soviet Union cut all road and rail links with the Allied sectors of Berlin, which was deep inside the Soviet controlled zone (East Germany). The Berlin Blockade had begun, and the Allied airlift also began the following day. The situation would remain in impasse until the Soviet Union eventually recognised the futility of prolongation, and lifted the blockade almost a year later, on 12th May 1949. All was not going to the Soviet plan elsewhere in Eastern Europe. After a fractious few months, Yugoslavia in 1948 found itself on the wrong side of Stalin, who on 28th June expelled the borderline communist country from the recently formed Cominform.

In Asia Pacific, the Republic of (South) Korea was formed on 15th August, followed on 8th Sep-

ISU-152 self-propelled assault howitzers cross Red Square during the same May parade. Note the 12.7mm DShKM anti-aircraft machine gun mountings.

tember by North Korea forming the Democratic People's Republic of Korea (DPRK / PRK). This was far from a distant concern for the Soviet Union, which at the time still had not insignificant numbers of troops located in the country. Elsewhere beyond the eastern borders of the Soviet Union, the Chinese brand of communism was spreading in Asia Pacific, with Chinese communist forces capturing Mukden in Manchuria as civil war raged in the region.

Conventional European received wisdom and school curriculum teaching has always suggested that the Soviet Union was a major threat to Europe in the immediate years after the end of World War Two. The potential for escalating conflict is undeniable, however from a Soviet perspective the immediate post-war focus was on spreading the Soviet brand of socialism by political means, particularly in Eastern Europe. But there was an alternative brand of communism not under Soviet control, which was literally fighting its way to power on the Soviet Union's eastern borders, in China, which was of greater concern, and far more enduring, than the machinations in Europe.

The GAZ-51 4x2 general service truck made its debut Red Square parade appearance in 1948. The GAZ-51 would be produced in massive numbers and serve in the Soviet Army as a general service load carrier and in many specialised variants. Early production vehicles were fitted with a cab assembled from sheet steel mounted over a wood frame, later replaced by a monocoque construction all-steel cab.

SU-76M self-propelled guns at the 1st May 1948 parade on Dvortsovaya Ploshchad (Palace Square) in Leningrad, followed by T-34-85 medium tanks. Photographer – Chernov.

Lend-Lease Allis-Chalmers HD-10W tracked artillery tractors towing 152mm Br-2 tracked guns across Red Square. Note the single axle bogie used for towing these unwieldy looking but immensely powerful "levelling" weapons.

7th November 1948 – 31st Anniversary of the Great October Socialist Revolution

The 7th November parade was taken by Marshal of the Soviet Union Semeon K. Timoshenko in the presence of Nikolai Bulganin as Soviet Defence Minister, with the parade commander being Marshal of the Soviet Union Kirill A. Meretskov. The parade commanders were in November 1948 mounted on black horses.

The T-34-85 medium tank, SU-100 medium and ISU-152 heavy assault guns continued to be the main heavy armoured vehicles displayed on Red Square, though the wartime ISU-122 was no longer demonstrated, its "tank hunter" role having been taken by the SU-100 on the T-34 medium chassis on which weapon type the Soviet Army standardised in the late 1940s and early 1950s.

From 1948, the Soviet Union began to consistently demonstrate on Red Square how its post-war military manufacturing capability was recovering, with new 4x2, 4x4 and 6x6 military transport vehicles from GAZ and ZiS being paraded on Red Square in November 1948 - the GAZ-51 and ZiS-150, GAZ-63 and ZiS-151 respectively. The GAZ-63 4x4 all-terrain version of the GAZ-51 entered series production in September 1948, joining the 4x2 GAZ-51 and the 6x6 ZiS-151 as the first post-war generation of Soviet general service load carrier vehicles. The ZiS-150 was in 1948 demonstrated in several versions, as a transport vehicle in VDV airborne forces markings with 16 "desantniki" paratroopers seated on

A T-34-85 lead tank with split turret ventilators crosses Red Square during the 31st Anniversary of the Great October Socialist Revolution parade, 7th November 1948. (RGAKFD)

bench seats in each vehicle, and as a potential post-war mounting for the BM-13 (BM-13-16) and BM-31 (BM-31-12) multiple rocket launchers (MRS). The ZiS-150 was ultimately replaced in the MRS role by the 6x6 ZiS-151, but for display purposes the ZiS-150 showed that the Soviet Union was rapidly recovering from the war and now had the capacity to produce new vehicle types for both military and civil application. The ZiS-150 was followed during the 1948 parade by the new GAZ-51.

Due to a shortage of sheet steel in the immediate post-war years, the first generation of post-war military transport vehicles displayed in the late 1940s, including the 4x2 GAZ-51, YaAZ-200 and ZiS-150, the 4x4 GAZ-63, and the 6x6 ZiS-151 were all fitted with cabs constructed from a combination of wood and steel. The 4x2 GAZ-51 vehicles paraded on 7th November 1948 were fitted with such cabs of partly wooden construction, replaced from 1956 by all steel cabs. Some vehicles were in the late 1940s fitted with twin 12.7mm DShKM anti-aircraft machine gun mountings in the rear cargo area for display purposes during Red Square parades.

The new 6x6 ZiS-151 was paraded on 7th November 1948, towing the 85mm M-1939 anti-aircraft gun. The early post-war production ZiS vehicles were as with GAZ vehicles fitted with cabs of wood framed construction. The new 100mm KS-19 anti-aircraft gun, which had good capability against newly emerging jet-powered aircraft, was regularly displayed on Red Square from 1948.

In a throwback to the war years, S-65 tracked artillery tractors with their open cab configuration towed 152mm Br-2 tracked howitzers through Red Square. The 1930s era S-65 had not been displayed on Red Square in 1945, with Lend-Lease Allis-Chalmers tractors having performed the

The M-2 (Mytischi-2) tracked medium artillery tractor had by 1948 replaced the Ya-12 in production and on Red Square. These M-2 tractors are towing pre-war 152mm M-1937 (ML-20) "Corps Duplex" heavy gun-howitzers.

The wartime S-65 tracked artillery tractor was occasionally displayed on Red Square in the immediate post-war years, having provided stellar if slow towing service for the duration of World War Two. The 210mm M-1939 (Br-17) and 305mm M-1939 (Br-18) heavy artillery pieces also made cameo appearances, split into barrel and gun carriage loads.

heavy artillery tractor role. In the first few post-war parades, Lend-Lease military vehicles were present, but these were quickly replaced by indigenous Soviet vehicles for both Soviet technological development and political reasons. The new M-2 tracked artillery tractor was also displayed in November 1948, towing the 152mm M-1937 (ML-20) gun-howitzer. *

Far from Red Square, on the other side of the world, events in Korea became a prime focus for the rival political blocs that were already aligning in 1948. The United States and the Soviet Union were both in 1948 in the process of removing their respective troops from Korea, which left a vacuum that proved more dangerous than when the country was occupied by rival occupying forces. As the year ended, the last Red Army (now Soviet Army) contingents left North Korea, though Soviet advisors would remain in the country throughout the forthcoming Korean War.

The ZiS-150 4x2 general service truck replaced the wartime ZiS-5 and ZiS-5V from 1948, with the first series production vehicles being demonstrated on Red Square in the late 1940s. These ZiS-150 truck are in VDV airborne forces markings and transporting sixteen paratroopers in each vehicle.

These GAZ-51 4x2 general service trucks crossing Red Square have the pre-1949 fabricated cab assembled from sheet steel formed over a wooden frame. A stamped monocoque construction steel cab was introduced from 1949.

* The first public debut of a limousine specifically adapted for military parade purposes was by the GAZ-M20B. Two such vehicles were used during a parade held in the Leningrad Military District (LVO) on 24th July 1948.

The ZiS-151 also made its Red Square public debut in 1948. The vehicle was the Soviet Union's first series production 6x6 all-terrain general service truck, based heavily on the American Lend-Lease Studebaker US6. These vehicles have the early production sheet steel over wooden frame cabs.

Some particularly rare vehicles made cameo appearances on Red Square in the late 1940s. An Establishment Lot of ZiS-150 vehicles was built configured as BM-13 and BM-31 multiple rocket launchers, but the chassis was not adopted for service.

Although demonstrated on Red Square, these ZiS-150 BM-13 multiple rocket launchers, and the ZiS-150 mounted BM-31 system demonstrated concurrently, were not adopted for service due to the recent availability of the more versatile 6x6 ZiS-151 as a more stable chassis for future MRS systems.

IS-3 heavy tanks on parade in Odessa, Ukraine on 7th November 1948. Red Square in Moscow was as always the default Soviet military parade location from an observer's perspective, but parades were held throughout the Soviet Union. The Commander of the Odessa Military District in the late 1940s was Marshal of the Soviet Union Georgy Zhukov.

Parades were regularly held in Kiev, Kharkov, Odessa and other cities in Ukraine. These SU-76Ms appear to be on parade in Kiev on 7th November 1948, though the original data card states Odessa. (RGAKFD)

SU-100s parade down Kreschatik, Kiev's main thoroughfare, in 1948.

SU-100s during the same 1948 parade in Kiev, with the destroyed buildings in the background providing testament to the massive destruction which Kiev suffered during the war.

1949

One of the defining moments of the Cold War occurred between the November 1948 and May 1949 Red Square parades. On 4th April 1949, the United States, Canada and several European countries, namely Belgium, Denmark, France, Great Britain, Iceland, Italy, Luxembourg, the Netherlands, Norway and Portugal formed a military defensive alliance - the North Atlantic Treaty Organisation (NATO). Later in 1949 President Harry S. Truman after some persuasion managed to have the Mutual Defence Assistance Program pushed through the US Congress, which allocated $1.4 billion in immediate military aid to these countries. The Western defensive alliance which is credited with keeping the peace in Europe in the second half of the 20th Century became a formidable military power, backed by US forces based in Europe, in particular Germany, long before the Common Market and the later European Union came into existence. Greece and Turkey would join NATO in 1952, which was from a Soviet perspective simply an additional irritant, however in 1955 the Federal Republic of Germany also gained membership to NATO, with permission to re-arm, which provoked a more defined reaction.

While defensive alliances were being formed in Europe against potential Soviet expansion plans, the greater potential for a major clash between "superpower" states was developing on the other side of the world, in Asia Pacific. Chinese communist forces were by January 1949 advancing steadily against the armies of Chiang Kai-shek, and by April had crossed the Yangtse River and were moving on Chiang Kai-shek's capital city - Nanking. The Chinese civil war was from a superpower perspective still considered for the moment as an internal Chinese issue. The situation in neighbouring Korea was however a multinational tinderbox, not least due to the foreign contingents based in the country, and their respective power influences. During an official trip to Moscow, the North Korean Premier Kim Il Sung on 7th March asked for Stalin's direct support in "liberating" South Korea.

Stalin diplomatically advised that there were agreements in place between the Soviet Union and the United States with regard to the 38th Parallel, and these agreements would be respected by the Soviet Union. Kim Il Sung left Moscow without Soviet support for his plans. The last American troops left South Korea on 29th June 1949, a few months after the Soviet troops had departed from the north of the country, leaving the Korean situation as a temporarily domestic issue.

Back in the Soviet Union, March 1949 saw the launch of Operation "Priboi" (Ocean Surf), the deportation of numbers of new Soviet citizens from Estonia, Latvia and Lithuania to GULAG* camps in Siberia. The initial operation was carried out in a four-day period from 25th to 28th March, with an estimated 90,000 people being moved using rail rolling stock and military vehicles from the Leningrad and Belorussian Military Districts. Progress in Lithuania was slower, with Operation "Osen" (Autumn) being carried out in 1951. The fundamental declared purpose of the deportations was collectivization of farming land, but there was also an element of removing the potential for armed resistance within these countries now under Soviet control. Such repressive measures were not solely related to the Baltic States - there would also be political purges in Leningrad during 1949.

While world events were unfolding, the British author Eric Arthur Blair, better known as George Orwell, in 1949 published his novel "Nineteen Eighty-Four" describing a dystopian futuristic world with society at constant war, a world of hate propaganda, government truth control and doublespeak, with the population under constant surveillance. The novel by the former Spanish Civil War veteran, teacher and BBC correspondent was loosely based on the perceived worst elements of the contemporary Soviet system, and generations of "Western" schoolchildren would read it as a novel rather than a prescient prediction of the future in their own countries.

---

* GULAG - Glavnoye Upravlenye ispravitelno-trudovykh Lagerei (Main Administration of Corrective Labour Camps)

1st May 1949

The Red Square 1st May parade in 1949 was taken by the new Soviet Defence Minister, Marshal of the Soviet Union Aleksandr M. Vasilevsky, who had taken up his new position on 24th March that year and would remain in the position until 1953, albeit with a change in title from 1950 to Minister of War. The parade commander was again the Commander of the Moscow Military District (MVO), Marshal of the Soviet Union Kirill Meretskov.

The T-34-85 remained the mainstay tank on parade in 1949, followed by infantry in trucks, infantry support artillery, towed mortars, and self-propelled artillery including the indefatigable ISU-152 self-propelled assault howitzer, while the parade featured the same new military transport vehicles as displayed in 1948.

The Berlin Blockade was lifted on 12th May 1949, and the Federal Republic of Germany established on 23rd May 1949, only three weeks after the May Day parade. From a political perspective, 1948 had been a year in which the Soviet Union was losing ground in Europe. At a strategic level, the Soviet Union had however between the May and November 1949 parades made significant progress with attaining what might be described as psychological balance in the emerging Cold War. On 29th August, the Soviet Union detonated its first atomic bomb, closing the gap with the United States in the nuclear "arms race". The means of delivering such weapons remained for both superpowers at the time the use of long-range bomber aircraft, but the gap in superpower atomic capability since the Hiroshima and Nagasaki bombings of 1945 had been narrowed, and was now entering an era whereby a nuclear attack by either superpower would meet with a nuclear response from the other, in what would in the later rocket years be termed "Mutually Assured Destruction" (MAD). The possession of nuclear weapons by both superpowers, later joined by other aligned nations, also brought new levels of behind the scenes pragmatism as a counter-balance to the public shows of political rhetoric displayed on both sides of the superpower divide.

The autumn weeks leading up to the 7th November parade in Moscow were again eventful in

The epitome of 1940s Soviet military might - IS-3 heavy tanks parade through Red Square in May 1951. This photograph, minus the background, became a definitive "recognition" photograph in US and NATO manuals during the Cold War.

the Far East. In September 1949, Stalin considered the unfolding situation in Korea, but any thoughts of direct Soviet military intervention were quietly shelved. The civil war in China that had been ongoing since 1945 was also moving towards its conclusion. Chiang Kai-shek's anti-communist forces had been forced to re-group in Taiwan, while the new Chinese communist leader Mao Zedong announced on 1st October 1949 the founding of the People's Republic of China. Thirty-two years after Soviet Russia had founded its fledgling Socialist State, China had taken a similar path, albeit with a brand of communism that would differ widely from the Soviet model. Whether the Soviet Union would cooperate militarily and politically with China against the market economy driven "Imperialist West" was in 1949 yet to be seen.

Back in Europe, the formation of the Federal Republic of (West) Germany on 23rd May 1949 was countered by the Soviet proclamation on 7th October that the former Soviet zone of influence in (East) Germany was now formalized as the independent German (Deutsche) Democratic Republic (GDR/DDR).

T-34-85 medium tanks at the same May 1949 parade. Note the "spider-web" road wheels and the minor differences in fuel tank mountings between the tanks. (RGAKFD)

7th November 1949 – 32nd Anniversary of the Great October Socialist Revolution

T-34-85 medium tanks dominated the beginning of the November 1949 Red Square parade, which was again taken by Soviet Defence Minister Marshal of the Soviet Union Aleksandr Vasilevsky. The tanks, moving in columns of four, were followed by M-2 tracked artillery tractors, which had now replaced the Ya-12 on Red Square, but continued to tow pre-war 152mm M-1937 (ML-20) corps gun-howitzers that had served the Red Army well throughout World War Two. There were other subtle changes in parade formation, with the new ZiS-150 4x2 truck, the post-war ZiS built replacement for the wartime ZiS-5, displayed in significant quantity on 7th November 1950.

In 1949, jet fighters again overflew the parade, accompanied by the debut Red Square appearance of a flight of Tu-4 strategic heavy bombers, the Soviet version of the venerable American B-29 "Superfortress" best known for dropping the two atomic bombs on Japan in August 1945. One of the Tu-4 bomber pilots was the commander of the Moscow region (MVO) of the VVS (the Soviet Air Force) Lieutenant-General Vasily Iosefovich Stalin (Dzhugashvili), son of the Soviet leader, who would overfly Red Square seven times during various parades as his father stood on the Lenin Mausoleum review stand below.

ISU-152 self-propelled assault howitzers pass the Hotel "Moskva" on Manezhnaya Square just before entering Red Square. Note the standard 12.7mm DShK anti-aircraft machine gun mounting.

The 4x2 GAZ-51 was in 1949 joined on Red Square by its 4x4 all-terrain derivative, the GAZ-63. These vehicles mount 12.7mm DShKM anti-aircraft machine guns for parade purposes. The cabs are still of the sheet steel over wood frame type, denoting pre-1949 production.

The M-2 tracked artillery tractor had by the late 1940s replaced the late wartime Ya-12 on Red Square, here towing the 152mm M-1937 (ML-20) gun-howitzer. The M-2 closely resembled the earlier Ya-12, the most discernable feature of the new type being the reconfigured and enlarged cargo area.

The BTR-152 wheeled APC was displayed on Red Square from 1951. The vehicle was basically an armoured ZiS-151 truck, but its introduction marked a major change in Soviet doctrine with regard to the concept of mechanised infantry.

The 1950s

The early 1950s was dominated by the Korean War, which broke out in June 1950 and would last until July 1953. The Korean War was the first of the post-war "proxy-wars" whereby the direct combatants were politically and military supported by their respective "superpower" and as yet to fully develop respective superpower blocs. Soviet military advisers were involved in the Korean War through their presence was denied for many years thereafter, while UN forces clashed directly with forces of the rising power in the post-war Asia-Pacific region - China. Elsewhere in the Far East the French, with US backing, arranged for the former Vietnamese emperor Bao Dai to return to Vietnam, which was at the time expected to result in a return to stability in the country.

On 14th February 1950, the American worst case communist threat scenario was confirmed when the Soviet Union and the newly formed communist government of the People's Republic of China signed a mutual defence treaty. After the death of Stalin in March 1953, a period of rapid de-Stalinisation in the Soviet Union would sweep away many of the excesses of that era, including some of its miscreants, in particular the head of the then governing MVD structure (formerly the NKVD), Lavrenty Beria, who would ultimately be dealt with by the Soviet Army. The 1950s in Europe was meantime dominated by the situation that arose in Hungary in the late autumn of 1956.

The first generation of post-war tanks and armoured vehicles entered series production and service with the Soviet Army during the 1950s. The immediate post-war T-44 was never displayed on Red Square, the T-54 directly replacing the T-34-85 on the cobbles of the square from 1957, with the parade debut of the T-54 being a full decade after it had entered service. A lack of indigenous wheeled scout and armoured personnel carriers in Red Army service during the war was rectified by the immediate post-war development of the BTR-40 and BTR-152 wheeled armoured vehicles, based respectively on the 4x4 GAZ-63 and 6x6 ZiS-151 chassis. The BTR-40 was also never displayed on Red Square; however the larger BTR-152 series became a parade regular for over a decade.

The 1950s also witnessed the regular display of the first post-war generation of military transport vehicles in all load classes, including the 4x2 GAZ-51 and YaAZ-200, the 4x4 GAZ-63, the 6x4 YaAZ-210G, the 6x6 ZiS-151 and the later production model ZiL-157, some of which had been seen in pre-series production form on Red Square at the very end of the 1940s.

The decade also saw the regular display of the Soviet Vozdushno-Desantnye Voiska (VDV) airborne forces as a regular part of Red Square parade contingents. Initially, VDV "desantniki" paratroopers were seated in ZiS-5V and latterly ZiS-150 trucks, with no heavy support weaponry.

By the end of the decade the first generation of mobile airborne heavy support weapons, the ASU-57 self-propelled gun, was being paraded on Red Square, soon followed by the more substantially armed, armoured and fully enclosed SU-85 (ASU-85) airborne self-propelled gun.

The final years of the 1950s also saw the introduction of the first generation of long-range tactical, surface to air and strategic rockets in addition to new generations of multiple rocket system as the Soviet Union entered the "missile years" under the direction of Soviet Premier Khrushchev. The development of rocket technology was widely applied in the late 1950s, and proudly demonstrated on Red Square, but it was the new strategic rockets unveiled in 1957 that caught the immediate attention of foreign military attachés and observers. The 1950s was a decade of rapid technological progress around the world, and in particular from within the primary competing superpowers, the United States and the Soviet Union. The Soviet Union rapidly developed military and civil rocket technology during the decade. The German V-2 (A-4) had by the late 1940s been successfully copied as the Soviet R-1 with a range of 270km. Such was the pace of development that on 7th November 1957 the new R-5M rocket with a range of 1,200km made its public debut on Red Square, being the first strategic rocket to be displayed in public by the Soviet Union. Meantime, the Soviet Union had on 27th August launched the 5,600km range R-7 rocket, the world's first successful ICBM flight.

The first Soviet surface to air missile (SAM) systems were also introduced in the late 1950s, with the S-75 (NATO: SA-2 Guideline) being demonstrated from 1957 and the enigmatic S-25 (NATO: SA-1 Guild) from 1960. The S-25 static pad-launch system was installed in a defensive ring around Moscow in the latter years of the decade. Originally thought by foreign observers to be a short to medium range mobile SAM like the S-75, it was only in later years understood that the rocket was deployed in a defensive circle on the "Bettony Krug" (concrete circle) around Moscow as a strategic defence for the Soviet capital.* The concurrent S-75 would appear earlier than the S-25 on Red Square, but would achieve fame and notoriety in May 1960 in the skies over Siberia, after which the potency of emerging Soviet rocket technology was no longer in doubt.

1950

The year 1950 was relatively quiet in the Soviet Union, with the events in Asia taking precedence in the world news. There were significant developments on Red Square, with generation changes of military technology beginning to be introduced. But from a superpower perspective, the signing of the Sino-Soviet Treaty of Friendship, Alliance and Mutual Assistance on 14th February 1950 was a further indication of changing post-war alliances, with the potential Western nightmare scenario of the largest "communist" nations of the world, the Soviet Union and China, finding common ground for cooperation and further development of their respective brands of communism in many areas of the world.

---

* The "Bettony Krug" was a ring road which ran well outside Moscow's suburbs, and made of concrete slabs - hence the description. It was originally laid down for servicing the city's strategic defence missile systems rather than for domestic transport purposes.

1st May 1950

The 1st May 1950 Red Square parade was again taken by Soviet Defence Minister Vasilevsky (whose position was changed to Minister of War from 1950 to 1953), with Vyacheslav Molotov, Georgy Malenkov, Lavrenty Beria and Marshal Semeon Budenny on the Lenin Mausoleum review stand. The armoured element of the parade included the T-34-85 medium tank and the SU-100 tank destroyer, followed by now standard post-war parade vehicles such as the new M-2 tracked artillery tractor, which had replaced the wartime Ya-12 in production at YaAZ in Yaroslavl and had its parade debut on Red Square in November 1948. The M-2, developed under the direction of chief designer Nikolai Astrov, famous for wartime light tank designs, closely resembled the Ya-12 but was more powerful and featured a redesigned cargo area. The name M-2 (Mytischi-2) was taken from the location of the plant in the northern suburbs of Moscow which had significant experience in the production of small and light tanks, and post-war would also produce armoured vehicles for the Soviet VDV airborne forces and air defence vehicle chassis.

The month following the May parade, on 25th June, North Korea invaded South Korea heralding the beginning of the Korean War. Within three days, the North Koreans had captured Seoul, and the United States began to move troops stationed in Japan into Korea, pushing the North Koreans back and soon thereafter crossing the 38th Parallel into North Korea. The international concern was always that of a direct conflict between the superpowers in the region, and by the time of the November military parade on Red Square this was a distinct possibility. By November 1950, Chinese forces had been committed directly to the war, and were pushing UN forces back beyond the 38th Parallel into South Korea, while American aircraft were flying sorties against Chinese airbases in Manchuria, for which bases the Soviet Union was providing strategic air cover. The dynamic situation in the Far East was looking distinctly dire in 1950, with a real likelihood of the war escalating exponentially beyond the borders of Korea, and with all the "superpowers" including the newly emergent China being directly involved.

These solo M-72 motorcycles are on Red Square as part of a Presidential Guard detachment rather than during a military parade.

The IS-3 remained a Red Square highlight into the early 1950s before being withdrawn, as the tank was being modernised (latterly as the IS-3M) and then exported.

The M-2 (Mytischi-2) medium artillery tractor was a Red Square parade regular in the 1950s, having replaced the very similar late wartime Ya-12.

ZiS-150 4x2 general service trucks in VDV airborne forces configuration. The early construction wood framed cabs are still evident.

The Yaroslavl built YaAZ-210G 6x4 wheeled artillery tractor was used by the Soviet Army in small numbers during the 1950s. These vehicles are towing 152mm D-1 howitzers.

THE SOVIET ARMY ON PARADE 1946-91

These ZiS-150 vehicles are armed with two tripod-mounted 12.7mm DShKM heavy machine guns with accompanying VDV airborne forces paratroopers, but the vehicles are unmarked.

May and November parades were also held in other Soviet cities. These early production IS-2 heavy tanks are on parade in the Belorussian capital, Minsk. The tank on the right has several shell impacts on the turret and has a rare "German" type muzzle brake. (Mikhail Baryatinsky)

7th November 1950 – 33rd Anniversary of the Great October Socialist Revolution

The venerable T-34-85 medium, and the IS-3 heavy tank as first seen on Red Square in 1946 provided the main armour display in November 1950. The IS-3 was by then already an anachronism however, as a direct result of the tank having been rushed into production in 1945. Although regularly paraded on Red Square, the IS-3 had in the meantime been gradually withdrawn from service for capital rebuild to eliminate defects, after which the tank was returned to strategic storage rather than service. The ISU-152 self-propelled howitzer was also still on display in November 1950 but would soon disappear from view as it also entered reserve status.

The 4x2 GAZ-51 and 6x6 ZiS-151 military general service vehicles were in November 1950 again joined by the 4x4 GAZ-63 and the 4x2 YaAZ-200, which Soviet sources indicate had occurred at the end of the 1940s, and by the 6x4 YaAZ-210G wheeled artillery tractor. The GAZ-63 as displayed in 1950 was a 4x4 all-terrain derivative of the 4x2 GAZ-51, both vehicles having been developed to prototype stage immediately pre-war, but with series production of both having been delayed until after the war so as not to disrupt existing production in wartime conditions. The early production model GAZ-63 displayed on 7th November 1950 featured a partially wooden cab construction, and was armed with a 12.7mm DShKM anti-aircraft machine gun installation in the truck cargo area for display purposes.

The early pre-series production YaAZ-200 paraded in November 1950 was displayed towing both the 100mm M-1944 (BS-3) anti-tank gun and the 122mm M-1938 (M-30) howitzer. The YaAZ-200 was the first post-war 4x2 truck developed to production stage at the YaAZ plant in Yaroslavl, which during the war had produced the Ya-12 tracked artillery tractor, replaced by the M-2 from the end of the 1940s as YaAZ converted to truck production. Series production of the YaAZ-200 would later be transferred to the MAZ plant in Minsk, where the vehicle was subsequently produced as the MAZ-200. The M-2 medium

IS-3s pass through Red Square on a wet and foggy 7th November 1950. The 7th November parades and their practice runs have often coincided with the first snows of winter.

and AT-T heavy tracked artillery tractors were both paraded regularly on Red Square from May 1949.

The ZiS-150 was displayed on Red Square in several versions in 1949, including in VDV airborne forces markings, with sixteen "desantniki" paratroopers in the rear cargo bed of each vehicle. Another new Red Square parade debut in 1950 was the 6x4 YaAZ-210G, which was demonstrated towing the 152mm M-1943 (D-1) field howitzer. The YaAZ-210G was primarily used as a ballast type artillery tractor and for towing full rather than semi-trailers.

M-2 tracked artillery tractors produced at MMZ in the Moscow suburb of Mytischi again towed wartime 152mm M-1937 (ML-20) Corps gun-howitzers through Red Square. While artillery tractors changed generation due to advances in mechanical technology, advances in towed artillery pieces were generally slower; hence pre-war artillery pieces were towed through Red Square by successive generations of pre-war and post-war artillery tractors. The 100mm KS-19 anti-aircraft gun was now being regularly paraded on Red Square, the newer weapon with its PUAZO off carriage fire control system increasing the capability of conventional anti-aircraft weapons to engage with increasingly faster jet powered fighter aircraft. The 100mm KS-19 would soon replace the wartime 85mm M-1939 and M-1944 weapons during Red Square parades. The ZiS-110B parade limousine meantime made its public debut in 1950, but in Vladivostok rather than Moscow, providing transport for Admiral of the Pacific Fleet N.G.Kuznetsov during a parade in the city.

M-2 medium artillery tractors towing 152mm M-1937 (ML-20) "Corps Duplex" heavy artillery pieces through Red Square, 7th November 1950. The banner in the background denoting the 33rd Anniversary of the 1917 Russian Revolution definitively confirms the date.

GAZ-63 4x4 trucks on display, 7th November 1950. These vehicles are armed with a tripod-mounted 12.7mm DShKM anti-aircraft heavy machine gun for display purposes.

The YaAZ-200 4x2 heavy load carrier was introduced into Soviet Army service from 1947 and was paraded on Red Square into the early 1950s. The vehicle was powered by a diesel engine, pioneering for Soviet military trucks at the time, and would be re-designated MAZ-200 after production was transferred to Minsk.

1951

As 1951 dawned, the war in Korea continued to dominate international relations, with the threat of escalation beyond the borders of Korea due to the superpowers being involved in a complex weave of allegiances. By 14th March, UN forces had recaptured the capital city Seoul. Meanwhile in the Soviet Union there were arrests of government officials in Georgia as dissent and corruption in equal measure in some Soviet Republics was dealt with by Moscow. On Red Square, 1951 would mark the Soviet Army closing the gap in mechanised infantry transport, which had always been a known and accepted deficiency, with the introduction of the BTR-152 wheeled APC.

1st May 1951

The 1st May 1951 parade, taken by Defence Minister (since 1950 Minister of War) Vasilevsky showed how rapidly the post-war Soviet Union was recovering and how the Soviet Army was one of the principal beneficiaries. The wartime T-34-85 medium and immediate post-war IS-3 heavy tanks were again the standard tank types on display, and together with the SU-100 self-propelled gun represented the armoured element of the columns that passed before the Lenin Mausoleum from which Iosef V. Stalin watched the procession. But in 1951 it was the softskin secondary vehicles that heralded the rapid changes in military manufacturing in the post-war Soviet Union. The

SU-100s parade through Red Square, 1st May 1950. These (Obiekt-138) SU-100s were built post-war at Plant №174 in Omsk and thereby have many detail differences from "Uralmash" vehicles. The small batch of SU-100s was built post-war at Plant №174 in Omsk primarily to retain the workforce and their skill-sets, hence production capacity, while the plant was being readied for series production of the T-54 tank production.

artillery towed through Red Square remained primarily of Second World War vintage, including the 122mm M-1938 (M-30) howitzer, the late war 100mm M-1944 (BS-3) dual-purpose gun, and immediate post-war weapons such as the 85mm D-44 divisional gun, but there were subtle changes in the parade line-up of the early 1950s. The wartime 152mm Br-2 tracked gun and 203mm B-4 tracked howitzer were now towed through Red Square by the new generation AT-T heavy tracked artillery tractor. The 37mm M-1939 (61K) and 85mm M-1939 (52K) anti-aircraft guns were now towed through Red Square by the 6x6 ZiS-151 Soviet built development of the Lend-Lease US6 Studebaker which has served the Red Army well in the latter months of the Second World War. The BM-13 and BM-31 MRS systems were now also mounted on the ZiS-151 rather than the Lend-Lease Studebaker US6.

The YaAZ-210G wheeled artillery tractor was again displayed in May 1951, towing the 152mm M-1943 (D-1) howitzer. At the time the YaAZ plant in Yaroslavl was developing more powerful 6x6 heavy trucks that were duly demonstrated on Red Square. Series production would soon however be handed over to the KrAZ plant, located at Kremenchug in Ukraine, with the later KrAZ-214 and KrAZ-255 series becoming the standard Soviet Army 6x6 all-terrain load carriers for the next decades.

The wartime Ya-12 tracked artillery tractor had by 1951 been long-since replaced by the new post-war M-2, but the new tractor continued to be displayed towing the pre-war 152mm M-1937 (ML-20) gun-howitzer. The new AT-T heavy tracked artillery tractor was meantime now being displayed on Red Square towing the pre-war 152mm Br-2 and 203mm B-4 tracked howitzers, a curious combination of a 1950s tracked vehicle towing 1930s vintage tracked howitzers which looked distinctly medieval when new - but were powerful and feared artillery weapons on a particularly stable firing platform.

The same Plant №174 Omsk production SU-100s from the rear. The Omsk built SU-100s differed from the Uralmash vehicles in detail. These SU-100s do not feature the crew personal effects stowage box standardised on post-war Uralmash SU-100s.

7th November 1951 – 34th Anniversary of the Great October Socialist Revolution

The 7th November 1951 parade repeated the 1st May format, but the 7th Nov 1951 Red Square parade witnessed the debut of the first Soviet series production armoured personnel carrier (APC) type - known as Bronetransporter (BTR) in Russian. The small BTR-40, which was a reconnaissance scout vehicle that also served as a small APC, was apparently never displayed on Red Square; however the larger BTR-152, based on a modified 6x6 ZiS-151 chassis, would become a standard feature of Red Square parades throughout the 1950s. The new BTR-152, the first Soviet designed wheeled APC to be series manufactured, was displayed on Red Square in 1950, towing the wartime 57mm ZiS-2 anti-tank and 76.2mm ZiS-3 dual-purpose guns that had served the Red Army to great effect during the war. The wartime 57mm ZiS-2 as towed through Red Square in 1950 by the new BTR-152 was not such an anachronism as it may have appeared. The 57mm weapon had excellent armour-piercing characteristics, with the calibre also being used for the 57mm S-60 anti-aircraft gun concurrently paraded on Red Square, and for the dual 57mm S-68 installation later mounted on the mobile ZSU-57-2. The 57mm calibre proved effective and durable with regard to armour penetration, and is still used by the modern Russian Army in the 21st Century.

The heavy armour remained as per the May parade, with the T-34-85 medium tank and SU-100 self-propelled gun joined as in May by the IS-3 heavy tank, with other recent new vehicles including the YaAZ-200 4x2 truck and the M-2 and AT-T tracked tractors towing the 152mm M-1937 (ML-20) and 152mm Br-2 tracked howitzers respectively. The airborne ASU-57 had entered production in 1951, demonstrating the rapidly increasing firepower being provided to the Soviet VDV airborne forces, but it was not immediately demonstrated in public, being displayed on Red Square only from 1957.

Days before the 7th November Red Square parade in Moscow, the United States had on 1st November tested a hydrogen bomb at Eniwetok Atoll in the Marshall Islands. Soviet defence spending increased immediately and exponentially as a result of the greater perceived threat, and by 1952 was 45% higher than in 1950 as the international superpower "arms race" became well advanced.

BTR-152s towing 76.2mm M-1942 (ZiS-3) dual purpose guns through Red Square, 7th November 1951.

1952

The main international focus at the beginning of 1952 remained the ongoing war in Korea. In Europe, Stalin on 10th March suggested to the United States and its NATO allies the possibility of allowing Germany a level of post-war independence, on condition of enforced German neutrality. The superpowers would in return disengage their military forces in the country. The suggestion did not meet with a positive response. A few weeks later, on 23rd July, Belgium, France, Italy, Luxembourg, the Netherlands and West Germany formed the European Coal and Steel Community, which would in the years ahead morph from a trade organisation to a construct called the European Union. In later years the latter would in turn morph into a remarkable resemblance to the command structure of the Soviet Union as East and West exchanged roles in the early 21st Century.

From a domestic administrative perspective, the designation of the controlling body of the Communist Party was in 1952 changed from VKP(b) to the slightly shorter and more wieldy KPSS or Communist Party of the Soviet Union (CPSU), while the Politburo was renamed the Presidium. Stalin was by 1952 meantime becoming increasingly paranoid with regard to those around him, perhaps not entirely without foundation.

1st May 1952

The 1st May 1952 parade taken by Minister of War Vasilevsky began with cadets of the military school of the Verkhnogo Sovieta (Upper Council) of the RSFSR and all of the usual military and defence related academies, (MVO) garrison troops and detachments from all the branches of the Soviet armed forces.

T-34-85 medium tanks and SU-100 self-propelled guns again represented the armoured might, followed in May 1952 by towed artillery including the still impressive wartime 152mm Br-2 tracked howitzer, which was in 1952 still being towed through Red Square, but now by the AT-T heavy tracked tractor rather than Lend-Lease Allis-Chalmers HD-10W or indigenous S-65 artillery tractors.

Soviet archive information with regard to the flypast in May 1952 is conflated. The 1st May 1952 parade was expected to include the public debut of the Il-28 frontal level bomber, but due to poor visibility over Moscow the flypast was grounded after the aircraft had taken off for the parade debut. The visibility deteriorated such that one aircraft crashed on the return flight and another was badly damaged on landing. Other archive information including footage purportedly of the parade shows a flypast, with Stalin's son Vasily, then Commander of the Air Forces of the Moscow Military District (MVO) performing circuits above Red Square.

THE SOVIET ARMY ON PARADE 1946-91

Plant №174 Omsk production SU-100s parade through Red Square in 1952. Note the late type commander's cupola, and seven track links bolted to the glacis.

From 1952, the ZiS-151 began to be displayed on Red Square mounting weapons system such as the 140mm BM-14 MRS, which replaced the wartime BM-13 "Katyusha". (Tank Museum 2472/D3)

Early production IS-2 heavy tanks on parade in Minsk, 1st May 1952. The IS-2 remained on parade in Minsk many years after it had last been seen on parade in Moscow.

Troops with wartime Moisin Nagant M-1891/30 rifles with cruciform bayonets fixed pass through Red Square on 1st May 1952. Overhead is a flypast by Soviet Tupolev Tu-4 bombers, the Soviet derivative of the American B-29 "Superfortress".

7th November 1952 – 35th Anniversary of the Great October Socialist Revolution

The 7th November 1952 parade represented the end of an era, being the last time the parade commanders would meet on Red Square on horseback. The parade was as usual taken by Minister of War (Defence Minister) Vasilevsky, with Marshal Semeon K. Timoshenko making the main speech after the meeting of the commanders on horseback on Red Square. The November 1952 Red Square parade was also the last that would be presided over by Iosef Stalin, who would die a few weeks before the following parade in May 1953, after a temporary return to the uncertain times endured by Soviet citizens during the purges of the late 1930s. A wave of anti-Jewish sentiment primarily related to senior government personnel ultimately led to what was known in the Soviet Union as the Doctor's Plot, with thirteen doctors arrested, the majority of whom had Jewish surnames. A wave of anti-Semitism followed* and a reign of terror against Jews, or more generally those that Stalin had personal issues with, would ensure in the months before Stalin's death in 1953.

With regard to military equipment displayed on Red Square, November 1952 was the parade debut of the new 140mm calibre BM-14 (BM-14-16) multiple rocket system (MRS) accepted into Soviet Army service in 1952. The BM-14 was based on the new 6x6 ZiS-151 chassis with a firing range of 10km, and replaced the wartime BM-13 system. The BM-14 remained the standard MRS in Soviet motorised rifle divisions until the deployment of the 9K51 "Grad" (BM-21) in the following decade.

BTR-152s on parade, 7th November 1952. The BTR-152 now provided armoured protection for infantry, with new combined arms mechanised warfare principles adopted accordingly by the Soviet Army.

---

* In Soviet internal passports ethnicity was documented, including the definition "Evree" for some Soviet citizens with specific Jewish heritage.

1953

There was a mix of international developments in 1953 that would over time have a significant effect on the Soviet Union and its international relationships. On 22nd April, Viet Minh forces moved into neighbouring Laos at the beginning of the Laotian Civil War, which would become inextricably linked to the developing war in Vietnam. On 27th July, the United Nations, China and North Korea signed an armistice, and the Korean War was officially at an end. South Korea refused to sign and remained technically at war with North Korea into the 21st Century when relations between South and North Korea again became a subject of concern for the world.

1953 was also an eventful year domestically in the Soviet Union. On 1st March, after the purge of the doctors involved in the "Doctor's Plot", Stalin turned on the Jewish population in Moscow, ordering their immediate expulsion from the city. He suffered a stroke the same day however, while at his dacha (country house) at Kuntsevo in the western suburbs of Moscow. There followed some significant subterfuge, which involved delays in attending to the stricken "Vozhd" or leader, which may have been due to fear of intervening, or by some accounts due to Lavrenty Beria's intent to ensure that Stalin did not recover. Stalin was pronounced dead several days later, on 5th March, on the day the Jews were to have been deported from Moscow. He was embalmed in the same manner as had been Lenin, by the same organisation, and on 9th March laid to rest in the Lenin Mausoleum in Red Square alongside his former revolutionary leader and mentor. The Lenin Mausoleum would for several years henceforth bear the name of both Lenin and Stalin, and the banners on the wall of the GUM department store on Red Square would also for some time reflect both leaders. Meanwhile a period of rapid de-Stalinisation would ensue after Stalin's death in 1953, which would continue until the end of the decade.

There were many rapid changes after the death of Stalin, one of the most important of which was an amnesty issued by the Presidium of the Supreme Soviet of the USSR (SM SSSR) on 27th March 1953 to many categories of prisoners held in the Main Administration of Corrective Labour Camps - known by the Soviet acronym GULAG, with over 1.5 million short-term military and political prisoners being released in the following three months.* The Ministerstvo Vnutrennykh Del (Ministry of Internal Affairs - MVD) was meantime merged with the Ministerstvo Gosudarstvennoy Besopastnosti (Ministry of State Security

The ZiS-110B parade limousine had replaced the horse by the time of the 1st May 1953 Red Square parade. The first Defence Minister to use such a vehicle was Marshal Nikolai Bulganin in 1953, followed by Marshal Georgy Zhukov from 1955. (Ogonok)

After the death of Stalin in 1953, his name was added under that of Lenin on the Mausoleum, from the review stand of which the Soviet hierarchy observed all Soviet Red Square parades.

---

* At the height of Stalin's purges the peak GULAG and penal system population - primarily criminals rather than political prisoners - is now believed to have been 1.7 million. Source: Andrei Martyanov - Losing Military Supremacy.

- MGB) into an enlarged MVD structure. One of the consequences of releasing large numbers of inmates from the GULAG system, which held some political prisoners but the majority of whom were the criminal underclass of society, was that there was a crime wave as the released inmates descended on Moscow. In the classic dictatorial manner of bringing a solution to an internally invented problem, Lavrenty Beria deployed MVD troops on the streets of Moscow to restore order. Many in the Soviet government, Khrushchev and Marshal Zhukov included, considered that Beria was himself the potential bigger problem rather than the solution, and feared that he was deploying MVD troops to stage a "putsch" (coup d'état). With Stalin dead and the process of de-Stalinisation underway in the Soviet Union, many of Stalin's most hated accomplices now found themselves in the position of those they had hounded during the Stalin years, in which clean up and retribution senior Soviet Army officers played a major role. Following from the actions described, the most notorious NKVD commissar of all time, Lavrenty Beria, having after the death of Stalin initially - and almost bizarrely - as First Deputy Premier been involved in a liberalisation of the Soviet regime was himself overthrown by Nikita Khrushchev in collaboration with Marshals Georgy Zhukov and Kirill Moskalenko.

Khrushchev arranged a special meeting of the Presidium on 26th June 1953, the primary purpose of which was to detain Beria, who was arrested with the direct involvement of the Soviet Army in the form of the aforesaid Marshals Zhukov and Moskalenko, with the compliance and inaction of internal security troops being ensured by the Soviet Army directed by Zhukov. The feared and hated Lavrenty Beria was tried on 2nd July, with Khrushchev personally denouncing him. Beria's predilection for the rape of young women kidnapped off the streets of Moscow was well known to the military and throughout the capital city. He was charged with and admitted to the rape offences, and was also accused among other things of working for the British, with his crimes being made public on 10th July. The headquarters of the Moscow Military District (MVO), best known to the general public for its participation in military parades on Red Square, was the scene of Beria meeting his fate. On the direct instruction of Khrushchev and Zhukov, Beria was executed by Soviet Army General Pavel Batinsky, after which unaccompanied women doubtless felt safer walking alone in the streets of Moscow. The announcement of Beria's execution was made public only on 23rd December 1953, though the exact timing and circumstances of his execution are contradictory. The MVD, specifically Beria's former NKVD accomplices, were also purged during this period. Khrushchev had gained significant prestige by his actions, ably aided by the command structure of the Soviet Army. The Soviet Union was rapidly moving forward from the days of repression under Stalin and better times were ahead, with the Soviet Army and Soviet Air Force being at the forefront of Soviet stability and prestige during what could have in other circumstances been very uncertain years.

The prestige of the conventional Soviet armed forces was however no more to Khrushchev's liking than it had been to Stalin before him. As Khruschchev, the rocket enthusiast, consolidated his position, he made the decision to reduce the size and power of the Soviet conventional armed forces, particularly the Soviet Army and Soviet Air Force. The Soviet Navy was less directly affected, as in Khrushchev's mind the Soviet Navy had its role to play in strategic rocket deployment. There were real concerns that a military coup could still happen in the country, with Marshal Zhukov on his forced retirement advising Khrushchev that even loyal supporters such as Marshal Moskalenko had talked openly of such a possibility. In the second half of the 1950s, Khruschchev reduced the manpower of the Soviet Army from 5.8 million to 3.7 million, an almost 50% reduction over a particularly short time period.

The Soviet Union on 12th August 1953 detonated its first thermo-nuclear hydrogen bomb at the Semipalatinsk test polygon in the Soviet

Republic of Kazakhstan, four years after the first Soviet successful test of an atomic bomb. The thermo-nuclear weapon had been devised by the Soviet scientist Igor Kurchatov at an institute bearing his name located in northwest Moscow, based on principles developed by the Soviet physicist Andrey Sakharov. Before March 1953, there had been three nuclear tests in the Soviet Union, but between August 1953 and December 1955 there would be sixteen, including three thermo-nuclear (hydrogen bomb) tests. That year, the German rocket engineer Helmut Gröttrup and his group who had been captured in 1945 and had worked on the Soviet rocket program were finally released and returned to Germany, having not worked on rockets for the previous two years to ensure they did not have the very latest sensitive information on Soviet developments to reveal on their arrival back in Germany. These German rocket scientists had spent eight years in captivity following a war with the Soviet Union that had lasted four years. The 1950s would also see the rapid development of Soviet nuclear delivery systems, with the first medium range strategic rockets being paraded on Red Square before the end of the decade.

1st May 1953

With Stalin dead, there was an initial period of reverence before the era of "de-Stalinisation" came into play. One immediate change on Red Square was the adding of Stalin's name to the Lenin Mausoleum, which by 1st May now featured the names of both former leaders, with Stalin's name under that of Lenin as founder of the Soviet State.

The party line-up on the review stand on top of the Lenin Mausoleum was in May 1953 largely civilian, including Georgy Malenkov as the new Soviet Premier and first secretary of the KPSS - the Communist Party of the Soviet Union (CPSU), Vyacheslav Molotov (of Molotov-Ribbentrop Pact fame) as Minister of Foreign Affairs, Beria as Minister of Internal Affairs (MVD), the Minister of the Verkhnogo Sovieta (Upper Council) Klimenti Voroshilov and a temporarily sidelined Nikita Khrushchev. The line-up was rather

These SU-100s are also Plant №174 Omsk production vehicles, fitted with the second (standard) version of the crew personal effects container.

shuffling in nature, as it was not entirely clear who would ultimately lead the post-Stalinist Soviet Union, and Malenkov would be short-term in his new position as Soviet Premier.

The parade began with a meeting of two ZiS-110B cabriolet parade limousines, for the first time replacing the horses that had been used for the traditional meeting of the parade commanders on Red Square since the days of the Russian Revolution. The parade was taken by Marshal Kirill S. Moskolenko standing in the rear of one of the ZiS-110B parade vehicles. Marching columns included military cadets and troops representing all branches of the Soviet armed forces, followed by the armoured and vehicular columns led by vehicles of the Tamanskaya Motorized Rifle Division.

The newly introduced GAZ-69 light vehicle which made its parade debut in May 1953 was used for leading the vehicular parade columns that year and would continue to do so for the next two decades. BTR-152s were again displayed on their own, and towing wartime 57mm ZiS-2 anti-tank guns, 85mm D-44 divisional guns and 160mm M-160 mortars. There were now also massed columns of new GAZ-51 4x2 general service trucks with seated infantry, YaAZ-200 trucks towing 100mm M-1944 (BS-3) dual-purpose guns, and 4x2 ZiS-150 trucks paraded in airborne marking with VDV desant paratroopers in the rear of each vehicle. ZiS-151 all-terrain trucks towed the 122mm M-1938 (M-30) and 152mm M-1943 (D-1) howitzers and mounted the BM-14 and BM-24 multiple rocket systems. M-2 tracked artillery tractors towed 240mm M-240 mortars through Red Square in 1953. The heavier AT-T tracked artillery tractor introduced at the turn of the decade continued to be used to tow 100mm KS-19 anti-aircraft guns which in combination with the latest PUAZO off-carriage directional control systems could engage aircraft including contemporary jet fighters.

The towed 85mm D-44 divisional gun as demonstrated in May 1953, was a replacement for the earlier 100mm M-1944 (BS-3), with a specialised VDV airborne forces auxiliary propelled version and the 85mm D-48 specialised anti-tank version also being demonstrated on Red Square in the 1950s and early 1960s. Although the 85mm D-44 divisional gun and its airborne auxiliary propelled SD-44 variant were lighter and marginally smaller in calibre than the wartime 100mm M-1944 (BS-3), the improved ammunition types with improved ballistic properties gave better armour penetration, such that the 85mm D-44 and D-48 were particularly useful weapons. The auxiliary propelled SD-44 variant also gave the emerging Soviet VDV

The 6x4 YaAZ-210G was used as an artillery tractor, here towing the 152mm M-1943 (D-1) howitzer through Red Square, and also for limited capacity tank transport applications.

airborne forces significant capability for engaging hard targets in support of airborne landings.

The 1st May 1953 parade would be the last public appearance of Lavrenty Beria, the feared chief of the enlarged MVD. As Khrushchev took the reins of power, he worked with Molotov and Zhukov to redress Beria's excesses. As earlier related, the much-hated chief of the secret police was arrested in June with the involvement of the Soviet Army, and together with several of his closest allies, was trialled in secret and was subsequently shot.

On 7th September Khrushchev became 1st Secretary of the CPSU. A new era of Soviet leadership very different from the Stalin years had begun, with Khrushchev bringing his own specific character traits to the country internally and also in its international relations.

On 25th September 1953, the Soviet Union began to return wartime German and Axis prisoners of war. They had been used on construction projects, including the building of the Moscow Metro, having spent many more years in the country as prisoners than they had served as combat troops.

Internationally, French forces were now engaged in combat with the Viet Minh in Vietnam, which would culminate in the Battle of Dien Bien Phu the following spring. The United States in November 1953 began sending aid to South Vietnam, and also began its embarkation towards on a new kind of war, pitching conventional forces against an elusive people's army enemy that was invisible in plain sight, in the paddy fields by day, and on the offensive by night. Cambodia had also moved to full independence during this period, and the region became set to become a main focus of American foreign policy for the next two decades.

On the other side of the world, on the island of Cuba, two revolutionary brothers, Fidel and Raul Castro had in July started the Cuban revolutionary movement, and in October led an attack on a military base in Cuba at the beginning of a local and drawn-out revolutionary conflict, which would less than a decade later bring the world superpowers to the brink of nuclear war.

7th November 1953 - 36th Anniversary of the Great October Socialist Revolution

The 36th Anniversary of the "Great October Socialist Revolution" was observed on 7th November 1953 by Khrushchev and other party members, standing on the parade review stand on the Lenin Mausoleum, now adorned with the names of both Lenin and Stalin. The parade was attended by foreign delegations, including from the world's newest emerging superpower - China.

The parade began as usual with the meeting of two ZiS-110B cabriolet limousines, followed by marching columns of cadets from military academies, and all the branches of the Soviet armed forces, some still armed with wartime era sub-machine guns. The parade was taken by Soviet Defence Minister Marshal of the Soviet Union Bulganin. The Tamanskaya Guards Motorised Rifle Division and Kantimirovskaya Guards Tank Division provided the majority of armoured vehicles on parade. Tank crews participating in the marching parade were also still armed with the wartime PPS-43, which remained a compact and versatile weapon for use by armoured vehicle crews.

The mechanised parade began as was standard in the 1950s with GAZ-69 parade lead vehicles as introduced the previous May leading massed columns of BTR-152 wheeled armoured personnel carriers (still the earliest variant with no central tyre pressure control system) followed by more

BTR-152s towing 57mm ZiS-2 anti-tank guns, 85mm D-44 divisional guns and 160mm M-160 mortars. M-2 tracked tractors towing 240mm M-240 mortars were followed during the parade by AT-T tractors with 100mm M-1949 (KS-19) anti-aircraft guns as in the previous parade line-up.

ZiS-150 4x2 trucks in VDV airborne markings paraded past the Lenin Mausoleum with VDV airborne infantry seated on benches in the rear of each vehicle, followed by 6x6 ZiS-151 trucks towing 152mm M-1943 (D-1) howitzers and BM-24 MRS, which were also mounted on the ZiS-151 chassis. A subtle change was that the cabs of these ZiS vehicles were now of monocoque all stamped steel construction as machine presses and thin section sheet steel became more readily available. AT-T tracked artillery tractors again towed 100mm KS-19 anti-aircraft guns, which with their associated PUAZO off-carriage fire control could intercept and destroy contemporary jet engine fighter aircraft. The November 1953 parade was accompanied by a flypast consisting of fighter, bomber and transport aircraft of the Soviet Air Force.

The 200mm BM-20-4 (BMD-20) MRS was also mounted on the 6x6 ZiS-151 chassis. The early production sheet steel over wood frame cabs on GAZ and ZiS vehicles were now replaced by cabs of all steel stamped and welded construction.

The GAZ-69 light vehicle entered production in 1953 and was immediately demonstrated on Red Square. These two door GAZ-69s are configured as VDV airborne forces vehicles.

The ZiS-110B, as seen here during a parade practice in the 1950s, was the standard parade limousine used by Defence Ministers and Parade Commanders during between 1953 and 1961.

1954

From a Cold War perspective, 1954 was an uneventful year, but domestically there were some internal changes in the Soviet Union, one of which, the signing of a single document relating at the time to a Soviet internal administration matter, would some sixty years later have a major impact on two former Soviet Republics, namely the Russian Federation and Ukraine.

On 27th February 1954, the Soviet mainstream newspaper "Pravda" announced the transfer by the Supreme Soviet of the USSR of the Crimean "Oblast" (region) to the Ukrainian Soviet Socialist Republic, because of: *"economic commonalities, territorial proximity, and cultural and communication links."* as espoused by Khrushchev at the time. The transfer of the Crimean peninsula of the Soviet Union on the Black Sea, home to the Soviet naval base at Sevastopol, was not at the time seen as being of great significance as it was a transfer between republics within the Soviet Union, but the administrative transfer would lead to a major clash between the Russian Federation and Ukraine in 2014, the results of which continue to reverberate through to the present day. The reasoning for the initial change in status was not entirely clear even at the time. The later Soviet 1959 Census showed that in that year the Crimean peninsula had a population of 268,000 ethnic Ukrainians and 858,000 ethnic Russians. The main industry in the region was tourism, with Crimea being the beneficiary of tourism from the rest of the Soviet Union. The other former "indigenous" population had been the estimated 300,000 strong Crimean Tatar community that had been deported from Crimea in May 1944 due to their alleged collaboration with the Nazis in 1941-43, with the Crimean Autonomous Republic becoming an Oblast or region (of the Soviet Union) in 1945. Khrushchev's benevolent gift of 1954 would be of no significance during the era of the Soviet Union, but there was significantly more logic to what is oft referred to as a "drunken whim" than Khrushchev (himself a Ukrainian) is often given credit for. The population of the RSFSR (the Russian Socialist Republic), together with Ukraine and Belorussia, represented a significant percentage of the overall Soviet population (nearly 80% at the end of the decade). There were still some elements of seething nationalism in Ukraine related to Ukraine's specific history in World War Two, and Khrushchev could not afford for this separation to grow. The economic links as stated were rather less significant than the political requirement to bind the core countries of the Soviet Union together. Crimea had a long history as a conflict zone, a borderland.* It was under Ottoman Empire control from 1478 until seized by Imperial Russia in the late 18th Century, and had been the battleground between Imperial Russia and Great Britain in the middle of the following century. It was the Russians that the British engaged at the Battle of Balaclava near Sevastopol, Crimea in 1854.** Concurrently with handing Crimea to Ukraine, Khrushchev also allowed the repatriation of the Balkars, the Chechens, the Ingush, the Kalmyks and the Karachai who had been deported from their homelands in 1943-44. Such a privilege was not extended to the Volga Germans or the Crimean Tatars. The handing over of Crimea to Ukraine, an inter-republic transfer within the Soviet Union, was an administrative matter of little relevance in 1954, but it would as stated lead to war between Russia and Ukraine in 2014.

Another administrative change, carried out

---

* The Russian term "krai" from which the name of Ukraine is evolved means "at the edge" or "borderland". It is derived from the Slavic word "Krayina", meaning frontier region.

** During the Crimean War, Russia's strongest ally was the United States of America, with widespread support within the American government, the public and the press for the Russians in their struggle against the British and French colonial powers. American doctors worked with the Russian Army in Crimea, and there were recruitment drives aimed at sending mercenary troops to assist the Russians, which did not however materialise into an American armed presence in Crimea.

in March 1954, was that the recently enlarged Ministry of Internal Affairs (MVD), which had been considered a threat to stability the year before under Beria prior to his arrest, was again split into two organisations. The MVD, with name unchanged, would henceforth be responsible for domestic crime and disorder, an armed police or militia organisation. The other, the Komitet Gosudarstvennoy Besopasnosti - The Committee for State Security, would be responsible for protecting the interests of the State at home and abroad. The latter organisation has always been best known by its acronym - the KGB.

In Vietnam, the Battle of Dien Bien Phu raged from March to May 1954, as the French attempted to cut Viet Minh supply lines into Laos. The French ultimately lost the battle, and the war, and their colonial years in the region came to an unseemly end. The United States was already providing assistance to South Vietnam, and would opt to inherit France's problems in the region. While the Soviet Union settled into a pattern of regular military parades demonstrating regular parade debuts of new military technology, events in Asia Pacific meantime continued to hold the focus of former colonial European powers and the United States.

As the Soviet Union celebrated the 1st May public holiday in 1954, the battle of Dien Bien Phu was coming to its conclusion in Vietnam, resulting in defeat for the French Expeditionary Corps in the 1st Indo-China War, and with it the end of French colonial influence in Indochina. Vietnam would soon be temporarily divided at the 17th Parallel demarcation line, with the Viet Minh communists in control of the north. As Moscow celebrated the 1st May holiday on Red Square, the French military experience in Vietnam was nearly at an end, and the American military experience in the country was about to begin.

On the superpower "arms-race" front, the United States in March 1954 successfully tested an air deployable hydrogen bomb, which raised the stakes again in the nuclear arms race between the post-war superpowers. While the handover of Crimea to Ukraine was in 1954 an entirely bureaucratic if positive procedure, with the later repercussions never considered at any level in the Soviet Union or abroad at the time, there was domestic unrest elsewhere in the Soviet Union in 1954, with riots in the GULAG system in the towns of Norilsk and Vorkuta, which required military intervention to suppress.

1st May 1954

The 1st May 1954 parade began with the traditional meeting of the parade commanders standing in their respective ZiS-110B cabriolet limousines, with the parade being again taken by Marshal of the Soviet Union Bulganin. The BTR-152 wheeled APC was demonstrated in large numbers, followed by ZiS-150 4x2 trucks in VDV airborne forces markings and M-2 tracked tractors towing both 100mm M-1944 (BS-3) dual purpose guns and 240mm M-240 heavy mortars. The GAZ-63 4x4 all-terrain variant of the GAZ-51 was displayed towing the 85mm D-44 divisional gun. The 130mm M-1946 (M-46) field gun had its public debut at the 1st May 1954 parade, being towed in travel order with the barrel withdrawn out of battery lock to reduce overall towing length. The weapon was significant in that in addition to firing HE-Frag and other ammunition to a maximum range of 27.2km, the weapon fired an armour-piercing round which could penetrate 230mm of vertical armour plate, not insignificant for a field artillery piece. The 130mm M-46 field gun would remain a parade standard for many years, being towed by the AT-S, then subsequently the ATS-59 and latterly the ATS-59G tracked tractor. Other towed artillery featured on Red Square in 1954 included the aforementioned 85mm D-44 divisional gun, which had replaced the late wartime 100mm M-1944 (BS-3) weapon. The BM-20-4 (BMD-20) MRS was also displayed in May 1954, mounted on the original ZiS-151 chassis.

The major highlight of the 1st May 1954 parade was in the air rather than on the ground, with the public debut of the Myasishchev M-4 (NATO: Bison) strategic bomber. The appearance was significant in that the M-4 was the first Soviet jet powered bomber with the cruising range to overfly the United States while transporting nuclear weapons. On 1st May the aircraft overflew Red Square escorted by MiG-15 and MiG-17 fighter aircraft, a year before the debut of the better known Tu-95 (NATO: Bear) turboprop powered long-range bomber.

BTR-152s pass through Red Square on 1st May 1954. The banner refers to the 300 year anniversary of the Treaty of Pereyaslav (today located in central Ukraine) in 1654, by which the local Cossacks swore allegiance to the Tsar of Muskovy, effectively the beginning of "formal" relations between what - centuries later - would become the Soviet Republics of Russia and Ukraine.

Defence Minister Marshal of the Soviet Union Bulganin in his ZiS-110B parade limousine, 1st May 1954.

7th November 1954 – 37th Anniversary of the Great October Socialist Revolution

The 11th November 1954 parade was as in May reviewed by the Defence Minister Marshal of the Soviet Union Nikolai A. Bulganin, with the parade commander being Kirill S. Moskalenko, who would become Marshal of the Soviet Army in 1955, with both standing in the rear of ZiS-110B cabriolet parade limousines. The new Soviet Premier Nikita Khrushchev watched from the parade review stand atop the Lenin Mausoleum together with the other Soviet hierarchy including Klimenti E. Voroshilov, V.M. Molotov, L.M. Kaganovich, A. I. Mikoyan, G.M. Malenkov and others.

The November 1954 parade again began with massed columns of BTR-152 wheeled APCs, followed by now increasingly obsolescent T-34-85 tanks and mechanised artillery including the 140mm calibre, sixteen rocket BM-14-16 and the 200mm calibre, four rocket BM-20-4 (BMD-20) MRS, both mounted on the ZiS-151 6x6 truck. The GAZ-69 was used for parade lead vehicle purposes, with other secondary vehicles including the ZiS-150 4x4 truck in VDV airborne forces markings and the M-2 tracked artillery tractor continuing to tow heavy artillery and 240mm mortars through Red Square.

The Red Square parade was overflown by Tu-95 long-range turbo-prop strategic bombers in November 1954. The Tu-95 was considerably slower than the jet engine powered Myasishchev M-4, but had longer range and could reach any city in the United States to deliver its nuclear weapon cargo.

Defence Minister Marshal of the Soviet Union Bulganin and Moscow garrison (MVO) Commander Moskalenko meet in the ZiS-110B parade limousines, 7th November 1954.

BM-20-4 (BMD-20) MRS with Guards symbols on the cab doors at the 37th Anniversary of the Great October Socialist revolution, 7th November 1954.

BM-14 MRS also with Guards symbols at the 7th November 1954 Red Square parade.

Early production BTR-152 wheeled APCs on parade, 7th November 1954. The vehicle was armed as standard with a pintle-mounted 7.62mm SGMB section machine gun.

1955

1955 was another landmark year with regard to declining Soviet-American relations and the drawing up of alliances on both sides of the political divide. On 22nd January 1955, the United States publically announced plans to develop inter-continental ballistic missiles (ICBMs) armed with nuclear warheads. The development of such rockets had in fact been underway for some time in both the United States and the Soviet Union, but the coming years would see the deployment of increasingly long-range rockets capable of delivering nuclear warheads with greater speed and less chance of interception than any long range turboprop or jet powered bomber aircraft.

1955 was also the year in which the Soviet bloc formalised its Cold War alliance partnerships, as NATO had done in 1949. The Warsaw Treaty of Friendship, Cooperation and Mutual Assistance was signed on 14th May 1955, creating what would become known as the Warsaw Pact. Although the Soviet Union was the founder member of the Warsaw Pact, and its controlling entity, the Warsaw Pact was not an entirely Soviet concept. The formation of NATO as a formal Western defensive alliance in 1949 was an obvious concern for the Soviet Union, but it was the German participation in NATO that was the catalyst for the formation of the Warsaw Pact. That West Germany was being allowed to both re-arm and join NATO caused consternation among the bordering nations that had suffered at the hands of Germany during World War Two. The security pact was initially driven by Czechoslovakia, which had initially looked to build a defensive pact with East Germany and Poland that would later become the Warsaw Pact.

The immediate post-Stalin years in the Soviet Union were meantime not entirely stable from a domestic perspective, as the country realigned from nearly three decades of the Stalin era. Soviet Premier Malenkov was forced to resign on 8th February 1955, being replaced by former Defence Minister Marshal Bulganin, with Marshal Georgy Zhukov being in turn made Defence Minister the same month. Zhukov had spent many years out of the limelight under Stalin, as his personal popularity and the pride of ordinary citizens in the Soviet Army had in the post war years not been seen as necessarily beneficial by Stalin or his sometimes far from loyal government ministers.

The year 1955 was nevertheless a relatively benign year within the Soviet Union. There were two events during the year however that would have an effect on the world superpowers in the year ahead, one in Europe and one in the Asia Pacific region. On 5th May 1955 (West) Germany had a change in status from occupied zone to that of the independent Federal Republic of Germany. The new country formally joined NATO four days later, on the 10th anniversary of the Allied Victory in Europe. The formation of NATO in 1949 as a defensive European and American alliance against external threats, Soviet or otherwise, had been well received in Europe, especially by those countries which would always find trouble meeting their financial defence commitments to the alliance. But the accession of Germany into NATO was an altogether different matter, as by default it allowed Germany to re-arm, albeit within the NATO alliance, and the re-arming of Germany had as previously described always been a major concern from both an Eastern European and a Soviet perspective. A line had been crossed. The other line that was written in stone from a Soviet perspective was that the reunification of Germany should not be allowed without guaranteed neutrality, lest Germany again be the cause of instability in Europe. Germany would reunify in 1989, and instability returned to Europe, almost as if by plan, in the years that would follow.

In the same year that events were unfolding in Germany, the Soviet Army removed its last troops from Austria. The final German prisoners of war held on construction projects in the Soviet Union returned home that year. In Great Britain meantime, the country also entered a new era, as the wartime British leader Churchill was finally replaced in office by Anthony Eden after his second post-war term as prime minister.

The United States was committed militarily via NATO to the defence of Western Europe, albeit with a large number of "buffer zone" Eastern European countries between the Soviet Union and Western Europe. There was thereby a considerable geographical "safety net" in place ensuring that there was little chance of direct superpower conflict in Europe. The United States was also content that the expansion of communism in Europe was at least now being held in check, which could not be said of the gathering storm in the Asia Pacific region. In February 1955, following the defeat of the French at the Battle of Dien Bien Phu, the United States sent its first "military advisors" to Vietnam in what would be the precursor to a two decade long involvement in the country.

1st May 1955

The 1st May 1955 Red Square parade was significant in that it was ten years to the day since Germany had presented its original conditional surrender to the Red Army "GenShtab" headquarters building located at Karlshorst in Berlin. The 1st May 1955 Red Square parade was thereby devoted to the 10th Anniversary of the Victory over Germany in the Second World War (VE Day), but celebrated on 1st May in 1955 rather than 9th May as it would be in subsequent anniversary years.

With Stalin now replaced as Soviet leader by Nikita Khrushchev, the May 1955 parade was reviewed by Marshal of the Soviet Union Georgy K. Zhukov, who had returned to favour, albeit temporarily. He reviewed the May parade in the capacity of Defence Minister of the USSR (which capacity he held from February 1955 to October 1957), with the parade commander being Marshal of the Soviet Union Kirill S. Moskalenko. Both officers stood in the rear of their respective ZiS-

Massed columns of BTR-152 wheeled APCs traverse Red Square, 1st May 1955. (Ogonok).

110B cabriolet versions of the ZiS-110, which had been introduced in 1953 for use by parade commanders at the beginning of Red Square parade ceremonies, replacing the tradition of earlier years where commanders met on horseback. Watching the parade from the review stand alongside Nikita S. Khrushchev were Soviet party leaders including K.E. Voroshilov, V.M. Molotov, A.I. Mikoyan, N.A. Bulganin and L.M. Kaganovich.

The parade was as since 1951 led by massed columns of BTR-152 wheeled APCs, with large columns consisting of lead vehicles and 24 BTR-152s in each section, followed by various towed artillery and multiple rocket systems including the 130mm M-46 field gun towed by the AT-S medium tracked artillery tractor, and the BM-14 (BM-14-16) and BMD-20 (BM-20-4) MRS, both mounted on the ZiS-151 6x6 chassis. One of the new weapons displayed from May 1955 was the 180mm S-23 gun-howitzer, a new calibre for ground forces, which was at the time mislabelled as the 203mm M-1955 by Western observers.

Above Red Square, the Tu-95 long-range turbo-prop bomber, which would remain in service as a long-range reconnaissance aircraft over 60 years later, long outliving the Soviet Union where it was developed, made another public appearance at a central Moscow Red Square parade.

On 9th May 1955, one week after the 1st May parade in Moscow, the United States and NATO admitted the Federal Republic of Germany into the NATO fold, and gave Germany permission to re-militarise as a bolster against the perceived Soviet threat in Europe. 1955 would be the defining year when the Eastern Bloc Cold War alliances were formalised to match the formation of NATO six years prior. Two weeks after the 1st May parade, a pact was signed on 14th May 1955 in Warsaw between the Soviet Union and seven allied countries in Eastern Europe as a counter to NATO. Named after the city where the pact was signed, the Warsaw Pact alliance consisted of Albania (which later withdrew), Bulgaria, Czechoslovakia, East Germany (GDR/DDR), Hungary, Poland and Romania and the Soviet Union, with the Warsaw Pact never expanding beyond its initial membership. The military command structure was however based in Moscow, with the Warsaw Pact being effectively controlled by officers of the Soviet General Staff.

On a wider world stage, the Soviet Union began to explore diplomatic and trade ties with

BM-14 MRS on the ZiS-151 chassis traverse Red Square on 1st May 1955. The definitive later all steel cab is apparent in this view.

countries which had become independent or had more independent status as the pre-war European colonial powers continued to lose their former overseas empires. During 1955, Khrushchev personally toured Afghanistan, Burma and the former jewel in the British colonial crown, India on diplomatic and trade missions. The relationship between the latter country and the Soviet Union would grow particularly close, with the training of many students, particularly engineering and medical professionals, in the Soviet Union - and an ever-increasing relationship with regard to the supply of military hardware, which has continued to the present day.

7th November 1955 - 38th Anniversary of the Great October Socialist Revolution

The November 1955 parade was as in May reviewed by Marshal of the Soviet Union Georgy K. Zhukov in his capacity of Defence Minister of the USSR, with the parade commander again being Marshal of the Soviet Union Kirill S. Moskalenko. Both officers as in May stood in the rear of ZiS-110B cabriolet versions of the ZiS-110 limousine.

The parade continued to demonstrate known weapons, such as the 130mm M-46 field gun and the 240mm M-240 heavy mortar towed by the M-2 artillery tractor, and the BM-14-16 and BM-20-4 (BMD-20) multiple rocket launchers systems. 1955 was also however a year of new Soviet artillery debuts on Red Square, not all of which were immediately obvious to Western observers. The 180mm S-23 long-range field gun, which had made its parade debut in May 1955 was for the second time towed through Red Square by the AT-T heavy tracked artillery tractor. The weapon, mounted on its twin-tyred gun carriage with transport dolly and distinctive pepper-pot muzzle brake was for many years mislabelled by Western military observers as the 203mm M-1955, following the reasonable logic that the weapon was the same calibre as the wartime 203mm B-4 tracked howitzer. What was known and clear long before either the calibre, or the official Soviet designation was revealed was that the weapon could out-range virtually all contemporary NATO towed and self-propelled artillery, and that it was nuclear capable.

Defence Minister Marshal Georgy Zhukov and Parade Commander Kirill Moskalenko in their respective ZiS-110B parade limousines, Manezhnaya Square, 7th November 1955. (Ogonok)

The ZiS-110B cabriolet version of the ZiS-110 was built in small numbers from 1949, with its parade debut being in Vladivostok in 1950 rather than Red Square in Moscow, where the tradition of using horses for the meeting of the parade commanders had continued until 1953.

M-2 medium artillery tractors towing 240mm M-1953 (M-240) heavy mortars across Manezhnaya Square, 7th November 1955. The innocuous looking 240mm M-240 mortar was nuclear capable. (RGAKFD)

BTR-152s lined up on Manezhnaya Square before the 7th November parade in 1955. Note the non-standard pintle-mounted 12.7mm DShKM heavy machine guns. GAZ-69A, GAZ-63 and BM-20-4 (BMD-20) vehicles are in the background.

1956

The year 1956 would prove to be rather more memorable in world history than some. The international news was dominated by the two military events, the Suez crisis in the Middle East and the Soviet invasion of Hungary in Europe.

Domestically in the Soviet Union, 1st Secretary of the CPSU Khrushchev publically denounced Stalin's crimes on 23rd February during the 20th Party Congress, accelerating the era of de-Stalinisation in the country. In 1956, the Soviet Union under Khrushchev's direction also continued the process of rehabilitating prisoners incarcerated in the Soviet GULAG system, which had begun with the Amnesty of March 1953 for non-political prisoners and political prisoners sentenced to less than five years internment. The GULAG system had peaked at approximately 2.5 million prisoners in 1950, and by the end of 1953 held approximately 500,000 less inmates. Mass releases back into society had begun in 1954.

The Soviet Army had served a useful purpose in the months after Stalin's death, and had admirably rid the country of arguably its greatest tyrant - Beria, but already by 1956 technology developments were causing a rift between government and the military. Khrushchev was a technophile, and the Soviet Union was now making great strides in rocket technology, with Khrushchev the ardent rocket enthusiast at the vanguard of this development. In addition to strategic rockets, there was also a drive to replace conventional ground and anti-aircraft artillery with rockets, and even to extend this to tank armament. Soviet military designers, particularly the tank design bureaus, were unconvinced, as was the Soviet Army, for it had been tanks and artillery that had been the Red Army mainstay weapons in World War Two, and the country continued to excel in the design of both. The Soviet government was not in entire alignment with the Soviet military by 1956 with regard to future weapon developments, and these differences would come to a head in 1957.

By November 1956, the world press was not focused on Soviet tanks making their regular annual parade in Red Square, but rather on newsreel broadcasts of the events unfolding in another European capital city, Budapest. The death of Stalin in 1953 and changing expectations in Eastern Europe had led to tensions in Hungary, exacerbated by a new reformist government, a poor harvest and fuel shortages in 1956. In the autumn of that year, the new Hungarian Prime Minister Imry Nagy began to implement far-reaching reforms, ranging from freedom of political expression of dissent, to press freedoms, to support for the trade unions. The reforms were similar to those being carried through in neighbouring Eastern European countries such as Poland, but they went further than authorised or condoned by the Kremlin. Nagy made two fundamental mistakes, the first being an assumption that the Soviet Union would accept his reforms and not intervene militarily, and the second was expecting that Western Europe would not stand back and watch if that occurred. He was proven wrong on both counts. Students and workers took to the streets of Budapest on 23rd October 1956, and after clashes with Hungarian police and Soviet troops, made a "16 Point" demand on the State for increased personal freedoms and removal of the secret police and Soviet control, following on from the similar actions in Poland which had resulted in some demands being granted. The following day, five Soviet Army divisions moved into Hungary, while the Soviet government debated whether to maintain those forces in Hungary indefinitely, or remove them again having made a point. The new Prime Minister Imre Nagy demanded Soviet tanks and troops that had moved into Budapest be removed from Hungary, to which request Khrushchev initially agreed. During the following week the Hungarian government under Nagy introduced new rules providing freedom of religion and freedom of speech. There had also been a revolt in Poland the same month, but this had been quickly suppressed and was overshadowed by the revolt in Hungary and the subsequent Soviet military reaction.

It looked as though moderate changes were to be allowed in Eastern Europe with Soviet acquiescence; however on 3rd November Nagy advised Khrushchev that Hungary also intended to leave the Warsaw Pact. The Soviet government attitude instantly hardened, and the following day, 4th November, as tanks were rehearsing for the Red Square parades in Moscow, an additional twelve motorised rifle and tank divisions moved into Hungary directed by Marshal Ivan S. Konev as Commander of Warsaw Pact Forces, supported by an estimated 1,130 tanks which had been pulled back to the Hungarian border only to be again operationally deployed in the environs of the capital city and in other regions of the country. The second assault named "Operation Whirlwind" was under the ultimate direction of Soviet Defence Minister Georgy Zhukov. The Soviet Army clashed with both civilian protesters and armoured units of the Hungarian Army on the streets of Budapest, with order restored by 10th November after a week of street clashes, following which a new and more compliant Prime Minister, Janos Kadar, was installed.

The Soviet Army had crushed civil and military resistance in Hungary using armoured units equipped with T-34-85 and T-54 medium tanks, IS-3 heavy tanks and ISU-152 self propelled howitzers to the clear streets of demonstrators, and engaging directly with Hungarian Army units backing the demonstrators. When the fighting was over on 10th November, over 2,500 civilians and approximately 700 Soviet Army troops had been killed, with an estimated 20,000 Hungarians wounded. Some 26,000 Hungarian demonstrators were subsequently put on trial, of whom approximately 13,000 were imprisoned. As many as 200,000 refugees subsequently fled Hungary for other countries in Europe. The deposed Hungarian Prime Minister Imre Nagy was arrested, put on trial, and executed in June 1958 together with another 229 people directly involved in the uprising. To the United States and Europe, the post-Stalinist Soviet Union looked very much like the earlier iteration. The Soviet invasion was perceived with scandal in the American and European press, but NATO declined to intervene in the internal affairs of a Warsaw Pact country. This was not least because events in Hungary were at the time considered secondary to events unfolding in Egypt, where France, Great Britain and the new State of Israel were engaged in the Suez crisis.

The week following the conclusion of events

in Hungary, Khrushchev made perhaps his most infamous comment while in his capacity of 1st Secretary of the CPSU at a meeting of foreign ambassadors at the Polish Embassy in Moscow on 18th November, raising the stakes in the nuclear "arms race". At a time of heightened tension, and referring to the opposing ideologies he made the statement: *"Myi Vas pokhoronim."*, which was translated literally as: *"We will bury you."* The comment was taken as a nuclear threat, but was as much a typical Russian direct quip, along the lines of "it's your funeral". His actual full statement was:

"Socialist states…base ourselves on the idea that we must peacefully co-exist. About the capitalist states, it doesn't depend on you whether or not we exist…If you don't like us, don't accept our invitations and don't invite us to come to see you. Whether you like it or not, history is on our side. We will bury you."

The statement was nevertheless what in American diplomatic parlance is called "unhelpful". Khrushchev would a year later become Soviet Premier, and the tone for the coming years had already been set.

As events were concluding in Hungary, new political and potential military clashes were in the making. In 1956, the United States began a program of U-2 reconnaissance aircraft flights over the Soviet Union, mapping areas of the country, in particular Siberia, in order to validate the industrial and military capability behind Khrushchev's statements on massive Soviet missile deployment and Soviet nuclear capability. The U-2 aircraft flew from an American base at Peshawar in Pakistan, and entered Soviet airspace over the Soviet Republic of Tajikistan. For four years these occasional flights would be without any diplomatic incident.

1st May 1956

The 1st May 1956 parade was significant in that for the first time there was live television transmission reportage direct from Red Square. The parade, taken by Defence Minister Marshal of the Soviet Union Georgy Zhukov, began with marching columns included students of the "M.V. Frunze" Military Academy, regiment of sailors, regiment of the "F. Eh. Dzerzhinsky" division and the usual mix of marching columns of military and academy units.

There were as in most years some subtle changes to the parade line-up, such as the BTR-152s on display now being the modified BTR-152V variant, with a driver adjusted central tyre pressure regulation system (CTPRS). The initial production BTR-152V used external air lines, which proved vulnerable to snaring on undergrowth, such that subsequent models had the air supply incorporated within the wheel hubs as technological development allowed.

The new AT-L tracked artillery tractor towed the 57mm M-1950 (S-60) anti-aircraft gun through Red Square. The early production AT-L (Izdeliye-5) as paraded in 1956 featured six small road wheels, the vehicle later being replaced in production by the modified and more commonly seen Izdeliye-5A version (with five large road wheels and no return rollers). The latter version was for many years erroneously referred to in Western countries as the AT-LM. The new AT-S medium artillery tractor was also demonstrated on Red Square in May 1956, towing the 130mm M-46 field gun. The distinctly utilitarian looking AT-S was developed at ChTZ in Chelyabinsk but assembled from 1953-62 at the Kurgan Machine Building Plant (KMZ) in the city of Kurgan. KMZ would in the following decade move from the production of tracked tractors to the assembly of tracked infantry combat vehicles, beginning with the BMP (BMP-1).

By the mid 1950s, a diverse range of new military equipment was being shown on Red Square as post-war designs began to replace wartime era equipment, with more modern weapons being

BTR-152V wheeled APCs cross Red Square, 1st May 1956. The BTR-152V featured larger profile tyres with a central tyre pressure regulation system (CTPRS) with external (and thereby vulnerable) air lines to the wheel hubs.

AT-L light artillery tractors towing 57mm M-1950 (S-60) anti-aircraft guns across Red Square, 1st May 1956. These AT-Ls are the early production and rarely seen "Izdeliye-5" variant with six small road wheels.

unveiled at the parades on an annual basis. From the mid 1950s the columns of tanks and heavy artillery were joined by new airborne forces heavy support weapons, new air defence artillery systems, anti-tank weapons and second generation multiple rocket launchers.

The T-54 was by the mid 1950s the default standard Soviet medium/main battle tank, while the IS-3 heavy tank was being replaced after a hiatus of some years by the T-10 heavy tank, but neither of these tanks would be seen on Red Square until 1957. Other new tanks such as the PT-76 amphibious light tank were also in service with the Soviet armed forces but were never paraded on Red Square.

The May 1956 parade had a significant focus on artillery, with anti-tank, anti-aircraft and multiple rocket launcher systems present in quantity. Less noticeably, the wartime era artillery pieces were replaced by post-war designs during the 1950s, including the 85mm D-44 divisional gun and its D-48 anti-tank gun variant, the 122mm D-74, 130mm M-46 and 152mm M-47 field guns, the 240mm M-240 mortar and other new weapons. These were duly towed through Red Square by the aforementioned new generations of wheeled and tracked artillery tractors including the light (AT-L) and medium (AT-S) tracked artillery tractors now complementing the AT-T heavy tractor which had been on display since the very beginning of the decade, all with better towing speeds than their wartime predecessors. The 57mm M-1950 (S-60) anti-aircraft gun which made its public debut through Red Square towed by the AT-L tracked tractor, would soon be followed by a self-propelled version, the ZSU-57-2. The military part of the 1st May parade was accompanied by a fly-past.

A few weeks after the Moscow 1st May parade, the IS-3 heavy tank that had been paraded so effectively in Berlin during the allied Victory Parade in September 1945 and for several years thereafter on Moscow's Red Square, was on 23rd July 1956 paraded in service with the Egyptian Army in Cairo. The IS-3 had in 1945 been a highly effective tank design from a ballistic and indeed a psychological perspective, but had proven troublesome in Soviet service, with high maintenance requirements and frequent stress cracking of the thickly armoured cast turret. After remedial development and modernisation the IS-3 had ultimately been replaced by the T-10 heavy tank, with the IS-3 being exported to the Middle East in the mid 1950s as the replacement T-10 entered Soviet Army service. Post-war production of the later T-34-85 medium tank had also been transferred to Czechoslovakia and Poland, with the SU-100 tank destroyer also being assembled in Czechoslovakia as the SD-100. These Warsaw Pact built armoured vehicles would be evident during the Suez Crisis, and in the Arab-Israeli wars of the coming years in the Middle East.

7th November 1956 – 39th Anniversary of the Great October Socialist Revolution

On 7th November 1956, the Soviet Union celebrated the 39th Anniversary of the Russian Revolution, with the parade again being taken by Marshal Georgy Zhukov in his capacity as Soviet Defence Minister. The display was in most respects identical to previous years. The traditional meeting of the parade command ZiS-110B cabriolet limousines was followed by a march by the orchestra of the Moscow Garrison (MVO) - some 800 musicians under the command of the chief conductor of the Soviet Army, General-Major I. V. Petrov. Marching participants from the usual ground forces, naval and air force academies and schools were joined by "desantniki" - VDV airborne forces of the Voenno-Vozhdushnaya Akademiya - the VDV Airborne Forces Academy. The fledgling Soviet airborne forces were growing exponentially in the 1950s as a post-war arm of the Soviet armed forces, and the new airborne divisions were being armed with some of the heaviest close-support weaponry of any airborne force worldwide.

The mechanised section of the parade as usual began with GAZ-69 light vehicles, which had since 1953 replaced the wartime GAZ-67 and earlier Lend-Lease Allied "jeeps" as column lead vehicles, followed by particularly large columns of BTR-152s, each of several successive parade sections being four columns wide and six rows deep. The 7th November 1956 parade witnessed the last public appearance of the 4x2 ZiS-150, again configured as VDV transport vehicles. The ZiS-150 was directly replaced in production by the ZiL-164, but the latter was never paraded on Red Square, where the emphasis from the mid 1950s was now on more powerful all-terrain transport vehicles rather than more mundane ostensibly road bound "tyl" or rear services load carriers. The new AT-L tracked artillery tractor was again displayed in its early "Izdeliye-5" configuration (with six small road wheels) towing the 240mm M-240 mortar and the 57mm S-60 anti-aircraft gun, accompanied by the significantly larger AT-T heavy tracked tractor towing the 180mm S-23 gun. The deployment of Soviet tanks and other armoured vehicles on the streets of Budapest in 1956 had however provided Western observers a closer than usual inspection of Soviet armoured developments in far from ceremonial circumstances.

Parade practice with ZiS-110B cabriolet parade limousines. The Red Square parades, the armoured elements of which lasted only a matter of minutes, were the result of weeks of painstaking practice and trial runs.

1957

After the momentous events of the previous year, 1957 was politically quiet. From a military standpoint it was however a watershed year, as Soviet rocket technology came of age in the public realm. November 1957 was also the 40th Anniversary of the Great October Socialist Revolution, so it was from a Red Square parade perspective a year for demonstrating the military might of the Soviet Union beyond the standard annual expectations.

In June, members of the Presidium (formerly the Politburo) led by Malenkov, Molotov and Kaganovich made an unsuccessful attempt to oust Khrushchev as 1st Secretary of the CPSU (which capacity Khrushchev held from 1953-64). Khrushchev would the following year also become Soviet Premier, a post he would hold until 1964, during which time subsequent world events and his personal leadership style would make the latter "Khrushchev era" particularly significant in world military history.

Khrushchev was convinced that the new strategic rocket technology, which made its public debut on Red Square in 1957, would provide the Soviet Union with all the deterrent capability the Soviet Union might require in the world, and at a nominal cost relative to the upkeep of the Soviet Army and Air Force. Differences of opinion regarding strategic development of the Soviet Army, and also its weapons, would lead to the Soviet Minister of Defence Georgy Zhukov being forced into retirement in October 1957. The Hero of the Soviet Union based on his World War Two military leadership had for the second time since the war been side-lined by politicians as the Soviet Army lost status to the new weapon of choice for deterrent purposes on Red Square. The tank was being replaced by the rocket system as the new showcase weapon for the world's military analysts to pursue. By the late 1950s, Khrushchev was also concurrently advocating a "peaceful co-existence" with the Soviet Union's international detractors, a military standoff or status quo, with Soviet rockets technology as the arbiter of that status.

Meantime, according to US Defence Department documents declassified in 1977, the year 1957 had been the perceived start date for a war with the Soviet Union based on a potential Soviet invasion of Western Europe and Asia. The scenario had been draw up in 1949 under the designation "Operation Dropshot"*, envisaging massive American nuclear retaliation on 200 targets in 100 Soviet cities and planned to destroy 85% of the Soviet Union's industrial capacity using long-range B-29 bombers in the pre-rocket age. While both superpowers planned for war but lived in peace, the year 1957 came and went with no Soviet invasion of Western Europe, and thereby no required response. Great Britain had a similar early Cold War "retaliation" plan, drawn up in late 1945 - four years earlier than the American plan - and designated "Operation Unthinkable", the detail of which was declassified in 1998. The British strategy devised at the behest of the wartime Prime Minister Winston Churchill envisaged a land engagement by 47 British and American divisions (50% of all available ground forces in Europe) with the Soviet Army in the region of Dresden in Soviet occupied Germany to: *"Impose the will of Western Allies on the Soviets."* at a time when the Soviet Army outnumbered Allied (later NATO) forces in Europe 4:1 in infantry and 2:1 in tanks. The somewhat optimistic plan to launch a surprise attack on the numerically superior Soviet Army was based on British concerns that once American forces left Europe, the Red Army (later Soviet Army) would seize the initiative and fill the vacuum. The plan envisaged a slow military strategic withdrawal, but concluded that the Royal Air Force would take a lead role in the long-range strategic bombing of the Soviet Union as envisaged in the later American plan. It was concluded however that Soviet retaliation would be massive, and directly on British territory, and the plans

---

* Operation World War Three. The Secret American Plan (Dropshot) for War with the Soviet Union in 1957. Anthony Cave Brown (editor). Arms & Armour Press. London. 1979.

were duly modified to a defensive "What If" strategy on the premise that the Soviet Army started to move west. As such offensive/defensive plans were made and remade, nothing of significance actually happened militarily in Europe during the last years of the 1950s with the exception of the events in Hungary. The memoirs of Field Marshal Lord Alanbrook make reference to Churchill's immediate post-war considerations regarding the Soviet threat, and British political plans for tackling the Soviet Army, which he and the British military command unsurprisingly concluded as being near lunacy. The British wartime leader would soon leave office.

1957 was the year when the Soviet Union began to show its rapidly developing rocket technology on Red Square. This technology would give the Soviet Union nuclear parity with the United States in the "arms-race", but it also again changed the status of the Soviet Army within the Soviet State. Khrushchev was in 1957 as concerned with the popularity of the Soviet Army and Defence Minister Georgy Zhukov as Stalin had been before him, and there were some concerns that the Soviet Army could still if so inclined stage a coup d'état in the same manner in which Beria had been suspected with his MVD (formerly NKVD) internal security forces. The maturing of rocket technology, particularly long-range nuclear systems, gave the Soviet Union not just a new weapon, but also an alternative to conventional Soviet Army tank and artillery forces, and to a lesser extent also an alternative for the Soviet Air Force. Zhukov would lose his position as Defence Minister in October 1957, and the Soviet Army would be drastically reduced in size from 5.8 million to 3.7 million personnel in the second half of the decade. By 1957 the tank was being considered an obsolete strategic technology, by Khrushchev if not necessarily by Soviet tank designers, and the Soviet Army as an expensive and high maintenance alternative to long-range rocket technology.

With regard to the maturing of rocket technology, 1957 was also from a technical perspective the watershed year between conventional and rocket artillery in the competition for technical prominence. The huge and impressive 2A3 and 2B1 tracked strategic artillery systems both had their concurrent public debut on Red Square in 1957, and they were exceptional massive and lumbering "crowd pleasers". They were however displayed alongside the first generation of mobile tactical level rockets, the 2K1 "Mars" and 2K2 "Filin" which though much smaller and less startling than the lumbering 2A3 and 2B1 weapons were able to more effectively deliver nuclear warheads over similar ranges while being mounted on far more versatile, and standard, tracked chassis.

1st May 1957

The 1st May 1957 parade, the last to be taken by Marshal Georgy Zhukov as Defence Minister, included the usual displays of marching troops and VDV "desantniki" airborne forces, followed by the mechanised display of tanks, airborne forces vehicles, light, medium and heavy artillery. The latter included mortars, towed by AT-L tracked tractors, and heavier artillery and anti-aircraft guns towed by AT-L light and AT-T heavy tracked tractors.

GAZ-69 light vehicles were again used for leading individual parade columns. The May 1957 parade was once again led by BTR-152s armed with pintle-mounted (and non-standard) 12.7mm DShKM machine guns for ceremonial purposes. Known vehicles such as the AT-S medium tracked tractors towed the 130mm M-46 field gun that doubled as a powerful anti-tank weapon, but it was the debut of new airborne and air defence vehicles that were of note in May 1957.

The public debut of the new Soviet VDV airborne forces ASU-57 self-propelled gun was in May 1957. The diminutive ASU-57 armed with the 57mm Ch-51 and later Ch-51M guns provided Soviet VDV airborne forces with a highly mobile and parachute deployable anti-tank vehicle, for which specialised "PRS" parachute descent platforms with rocket assisted braking were developed.

The usual display of well known conventional military vehicles was overshadowed by the parade debut of the 2A3 and 2B1 super-heavy strategic artillery systems, making a definitive statement on the ability to deliver nuclear shells on the tactical battlefield. It was the 2A3 and 2B1 strategic tracked artillery pieces that caught the public imagination in 1957, albeit Khrushchev the rocket enthusiast was unimpressed, as he was with all conventional artillery. The huge tracked self-propelled strategic weapon systems looked near identical, but one was a long-range mortar and the other a long-range gun. Two of each weapon type were paraded through Red Square; they were however accompanied by the new tactical rocket systems which also had their parade debut the same year. The pace of rocket technology development in the 1950s was such that the 2A3 and 2B1 had been effectively replaced by the first generation of the new tactical rockets (OTRs in Russian) - the 2K1 "Mars" and 2K2 "Filin", even as they made their parade debut on Red Square.

A new self-propelled air defence system for armoured formations, the ZSU-57-2, also made its debut appearance in May 1957. The ZSU-57-2

A 2B1 "Oka" mortar (foreground) and 2A3 "Kondensator" gun (background) move across Manezhnaya Square towards Red Square. This photograph was taken from the site of the former US Embassy. (Tank Museum 2472/E3)

BTR-152s moving down Gorky Street past the Central Telegraph building towards Red Square, 1st May 1957. (RGAKFD)

The 2B1 SPU vehicle mounted the 2B2 420mm strategic mortar with a barrel length of 20 metres and a range of 45km. The 2B1 had a low profile frontal cab arrangement as compared to the tandem cab of the 2A3.

A 2A3 "Kondensator" self-propelled strategic gun moves down Gorky Street towards Red Square. The impressive looking 2A3 gun and the similar looking 2B1 mortar made their concurrent public appearance in 1957.

was based on a significantly modified T-54 tank chassis and armed with a twin 57mm S-68 parallel gun installation mounted in a large open turret. The ZSU-57-2 anti-aircraft vehicle was the first such vehicle to be operationally deployed with the Soviet Army, the earlier ZSU-37 having been built in a small trials batch only, and the subsequent ZSU-37-2 (2A1) "Enisei" having also not entered series production.

Among the other new weapons systems making a public debut on 1st May 1957 was the 2P5 launch vehicle for the 2K5 "Korshun" rocket system, also known as the BM-25, which could fire six 250mm ZR-7 rockets to a range of 55km. Mounted on the YaAZ-214 6x6 truck chassis (renamed KrAZ after the move of production from Yaroslavl in Russia to Kremenchug in Ukraine), the 2P5 "Korshun" SPU vehicle actually had greater non-nuclear offensive capability than the massive and lumbering 2A3 and 2B1 tracked strategic artillery pieces displayed on the same day, but being mounted on a relatively mundane by comparison 6x6 truck the system went almost unnoticed, and for many years it was from a foreign intelligence perspective one of the more enigmatic Soviet "multiple rocket launcher" systems. The 1st May 1957 parade was by tradition accompanied by a flypast, with a combination of jet engine and propeller driven aircraft.

As was a frequent occurrence during the Cold War era, a single defining event occurred in the Soviet Union between the May and November 1957 military parades, which would have a major effect on relationships between the country and the United States, and would further drive the "arms race". On 4th October 1957, the Soviet Union successfully launched the "Sputnik-1" orbiting satellite into space. The deployment of "Sputnik" was an immense technological achievement of which the Soviet Union was justifiably proud. But from a military standpoint, the message received in Washington was clear. The following month, on 3rd November, Laika the dog also made a journey into space on board "Sputnik-2", the first living creature to do so, though unfortunately without a return ticket. The apparently technologically backward communist state, run by a former collective farm manager, now seemed to have the edge in rocket technology over the United States and its European allies, where the strategic technology now being utilized by both sides of the divide had been developed in Nazi Germany just over a decade previously. The first shivers of the coldest winters of the Cold War were apparent in Western capitals around the world.

The first American satellite launch attempt, on 6th December, resulted in an explosion on the launch pad, as was a common occurrence with both superpowers during development of such systems. The US government Gaither Committee meantime began to talk up what would later be referred to by President John F. Kennedy as the "missile gap". The report by the same name exaggerated Soviet missile technology and numbers for American defence budget approval purposes as was the norm; however as was clear from subsequent Red Square parades the threat was real even if the numbers might have been exaggerated on the American side, and the technological capability exaggerated on the Soviet side. President Eisenhower (US President 1953-61) received a copy of the Gaither Report, which called for an increase in Strategic Air Command long-range bomber sorties (the B-52 strategic bomber had recently entered service), the emplacement of inter-continental ballistic missiles (ICBMs) in hardened concrete launch silos, and the building of nuclear command centres and fallout shelters in the United States as a response to the Soviet threat.

While the United States worried about Soviet strategic military capability now having the theoretical ability to reach American shores, forthcoming conflict again lay elsewhere than with the Soviet Union. In the Democratic Republic of North Vietnam, Ho Chi Minh and his commanders began to organize for guerrilla warfare in South Vietnam. The guerrilla fighting force being organized in Vietnam at the end of the 1950s would in the years to come have a far greater direct impact on the United States than rival superpower technology developments. The organization was called the Viet Cong.

The 2P2 SPU vehicle for the 2K1 "Mars" tactical rocket (OTR) system firing the ZR-1 "Sova" rocket was displayed concurrently with the 2A3 and 2B1 "conventional" artillery systems. By 1957 rocket technology had effectively replaced both the 2A3 and 2B1 in terms of range and nuclear delivery capability, but the latter vehicles were nevertheless great "crowd pleasers" on Red Square. (Tank Museum 2472/E6)

A T-54 crosses the Krymsky Bridge near Gorky Park, on its return from Red Square. The T-54 made its public debut on Red Square in 1957 - almost a decade after the tank had entered series production. This early T-54 M-1951 tank has a clean gun barrel without counterweight (the latter denoting the use of gun stabilisation) or bore evacuator, both of which followed.

7th November 1957 – 40th Anniversary of the Great October Socialist Revolution

The 7th November 1957 Red Square military parade celebrated the 40th Anniversary of the Great October Socialist Revolution, and as such the parade was a significant commemorative event, with the public debut of all manner of new tanks, armoured and support vehicles. Significantly, it also occasioned the November parade debut of several new rocket types. By the mid 1950s the superpower nuclear arms race was moving from conventional long-range delivery by aircraft to the introduction of long-range rocket systems, with both countries developing such weapons at an exponential rate. In August 1957 the Soviet Union had tested its first long-range nuclear rocket system, the 1,200km range R-5M MRBM (NATO: SS-3 Shyster), which had its public debut on Red Square on 7th November that year - the first strategic weapon to be displayed in Moscow. A large number of other new rocket systems, surface to surface, surface to air and strategic were also unveiled during the 7th November parade, which heralded the "rocket age" in the Soviet Union, for which Moscow's Red Square was the public showcase.

The 7th November 1957 parade was reviewed by the newly appointed Soviet Defence Minister Marshal Rodion Ya. Malinovsky, who had only days before replaced Georgy Zhukov after his forced retirement at the insistence of Khrushchev. Marshal Malinovsky would remain in the position of Soviet Defence Minister until 1967, and would take the Red Square parades during the most eventful years of the Cold War. The parade commanders per tradition met at the beginning of the parade in two ZiS-110B cabriolet limousines.

With the parade being the 40th Anniversary of the Great October Socialist Revolution, there was an international line-up of communist world leaders alongside the Soviet leadership on the

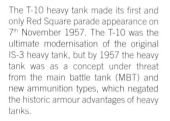

The T-10 heavy tank made its first and only Red Square parade appearance on 7th November 1957. The T-10 was the ultimate modernisation of the original IS-3 heavy tank, but by 1957 the heavy tank was as a concept under threat from the main battle tank (MBT) and new ammunition types, which negated the historic armour advantages of heavy tanks.

Lenin Mausoleum review stand, which was in 1957 still labelled with the names of both Lenin and Stalin. The Chinese leader Mao Tse Tung and the Vietnamese leader Ho Chi Minh stood alongside Khrushchev, braced against the November cold as the parade passed in front of them. These two leaders would play a key role in a developing regional conflict that would rapidly become the Cold War proxy conflict then developing in Vietnam.

The Kantemirovskaya Tank Division and the Tamanskaya Motor Rifle Division per tradition provided the armoured might on display on Red Square in November 1957, but there were both minor and some significant changes in the line-up of vehicles and weapons systems displayed on 7th November 1957. The parade columns were led by the new GAZ-69 light vehicle as introduced in 1953, with the BTR-152s now displayed being the later BTR-152V model with driver controlled central tyre pressure regulation, for parade purposes again fitted with non-standard pintle-mounted 12.7mm DShKM heavy machine guns in lieu of the standard 7.62mm SGMB. The BTR-152V could transport a full infantry section of 17 fully armed troops in addition to the vehicle crew.

The first major change in the parade line-up in November 1957 was however with regard to the tanks on display. The T-54 medium/main battle tank (MBT) finally had its Red Square parade debut on 7th November 1957, a decade after it had entered service, with the tank replacing the venerable but now increasingly obsolescent T-34-85 and the limited production T-44 in Soviet Army service. The T-54 would become the default symbolic "Soviet tank" of the Cold War era but is one of those tanks that, as with the T-34 medium and KV heavy tanks in November 1940 and May 1941 was not immediately paraded on Red Square for international observation. The IS-3 heavy tank, which had such a shock impact when publically unveiled at the Allied Victory Parade in Berlin in September 1945, had meantime been noticeable by its absence

The ZSU-57 self-propelled anti-aircraft gun system had made its Red Square debut appearance in May 1957 and was seen again in November, and for several years thereafter. The vehicle mounted the 57mm S-68 gun system (i.e. two paired S-60 guns) on a modified and lightened T-54 tank chassis.

from Red Square since the very early 1950s. The tank had been rushed into production in 1945 but had proven capricious in service, as a result of which many were rebuilt, ultimately as the later IS-3M, which was thereafter maintained in strategic storage and not used operationally, or ever displayed on Red Square. The tank was to have been replaced by a new design, the IS-5, which during development morphed into the IS-8 and ultimately the IS-10. The new Soviet heavy tank entered service as the T-10 heavy tank rather than the IS-10 (Iosif Stalin-10) as a consequence of the de-Stalinisation of the mid 1950s, and made its public debut (and only parade appearance) on 7th November 1957 together with the T-54. The T-10, as equally impressive as it was elusive, was the last Soviet heavy tank to be fielded by the Soviet Army. The tank design was a vast improvement over the IS-3M, but as with heavy tanks worldwide it had by the mid 1950s been overtaken by rapid advancements in military technology. The heavy tank was by 1957 being made redundant worldwide by the introduction of the universal Main Battle Tank (MBT), the availability of new conventional ammunition types, and the introduction of anti-tank guided rockets that had vastly improved armour penetration and could be mounted on relatively light vehicles.

The BM-24T was a tube-launched version of the BM-24 MRS, mounted on the chassis of the AT-S artillery tractor. The concept was to provide a weapon system with the capability to accompany armoured units across any terrain.

The 2A3 "Kondensator" strategic nuclear artillery weapon, on its partly T-10 derived Obiekt-271 chassis, was displayed on Red Square from 1957 until 1963, alongside the 2B1 "Oka" strategic nuclear mortar. The 406mm 2A3 strategic gun fired a 570kg nuclear shell to a range of 25.6km. (Mikhail Baryatinsky)

The relatively diminutive ASU-57 self-propelled gun, which had its public debut in May 1957, was also displayed again on Red Square in November, and for several years thereafter. The 57mm Ch-51M gun provided an element of mobile anti-tank support for Soviet VDV airborne forces. (Mikhail Baryatinsky)

New parade debuts in 1957 were not confined to the T-54 and T-10 tanks. The new BTR-50P tracked APC also paraded in November finally gave Soviet infantry an armoured vehicle that could keep pace with tank formations across open terrain while providing reasonable armour protection. For parade purposes a 12.7mm DShKM heavy anti-aircraft machine gun was pintle-mounted at the front of the open roofed fighting compartment of the BTR-50P vehicles displayed on Red Square.

The Soviet VDV airborne forces were rapidly rising to prominence in the 1950s and were a regular feature of Red Square parades. The two-door GAZ-69 was from 1957 paraded through Red Square in large numbers with VDV "desantniki" seated in the rear. The Soviet VDV airborne forces had for several years been provided with their first purpose designed tracked self-propelled gun however, in the form of the diminutive ASU-57, which was first paraded on 1st May and again on 7th November 1957, armed with the later Ch-51M gun with the more conventional double-baffle muzzle brake.

Ground forces artillery on display in November 1957 included the now parade standard 130mm M-46 field gun towed by the AT-S tracked tractor and the Red Square parade debut of the BM-24T MRS, also mounted on the same AT-S chassis. The particularly utilitarian looking AT-S tracked artillery tractor had been developed at the ChTZ tank plant in Chelyabinsk to provide all-terrain artillery support to tank divisions, and it very much looked as if it had been designed at a tank plant. The BM-24T on its AT-S tracked chassis was displayed only until the end of the decade before being replaced by more modern systems. The later "Izdeliye-5A" version of the AT-L light tracked artillery tractor, designated AT-LM at the time in Western sources, was displayed towing the 240mm M-240 heavy mortar, and the AT-T was displayed towing the 180mm S-23 gun.

One of the new rocket systems that would make the BM-24T MRS obsolescent was the new 2K5 "Korshun" (BMD-25) wheeled MRS (OTR), which made its second appearance on Red Square in November 1957. The 2P5 launch vehicle for the 250mm calibre 2K5 "Korshun" MRS was originally mounted on the 6x6 YaAZ-214 chassis, though the standard mounting was the same vehicle re-designated KrAZ-214 after production was transferred from Yaroslavl in Russia to Kremenchug in Ukraine. The ZR-7 rocket used with the 2K5 system had a range of 55km, far exceeding that of the wartime BM-13 and BM-31 systems, and matching the range of the 2A3 and 2B1 tracked strategic artillery pieces demonstrated during the same parades in the late 1950s and early 1960s.

New air defence systems also had their public debut on 7th November 1957. The already well

The 2P5 launch vehicle for the 2K5 "Korshun" MRS was based on the YaAZ (later KrAZ)-214 6x6 chassis. The purpose of the vehicle was at the time somewhat enigmatic, but it is now known to have been a tactical or OTR system rather than a conventional MRS.

known 57mm M-1950 (S-60) anti-aircraft gun was towed through Red Square by the new AT-L artillery tractor, together with the larger calibre 100mm KS-19 anti-aircraft gun, which could engage jet fighter aircraft at high altitude, towed by the significantly larger AT-T heavy tracked artillery tractor. These towed anti-aircraft weapons were joined in November 1957 by the new ZSU-57-2 tracked self-propelled anti-aircraft gun (SPAAG) which was again displayed after its public debut in May.

The massive and unwieldy 406mm 2A3 "Kondensator" and 420mm 2B1 "Oka" strategic artillery pieces made their second parade appearance on 7th November 1957, with two vehicles of each type being again displayed on Red Square. The weapons were particularly impressive as parade vehicles, but Khrushchev the Soviet Premier and rocket enthusiast remained unimpressed, apparently calling the large conventional tube artillery trundling through Red Square: *"the ultimate expression of unchecked military stupidity."* Khrushchev was renowned for his bias towards any and all forms of rocket artillery, but these unwieldy weapons were nevertheless showpieces with little effective capability beyond the confines of Red Square. The presence of these lumbering giants was dramatic; however the rocket systems that preceded them onto the square were actually the next generation replacement for such systems that had been outclassed by rocket technology even during their final development. The "marketing" effect for the attendant foreign military attachés and the foreign press was nevertheless as required and the conventional, if huge, artillery pieces served their intended purpose. The 2A3 "Kondensator" self-propelled gun and 2B1 "Oka" self-propelled mortar were paraded annually until 1963, but were effectively redundant before they were introduced, their intended role having been taken by the 2K1 "Mars" and 2K2 "Filin" (NATO: FROG - Free Rocket Over Ground) Operational Tactical Rocket (OTR) systems which also had their public debut in 1957. The new OTR rocket systems were displayed on Red Square on 7th November ahead of the significantly larger 2A3 and 2B1 "atomic cannon" tracked artillery systems they were destined to replace, in all likelihood because the impact level of the "conventional" artillery systems was far greater from a visual perspective due to their overall dimensions and sheer "presence". Starting from 1957 strategic weapons would be the final systems paraded through Red Square, these being entirely rocket based after the retirement of the 2A3 and 2B1 from Red Square parades after November 1963. Only four examples of each of these systems were ever built.

The new operational (OTR) and short-range nuclear rockets that made their public debut together with the 2A3 and 2B1 "conventional" tracked artillery pieces, signalled a new generation of rocket based military technology. The 2P2 SPU vehicle for the 2K1 "Mars" rocket system with its ZR-1 rocket, and the larger 2P4 SPU for the 2K2 "Filin" rocket system with its ZR-2 rocket both had their public debut during the November 1957 parade. The 2P2 SPU vehicle was based on the same chassis as the PT-76 amphibious reconnaissance tank, with the 2P4 SPU vehicle being based on an ISU-152K derived Obiekt-804 SPU chassis. Both were nuclear capable, with a 10kT warhead and with respective ranges of 17.5km and 25.7km. All such rockets would be generically designated "FROG" by NATO, though several different types were deployed mounted on differing chassis over the following years, with the different early rocket types often conflated by NATO sources.

The result of Soviet surface to air missile technology developments was also beginning to be shown on Red Square, with 1957 being the debut year during which these new rockets would also be introduced for public and press consumption. Another rocket displayed at the November 1957 parade was the S-75 "Dvina" (NATO: SA-2 Guideline), which had its parade debut three years before the S-25 "Berkut" (NATO: SA-1 Guild) system which was statically deployed around Moscow as a strategic defence perimeter. By the time of the 7th November 1960 Red Square parade, the latterly better known and understood S-75 would be world famous due to its major role in the Cold War elsewhere than Red Square on the day of the 1st May parade earlier that year. The S-25 and S-75 SAM systems would become standard participants in Red Square parades for the following two decades. The S-75 was originally towed through Red Square by the ZiS-121B tractor truck version of the ZiS-151, which was soon replaced by the ZiL-157V.

The highlight (or from a Western military attaché observer perspective, the low point) of the November 1957 parade was the November public debut of the R-5M (8K51) (NATO: SS-3 Shyster) medium range ballistic missile (MRBM). The 300kT nuclear warhead, 1,200km range R-5M rockets were towed through Red Square on their transport trailers by AT-T tracked artillery tractors. Based in East Germany, the ostensibly mobile and pad launched R-5M could target all the capital cities of Europe and this was clearly understood by both superpowers. Strategic rockets systems would from 1957 become a standard highlight of future Red Square parades.

The aircraft flypast planned for the November 1957 parade was, not for the first or last time, cancelled due to low cloud and poor visibility. Though it was not known at the time, aircraft displays would not appear again over Moscow for another 38 years, the next aviation flypast accompanying a military parade being only on 9th May 1995, and above Red Square only in the first decade of the 21st Century.

The S-75 "Dvina" (NATO: SA-2 Guideline) surface to air missile (SAM) was displayed on Red Square from 1957, initially towed by the ZiS-121B 6x6 tractor truck. The S-75 would become world famous over Sverdlovsk, Siberia on 1st May 1960.

The 40th Anniversary of the Great October Socialist Revolution saw the parade debut of strategic rockets on Red Square, starting with the 1,200km range R-5M, towed by the AT-T heavy artillery tractor.

Until 1957, Soviet long-range nuclear weapons delivery was demonstrated by means of the various bomber aircraft that had participated in fly-pasts over Red Square during both the May and November annual military parades. That long-range delivery potential was from 1957 demonstrated on the ground by the new and rapidly developing strategic rocket systems that were now being shown on Red Square. 1957 was the watershed year when the focus of projection of Soviet military might moved from the tank to nuclear armed medium range, and soon to be deployed intercontinental range, rocket systems. The decade of rapid rocket technology development, in which the role of Soviet Premier Khrushchev would be particularly influential, had begun, and it would prove the most dangerous decade of the entire Cold War era.

The AT-T heavy tractor was used to tow the 1,200km range R-5M, introduced on Red Square in November 1957 and soon thereafter the 2,100km range R-12, which was introduced in 1960. The latter rocket was almost identical to the former, but was approximately one metre longer.

The 2P4 "Tuilpan" SPU vehicle for the 2K2 "Filin" OTR system firing the ZR-2 rocket also made its Red Square parade debut in 1957, concurrent with the 2K1 "Mars" OTR based on a lighter chassis related to the PT-76 amphibious light tank.*

---

* The 2K2 "Filin" OTR is also referred to in many Russian sources as the 2K4 "Filin". The GRAU Index 2K4 specifically refers to the "Drakon" ATGM system however, hence the 2K2 designation is used throughout this book.

1958

The year 1958 was the first of the "Khrushchev" years, with Nikolai Khrushchev becoming the Soviet Premier on 3rd March in addition to his previous role of 1st Secretary of the CPSU. While the year was relatively quiet within the Soviet Union, and in Europe, events were unfolding on an island in the Caribbean close to the United States. In May of 1958 the rebel group led by Fidel Castro and his brother Raúl ramped up their insurgency campaign against the Batista government. By the end of the year Castro's forces were advancing on the capital city of Havana. At the time this was largely irrelevant from a superpower perspective, but the island would soon become synonymous with the Cold War.

The seemingly unlikely combination of Soviet missiles and a Caribbean island developing into a potential superpower clash might have appeared whimsical in 1958. But the subject of Soviet missile technology advances was already embedded in the American political psyche. During his Senate election campaign American Senator John. F. Kennedy on 14th August 1958 first used the aforementioned term "missile gap" referring to a purported Soviet superiority in such weapons based on what was later understood to be inflated US Air Force numbers. Kennedy continued to talk of the "missile gap" as he ran for election as President in 1960, and indeed missiles would prove a central theme during his later presidency. The SM-75/PGM-17 "Thor" intermediate range ballistic missile had entered production in the United States in 1958, with Great Britain planned to receive 60 of these systems beginning in September 1958, which would be operated by newly formed Strategic Missile Squadrons within the Royal Air Force. The rockets were to be operated by the Royal Air Force but with the nuclear warheads under American control, with the first "Thor" missile being delivered to Great Britain in September that year. This, together with similar plans for strategic rocket deployment in Italy and Turkey moved NATO strike capability much closer to the borders of the Soviet Union, with the attendant retaliatory dangers for the populations of Western Europe and Turkey. The Soviet Union would respond in kind to the deployment of these weapons, but in the Caribbean rather than in Europe.

Domestically, life was meantime improving for the average Soviet citizen under Khrushchev, with the rapid construction of concrete panel apartment blocks (names "Khrushovki" after the Soviet leader), improvements in the provision of hospital treatment and education, low utility costs and the increasing appearance of domestic goods such as fridges and televisions. Meat consumption increased by 50% from 1958 to 1965, and the population was not subject to the adverse terrors of the Stalin years. The Soviet Union was on the surface at peace both internally and with the outside world. Considering the recently resolved security concerns with regard to Beria and the MVD when under his direct control at the beginning of the decade, the Soviet Presidium nevertheless continued to cordon off the centre of Moscow on 1st May and 7th November parade days to prevent any spontaneous protests, such that the Red Square parades thereby remained as before a closed event for the select few rather than the general public.

1st May 1958

The 1st May 1958 parade was commanded by Soviet Defence Minister Marshal of the Soviet Union Rodion Ya. Malinovsky, standing in the rear of a ZiS-110B cabriolet limousine. With new weapons in practically all classes having made their parade debut appearance in 1957, there were unsurprisingly no parade debut surprises in May the following year. The May 1958 parade, being combined with the civil demonstration, was significantly smaller in size than in 1957, but again included some newly introduced Soviet weapons such as the diminutive ASU-57 light airborne self-propelled gun, armed with the later Ch-51M gun with its conventional double-baffle muzzle brake. The new AT-P semi-armoured artillery tractor was however displayed towing the 85mm D-48 anti-tank gun, while the larger AT-L, AT-S and AT-T tracked tractors towed the 240mm M-240 heavy mortar, 130mm M-46 field gun and 100mm KS-19 anti-aircraft gun respectively. MRS rocket systems included the now parade standard ZiS-151 mounted BM-14, the BM-20-4 (BMD-20) MRS and the tracked BM-24T version of the otherwise truck mounted BM-24.

The wartime BM-13 "Katyusha" MRS was replaced by several modernised systems from the mid 1950s, including the ZiS-151 mounted BM-14 (BM-14-16) seen here during the 1st May 1958 parade.

ASU-57s pass before the Lenin Mausoleum, with Stalin's name below but more prominent than that of Lenin. The parachute deployable ASU-57 was the first Soviet production AFV designed specifically as a heavy support vehicle for Soviet VDV airborne forces. Note the separation between the military and civilian hierarchy on the Lenin Mausoleum review stand.

7th November 1958 – 41st Anniversary of the Great October Socialist Revolution

The 7th November 1958 military parade was almost identical to the November 1957 event, and again taken by Marshal Malinovsky as Defence Minister. The T-54 introduced the previous year was again on display, but after its cameo appearance in November 1957 the T-10 heavy tank would never again be displayed on Red Square. The new T-55 had been accepted for service with the Soviet Army on 24th May 1958, only six months after the earlier T-54 had made its public debut on Red Square having been in service with the Soviet Army in various production variants for the previous decade. The T-55 tank would make its own debut parade appearance after a shorter service period than its predecessor, but would nevertheless not appear on Red Square until 7th November 1962. Whereas rockets were sometimes displayed in Moscow for effect while still under development, tank types continued to have their public debut on Red Square years after entering service with the Soviet Army.

The Soviet VDV airborne forces ASU-57 self-propelled gun was again paraded in November, soon to be joined by the larger, more powerfully armed and fully enclosed SU-85 (ASU-85) that was also accepted into service with Soviet Army VDV forces in 1958, supplementing the earlier ASU-57. The SU-85 (ASU-85) airborne assault gun would become a parade standard during the 1960s. The ZSU-57-2, which had been introduced on Red Square in 1957 was now a regular parade participant, as was the 180mm S-23 field gun towed by the AT-T tractor, and the tracked BM-24T multiple rocket system based on the AT-S tracked tractor, which would be a relatively short-lived operational system.

ZSU-57-2 self-propelled anti-aircraft gun systems parade through Red Square, 7th November 1958. The ZSU-57-2 was based on the T-54 tank chassis, but with significantly lightened armour, four road wheel pairs and a turret fabricated of sheet steel mounting the 57mm S-68 paired gun installation. (RGAKFD)

Soon after the November 1958 parade, Khrushchev subsequent to the obvious displays of strategic rockets on Red Square beginning in 1957 and repeated in 1958 decided on 4th December to ramp up Soviet rhetoric on the strength and disposition of Soviet long-range rockets. On that date he made the public pronouncement that the Soviet Union had begun series assembly of nuclear-armed intercontinental rockets (ICBMs) with a range of nearly 13,000km. The US had experienced technical problems with the initial test launch of their "Titan" rocket the same month, and there was understandable American and NATO concern over the apparent disparity. The R-5M as then being displayed on Red Square had a relatively short range of 1,200km however, and the as yet unseen R-12 and R-14 rockets that would become the bane of the United States when sent to Cuba in 1962, had ranges of approximately 2,100km and 4,000km respectively. Khrushchev was in 1958 at best being optimistic with regard to the range of the Soviet Union's "ICBMs", however as events in the not too distant future would prove, the range was easily closed by moving the rockets closer to their target loaded on cargo ships.

Two 2B1 "Oka" strategic mortars follow two 2A3 "Kondensator" strategic guns through Red Square, 7th November 1958. The 2A3 and 2B1 were overall similar in appearance but quite distinct weapons, both based on extended and modified T-10M heavy tank chassis, the Obiekt-271 and Obiekt-273 chassis respectively.

These AT-L light artillery tractors towing 240mm M-240 heavy mortars through Red Square are of the later "Izdeliye-5A" type, with five large cast road wheels rather than the six smaller road wheel and return roller combination.

The 8U218 launcher vehicle for the early 8K11 system, known as "Scud-A" by NATO resembled the earlier (and currently displayed) 2K2 "Filin" system, but was significantly improved in range and other characteristics, not least its nuclear warhead capability. The launch vehicle was based on the Obiekt-803 chassis. (Igor Zheltov)

1959

The year 1959 was from a Soviet perspective yet another uneventful year domestically, with more cordial than usual relationships with the United States, the proverbial calm before the storm. On 24th July Khrushchev and American Vice President Richard Nixon met in Moscow for talks on the elimination of foreign military bases while also as an aside comparing Soviet and American living standards and domestic appliances. This was followed by meetings with President Dwight D. Eisenhower at Camp David, a location that would in later years become synonymous with international peace talks. The year ended in the Soviet Union as it had begun, in relative quiet. Two unrelated events far from the Soviet Union would however determine the relationships between the superpowers in the next years. One would lead to a sharp and short crisis, the latter to a protracted war that would dominate American politics for the next two decades. By the end of the first week of January 1959, Fidel Castro was in control of Cuba and Khrushchev's boast of having rockets that had the range to hit the United States would soon be fulfilled, albeit with a long sea journey followed by a relatively short flight time rather than technical fulfilment of Khrushchev's December 1958 pronouncement. Meanwhile, in Asia Pacific, Ho Chi Minh having been spurned in Paris some years prior declared a People's War in March 1959 to unite Vietnam, and American involvement in a conflict inherited from France would grow exponentially in the years ahead.

The 1950s had been a decade during which the armed camps of the Cold War were formed, alliances made, and technology developed to a level whereby rockets had succeeded tanks as the symbol of projected Soviet military might. The early 1960s were to prove the greatest test of the relationship between the two respective armed camps, and of the restraint now required of the superpower world leaders in a world where Armageddon was possible in minutes rather than requiring a protracted war.

In Eastern Europe, the Baltic States of Estonia, Latvia and Lithuania, which would later be instrumental in the ultimate downfall of the Soviet Union, were in the late 1950s witnessing significant industrialisation and economic improvement under Soviet control. All three countries considered themselves as occupied, and this political position would not change over the years, but the economic ties to the Soviet Union and the benefits this brought were significant. The domestic populations of the Baltic Republics were also changing however, as Russian professionals moved into the Baltics together with the new factories and Soviet investment. By 1959, nearly 30% of the population of Latvia was of Russian origin, the Baltic nation trade-off in the Soviet era being the economic and industrial benefits that came with the perceived occupation by the Soviet Union.

1st May 1959

The military section of the 1st May 1959 Red Square parade was again taken by Marshal Malinovsky as Defence Minister. The parade per tradition included marching columns from the respective ground, air and naval armed forces of the Soviet Union, together with students in uniform from the "M.V. Frunze" Military Academy, the Caspian Naval School and Suvorov cadets from the city of Tula amongst many others. The parade was, as in May 1959, accompanied by a military orchestra conducted by the senior conductor of the Soviet Army Colonel N. Nazarov.

The mechanised parade included T-54 tanks and armoured vehicles of the Guards Kantemirovskaya Tank Division and the Guards Tamanskaya Motorised Rifle Division, but there were as in 1958 no major revelations during the May 1959 parade.

A 2A3 "Kondensator" self-propelled strategic artillery system passes St. Basil's Cathedral as it leaves Red Square.

7th November 1959 – 42nd Anniversary of the Great October Socialist Revolution

From a military observer's perspective, 1959 was another benign year on Red Square, and the final November parade of the 1950s, again taken by Marshal Rodion Ya. Malinovsky as Defence Minister, also held no surprises, though certain trends that would have a major impact in the following decade were beginning to emerge. The marching parade by the Soviet armed services and military schools such as by tradition the "M.V. Frunze" Military Academy was as always followed by the mechanised display of armoured vehicles, artillery and rocket systems. The tracked BM-24T MRS mounted on the curiously antiquated looking AT-S medium tracked tractor chassis was again paraded in 1959, together with more modern vehicles such as the AT-L (Izdeliye-5A) light tractor towing the 240mm M-240 heavy mortar. The ZSU-57-2 air defence system with its twin barrelled 57mm S-68 guns was displayed again, but since 1957 there had been a dramatic shift from conventional gun to rocket technology, and this would increase exponentially from the very

By the end of the 1950s, new generations of military vehicle were entering service with the Soviet Army. The BTR-50 tracked APC and the BRDM (BRDM-1) reconnaissance vehicle would be paraded annually throughout the 1960s, with the parade debut in Moscow being in 1961.

beginning of the following decade. Already by November 1959, new generations of multiple rocket launchers, such as the ZiS-151 mounted BM-14 (BM-14-16) MRS had become parade standard features, as were "OTR" (NATO: FROG) surface to surface (SSM) rockets, surface to air (SAM) rockets and increasingly longer-range ballistic missiles.

The 1950s ended with the formalisation on 17th December 1959 of a new branch of the Soviet armed forces created by a Resolution of the Council of Ministers and named the "Raketnye Voiska Strategicheskogo Naznachenya - the Strategic Rocket Forces, usually abbreviated to RVSN. The late 1950s had seen the deployment of the first short and medium range nuclear-armed rockets. The 1960s would see the development of intercontinental range rocket systems, and the replacement of conventional long-range artillery with tactical rockets as a delivery means on the nuclear battlefield. Soviet military might in the 1950s had still been defined on Red Square by tank forces, but in the 1960s rocket technology would assume the role of the ultimate Soviet military deterrent.

The BM-24T was a relatively short-lived weapons system, as the wheeled BM-24 version mounted on the marginally less all-terrain capable 6x6 ZiS-151 and latterly 6x6 ZiL-157 chassis, provided the same artillery support on a less high-maintenance chassis with much better road speed.

2P4 "Tuilpan" rocket launcher vehicles for the 2K2 "Filin" tactical rocket (OTR) system during parade training. Soviet OTR systems, of which there were several very similar types, were generically designated "FROG" and later "Scud" by NATO.

The SU-85 (ASU-85) airborne self-propelled gun replaced the earlier ASU-57 on Red Square parades for the duration of the 1960s and into the early 1970s. These vehicles are on display on 7th November 1968. Photographer - Boris Volovenko

The 1960s

The early 1960s was the height of the Cold War era, at least in the public domain, and also the closest point that the two rival camps came to outright nuclear war. Central to this developing theme, the 1960s was also the decade whereby rocket developments started in the early 1950s matured into service deployment. Driven in part by technology, in part by ideology directed by the rocket enthusiast Khrushchev, the Soviet Union deployed all manner of rocket systems during the 1960s. Ever more powerful rocket based technology was displayed on Red Square, now requiring an additional lexicon for description purposes, including surface to air missile systems (SAMs), OTR surface-to-surface tactical rockets (SSMs), Medium and Intercontinental Range Ballistic Missiles (MRBMs and ICBMs,) and Anti-Ballistic Missiles (ABMs). The defining essence of Red Army and Soviet military might had since the inception of the Red Square parades always been based on displays of tanks and artillery. Both would however be overshadowed by rocket technology in the 1960s, and particularly by the massive new MRBM and ICBM rockets, as the new definition of that Soviet military might. The 1960s was to be the rocket decade on Red Square, and Soviet rockets would be in the public imagination worldwide. This was amply demonstrated during the very first military parade of the decade on 1st May 1960.

Although dominated by demonstrations of rocket technology on Red Square, the 1960s was also a decade of significant progress in the development of tank and other armoured vehicle designs, with the introduction of new vehicle types such as the BMP mechanised infantry combat vehicle, a vehicle type introduced by the Soviet Union and duly adopted by NATO as mechanised combat methodology continued to evolve during the Cold War.

The BTR-152 wheeled APC as displayed throughout the 1950s was replaced on Red Square in the early 1960s by the revolutionary BTR-60, introduced into Soviet Army service in 1961. The tracked BTR-50 series would later in the decade be complemented and ultimately replaced by the BMP (BMP-1) infantry combat vehicle. The T-54 would be replaced by the T-55 on Red Square in 1962, with the new T-62 following only three years later. The 1960s was a time of rapid change in military technology, and this was amply reflected in the Red Square parades. On an artistic note, the posters and symbols decorating the walls of the GUM department store building on Red Square during the 1960s parades were of grandiose proportions and particularly colourful compared to the more austere 1950s, the posters of the 1960s depicting socialist workers at work and play. The 1960s are regarded in some Western countries as the best of times from a social perspective, and the post-Stalin 1960s were perhaps also the best years of the Soviet Union.

Among the new tanks and rockets paraded on Red Square in the 1960s there were also subtle changes to the design of armoured vehicles in Soviet Army service, reflecting adaptation to the requirements of operation in a nuclear, biological and chemical (NBC) battlefield environment. In the mid 1960s the wheeled BTR-60 and earlier tracked BTR-50 APCs were both provided with overhead armour and NBC systems, replacing the previous generations of open vehicles. In contrast with the United States and some NATO countries, most Soviet artillery remained towed until the early 1970s, and from the 1940s through the 1960s Soviet artillery was towed by successive generations of tracked and latterly wheeled artillery tractors, with the exception being multiple rocket launcher systems, which were mounted on autonomous wheeled chassis. The Soviet Union actually developed an entire range of tracked self-propelled conventional artillery in the late 1950s and 1960s, but most systems did not enter service. It was not until the GRAU "2S" series of self-propelled weapons entered service in the early 1970s that this situation was rectified.

The late 1960s also saw the introduction of an entirely new military vehicle type, the BMP mechanised infantry combat vehicle (MICV), which made its public debut in November 1967. The BMP was able to enter combat alongside tanks while giving infantry the capability to fight from within the vehicle, which could provide covering fire against hard and soft targets on the battlefield.

The second half of the 1960s saw the most extensive parades of nuclear missile technology ever held on Red Square, with new generations of long-range ICBMs capable of reaching not only any city in Europe but also directly targeting the United States. Concurrently with these developments the A-350Zh rocket for the A-35 Anti-Ballistic Missile System (NATO: ABM-1 Galosh) was demonstrated on Red Square alongside the displays of nuclear offensive strike capability. The latter anti-ballistic missile (ABM) system was in fact an ongoing work in progress, initially known in the Soviet Union as the "System A-35", with the thermo-nuclear warhead armed rocket being designated A-350Zh. It was intended for deployment in a defensive ring around Moscow in a similar manner to the S-25 "Berkut" SAM system, but with a far greater strategic defence capability.

The decade that began with the coldest depths of the Cold War, and which peaked with the Cuban Missile Crisis, also ended with the first signs of détente between the superpowers. Alarmed by the exponential increase in Soviet nuclear strike capability, in terms of both range and yield, coupled with the apparent deployment of defensive ABM rocket systems around Moscow, US President Lyndon B. Johnson in January 1967 called for strategic arms limitation talks (abbreviated to SALT) with the Soviet Union. These protracted talks got underway in Washington the same year during a Soviet State visit by Soviet Premier Aleksey Kosygin, and were continued in 1969 by their respective successors Leonid Brezhnev and American President Richard Nixon in the neutral location of Helsinki in Finland. The 1960s was the most intense decade of the entire Cold War, but it also heralded an era of détente in the following decade as the nuclear superpowers reached equilibrium in their capability to destroy each other with the entire planet as collateral damage.

1960

A single incident defined the relationship between the superpowers in 1960, and this incident happened on the very day the Soviet Union was celebrating the traditional annual 1st May workers holiday. The Cold War superpowers were in 1960 entering the most dangerous decade of the entire Cold War.

1st May 1960

The May Day parade of 1960 was unusually overcast for May, and was also conducted in the eye of the proverbial storm. The date would be marked as a major event in the history of the Cold War, with events elsewhere in the Soviet Union being more historically significant than what was happening on the ground on Red Square. The 1st May 1960 Red Square parade is the only Soviet parade that did not according to anecdotal evidence run precisely to schedule, and for a particularly valid reason.

On the morning of 1st May 1960, as Soviet First Secretary of the CPSU and Soviet Premier Khrushchev stood on the review stand above the Lenin Mausoleum on Red Square for the annual May Day parade, and the civil and military contingents of the parade were assembled on Red Square as usual, there was an unprecedented delay in the schedule. As Defence Minister Marshal Malinovsky prepared to take the parade, Khrushchev stood on the Lenin Museum review stand, still marked with the names of both Lenin and Stalin, with other things on his mind than ceremonial military parades. The same morning, an American Lockheed U-2A high altitude spy plane piloted by former US Air Force (and since 1956 CIA Grade GS-12) pilot Francis Gary Powers was en-route from Peshawar in Pakistan across western Siberia, on a joint USAF/CIA mission photographing Soviet sites, and in particular the Chelyabinsk-65 nuclear facility. Powers had taken off from a military airbase at Peshawar and entered Soviet airspace over Tajikistan. His aircraft had continued

The progress of rocket technology at the end of the 1950s was such that the 1,200km range R-5M was by 1960 already being supplemented on Red Square by the 2,100km range R-12, both towed by the AT-T tracked artillery tractor.

AT-T tracked artillery tractors towing the 130mm M-46 field guns down Gorky Street towards Red Square.

on a trajectory that would ultimately take him over the Siberian city of Sverdlovsk, safe in the knowledge that the Soviet Union did not possess surface-to-air rocket systems capable of reaching his flying altitude (the U-2A could fly at a maximum altitude of 21,000m). Soviet fighter aircraft had already attempted to intercept the U-2A aircraft without success as Powers continued his mission above Siberia. Meantime in Moscow, as the Red Square parade waited to start, the popular legend is that an obviously distracted Khrushchev pondered whether to give the order to shoot down the aircraft with V-750 rockets of the S-75 "Dvina" (NATO: SA-2 Guideline) SAM system. Anecdotal evidence from interviewed parade participants indicates that the parade was held up for a few minutes as Khrushchev conferred on the decision to launch S-75 "Dvina" system rockets against the U-2A then flying high above Siberia. The assembled troops apparently witnessed the animated Khrushchev give the command "sbit!" (literally "shoot it down!") from the review stand leaving the parade commander to consider momentarily to whom the command was directed. With the assembled troops doubtless metaphorically shrugging their shoulders, the parade then began. The events that followed over Siberia are now a major part of Cold War history. As the 1st May celebrations were beginning in Moscow, the U-2A piloted by Powers was shot down by a S-75 "Dvina" system rocket over Sverdlovsk. The actual missile launch was apparently at 08:53 rather

A 2P4 "Tuilpan" launch vehicle for the 2K2 "Filin" OTR passes before the Lenin Mausoleum, 1st May 1960. (Time Life)

2P4 "Tuilpan" (Obiekt-804) launch vehicles for the 2K2 "Filin" OTR system parade through Red Square, 1st May 1960, directly followed by the 8U218 (Obiekt-803) launch vehicles for the 8K11 OTR. (Mikhail Baryatinsky)

The AT-T was used to tow both the R-5M (seen here) and later R-12 strategic rockets through Red Square. The rockets were near identical, but the R-12 had a longer fuselage and slightly fluted base section.

than 09:53 Moscow time, which casts some doubt on the actual timing of activities at Red Square, but what is indisputable is that as the parade was preparing to start, Francis Gary Powers was parachuting to earth and captivity as his aircraft U-2A #56-6693 descended to the ground in pieces. The incident was another shock to United States and NATO commanders, in that it was now clear that Soviet technology was progressing faster than expected and that the Red Square demonstrations were backed by real advances in military capability. When asked many years later by a journalist what height he had actually been flying at when shot down by the Soviet rocket, Powers apparently replied with good humour "clearly not high enough".

After the incident, the US initially claimed that the U-2A was collecting weather data for NASA and had accidental strayed deep into Soviet territory. Unbeknown to the United States, the Soviet Union had recovered the on-board cameras and developed the film showing images of the sites that Powers had photographed from high altitude. The Soviet ability to shoot down a spy plane at an altitude NATO had considered well beyond the range of Soviet rocket technology was a hard lesson for the United States, and in the Soviet Union heralded in a decade of exponential rocket technology development, initially at Khrushchev's personal insistence.

Meanwhile, back on Red Square, the 1st May parade began with the now standard meeting of two parade limousines that had performed such a parade role since 1953, but with the ZiS-110B from 1960 replaced by the ZiL-111V, a cabriolet version of the ZiL-111 of which only 12 were hand built in 1960-62. The ZiL-111V would serve in the parade commander transport role for the rest of the 1960s.

The T-54 was the main battle tank type on display in May 1960, followed by towed and self-propelled artillery systems including the long in service 85mm D-48 anti-tank gun towed by the new semi-armoured AT-P light artillery tractor and the at the time less than clearly understood 2P5 launch vehicle for the 2K5 "Korshun" MRS.

The 2K1 "Mars" and 2K2 "Filin" OTR battlefield rocket systems had by 1960 begun to replace long-range strategic artillery as the weapon of choice on the tactical battlefield, and these were displayed in May 1960 together with the tracked 2A3 and 2B1 strategic artillery vehicles that they had by 1957 effectively already replaced in service. These short-range battlefield delivery rockets were generically designated "FROG" (Free Rocket Over Ground) by the US DoD and NATO, though there was conflation between "Mars" and later tracked "Luna" rockets that used a similar VgTZ built light tracked chassis, related to the chassis used by the PT-76 amphibious light tank and BTR-50 tracked APC.

The ASU-57, ZSU-57-2 and S-25 and S-75 SAM systems were all now displayed as standard parade vehicles. The 180mm S-23 field gun, with its new calibre for ground forces, was again towed through Red Square by the AT-T artillery tractor, as it had been since its parade debut in 1955. The weapon was still at the time assumed by NATO observers to be 203mm calibre, which had been a default Soviet heavy weapon calibre since the early 1930s. The May parade culminated with AT-T tractors towing the R-5M short-range ballistic rocket on their transport trailers across Red Square.

The R-5M in an image typical of those provided in Western intelligence recognition files in the early days of photocopier technology.

7th November 1960 – 43rd Anniversary of the Great October Socialist Revolution

The shooting down of an American U-2A spy plane over Sverdlovsk at the time of the 1st May Red Square parade in Moscow was not conducive to warm Soviet-American relations, and for that and other reasons relationships between the Soviet Union and the United States deteriorated badly between the May and November 1960 parades. The planned mid-year summit between Premier Khrushchev and President Eisenhower was inevitably cancelled as a consequence of the events of 1st May. The United States had meantime continued reconnaissance flights over Soviet territory, and in July an American RB-47 reconnaissance aircraft had also been shot down over the Barents Sea, but without the attendant publicity that the May incident had received. The same month, in what at the time seemed unrelated to the big picture of superpower relationships, the Soviet Union announced that it would purchase 700,000 metric tonnes of sugar from Cuba, and would also supply the island with Soviet weaponry. In the public domain, the ever-flamboyant Khrushchev had in October 1960 meantime lost his temper at a United Nations conference in what became known internationally as the "shoe incident".

The November 1960 parade was again reviewed by the Soviet Defence Minister Marshal of the Soviet Union, Rodion Ya. Malinovsky, with the parade commander being the newly appointed Moscow Military District (MVO) commander; Soviet Army General Nikolai Ivanovich Krylov. Both officers now stood in the rear of their respective ZiL-111V cabriolet parade cars rather than the ZiS-110B that had been retired after seven years in the role.

Vehicles on parade on 7th November 1960 included the BTR-50P tracked amphibious armoured personnel carrier, and well known parade regulars such as the AT-T heavy tracked artillery tractor towing the 180mm S-23 field gun. There were some subtle but significant changes in the weapons on parade, with the public debut

BTR-50P tracked APCs traverse Manezhnaya Square on a rainy 7th November 1960. The open BTR-50P would soon be replaced by the closed BTR-50PK with an element of NBC warfare protection.

A 420mm 2B1 "Oka" tracked strategic mortar follows a 406mm 2A3 "Kondensator" strategic gun down Gorky Street towards Red Square 7th November 1960.* (Mikhhail Baryatinsky)

in 1960 of the static launched S-25 (205) "Berkut" (NATO: SA-1 Guild) SAM system, joining the static launched but trailer transportable S-75 "Dvina" (NATO: SA-2 Guideline) SAM system which had its parade debut in 1957.

The S-25 "Berkut" SAM system was accepted into service in May 1955, having been developed for static battery deployment in a defensive ring around the Soviet capital Moscow. The S-25 system and its V-300 rocket was one of those missiles the exact purpose of which was not for some time understood by foreign military analysts. For Red Square display purposes the S-25 was mounted on its PR-3M TZM trailer, which transported the V-300 missile and associated fuel. It was initially towed by a ZiS-121B tractor truck version of the ZiS-151 6x6 truck, latterly replaced by the PR-3M3 TZM trailer towed by the production replacement ZiL-157V tractor truck. As of 1960 both the S-25 and the S-75 SAM systems were towed on their respective PR-3 and PR-11 series TZM trailers by the ZiL-157V 6x6 tractor truck rather than the earlier ZiS-121B semi-trailer tractor version of the ZiS-151.

November 1960 was also the parade debut of the R-12 (8K63) (NATO: SS-4 Sandal) MRBM rocket, with four of the new R-12 rockets being towed by AT-T tracked tractors across the square. The R-5M and R-12 rockets looked near identical, but the latter had a range of 2,080km - double that of the R-5M introduced only three years prior.

S-25 "Berkut" (NATO: SA-1 Guild) SAM systems being towed across Red Square by ZiL-157V semi-trailer tractor-trucks, 7th November 1960. (Time Life)

8U218 launch vehicles for the 8K11 OTR system depart Red Square. The 8K11 was the first "Scud" system, the "Scud-A" as defined by NATO and Western countries.

* The photograph is labelled 1960, but the BRDM in the background was not displayed on Red Square until 1961, suggesting the latter date may be correct.

1961

1961 would be another significant year in the Cold War era, and would be the year that the defining symbol of the Cold War in the European public consciousness would come into existence. In August 1961, the drift of professionals and workers from the German Democratic Republic (GDR/DDR) to West Germany across the divide in Berlin was brought to an abrupt halt when Premier Khrushchev that month gained agreement from the Soviet Presidium to build a wall dividing the Soviet sector of occupied Berlin from the sectors held by the other former wartime Allies.* In light of the events of 1960, the Soviet Union also restarted nuclear testing. A critical development during 1961, which would lead to the greatest "near miss" of the Cold War the following year, was the deployment by the United States Air Force of "Jupiter" medium range ballistic rockets in Italy and Turkey. The rockets based in Turkey had a range of 2,400km and were thereby a direct threat to the major cities of the Soviet Union. In response to these American rocket deployments, Soviet R-12 and R-14 rockets would the following year be despatched to an island in the Caribbean near the Florida coast of the United States - Cuba.

1st May 1961

On 1st May 1961, the Soviet Union celebrated May Day by tradition with a parade on Red Square, with Marshal Malinovsky again taking the military component of the parade. But not for the first time it would be recent events that provided background focus on the equipment displayed during the military parades on Red Square. On the Lenin Mausoleum, still adorned with the names of both Lenin and Stalin, with the former above the latter, dignitaries standing alongside Premier Nikita Khrushchev included the Soviet Cosmonaut Yuri Gagarin, who had on 12th April 1961 left the earth's atmosphere on-board the Soviet spacecraft "Vostok-1" and completed an orbit of the earth, landing precisely 108 minutes later. The Soviet Union had completed the first manned space flight, the country was collectively elated, and that single achievement for some time put

The curious looking 2P30 SPU vehicle for the 2K17 coastal defence system firing the 4K95 (FKR-2) cruise missile made its public debut on 1st May 1961.

---

* Although Khruschev is "credited" with building the Berlin Wall, it was Walter Ulbricht, the 1st Secretary of the Socialist Unity Party of the GDR/DDR that had been demanding its construction. The data are conflated, but it would appear the USSR agreed to rather than directly facilitated the action.

The 2P30 SPU vehicle for the 2K17 coastal defence cruise missile system was based on a modified ZiL-135K chassis with a new, angular cab. The significance of the system, known by NATO as the SSC-1a "Sepal/Shaddock" was not entirely understood at the time of its initial appearance. It was in fact designed to sink large surface warships far from Soviet shores.

the Soviet Union ahead of the United Sates in the "Space Race". Following on from the launch of the "Sputnik" (Sputnik-1) satellite in 1957, Gagarin's space flight in 1961 provided categorical proof that, inconceivable as it might seem, the Soviet Union was perhaps actually ahead of the United States in rocket technology and thereby the Cold War "arms race". The "Vostok" rocket development program had two purposes, one of which was manned spaceflight, which had in April 1961 been successfully achieved to popular acclaim. The other undeclared aim was the deployment of reconnaissance satellites under the "Zenit" program. The first Soviet military parade of 1961 in this regard set the scene for the decade, which would be dominated by rocket technology and its deployment in space, and on an island in the Caribbean on the earth below.

The mechanised part of the military parade was led by GAZ-69 lead vehicles as in previous years, followed directly by the introduction of a new armoured scout car, the BRDM, which led the armoured contingent of the parade. The BRDM was a front-engined, highly mobile reconnaissance vehicle, which was fitted with four retractable chain driven wheels located between the main road wheels to prevent the vehicle from "bottoming out" in rough terrain. It was later re-designated BRDM-1 after the introduction of the BRDM-2 a few years later. The BRDM was also fitted with several anti-tank guided missile (ATGM) systems and became a potent tank-killer in the latter role, with these ATGM vehicles also being paraded on Red Square. May 1961 was the final parade appearance of the BTR-152 wheeled APC series, in the form of the later BTR-152V production version. The BTR-152 series would be replaced by the radical BTR-60 design from November 1961.

Other parade standards such as the BTR-50P, the ZSU-57-2, the massive 2A3 and 2B1 tracked strategic artillery weapons and the 2K5 "Korshun" MRS (OTR) continued to be displayed, but again there were subtle changes in the parade line-up in 1961. The 8U218 (Obiekt-803) SPU vehicle for the 8K11 OTR system was again demonstrated on Red Square in May 1961, having debuted in 1960 and already replacing the

2K2 "Filin" system, which had debuted on Red Square only four years earlier. The systems looked very similar, but the 8K11 system featured the option of a new R-11M rocket with a 10kT nuclear warhead in addition to a conventional rocket, mounted on an entirely new SPU launch system. The S-25 "Berkut"and S-75 "Dvina" SAM systems were now displayed together, and would remain parade staples until almost the last Soviet era Red Square parade.

The 2P30 SPU vehicle for the 2K17 system firing the S-5 (4K95) cruise missile also made its debut at the 1st May 1961 Red Square parade. The curious looking vehicle developed at ZiL in Moscow was a mystery to foreign intelligence sources at the time, and was generally labelled "Sepal" or "Shaddock" in the West for the duration of the Cold War. The parade finished with the display of four R-5M strategic rockets, towed through Red Square by AT-T tracked tractors.

Relations between the Soviet Union and the West would significantly deteriorate in the summer and autumn months of 1961 between the May and November parades. The centre of conflict was as noted Germany, with work on building the Berlin Wall starting on 13th August 1961. The Berlin Wall would become the ultimate symbol of the Cold War, dividing East and West Berlin and the East from the West in principle. The Berlin Wall would remain in place for almost three decades.

7th November 1961 – 44th Anniversary of the Great October Socialist Revolution

Days before the 44th Anniversary Great October Socialist Revolution parade of 7th November 1961, as training was underway in the Moscow suburbs, Stalin was exhumed from the Lenin Mausoleum and reburied in the garden behind the mausoleum under the Kremlin wall. Stalin's name was also removed from the mausoleum, the signage reverting back solely to the name of Lenin as it had been before Stalin's death in 1953.

On 7th November 1961, Soviet Premier Nikita Khrushchev stood on the review stand with other Soviet leadership including Leonid I. Brezhnev, with the parade taken by Soviet Defence Minister Marshal Rodion Ya. Malinovsky. November 1961 was primarily an infantry parade, with large columns and a more limited armour contingent. Marching columns included students from the "M.V. Frunze" Military Academy, the "N.E. Zhukovsky" Air Force Engineering Academy, the Moscow Border Guards Academy and the tank forces, the military-political academy and Moscow "Suvorov" academies.

GAZ-69s led the armoured vehicle parade columns, which began with the public debut of an entirely new type of wheeled armoured personnel carrier, the BTR-60P, which was a revolutionary vehicle compared to the BTR-152 it was destined to replace. Whereas the BTR-152 was basically an armoured truck, the BTR-60P (Plavayushy - amphibious) was a purpose designed wheeled APC. The BTR-60P represented a quantum leap in Soviet mechanised infantry deployment. The vehicle had highly faceted armour, was fully amphibious - being propelled in water by a hydro-jet system - and was powered by two GAZ-49 petrol engines, each driving the road wheels on one side of the vehicle, such that it could continue to operate on one engine or with damaged roadwheels.

The tracked BTR-50P was again displayed in November 1961 still in open configuration, being complemented by the fully enclosed and NBC capable BTR-50PK from 1962. Mobile short-range air defence was represented by the ZSU-57-2 self-propelled air defence system. The 2A3 and 2B1 strategic weapons remained the great "crowd pleasers" on Red Square, even though they had already been effectively replaced by the 2K1 "Mars" and 2K2 "Filin" OTR systems as they made their parade debut in 1957. By 1961 these early OTR systems had been joined by the next generation 8U218 and the 2P19 on the Obiekt-803 and Obiekt-810 chassis respectively, and were by 1961 already coming to the end of their parade life. On 7th November 1961, four 2P19 SPU vehicles mounting the R-17 (8K14) rocket for the 9K72 "Elbrus) (NATO: SS-1 Scud-B) made their parade debut on Red Square, as the rocket generations rapidly overtook each other in Soviet Army service and on public display.

Less apparent than the provision of overhead armour on secondary combat vehicles on Red Square from the beginning of the 1960s was that vehicles were now also being fitted with infrared night vision equipment for both the main armament systems and for driving, providing the Soviet Army with a new level of night fighting and poor weather operational capability. Such fitments became increasingly common on vehicles displayed on Red Square from this time.

One of the most unusual looking and enigmatic vehicles to parade through Red Square made its second appearance in November 1961 having made its parade debut in May. As would become clear to Western observers only later, the 2P30 was the SPU vehicle for the 2K17 coastal defence cruise missile system firing the FKR-2* (4K95/S-5) cruise missile. The curious looking vehicle, with a launch container mounted on the rear of a Zil-135K chassis with a new and angular cab was a mystery to foreign intelligence analysts when initially unveiled, and for some considerable time thereafter. The November 1961 parade ended with four R-12 medium range strategic rockets - usually abbreviated to MRBM - being towed through Red Square by AT-T tractors. The R-12 rocket would soon thereafter become world famous, by deed if not by name.

The 2A3 "Kondensator" (foreground) and 2B1 "Oka" (background) remained on display until 1963 despite having been made obsolescent by the OTR and strategic rockets displayed concurrently since 1957. (Aleksandr Koshavtsev)

---

* The 2K17 shore defence system fired the FKR-2 (Frontalnaya Krilataya Raketa - Frontal Cruise Missile - 2), the cruise missile also being known by the GRAU designation 4K95, and as the S-5. It was developed from a Soviet naval system.

THE SOVIET ARMY ON PARADE 1946-91

The 2P19 on the Obiekt-810 chassis closely resembled the earlier but concurrently displayed 8U218 SPU vehicle, but was the SPU vehicle for the 8K14 system and its R-17 rocket.

The 2P4 "Tuilpan" SPU vehicle for the 2K2 "Filin" OTR system was the first such vehicle to be displayed on Red Square. It was rapidly replaced by the 8K11 and 8K14 OTR systems, with all three being displayed concurrently for some years.

BTR-50P tracked APCs disperse having traversed Red Square, 7th November 1962. The open BTR-50P would soon be replaced by the enclosed BTR-50PK. (Mikhail Baryatinsky)

The BRDM (BRDM-1) reconnaissance vehicle made its Red Square public debut in 1961. The vehicle was amphibious and had retractable chain driven aircraft type wheels to assist travel in difficult terrain.

1962

1962 would prove a momentous year on the world stage, and the year that the Cold War came closest to becoming hot. World focus would in late 1962 concentrate on the Caribbean island of Cuba, albeit recently declassified information emanating from both the Russian Federation and the United States indicates that an equally disastrous "near miss" would occur much later in the Cold War, in 1983.

For the Soviet government, the developing international political situation with the United States and its NATO allies was in early 1962 secondary to events closer to home, there being potentially serious domestic issues for the Soviet government to contend with that year. Shortages of meat, butter and other staple foods in some regions of the Soviet Union led to demonstrations against the local government, with riots in Chelyabinsk in Siberia - the "Tankograd" tank manufacturing centre of World War Two - and in Kiev and Riga, the capital cities of the Soviet Republics of Ukraine and Latvia respectively. In June, riots in Novocherkassk resulted in local politicians - and also the police who intervened - being collectively lynched. The restoration of order required direct intervention by the Soviet Army. Meanwhile, in stark contrast with the unrest in some individual cities, a degree of unprecedented openness was occurring in the Soviet Union, with a new tolerance of expression, and limited protest against the existing order being allowed in the area of arts and entertainment. The most public manifestation of this as seen from abroad was the publication by the former GULAG inmate Aleksandr Solzhenitsyn of his novel "One Day in the Life of Ivan Denisovich" which described a typical day in the life of an everyday Soviet citizen on the wrong side of the State system. The book was internationally acclaimed, and cracked open the window on the inner workings of the Soviet State to the outside world. From a Soviet perspective, it was indicative, particularly considering the internal issues of the time, that the Soviet State allowed that window to be opened for inspection and comment by everyday readers in the outside world. It had been only recently that the writer Boris Pasternak, author of the book "Doctor Zhivago" had a more troublesome time related to his manuscript smuggled out of the country and published in Italy, for which he had ultimately been presented the Nobel prize for literature in 1958.

At the beginning of the year at least one American citizen was pleased with developments in the Soviet Union. On 10th February Francis Gary Powers was released from captivity and exchanged for the Soviet KGB Colonel and spy Vilyam Fisher (better known in the West as Rudolf Abel) on the Glienicke Bridge in Berlin. Powers, who clearly had a wry sense of humour, had been well treated and advised that he had learned carpet weaving during his incarceration, though he would resume his career as a test pilot despite his newly acquired alternative skills. More ominously according to the somewhat curious narrative as released to the American public as the official version of events, another American also returned to the United States from the Soviet Union in the summer of 1962. A former American marine who had apparently defected to the Soviet Union in 1959 and had been living in the Belorussian capital Minsk where his work as a machine operator was not to his expectations returned to the United States on 1st June with his Russian wife Marina. He moved to the city of Dallas, Texas and for a time lived there quietly, with clearance to work at military facilities, including a U-2 base. His name was Lee Harvey Oswald.

By September 1962, the Soviet Union was sending military hardware to Fidel Castro's government in Cuba to ward off a potential American invasion of the new fledgling state under new management. By October the situation had become formalised as the Cuban Missile Crisis.

1st May 1962

The 1st May 1962 military parade again taken by Soviet Defence Minister Marshal Malinovsky was unremarkable, with a display of T-54 tanks and BTR-50P tracked APCs of the Guards Kantemirovskaya Tank Division, BTR-60P wheeled APCs of the Guards Tamanskaya Motor Rifle Division, air defence systems and as in November 1961 a display of R-12 ballistic rockets as the parade finale. Although the 1st May 1962 parade was in of itself unremarkable, what was going on in the background certainly was. The year between May 1962 and May 1963 would be momentous. The events that unfolded during this short time period are regarded by most military historians as the closest point, the later disclosed events of 1983 aside, that the United States and the Soviet Union came to nuclear war during the entire Cold War era.

BTR-60P wheeled APCs traversing Red Square, 1st May 1962. Note the non-standard pintle-mounted 12.7mm DShKM heavy machine gun and standard 7.62mm SGMB weapons. (RGAKFD)

The SU-85 (ASU-85) VDV airborne forces close support gun mounted the 85mm D-70 tank gun in a fully enclosed casemate-type fighting compartment. (Tank Museum 2467/E5)

The AT-T tracked artillery tractor was used to tow the R-5M strategic rocket during Red Square parades, and from 1960 also the longer range but almost identical R-12 rocket, as seen here.

AT-S medium tracked artillery tractors with 130mm M-46 field guns await parade start orders on Red Square. The AT-S was developed at the ChTZ tank plant in Chelyabinsk but built at KMZ in Kurgan.

The Cuban Missile Crisis

A few weeks before the 1st May 1962 parade in Moscow, a new Soviet rocket division had been formed. There was nothing particularly remarkable about this in the context of a nation that was rapidly deploying rocket technology, but the deployment of the 51st Rocket Division, formed in April 1962 under the command of Divisional Commander I. D. Stotsenko, would be written into world history. As formed, the 51st Rocket Division consisted of five regiments, three of which were to be equipped with 8 PU erector/launchers each for the 2,100km range R-12 SRBM, and two regiments with 8 PU erector/launchers each for the 4,500-5,500km range R-14 MRBM, for a planned nominal total of 36-40 PU launchers for the R-12 and R-14 nuclear armed rockets. The 51st Rocket Division was to be deployed abroad under the auspices of "Operation Anadir". The destination was an island straddling the Gulf of Mexico and the Caribbean Sea - Cuba. Once deployed, the relatively short-range R-12 rockets were capable of striking 33% of the mainland territory of the United States. The larger and longer-range R-14 rockets were meantime capable of targeting any city in the United States and a large part of the land territory of Canada.

On 9th September 1962, as early parade rehearsals were underway in Moscow for the 7th November 1962 parade, the motor vessel "Omsk" docked at the Cuban port of Casilda and discharged its cargo of six R-12 rockets. A further 24 ships would arrive in Cuba between 9th September and 22nd October, delivering a total of 42 R-12 rocket systems, consisting of 36 operational rockets with nuclear warheads and 6 training rockets. The rockets were supported in Cuba by a not entirely small contingent of 1,404 Soviet officers and 6,462 other ranks and specialists attached to the 51st Rocket Division on the island. On 4th October, the motor vessel "Indigirka" docked in Cuba and offloaded its cargo of 60 nuclear warheads for both the R-12 and R-14 rockets. Within 24 hours of the nuclear warheads being disembarked, the 51st Division had 24 nuclear-armed R-12 rocket systems ready for launch.

In October 1962, American U-2 reconnaissance aircraft flying high over Cuba photographed concrete rocket launch pads being prepared on the island. These were not laid out in the traditional "star" format used by anti-aircraft missile systems such as the S-75 "Dvina" (NATO: SA-2 Guideline) that had recently downed Francis Gary Power's U2A aircraft over Siberia, but were being built for larger, short and medium range ballistic missile systems. President Kennedy was informed of the situation on 16th October. The American reconnaissance photographs of Soviet ships and their deadly cargoes had meantime set in motion a frenzy of activity in the American White House, and as of 22nd October the United States Navy began a blockade of Cuba. The blockade stopped delivery of the smaller quantity of longer-range R-14 rockets, but the shorter range, and nuclear armed, R-12 rockets were ready to launch from their Cuban launch sites locations two weeks before the blockade on the longer-range R-14 rockets had taken effect.

The urgent negotiations that followed are outwith the scope of this study; however the tense situation was resolved in the final days of October 1962. It was only many years later that the agreements made behind the scenes between the Soviet Union and the United States were made public. Fidel Castro had asked Khrushchev to bomb American cities during the crisis, which favour Khrushchev had neglected to fulfil. A top secret agreement between Premier Khrushchev of the Soviet Union and President Kennedy of the United States, and actually named "The Secret Deal" - and which was made public only many years later - determined that in return for the Soviet Union removing its rockets from Cuba, the United States guaranteed not to invade the island. Further, and fundamental to the Soviet principal interest in the matter, the US agreed to cancel deployment of the "Jupiter" MRBMs for which launch sites were under preparation in Turkey and Italy, nor would it complete delivery of the 60 SM-75/PGM-17A "Thor" MRBMs planned for installation in Great Britain under the codename "Project Emily", the first of which had been delivered by air transport to No.77 (SM) Squadron based at RAF Feltwell in Norfolk on 19th September 1958.

On 28th October 1962, Divisional Commander Stotsenko received orders to decommission all operational R-12 launch positions in Cuba, which was duly completed by 31st October 1962, precisely one week before the next 7th November military parade in Moscow. All rockets had by 2nd November been loaded back on ships, with the first five rockets departing the Port of Mariel (Havana) on 5th November on the motor vessel "Dvinogorsk". As the 7th November parade was being held in Moscow in 1962, the world was receding from the brink of potential nuclear war. The Cuban Missile Crisis might also be considered as an inevitable high stakes political standoff, the ultimate brinkmanship considering the threats, counter-threats and outcome, but the world had survived the nearest it had come during the Cold War to nuclear conflict. The last ship transporting R-12 rockets departed the Port of Casilda on 9th November on the motor vessel "Leninsky Komsomol". The Cuban Missile Crisis, which had effectively begun in Turkey rather than Cuba, was over, and behind the public sabre-rattling and the fear mongering, the level of pragmatism displayed by both sides of the divide was remarkable by modern standards. Domestically, and internationally, the Soviet Union, and Khrushchev personally, were seen however to have backed down on a Soviet created incident. Khrushchev's status was in consequence significantly damaged at home in the Soviet Union. In later years as the evidence was released by both the United States and the Soviet Union, it became clear that the Cuban Missile Crisis had been far more complex than the small matter of a regional revolution on an island in the Caribbean. And the superpower solution had also been far more diplomatic than could have been imaged by the general public based on what information had at the time been released to the mainstream press.

7th November 1962 – 45th Anniversary of the Great October Socialist Revolution

The 45th Anniversary of the Great October Socialist Revolution military parade held on Red Square on 7th November 1962 was set against the background of a potential nuclear conflict having been averted only days before. Nikita Khrushchev stood on the Lenin Mausoleum and reviewed the passing columns of marching troops and military vehicles as Defence Minister Marshal Malinovsky took the parade from the square, with others on the tribunal again including Leonid Brezhnev.

The BTR-60P wheeled "Bronetransporter" was displayed for the second year on Red Square. The original open roofed version would be quickly replaced by modernised versions with overhead armour and NBC protection, namely the BTR-60PA (known in the West as the BTR-60PK) and later BTR-60PB. The BTR-60 was a particularly successful design, the basic design principles of an 8x8 configuration fully amphibious wheeled APC evolving over the decades into the BTR-80 and BTR-82A series, which are in service with the modern Russian Army. The earlier tracked BTR-50P "Bronetransporter" had meantime already been replaced in production by the BTR-50PK with overhead armour, reflecting the new nuclear age. The new BTR-50PK version made its parade debut on 7th November 1962, alongside the earlier production BTR-50P.

The late 1950s and early 1960s was a time of rapid development in tank technology, and consequently the T-55 MBT made its public debut on Red Square on 7th November 1962, only five years after the parade debut of the T-54, while the new T-62 was also entering series production and would soon also make a parade appearance on Red Square. The early production T-55 resembled the final T-54B version of the earlier T-54, and at a distance was almost indistinguishable from the earlier design, but the T-55 was an entirely new tank development that would serve the Soviet Army for the next two decades.

The 2P16 SPU vehicle for the 2K6 "Luna" OTR short range tactical rocket system made its public Red Square debut in November 1962, displayed in two versions, armed respectively with the ZR-9 and the ZR-10 rocket - the latter ZR-10 rocket having a nuclear warhead. The 2P16 was almost identical to the earlier 2P2 SPU vehicle for

BTR-50PK tracked APCs during final parade practice at the former Khodynka airfield in northwest Moscow. The BTR-50P and new BTR-50PK fully enclosed version were displayed together in 1962.

BTR-60P wheeled APCs moving down Gorky Street for the 7th November 1962 Red Square parade. The non-standard 12.7mm DShKM installation was for parade purposes only.

The T-54 had its Red Square public parade debut in 1957. Only five years later, it was joined on Red Square, and then quickly replaced by the T-55.

the 2K1 "Mars" rocket system but was a modified design mounted on the same base chassis. The early ISU-152K chassis derived 2P4 "Tuilpan" SPU vehicle for the 2K2 "Filin" OTR was now displayed on Red Square alongside the newer 8U218 SPU for the 8K11 OTR system with its R-11M nuclear armed rocket option and the 2P19 SPU vehicle for the 8K72 system with its R-17 (8K14) rocket. These vehicles also looked similar, but the latter had a significantly increased range and nuclear delivery capability.

The ZSU-57-2 tracked self-propelled air defence system was again paraded in November 1962, however a new and highly potent short-range air defence system was accepted for service on 5th September 1962 that would soon be paraded alongside the ZSU-57-2, and would ultimately replace it. The ZSU-23-4 that would appear on Red Square from 1965, was armed with four radar controlled 23mm ZU-7 guns that would prove lethal against low-flying aircraft and helicopters as it made its international combat debut in wars in the Middle East in the years ahead.

The fully enclosed and air transportable SU-85 (ASU-85) was from 1962 a standard parade feature on Red Square, replacing the lighter armed and armoured, but parachute deployable ASU-57 as the primary VDV airborne forces heavy ground support weapon.

Air defence systems included the now parade standard S-25 "Berkut" and S-75 "Dvina" SAM systems, both towed by ZiL-157V 6x6 tractor vehicles on their respective PR-3 and PR-11 series TZM transport reload trailers. The latter S-75

T-54B tanks move down Gorky Street towards Red Square, 7th November 1962. The T-54B and T-55 were paraded together in 1962. (RGAKFD)

A T-55 on the return run from Red Square after its parade debut, 7th November 1962. Note the 12.7mm DShKM anti-aircraft machine gun mounting (Tank Museum 2948/C4)

(NATO: SA-2 Guideline) surface to air "SAM" rocket system was now world-famous as a consequence of the May 1960 U-2 incident over Siberia.

The somewhat obsolescent 2A3 "Kondensator" and 2B1 "Oka" strategic artillery weapons were still being paraded through Red Square in 1962, and remained as impressive as ever. Both systems had however already been replaced by the new OTR tactical rocket systems displayed during the same parades. The curious looking (and at the time of service largely enigmatic) 2P30 SPU vehicle for the 2K17 coastal defence missile system and its 4K95 (S-5) rocket was displayed for the second year, its precise role in 1962 remaining largely un-clarified. The Red Square parades were now also joined by submarine launched rockets, beginning with the R-13 (D-6) (NATO: SS-N-4 Sark) towed by AT-T tracked tractors in Soviet Navy markings.

At the end of the parade, four R-12 MRBMs were again towed through Red Square by AT-T tracked tractors. The American military attachés watching the display on Red Square on 7th November 1962 were able to observe the R-12 rockets from a more detached "touristic" observers perspective, than was the case when reviewing U-2 reconnaissance plane photographs of the same rockets located on their launch stands in Cuba only a matter of days before.

1963

After the near nuclear debacle in late 1962, the following year was by contrast particularly quiet on the diplomatic front between the superpowers. As an afterthought to the Cuban Missile Crisis, a "hot line" phone system was set up in 1963 for direct communication between the leadership of the Soviet Union and the United States. An agreement was also reached between the Soviet Union, the United States and Great Britain with regard to halting atmospheric nuclear testing. The overall strategic stance of the superpowers had not changed, but their newfound willingness to cooperate reflected the realities of what had been narrowly avoided in the recent months.

1st May 1963

The 1963 May Day Parade was only six months after the Cuban Missile Crisis that had come close to a potentially nuclear conflict. While for foreign military observers the annual parades of Soviet rockets moving through Red Square had been informative; having these rockets deployed on Cuba a matter of minutes flying time from all major American cities including Washington was clearly a more overt demonstration of Soviet response capability than the United States could tolerate. The direct crisis had long passed by May 1963, but the nuclear arms race only intensified over the next years, now that the Soviet Union had technically caught up in the subject, and had proven at least for defence budget purposes a clear and present danger to the United States. To add to the flavour of the day, particularly bearing in mind the events of recent months, the President of Cuba, Fidel Castro, was present on the review stand above the Lenin Mausoleum for the 1st May 1963 Red Square parade.

The May 1963 military parade was reviewed by Marshal of the Soviet Union, Rodion Ya. Malinovsky, with the parade commander being the Moscow Military District (MVO) commander, General A. P. Beloborodov, with both per tradition standing in the rear of cabriolet parade limousines, now the ZiL-111V. Only twelve of these 190km/h capable limousines were hand built, specifically for military ceremonial purposes.

The mechanised section of the parade was as standard undertaken by the Guards Kantemirovskaya Tank Division and the Guards Tamanskaya Motor Rifle Division. GAZ-69 vehicles led the parade columns, with the T-55 tank now having replaced the T-54 as the main tank type on display.

The BTR-60P was still displayed in its original open configuration, however the tracked BTR-50P was now joined by the BTR-50PK with overhead armour and NBC battlefield capability, with the two successive types being displayed together until November 1964.

Soviet VDV airborne forces again demonstrated the new SU-85 (ASU-85). The larger, heavier airborne support vehicle armed with an

The BTR-50P and BTR-50PK were by 1963 displayed together on Red Square, with the BTR-50PK replacing the earlier production version from 1965. (Mikhail Baryatinsky)

85mm D-70 dual purpose gun now provided significantly increased firepower support to VDV airborne forces compared with the earlier ASU-57. Although the airborne assault gun was labelled as the ASU-85 by the US and NATO until after the fall of the Soviet Union, the vehicle was actually designed as a dual role ground/airborne forces assault gun, and was designated SU-85 rather than ASU-85 in the Soviet Union. The SU-85 (ASU-85) continued to represent VDV airborne forces heavy support armament until the mid 1970s.

Artillery on display in May 1963 included the 130mm M-46 and 180mm S-23 field guns, towed by the AT-T artillery tractor, the combinations having been a parade regular on Red Square since 1955. Anti-aircraft rockets included the new 2K11 "Krug" on the Obiekt-123 self-propelled tracked chassis, and the S-25 and S-75 SAM systems, both towed since November 1960 by the ZiL-157V tractor truck. The 2K11 "Krug" had been developed concurrently with the S-75, but due to technical delays had been introduced into Soviet Army service later than the static launched S-75 "Dvina" system.

1963 was the final year in which the 2A3 and 2B1 strategic artillery systems would be displayed, now entirely replaced by the "Mars", "Filin" and later generation "Luna" OTR tactical rockets that had effectively superseded them before they had made their first parade appearance in 1957. Khrushchev looked down from the Lenin Mausoleum review stand at his dream of having conventional artillery replaced with rockets to project Soviet military might now fulfilled on Red Square. The 2P16 SPU vehicle for the 2K6 "Luna" OTR rocket had now replaced the 2P2 SPU vehicle for the earlier 2K1 "Mars" on Red Square. The 2P30 SPU vehicle for the 4K95 (S-5) cruise missile system was displayed, with its exact purpose still undefined at the time by foreign intelligence analysts.

The parade ended with the default strategic interest for foreign attachés on Red Square during the 1960s, namely the growing display of ever-larger rocket systems at the end of the parade. GAZ-69 vehicles with naval flags led AT-T tractors towing R-13 (D-6) (NATO: SS-N-4 Sark) submarine launched SLBMs, a seagoing means of nuclear delivery far more reliable and difficult to intercept than an aircraft, as also favoured by NATO countries, and first demonstrated on Red Square in 1962. The parade concluded with AT-T tracked artillery tractors towing R-12 (8K63) (NATO:

AT-T heavy artillery tractors towing 180mm S-23 field guns with the barrels out of battery lock for transport purposes, 1st May 1963.

AT-T artillery tractors towing 180mm S-23 field guns across Red Square, 1st May 1963.

An R-13 (D-6 system) (4K50) submarine launched ballistic missile (SLBM) system on display, Red Square, 1st May 1963. The NATO designation for this system was SS-N-4 Sark. Photographer - Stan Wayman (LIFE)

SS-4 Sandal) rockets through Red Square, the same rocket type that had been operationally deployed on Cuba. To reinforce the point to observers present or watching from abroad, eight R-12 rockets were towed past the Lenin Mausoleum as Castro looked on, rather than the two or four such rocket systems displayed in earlier years.

The Soviet Union in 1963 also continued to forge ahead in the "Space Race" with the United States. On 16th June 1963, the "Vostok-6" spacecraft was launched, the last of the "Vostok" rocket program. On board was the female cosmonaut Valentina Tereshkova, who became the first woman in space, making a broad statement to the world as to unquestionable Soviet fortitude, Soviet female courage and Soviet technological capability.

7th November 1963 - 46th Anniversary of the Great October Socialist Revolution

The November 1963 military parade was without surprises, rather continuing the standard parade format that had been effective in displaying military might at the end of 1962 when the world had narrowly averted a nuclear exchange - assuming that the contemporary press reports rather than the diplomacy in the background are to be accepted as the primary source material. As the flamboyant Khrushchev watched the parade columns pass in front of him from the Lenin Mausoleum review stand, his time as leader was coming to an end. In the background, his party was in the process of arranging his removal from office due to his increasingly erratic behaviour, sometimes referred to without any sense of irony as his "individualism".

Next to him stood his ultimate successor, Leonid Brezhnev. The November parade was as in May taken by Soviet Defence Minister Marshal Malinovsky, with the parade commander again being the MVO commander General Beloborodov.

There were many new vehicles on display on the cobblestones of Red Square in November 1963. The 2P27 and 2P32 anti-tank rocket launcher vehicle versions of the BRDM armoured car were displayed together in November 1963. These systems would, as with similar systems in other countries, bring fundamental changes to the armoured battlefield, as the lightly armoured and highly mobile launch vehicles mounted anti-tank rockets that could destroy any known tank includ-

The base BRDM (BRDM-1) introduced in 1961 was paraded on Red Square for the rest of the decade.

ing heavily armoured heavy tanks, which largely negated the former advantages of the heavy tank on the battlefield. This, together with the appearance of the Main Battle Tank (MBT) and improved ammunition and armour in the 1960s led to the extinction of the heavy tank as a design, in the Soviet Union and around the world.

T-55 tanks of the Guards Kantemirovskaya Tank Division which had made their public debut the year before were again displayed, following the BTR-60P and BTR-50P and now also BTR-50PK parade regulars on to Red Square. Some less common vehicles again seen in 1963 included the AT-P semi-armoured light artillery tractor towing the 85mm D-48 anti-tank gun. The D-48 was a modified version of the 85mm D-44 Divisional Gun, and both types were displayed on Red Square in different years, with the main recognition feature being that the D-44 had a double baffle muzzle brake, whereas the D-48 anti-tank gun had a multiple slot muzzle brake.

AT-T tractors towing 180mm S-23 field guns and wheeled MRS including the YaAZ-214 (later KrAZ-214) mounted 2K5 "Korshun" and ZiL-157 mounted BMD-20-4 (BMD-20) were followed by the now standard ZSU-57-2 SPADS and the S-25 "Berkut" and S-75 "Dvina" SAM systems towed by ZiL-157V tractor vehicles. These air defence systems were now joined by the public debut of the Izdeliye-400 "Dal" long-range SAM system, which was one of the most enigmatic rockets to ever be displayed on Red Square. The "Dal" rocket was originally towed through Red Square on its PR-41A transport trailer by the by MAZ-502V 4x4 tractor, later replaced by the 6x6 Ural-375S. The system looked almost identical to the S-75 SAM, but was significantly larger.

The early 2P4 "Tuilpan" SPU launch vehicle for the 2K2 "Filin" tactical rocket was displayed together with both the newly introduced 8U218 SPU for the 8K11 system and its R-11/R-11M rocket, and the 2P19 - three very similar looking but sequential generations of OTR ground to ground tactical rocket systems all displayed concurrently. The latter systems looked relatively similar to the earlier 2P4 SPU vehicle, and were also mounted on an ISU-152K derived chassis but with a uniform diameter rocket with a conical warhead mounted on an open launch frame on both versions. November 1963 was the final parade appearance of the tracked 2A3 "Kondensator" and 2B1 "Oka" self-propelled strategic artillery weapons, the role of which had been succeeded by the new and concurrent OTR tactical rocket systems now being displayed on Red Square. Other rocket systems included the 2P30 SPU vehicle for the 4K95 (FKR-2/S-5) coastal defence missile system, AT-T tractors towing R-13 (D-6 system) (NATO:

SS-N-4 Sark) and R-29 (4K75) (NATO: SS-N-8 Sawfly) submarine launched strategic rockets - helpfully described by the commentator as "giant rockets" - and a parade finale by four R-12 (8K63) strategic rockets also towed by the AT-T tracked tractor. The R-12 (8K63) MRBM remained in 1963 the most powerful rocket on display, but was about to be joined on Red Square by newer and significantly larger and longer-range rockets.

The Soviet Union and the United States were by the end of 1963 both meantime reviewing their recently tense relationship in light of the proximity to nuclear war that had only narrowly been averted. The vacuum that this short period of reflection and détente provided was however filled from an American perspective by events in Asia Pacific and also at home. By October 1963, the United States had increased its military deploy-

The BRDM was used as the chassis for three anti-tank rocket guided missile (ATGM) launcher vehicles; the 2P27, 2P32 (seen here) and the later 9P110.

The 2P32 (NATO: AT-2 Swatter) launch vehicle was designed to engage tanks at relatively long-range. The four rocket launcher system was retracted under light armour in transport mode.

ment in Vietnam to 16,300 combat troops, albeit with optimistic plans to have all forces withdrawn by the following year. While the United States was concerned with communism in Asia Pacific, the former American national communist who had defected to the Soviet Union in 1959 and then returned apparently without much question to live in Dallas the previous year became known to the world. On 22nd November 1963 according to the official US narrative, he opened fire on a motorcade travelling through Dallas city centre with an Italian made Carcano 6.5mm Model 91/38 rifle purchased by mail order. Lee Harvey Oswald was successful in assassinating his target, the President of the United States, John F. Kennedy.*

The BRDM 2P32 was the launch vehicle for the 2K8 "Falanga" ATGM system. (Steven J. Zaloga)

The SU-85 (ASU-85) was regularly paraded on Red Square throughout the 1960s and early 1970s. Note the infrared night fighting equipment on these vehicles.

The "Izdeliye-400" or "Dal" (NATO: SA-5 Griffon) long-range air defence missile system was towed through Red Square on its semi-trailer TZM by the MAZ-502V tractor truck when introduced onto Red Square in 1963. The "Dal" system was never operationally deployed. (US DoD)

---

* The assassination of President Kennedy by Lee Harvey Oswald is the official narrative of events. Oswald was himself killed two days later and much background material known to the US government remains classified. At the time of his assassination, Kennedy was attempting to reach rapprochement with the Soviet Union and bring an end to the Cold War.

1964

The main political event in the Soviet Union in 1964 was the replacement of Khrushchev as Soviet Premier. On being recalled to Moscow from holiday for a meeting of the Presidium called by Leonid Brezhnev, Khrushchev, by then 70 years old, stoically accepted his fate, and by 14th October had retired, officially for health reasons. He was initially replaced as Soviet Premier by Aleksei Kosygin, with Leonid Brezhnev as the 1st Secretary of the CPSU. The same day, a team of three cosmonauts was launched into space and performed an orbit of the planet before returning to earth in another demonstration of Soviet progress in both rocket development and space exploration.

1st May 1964

The 1st May 1964 parade was again taken by Marshal of the Soviet Union Rodion Ya. Malinovsky, with the parade commander being the MVO commander Afanasy P. Beloborodov. Nikita S. Khrushchev stood on the review stand for what would be his last Red Square parade review as Soviet Premier. Leonid. I. Brezhnev, the party official who would be his ultimate replacement, stood alongside him on the review stand, having begun the machinations in March that would result in Khrushchev's removal from office in October that same year. Others on the review stand in May included A.I. Mikoyan and A.N. Kosygin.

Following the traditional marching columns, the mechanised parade began on 1st May with columns of GAZ-69 and GAZ-69A light vehicles, followed by BRDM armoured cars in columns four vehicles wide.* BTR-60 wheeled APCs followed in both open roofed BTR-60P and fully enclosed PA versions, followed by the tracked BTR-50 also in both open BTR-50P and fully enclosed BTR-50PK versions. The subtle generation change from open vehicle to closed type provided an element of NBC battlefield capability and protection for motorised infantry in Soviet tank and motorised rifle divisions.

The main tank on display was again the T-55 main battle tank, which had replaced the T-54 on Red Square from 1962. VDV airborne forces were represented by the SU-85 (ASU-85) self-propelled gun, which was then entering general service. Well-known artillery followed, in the form of AT-T tractors towing 130mm M-46 and 180mm S-23 field guns. Multiple rocket launchers were represented by the BM-24 and BM-20-4 (BMD-20) both mounted on the ZiL-157 chassis, and again the YaAZ (later KraZ-214) 2P5 SPU vehicle for the 2K5 "Korshun" MRS. The 40 round 122mm 9K51 (BM-21) "Grad" MRS was accepted into service with the Soviet Army in 1963, based on the powerful 6x6 Ural-375D all-terrain truck, and this new system would soon replace all other medium calibre multiple rocket systems on Red Square.

Air defence was again represented by the ZSU-57-2 self-propelled air defence system (SPADS) and S-25 and S-75 SAMs towed by ZiL-157V tractor trucks on their respective PR series transport trailers. They were joined by the Izdeliye-400 "Dal" long-range surface to air missile introduced on Red Square the previous year, towed by the 4x4 MAZ-502V tractor, and the 2P24 SPU for the 8K11 "Krug" SAM system. The former resembled the S-75 as detailed earlier, but was significantly larger and as its name "Dal" (far) suggested, was intended for long range interception of fast moving jet aircraft. The four 2P24 SPU vehicles for the 2K11 "Krug" SAM system were also a major development. The 2K11 "Krug" (circle) SAM system was provided with dedicated tracked location and intercept radar systems, with the 2P24 SPU

---

* The BRDM was later re-designated BRDM-1 to distinguish it from the BRDM-2.

The BRDM, which had its public debut on Red Square in 1961, was a purpose designed fully amphibious reconnaissance vehicle.

vehicles mounted on a highly mobile tracked Obiekt-123 chassis, such that the 2K11 SAM system could accompany tank and motorised rifle divisions over most terrain with the rockets in ready to launch configuration.

Tracked 2P16 SPU vehicles for the 2K6 "Luna" tactical rocket system, replacing the earlier 2K1 "Mars" system, and mounted as before on a chassis related to that of the PT-76 amphibious light tank were followed by the 2P30 SPU vehicle for the 2K17 system firing the 4K95 (S-5) (NATO: Sepal/Shaddock) cruise missile, the latter in 1964 remaining as enigmatic as when first displayed. AT-T tractors towed the Soviet naval R-13 and R-29 SLBM rockets, with the parade finale being the now well-known rocket stand launched R-12 (8K63) MRBM.

While on 1st May 1964 the cameras were as always focused on Red Square, a military parade was held in Kiev that included some historically significant but never seen elsewhere weapons, not least later developments of the original Soviet R-1 rocket system which was a direct descendant of the technology inherited from the German V-2 (A-4) towed by the AT-T tractor along Kiev's main thoroughfare, Kreshchatik. Such cameo appearances of unusual or rare weapons were not infrequent during parades held in the capital cities of the Soviet Republics and other major Soviet cities.

Later in 1964, events in Asia Pacific would unfold that would distract the United States from the Soviet threat, perceived or real, for the next decade. On 4th August an American warship, the USS Maddox, was according to information relayed at the time as accurate, engaged in a battle with North Vietnamese motor-torpedo boats in what was known as the "Gulf of Tonkin" (USS Maddox) incident. The incident has since been refuted as a false flag operation, however the result was that the United States would quickly be drawn into a war in the country that proved impossible to fight with conventional forces, and became increasingly unpopular at home as the death toll mounted.

The year 1964 saw the public debut of the R-14U (8K65U) strategic rocket, towed by the new MAZ-535A 8x8 wheeled artillery tractor, which replaced the AT-T tracked tractor in many roles on Red Square from that year. (Aleksandr Koshavtsev)

The R-14U MRBM was the silo-launched version of the R-14 rocket that had almost been delivered to Cuba in 1962 to complement the shorter-range R-12 rockets which had been landed and emplaced. The R-14U (NATO:SS-5 Skean) had a range of 4,500-5,500km.

7th November 1964 – 47th Anniversary of the Great October Socialist Revolution

Nikita Khrushchev was removed from office on 13th October due to his "ill health" and by the time of the 7th November 1964 parade, he had been replaced in the role of Soviet Premier by Leonid Brezhnev. Brezhnev would remain in place as Soviet Premier for the next eighteen years, a period that from the perspective of the Russian and Soviet population was perhaps the most stable and overall benign and hopeful period in Soviet history. Brezhnev in 1964 announced an additional State holiday, "Victory Day" to commemorate the end of World War Two in Europe, with the first such military parade being scheduled for 9th May 1965.

The November 1964 parade, which was taken per 1960s tradition by Marshal Malinovsky included many new military vehicles, and is also the occasion that longer-range ballistic and defensive rockets began to appear on Red Square. The parade began with GAZ-69 lead vehicles followed by the standard BRDM reconnaissance vehicle, and also the new 2P32 launcher vehicle for the 2K8 "Falanga" system firing the 3M11 "Fleyta" anti-tank guided missile (ATGM) (NATO: AT-2 Swatter). These powerful guided anti-tank missiles provided significant anti-tank capability on a relatively light chassis, and were instrumental (in the Soviet Union and elsewhere) in negating the raison d'être effectiveness of the heavy tank as a weapon type. The earlier BRDM mounted 2P27 launcher vehicle for the 2K16 "Schmel" (NATO: AT-1 Snapper) ATGM had meantime made only a cameo appearance on Red Square, before being immediately replaced by the 2P32 vehicle.

The open BTR-50P and closed BTR-50PK were displayed together for the last time as the earlier open armoured vehicles were replaced by closed NBC battlefield capable designs, and the subtle generation change was complete.

The 2P16 SPU vehicle for the "Luna" OTR was displayed with both ZR-9 conventional and ZR-10 nuclear warhead rockets, and the larger ISU-152K chassis based 8U218 (Obiekt-803) and 2P19 (Obiekt-810) SPU vehicles were again

The 2P32 launch vehicle for the 2K8 "Falanga" ATGM system mounted on the BRDM chassis moving towards Red Square, 7th November 1964.

displayed together as Soviet OTR tactical rockets underwent rapid generation changes as displayed on Red Square.

Ground and air defence artillery and rocket systems were as for the May parade, including the ZSU-57-2 self propelled anti-aircraft gun, the S-25 and S-75 and 2K11 SAM systems, and the Izdeliye-400 "Dal" towed by the MAZ-502V. 1964 was also the year when the Soviet Union began to exponentially ramp up the displays of strategic nuclear rockets to project military might from the cobbles of Red Square. The R-12 (8K63) had only a few years earlier been the most dramatic weapon shown on Red Square, or for that matter demonstrated in Cuba, but by 1964 the R-12 was joined by much larger rockets. Naval (submarine launched SLBM) R-13 (D-6) and R-29 rockets would from 1964 become a parade standard on Red Square. Parade debuts in November 1964 included the R-14 (8K65) ICBM, the A-350Zh (5V61) rocket for the A-35 "Aldan" anti-ballistic missile system towed by a 10x10 MAZ-537V tractor/powered trailer combination, and finally the huge GR-1 "Global Rocket" ICBM, which will be described later.

As another sign of rapidly developing Soviet technology, the AT-T tracked tractors which had towed the R-5M, R-12 and other ballistic rockets through Red Square were by the mid 1960s being replaced by the wheeled MAZ-535A 8x8 ballast tractor and MAZ-537V 8x8 semi-trailer tractor, both of which had their Red Square parade debut in November 1964. The MAZ-535A ballast and

A BTR-50P tracked APC passes the Hotel Moskva before entering Red Square, 7th November 1964; the last appearance of the original production version of the vehicle.

The MAZ-535A 8x8 ballast tractor (seen here) and related MAZ-537V 8x8 semi-trailer tractor replaced the AT-T tracked tractor in most Red Square towing roles from 1964. (Tank Museum 2479/A1)

A MAZ-537 in VMF (Russian Navy) markings tows an R-29 (4K75) SLBM system through Red Square. The system was known by NATO as the SS-N-8 Sawfly.

From 1964, silo based intercontinental range rockets also appeared on Red Square. A MAZ-537V 8x8 towing a R-26 (8K66) ICBM past the Lenin Mausoleum, November 1964.

THE SOVIET ARMY ON PARADE 1946-91

MAZ-537V semi-trailer tractors towing the new A-35, R-14 and GR-1 rocket systems were in of themselves large vehicles compared to the tracked AT-T tractors which had preceded them, and the move towards highly mobile multi-axle wheeled all terrain vehicles would in the years ahead have a significant role in mobilising the Soviet Union's rapidly developing strategic rocket forces.

2P30 SPU vehicles for the 2K17 coastal defence cruise missile system parked on Gorky Street awaiting parade start orders. The vehicle was based on the 8x8 ZiL-135K chassis, and had a distinctive cab arrangement.

The concurrent 8U218 and 2P19 (seen here) OTR launch vehicles were displayed together with the earlier 2P4 for the last time in November 1964. The 2P19 was generically designated by NATO as the "Scud-B".

A MAZ-535A towing an R-14U MRBM (NATO: SS-5 Skean) returns from a Red Square parade. (Aleksandr Koshavtsev).

1965

From a political perspective, all remained relatively quiet in the Soviet Union in 1965, with the Soviet hierarchy concerned with cosmetic internal matters such as changing the name of the Presidium back to the Politburo at the 23rd Party Congress. Within the Soviet Bloc internationally, economic reforms were being tolerated in some Warsaw Pact countries, particularly in Hungary and Poland, with the latter country even being allowed to obtain Western credit to invest in its own manufacturing potential. As interest rates were increased in the 1970s this would have a profound effect on the Polish economy, sparking the protests and political changes in Eastern Europe that would ultimately bring down the Soviet Union.

After the Soviet consolidation years of the 1950s in Europe, and the near clash of superpowers during the Cuban Missile Crisis of 1962, the Soviet grip on Europe appeared to be loosening slightly. From a historical military perspective, 1965 was meantime a major commemorative year for the wartime Allies including the Soviet Union, being the 20th Anniversary of the end of the Second World War in Europe. As such, the two military parades held in Moscow that year were a Victory Parade held on 9th May in lieu of a military element to the 1st May celebrations, and the traditional revolutionary parade in November. Both parades included the 1960s traditional mix of tanks, armoured vehicles and strategic rocket technology, which in 1965 were impressive even by traditional Soviet standards, primarily due to the increasing displays of new strategic rocket systems. The year was however relatively benign from a Cold War perspective, with the attention of the US government and the American public remaining focused on the escalating war in Vietnam rather than the relatively quiet situation in Europe.

9th May 1965

In May 1965, the Soviet Union celebrated the 20th Anniversary of Victory over Germany and the end of the war in Europe - Victory in Europe or VE Day as known throughout the world. Being a major anniversary, the military parade staged in May 1965 was particularly extravagant, larger in scale than even the original June 1945 Victory Parade in terms of the number of military vehicles paraded through Red Square. The parade featured a very large number of different weapons systems, with a subtle generation change in evidence, as older weapons such as the ZSU-57-2 tracked air defence system and the R-12 ballistic rocket were replaced by newer systems, with both old and new being displayed together in 1965 as the generation change was underway. The tradition of a minute of silence for the war dead was also introduced in the Soviet Union in May 1965.

The 9th May VE Day parade content was as for the usual May and November parades, but with the marching columns including war veterans parading through the square. For the first time, the original flag raised over the Reichstag in 1945 was paraded through Red Square, with Heroes of the Soviet Union Konstantin Ya. Samsonov, Meliton V. Kantariya and Mikhail A. Egorov - who had raised it on the Reichstag roof participating in the parade celebrations.*

Among the Soviet hierarchy observing the parade was Leonid Brezhnev, who had taken office as General Secretary of the CPSU on 14th October 1964. The one high-ranking veteran conspicuous by his absence was Marshal of the Soviet Union Georgy Zhukov, who having found himself out of favour not for the first or even the second time in the post-war Soviet Union, was not invited to par-

---

* At the time of raising the Soviet flag over the Reichstag, Captain Samsonov was accompanied by four others, Junior Sergeant Kantariya, Sergeant Egorov, Captain Stepan Neustroyev and Sergeant Major Ilya Syanov.

2P24 launch vehicles for the 2K11 "Krug" (Circle) SAM system traverse Red Square. The mobile air defence system was developed concurrently with the static launched S-75 "Dvina", but proved significantly more complex to perfect hence its later introduction into service.

ticipate. The parade was as usual taken by Defence Minister Marshal Rodion Ya. Malinovsky. As part of the commemorations in May 1965, seven Soviet cities, namely Brest, Leningrad, Kiev, Moscow, Odessa, Sevastopol and Volgograd were awarded the status of "Hero Cities" of the Great Patriotic War, and a medal was struck for the 20th Anniversary of Victory in the Great Patriotic War 1941-45, which was awarded to 15 million people.

The parade commander vehicles were again in ZiL-111V parade limousines. The marching columns included students and staff of the "M.V. Frunze" Military Academy, the "Malinovsky" Tank and Armoured Forces Academy, the "V.V. Kuibyshev" Military Engineering Academy, the parade regiment of the Air Force Academy, staff of the "N.E. Zhukovsky" Aviation Academy, the "F. Eh Dzerzhinsky" Naval Engineering School, and the Moscow "F. Eh Dzerzhinsky" Border Guards School, and many others.

The mechanised section of the Victory Parade began with horse drawn "tachanki" machine-gun carts from the revolutionary era, with the armoured columns that followed being led by GAZ-69 light vehicles. The original BRDM was again displayed, also now known as the BRDM-1 to distinguish it from the later BRDM-2, which had entered series production in 1963. The original BRDM scout vehicle would soon be removed from parades, though the ATGM versions would remain on display until replaced by BRDM-2

mounted versions in the early 1970s. The standard reconnaissance version of the BRDM-2 would not be paraded on Red Square, one of many parade nuances where some vehicle types were not necessarily put on public display. The earlier BTR-40 was also never displayed on Red Square, but was for-instance paraded in Kuibyshev (today Samara) on 9th May 1965, such that the annual events on Red Square were but one snapshot of what was being displayed during military parades in cities throughout the Soviet Union.

The BRDM 2P32 "Falanga" (NATO: AT-2 Swatter) and newer 9P110 "Malyutka" (NATO: AT-3 Sagger) ATGM vehicles were paraded together in May 1965. It was originally considered by Western sources that the 9K11 "Malyutka" firing the 9M14 rocket was a replacement for the 2K8 "Falanga" as the latter had been seen earlier. It was later understood that the "Falanga" firing the 3M11 rocket was a long range ATGM with a different over-watch role to the direct support "Malyutka".

Armoured vehicles of the Tamanskaya Motor Rifle Division followed, with the BTR-60PA* displayed, armed with a pintle-mounted (and non-standard) 12.7mm DShKM instead of the 7.62mm SGMB for parade purposes, followed by the BTR-60PB, with a turret mounted 14.5mm KPVT heavy machine gun, which would become the default Soviet wheeled BTR for many years to come.

Only the later BTR-50PK version of the BTR-

---

* The BTR-60PA was designated BTR-60PK by the US and NATO during the Cold War era.

50 tracked APC series was paraded in 1965, now fitted with overhead armour. The replacement for the BTR-50 series, an entirely new vehicle type designated the BMP, was meantime being prepared for full series production in 1965, though the BTR-50 series would remain a participant on Red Square parades until the early 1970s.

The T-55 tanks of the Kantemirovskaya Tank Division which had made their public debut only in 1962 were in 1965 already supplemented on Red Square, only three years later, by the public debut at the 9th May 1965 Victory Parade of the new T-62 MBT, which had been accepted into Soviet Army service in 1961. The T-55 and T-62 were paraded together in May 1965.

Artillery displayed in May 1965 included the 130mm M-46 and the 180mm S-23 field guns, now towed respectively by the ATS-59 medium and AT-T heavy tracked artillery tractors, followed by wheeled MRS including the BMD-20 (BM-20-4) mounted on the ZiL-157 chassis and the 2P5 launch vehicle for the 2K5 "Korshun", now accompanied by the new BM-21 "Grad" 40 round MRS mounted on the powerful 6x6 Ural-375D chassis, which would become the default Soviet Army MRS paraded on Red Square until the last Soviet era Red Square parade in November 1990.

Air defence systems were represented by the ZSU-57-2 self-propelled anti-aircraft vehicle, which was in 1965 displayed together with its ultimate replacement, the ZSU-23-4 "Shilka", mounting four 23mm 2A7 machine guns together with an engagement radar system on a new tracked GM-575 chassis. Air defence rocket systems (SAMs) were represented by the 2P24 SPU vehicle for the 2K11 "Krug" (NATO: SA-4 Ganef) SAM system which was accepted into service with Soviet Army in 1964, and the parade regular S-25 "Berkut" and S-75 "Dvina" SAM systems, the ZiL-157V having by 1965 long replaced the earlier ZiS-121B as the semi-trailer tractor for both SAM system types. These well known and understood SAM systems

The Obiekt-815 SPU vehicle for the RT-15 as displayed on Red Square in May 1965 was a major technological advancement, being the first self-propelled independent mobile MRBM.

were followed by four Ural-375S 6x6 tractors towing Izdeliye-400 "Dal" long-range SAM systems on their PR-41A TZM semi-trailers, the Ural-375S having replaced the earlier MAZ-502V 4x4 tractor truck as tow vehicle. The "Dal" long-range SAM was at the time sometimes confused by Western intelligence with the almost identical but significantly smaller S-75 (NATO: SA-2 Guideline) system.

The relatively rare ATS-59 tracked artillery tractor made an appearance in 1965, displayed on Red Square towing the 130mm M-46 field gun, and in a belated cameo appearance the wartime 152mm M-1937 (ML-20) heavy gun-howitzer. The ATS-59 medium tracked artillery tractor had replaced the somewhat prehistoric looking AT-S, but would be quickly replaced by the ATS-59G, which returned to the larger cab arrangement of the AT-S that could accommodate both the vehicle and gun crew.

The ASU-85 (known in the Soviet Union as the SU-85 without the A (airborne) prefix, was demonstrated as usual on Red Square in 1965, but was now accompanied by columns of GAZ-66B 4x4 trucks, the vehicle being a modified and lightened variant of the standard GAZ-66, towing anti-tank weapons and the RPU-14 towed multiple rocket launcher, bringing increased levels of ground support for airborne forces. The standard military version of the GAZ-66 4x4 truck was never displayed on Red Square.

The 2P19 (NATO: Scud-B) OTR SPU vehicle was displayed, being very similar in appearance to the earlier 8U218 SPU vehicle with which it was concurrently displayed, but with differences in regard to the launch system and details such as the exhausts mounted on the vehicle sides. The later 9P113 (9K52) "Luna-M" on its 8x8 BAZ-135 chassis, 9P117 (9K72) "Elbrus" on its 8x8 MAZ-543A chassis and the Front level 9K76 "Temp-S" also on a MAZ-543A chassis were also evident in 1965, as they would be on Red Square for many years to come.

Four of the curious 2P30 SPU vehicles for the 2K17 (NATO: Sepal/Shaddock) coastal defence cruise missile mounted on the ZiL-135K chassis were followed by AT-T tractors towing R-13 (D-6) submarine launched ballistic missiles (SLBMs) that were intended for operational deployment off the American coast if required.

The R-12 (8K63) (NATO: SS-4 Sandal) rocket had its last parade appearance in 1965, towed as usual by the AT-T tracked artillery tractor, followed by two R-14U (8K65U) (NATO: SS-5 Skean) silo-launched MRBMs towed by the next generation of heavy tractors, in the form of the wheeled 8x8 configuration MAZ-535A and MAZ-537V. The R-14/R-14U was a three-stage, solid fuel rocket system, which could remain in a silo installation in ready to launch configuration for many years without the need for removal and maintenance. It was also the earlier pad-launched R-14 which had almost successfully completed the recent journey by sea to Cuba, and for which the nuclear warheads had been landed safely on the island when the international crisis finally broke.

The May 1965 parade also saw the Red Square debut of the mobile RT-15 MRBM, initially mounted on the Obiekt-815Sp1 SPU vehicle based on a heavily modified T-10 tank chassis developed at the LKZ plant in Leningrad. Though far from the largest rocket on display, the RT-15 was significant in that it was mounted on a tracked SPU vehicle and was a particularly mobile launch system, capable of rapid redeployment to avoid detection or retaliation strikes. As such the system was more of a threat than some of the larger and longer-range systems displayed which were fired from fixed launch sites.

Towards the end of the parade, two A-350Zh rockets for the A-35 (NATO: ABM-1 Galosh) Anti-Ballistic Missile (ABM) system were displayed, towed by MAZ-537V tractors with 4x4 powered trailers, followed by MAZ-537s towing R-14 (8K65) and R-26 (8K66) ICBM rockets. The parade ended with the display of two huge GR-1 (8K713) rockets, which were towed backwards through Red Square by MAZ-535A 8x8 tractor vehicles. The GR-1 (Globalnaya Raketa

- Global Rocket -1) was perhaps the most misunderstood of all rocket systems ever paraded on Red Square. The 117 metric tonne launch weight rocket was designed to be launched into space orbit and re-enter anywhere in the world with a range capable of targeting any city worldwide, hence the designation. In fact it was technically over-ambitious for its day, and never actually left the ground other than when being towed on its transport trailer through Red Square, but was a particularly large and impressive weapon for international marketing purposes.

7th November 1965 - 48th Anniversary of the Great October Socialist Revolution

The 7th November 1965 Red Square military parade was from a military observation point of view as interesting as the May event, with the November parade also being used to showcase the latest in Soviet military technology, particularly long range strategic weapons, some of which were operationally deployed, and others claimed to be for political expediency purposes. The highlight of the 48th Anniversary parade was the appearance of the already known RT-15 MRBM and the new RT-20P ICBM systems (or rather their fibreglass TPK transport containers) mounted on tracked chassis derived from the T-10 heavy tank series, together with other strategic rockets including the solid fuel R-14U and R-26 rockets and the parade finale GR-1 "global range" rocket.

The 7th November 1965 parade was again reviewed by the Soviet Defence Minister, Marshal of the Soviet Union Rodion Ya. Malinovsky, with the parade commander being Hero of the Soviet Un-

This photograph of the November 1965 Red Square parade, shows how rapidly changes were introduced in the 1960s. The MAZ-502V had by 1965 already been replaced by the Ural-375S as a tractor truck for the Izdeliye-400 "Dal" SAM system, and the MAZ-535A and MAZ-537V 8x8 wheeled tractors had replaced the tracked AT-T for heavier rocket systems.

A column of BTR-60PA wheeled APCs practice at the Alabino military base near Moscow for the 7th November 1965 Red Square parade.

The 9P110 was the final ATGM vehicle based on the original BRDM chassis, mounting six 9M14 "Malyutka" rockets for the 9K11 system.

2P25 SPU vehicles for the 2K12 "Kub" (Cube) SAM system await parade start orders on Moscow's Gorky Street. The 2P25 was based on the GM-578 tracked chassis.

ion A.P. Beloborodov. There were 26 battalions of marching infantry followed by armoured vehicles from the Kantermirovskaya Tank Division and the Tamanskaya Motorised Rifle Division.

The parade began with GAZ-69 column lead vehicles followed by massed formations of BRDM reconnaissance and BRDM 9P110 (9K11) (NATO: AT-3 Sagger) and 2P32 (2K8) "Falanga" (NATO: AT-2 Swatter) ATGM vehicles on the BRDM chassis as in May, with all armoured vehicles being in columns of four.

The BTR-60PA and BTR-50PK as displayed in November 1965 now represented a modified generation of wheeled and tracked APCs for motorised rifle and tank divisions respectively, both vehicle types now being provided with overhead armour allowing closed-down operation in an NBC environment.

The Soviet VDV airborne forces were represented by GAZ-69 vehicles painted in airborne forces markings and with "desantniki" paratroopers seated in the rear of each vehicle, with artillery ground support represented by the SU-85 (ASU-85) airborne self-propelled gun. The SU-85 was a significant increase in firepower over the earlier, and diminutive ASU-57, but the original drop pallet system allowing the later SU-85 (ASU-85) to be parachute deployed was not taken into service, and so the SU-85 remained an airborne forces weapon suitable for air landing by military transport aircraft rather than parachute drop deployment.

The 2P5 MRS (OTR) for the then still rela-

During the large scale parades of the 1960s Manezhnaya Square was used in addition to Gorky Street as a marshalling area for columns of "tekhnika".

The Izdeliye-400 "Dal" long-range SAM prototype resembled the smaller S-75 "Dvina" which gained fame in May 1960, but was significantly larger in scale.

RT-2 (8K98) silo-launched ICBMs await start instructions on Moscow's Gorky Street. The rocket was designated SS-13 "Savage" by the US and NATO.

9P120 SPU vehicles for the 9K76 "Temp-S" (NATO: SS-12 Scaleboard). The Front level rocket was based on the MAZ-543A 8x8 chassis await parade start orders.

tively opaque 2K5 system, mounted on the YaAZ-214 (later KrAZ-214) 6x6 chassis made its final parade appearance in November 1965, with the role thereafter being taken by the universal 9K51 (BM-21) "Grad" MRS.

Following the airborne vehicles, the T-62 MBT made a November parade appearance having made its public debut on Red Square in May. The new tank, armed with a smoothbore 115mm U-5TS (2A20) tank gun with a newly developed fin-stabilised sub-calibre anti-tank round within its ammunition complement was defined as a long-range over watch tank-killer in the manner of the secretive SU-122-54 or even earlier SU-100, rather than a direct replacement for the T-55 MBT which had itself appeared on Red Square only three years prior. The rivalry between tank design bureaus that led to this nuanced distinction between certain Soviet tank designs is in of itself a complex subject that is only now becoming clearer to researchers in the Russian Federation and abroad. A column lead T-62 was followed by twenty T-62 MBTs onto the square.

In a common theme where two generations of weapon type were deployed on Red Square simultaneously as one generation was leaving the public domain on Red Square and the other entering it, the ZSU-57-2 anti-aircraft gun system was in November 1965 displayed together with the new ZSU-23-4 that would ultimately replace it, with the ZSU-23-4V leading the earlier ZSU-57-2 vehicles in the parade line-up. Longer-range

An Obiekt-815 SPU vehicle for the RT-15 land-mobile MRBM during parade practice. The first SPU vehicle, mounting a transport container, was demonstrated on Red Square in 1965 and 1966. It was subtly replaced by a modified variant, designated 8U253 (15U59), from 1967.*

AT-P semi-armoured artillery tractors towing 85mm D-48 anti-tank guns down Gorky Street towards Red Square.

anti-aircraft defence was provided for in the form of the 2P24 SPU vehicle for the 2K11 "Krug" SAM system, again displayed immediately after the gun armed defensive weapons. The 2K12 "Kub" SAM system would also make its public debut at the November 1965 parade.

The relatively diminutive AT-P light artillery tractor was again displayed in November 1965, towing the 85mm D-48 anti-tank gun. The rarely seen ATS-59 tracked medium artillery tractor, which had entered service in 1962, was also paraded on Red Square on 7th November 1965, towing the 130mm M-46 field gun. The ATS-59 was a major modification of the design principles incorporated in the earlier AT-S, but its small two-man cab proved impractical in service, and the later ATS-59G returned to the full gun crew cab layout of the original AT-S. The larger AT-T heavy tractor towed the now more clearly understood 180mm S-23 field gun during the same parade.

The ZiL-157V had rapidly replaced the earlier ZiS-121B as the standard tractor vehicle for the trailer mounted S-25 and S-75 SAMs, and as the transport chassis for the S-125 PR-14 TZM vehicle, with the following "Izdeliye-400" (Dal) long-range SAM towed on Red Square by the now standard Ural-375S tractor vehicle rather than the earlier 4x4 MAZ-502V.

Surface-to-surface (OTR) rockets and strategic rockets followed the anti-aircraft systems as the

SU-85 (ASU-85) airborne self-propelled guns parade through Red Square, 7th November 1965. (Mikhail Baryatinsky)

* Two variants of the RT-15 SPU vehicle were demonstrated on Red Square, both mounted on the Obiekt-815 chassis. The first, Obiekt-815Sp1, was shown in 1965-1966. The second, designated 8U253 and later 15U59, was demonstrated from 1967.

traditional parade finale. The OTR rockets were represented by the tracked 2P16, and the larger ISU-152K chassis based 8U218 (Obiekt-803) and later 2P19 (Obiekt-810) SPU vehicles, and the wheeled 9P113 "Luna-M" mounted on its 8x8 ZiL-135 (BAZ) chassis, and finally by the wheeled 9P117 (9P117M) SPU vehicles for the 9K72 "Elbrus" OTR, mounted on the MAZ-543A chassis. The early OTR vehicles were generically designated as "FROG" and "Scud-A", the latter 9P117 as the "Scud-B" by NATO. The change from tracked to wheeled chassis for OTR systems was significant, in that wheeled chassis provided better road speed and range and were less vibration prone, and the Soviet Union had developed wheeled vehicles with the same mobility that could earlier be provided only by tracked vehicles.

Two 2P30 cruise missile launch vehicles for the 2K17 coastal defence cruise missile system followed, mounted on their ZiL-135K 8x8 chassis with their very specific angular cabs. The 2P30 was generically designated "Sepal" or "Shaddock" by NATO, the changing designations reflecting ongoing uncertainty at the time as to the exact purpose of the system. In later years it was clarified as a coastal defence cruise missile system for engaging naval surface targets. The ZiL-135K chassis was originally built in Moscow before production of the vehicle type was moved to Bryansk. The huge A-350Zh* rockets for the A-35 ABM system followed, towed by MAZ-535A tractors, separated from the other strategic rocket systems later paraded through the square in November 1965.

The year 1965 was the first of the full-scale Red Square parade "rocket years", with displays of all manner of short, medium and intercontinental range rockets. AT-T tractors towed R-13 (D-6) and R-29 submarine launched rockets, followed by the tracked and thereby land re-deployable RT-15 MRBM and RT-20P ICBM systems.

The RT-15 (8K96) MRBM and RT-20P (8K99) MRBM rockets - the most powerful land-mobile MRBM and ICBM systems in the Soviet arsenal, both mounted on T-10M heavy tank derived tracked chassis were both displayed in November 1965, where the large and obviously land mobile rocket systems caused considerable consternation, particularly the latter RT-20P, which

Two parade finale GR-1 (8K713) rockets follow two R-26 (8K66) rockets leaving Red Square across the river Moskva. The sheer size of the GR-1 rockets even compared to the huge R-26 ICBMs moving before them is evident.

---

* The A-350 series rockets for the A-35 ABM system displayed on Red Square were located within their 5P81 TPK transport containers. The rockets were launched from large pivoted launch stands.

The GR-1 (8K713) "Globalnaya Raketa" (Global Rocket) was one of the most enigmatic rocket systems ever displayed on Red Square. The planned orbital rocket was scrapped as being technically unfeasible before it began its regular Red Square parade appearances.

Also displayed on Red Square on 7th November 1965 was the 15U51 SPU vehicle for the RT-20P, also known as the 8K99 / 15P699 (NATO: SS-X-15 Scrooge) land mobile ICBM complex. (RGAKFD)

was the first truly mobile land deployed ICBM system. The SPU vehicles for the RT-15/8K96 rocket (NATO: SS-X-14 Scapegoat/Scamp) on the Obiekt-815Sp1 chassis demonstrated on Moscow's Red square on 7th November 1965 were developmentally more significant than the larger silo mounted systems towed concurrently through the square. With the systems being road and terrain mobile, initial detection and any retaliatory strike against these launch systems was exponentially more difficult to achieve. The SPU vehicles displayed in 1965 were the first prototype chassis, developed at the KB-3 design bureau within the Leningrad Kirov plant (LKZ) under the direction of Zh. Ya. Kotin for operational trials to determine the practical issues with the systems, from mobility to the time required to prepare for launch to the required technical maintenance for the system in military service. As displayed in Red Square the vehicles were fitted with fibreglass transport containers (TPKs) within which the rockets would normally be transported. In August 1965 the design specifications for the system had been modified such that the tracked TU / SPU vehicle was now designed to both transport and launch the rockets. In consequence, as the two original Obiekt-815Sp1 prototypes were being demonstrated on Red Square with their fibreglass TPK containers, work was underway to significantly modify the prototype vehicles to both transport and launch the RT-15 missile. The TU / SPU and its RT-15 rocket system were originally known in the West by the NATO designation "Scamp", later as the SS-X-14 "Scapegoat", subsequently modified to SS-X-14 "Scamp/Scapegoat" when it was later understood that the designations referred to one and the same Soviet rocket system. The RT-20P 8K99 ICBM (NATO: SS-X-15 Scrooge) in its huge TPK container was displayed at the same parade, mounted on the Obiekt-820/821 SPU vehicle chassis, also developed at LKZ in Leningrad on an extended T-10M chassis.

The parade finale consisted of a large range of strategic rocket systems, with a line-up of two each of the static silo-launched R-14, the RT-2 and R-26, all towed through Red Square by MAZ-535A and MAZ-537V 8x8 tractors, and finally two MAZ-535 tractors towing the disingenuously named GR-1 "Global Rocket". The GR-1 had a theoretical orbital range of 40,000km, hence the designation, but as the years passed it was admitted that the highest altitude achieved by the rocket was on the back of its transport trailer on Red Square, Soviet "maskirovka" at its finest.

Although the 7th November military parade included a variety of new military vehicles, some of which were ground breaking in terms of military technology, it was the massive strategic rocket systems that caught the attention of the assembled foreign military attachés and Western press, as was doubtless the clear intent. The missiles were deployed on Red Square to make it clear that the Soviet Union now had parity with the United States in nuclear weapons technology and its deployment, and that the Soviet State now considered itself as an equal partner in any ensuing political discussions. The deployment of such long-range ICBMs on Red Square, some capable of reaching the United States mainland, was done to make a deliberate and provocative statement. The reaction from the United States was not long in coming, and would bring the two superpowers to a more pragmatic and less rhetoric-laden negotiating status in the years ahead. The Soviets, and now the Russians have always been good at "schakhmaty" (chess) and this was a strategic chess game being played on Red Square with negotiations directly resulting from the deployments on the square.

An AT-P semi-armoured tracked artillery tractor with 85mm D-48 anti-tank gun returning to base from the Red Square parade of 7th November 1965. (Mikhail Baryatinsky)

A BTR-60PA (PK in NATO terminology) wheeled APC returning from the 7th November parade. (Mikhail Baryatinsky)

The ATS-59 was the replacement for the archaic looking but powerful AT-S, but the small cab left the artillery crew literally out in the cold. (Mikhail Baryatinsky)

The enigmatic 2P5 launcher vehicle for the 2K5 "Korshun" was originally based on the YaAZ-214 6x6 chassis, later produced in Kremenchug as the KrAZ-214. The distinguishing feature of the earlier YaAZ vehicle was the trademark chrome Russian bear on the engine bonnet. (Mikhail Baryatinsky)

A 2P32 launch vehicle for the 2K8 "Falanga" ATGM system returns from Red Square, 7th November 1965. (Mikhail Baryatinsky)

1966

The Soviet Union in 1966 continued to be outwith the immediate attention of the United States after the Cold War "peak" of the Cuban Missile Crisis, with American focus remaining very much on events in Asia Pacific. By April 1966, the number of American troops in Vietnam had reached 250,000, and by the end of the year would rise exponentially to 385,000. While Soviet relations with the United States were stable, the relationship with China was changing. The Red Guard would take control in the country from August 1966, subsequent to which China's relations with the Soviet Union would deteriorate rapidly. One of the Soviet domestic highlights of the year was the signing of a contract with the Italian FIAT company on 4th May to build a new car plant in the city of Toliatti, where the FIAT-124 would be built as the VAZ series of passenger cars, known in the Soviet Union as the "Zhiguli" (named after the hill range near Kuibyshev) and abroad as the "Lada". It was precisely four decades since FIAT had assisted the Soviet Union to produce its first indigenous series production truck, the AMO F-15, based on the FIAT-15ter, which had given the Red Army its first locally produced military transport vehicle, and that automotive relationship with the Soviet Union continued to be particularly influential.

1st May 1966

The 1st May 1966 parade commander was General A.P. Beloborodov, with the parade being received by Marshal of the Soviet Union Rodion Ya. Malinovsky. Soviet Premier Leonid Brezhnev stood on the Lenin Mausoleum review stand, accompanied by Prime Minister Kosygin and many other Soviet dignitaries. The marching columns were as usual from the Tank Forces Academy, cadets of the Sevastopol Higher Naval Engineering School, Soviet VDV airborne forces, and all the usual military units that participated in such displays. After the massive 1965 Red Square parade with its huge displays of new rocket technology, there were once again no major surprises on Red Square in May 1966, rather a reinforcement of the weapons displayed the previous year. The armour on display included BTR-60PA and PB vehicles of the Tamanskaya Motorised Rifle Division displayed together, with the latter version becoming the definitive wheeled APC in Soviet Army service.

Conventional artillery consisted of 85mm, 130mm and 180mm weapons, with the 130mm M-46 being again towed by the relatively short-lived ATS-59, and with the 9K51 (BM-21)

T-62 main battle tanks traverse Red Square, 1st May 1966. The T-62 would participate in Red Square parades from 1965 until November 1974.

"Grad" MRS on the powerful Ural-375D 6x6 chassis now being the default MRS on display, replacing several earlier systems.

Tactical OTR rocket systems were again represented by eight 8U218 and eight 2P19 SPU vehicles paraded together on their ISU-152K derived chassis, and the lighter 2P16 SPU vehicle based on the same chassis as the PT-76 amphibious light tank. The ZiL-135K chassis mounted 2P30 SPU vehicles for the 2K17 system firing the FKR-2 (4K95/S-5) cruise missile, still only known at the time by its NATO designator SSc-1a "Sepal/Shaddock" made their regular appearance.

The air defence systems displayed were also a repeat of the previous year, as were the larger strategic rockets. The A-350Zh (5V61) rocket for the A-35 ABM rocket system remained an impressive weapon display, as it would throughout

The ungainly looking 2P30 SPU vehicle for the 2K17 coastal defence cruise missile system was paraded annually from 1961 until the end of the decade. After production of the ZiL-135 8x8 chassis was transferred from Moscow to Bryansk, the vehicle was renamed BAZ.

2P19 SPU vehicles for the 9K72 OTR system, known to Western observers as the "Scud-B".

the late 1960s. The tractor/trailer combination used with the A-350Zh consisted of a MAZ-537V 8x8 tractor coupled with a 4x4 trailer powered by a driveshaft from the prime mover vehicle. Two RT-15 rockets, which were not at the time directly associated with being the rockets from the tracked RT-15 concurrently displayed on Red Square, were towed behind MAZ-537V 8x8 tractors immediately following the Obiekt-815Sp1 SPU vehicles for the RT-15. The RT-2 rocket, which looked similar to the RT-15, but was significantly larger, was also towed through Red Square during the same parade on its three-axle trailer. As was the norm from 1965, the parade finale consisted of two highly impressive but already cancelled prototype GR-1 (8K713) ICBMs.

Izdeliye-400 "Dal" SAM systems, now towed by the 6x6 Ural-375S, followed by A-350Zh ABM rockets towed by 8x8 MAZ-537V and 4x4 powered trailer combinations crossing Red Square mid-parade.

The 9K51 (BM-21) "Grad" MRS would be a parade regular from the mid 1960s until the last ever Soviet era parade in November 1990. The original Ural-375D 6x6 chassis was replaced in the late 1980s by the diesel powered Ural-4320.

7th November 1966 – 49th Anniversary of the Great October Socialist Revolution

The 7th November 1966 parade was taken by Marshal of the Soviet Union Rodion Ya. Malinovsky, his last parade appearance after ten years as Defence Minister. The parade began with an orchestra with drummers, followed by cadets of the "M.V. Frunze" Military Academy, the " N.S. Nakhimov" Higher Naval Technical School, and cadets of the All-Arms Technical School of the SM SSSR amongst the marching processions from all the Soviet service arms and main training establishments.

BTR-60PAs of the Guards Tamanskaya MRD were displayed in large numbers, followed by tracked BTR-50PKs, representing the mid 1960s generation change from the open vehicles of the turn of the decade to vehicles that could be closed down for operation in an NBC environment.

The air defence systems on display continued to be the staple ZiL-157V towing the V-300 (5V7) rockets for the S-25 "Berkut" (NATO: SA-1 Guild) SAM system and the V-750 rocket for the S-75 "Dvina" (NATO: SA-2 Guideline), with mobile systems represented by the 2P24 launch vehicle on the Obiekt-123 chassis for the ZRK 2K11 "Krug" SAM, which had a range of 11-45km and an engagement altitude of 3-24km.

The now common large-scale deployment of ground-to-ground "OTR" and strategic missiles continued in 1966, including the 8U218 (Obiekt-803) SPU vehicle for the 8K11 OTR system with its R-11/R-11M rocket, the newer 2P19 (Obiekt-810) SPU vehicle for the 9K72 OTR system and the ever-enigmatic 2P30 launch vehicle for the 2K17 coastal defence cruise missile system on its ZiL-135K chassis. The A-350Zh (5V61) ABM rocket, or rather its TPK container, was displayed, and as in 1965, two RT-15 MRBMs were again shown mounted on the original Obiekt-815Sp1 tracked chassis, followed later in the parade by two RT-20P land mobile ICBMs.

The R-36 (NATO: SS-9 Scarp) ICBM displayed on Red Square since 1965 was by contrast with some other rocket systems shown a genuine in-service ICBM, with a range of 11,000km, which now delivered somewhat belatedly on Khrushchev's earlier promise with regard to rocket developments capable of striking the United States. Developed in accordance with a Resolution dated 12th May 1962, the R-36 was formally accepted for service with the Soviet RVSN strategic rocket forces in May 1966, the R-36 being towed across Red Square by the new 8x8 MAZ-535A series wheeled tractor before this formal acceptance. The early R-36 was later modified as the R-36M, also known as the 15A14/15A18) (NATO: SS-18 Satan), but only the original R-36 was displayed on Red Square.

The Izdeliye-400 "Dal" long-range SAM system was largely enigmatic for foreign observers during its Red Square career, being frequently confused by military analysts with the smaller S-200 system which was never paraded on Red Square.

The 15U51 SPU vehicle for the 15P699 RT-20P land-mobile ICBM system was built at the specially developed Obiekt-821 chassis at the Leningrad Kirov Plant in Leningrad, using mechanical components of the T-10M heavy tank.

2P30 SPU vehicles for the 2K17 coastal defence cruise missile system pass before the huge banner to the founder of the Russian Revolution, Vladimir Ilyich Lenin.

The sheer size of the GR-1 "Globalnaya Raketa" is evident in this view. These rockets were always used as a parade finale. Note that they are towed backwards by their MAZ-535A 8x8 tractor vehicles.

8U218 SPU vehicles for the 8K11 OTR rocket return from Red Square, 7th November 1966. The 8U218 and later 2P19 were near identical in appearance. (Mikhail Baryatinsky)

A column of V-300 (205/5V7) rockets for the S-25 "Berkut" Moscow defence ring missile towed by ZiL-157V tractor trucks returning from the Red Square parade of 7th November 1966. (Mikhail Baryatinsky)

A column of 2P30 SPU vehicles for the 2K17 coastal defence cruise missile system returning from the 7th November 1966 Red Square parade. (Mikhail Baryatinsky)

1967

1967 was again another year of relative restraint with regard to relationships between the global superpowers. There were however some concerns in the Kremlin with regard to the developing situation in Czechoslovakia, which had begun economic reforms in the manner already being undertaken by Hungary and Poland, but on a much more aggressive basis. Soviet Premier Brezhnev did not however want a repeat of the 1956 Hungarian experience, and in December 1967 rejected a proposed Soviet intervention in the country.

War returned to the Middle East in 1967, with the Six Day War in June being fought between Isracl and Egypt, Syria and Jordan. American and British supplied Israeli tanks and equipment were engaged against Soviet supplied equivalents in what was from a superpower perspective a proxy-war proving ground scenario.

In Asia Pacific, the Vietnam War continued to escalate, with 464,000 American troops engaged in the country by the end of the year, which was almost 25% of the number deployed in Europe during the latter stages of World War Two. The Vietnam War was by 1967 far from a limited regional conflict.

1st May 1967

The 1st May 1967 parade was taken by the new Soviet Defence Minister, Marshal of the Soviet Union Andrey A. Grechko, who had become Soviet Defence Minister on 12th April that year. The parade commander was General Lieutenant E.F. Ivanosky, the deputy commander of the Moscow MVO, with both commanders standing in the rear of their respective ZiL-111V parade limousines. Marshal Grechko would be Soviet Defence Minister for the following decade, leaving his position only in 1976.

Marching columns on 1st May 1967 included troops from the Guards "Putilovsky-Kirovsky" PVO (air defence) unit, and cadets of the "A.S. Popov" Higher Naval Radio-Electronics School. The parade was led by columns of M-72 motorcycle combinations, with GAZ-69 vehicles leading the individual armoured vehicle columns.

A MAZ-537G in VMF (naval) markings towing an R-29 (NATO: SS-N-6 Sawfly) SLBM through Red Square. (Aleksandr Koshavtsev)

Airborne forces were represented by the SU-85 (ASU-85) self-propelled gun. Air defence vehicles included the ZSU-23-4V SPADS followed by the 2P24 SPU vehicle for the 2K11 "Krug" SAM. Tactical OTR rockets were represented by the 8U218 followed by the 2P19, the very similar vehicles both being generically described as "Scud" by NATO. The strategic rocket systems were also as for the previous year, including the R-14, R-26, R-36, GR-1 and the A-350Zh rocket for the A-35 ABM system.

The month following the May 1967 Red Square parade would see the outbreak of the Six Day War in June 1967 with Egypt (the United Arab Republic), Jordan and Syria, and with more distant Algeria and Iraq also peripherally involved, all engaged against the less than two decade old State of Israel. The shortest conflict in 20th Century post-war history witnessed Soviet built T-34-85, T-54, T-55 and IS-3M tanks pitched against Israeli tanks including British supplied "Centurion" and upgraded M-51 "Super Sherman" tanks armed with British 105mm tank guns. As many as 2,500 tanks were engaged in the short conflict during which 73 Syrian tanks were destroyed, including a handful of the modern T-54 and T-55 types, during fighting concentrated in the Golan Heights. Israel lost 160 "Super Sherman" and British "Centurion" tanks during the same conflict, which was a major "proving ground" for all the nations that had supplied modern post-war tanks to the respective combatant countries.

MAZ-537V tractor trucks towing R-26 (8K66) ICBMs through Red Square.

The 2P30 SPU vehicle for the 2K17 coastal defence cruise missile system was well known by 1967, but no less enigmatic than it had been in 1961.

Two A-35 anti-ballistic missile systems (or rather 5P81 TPK transport containers for the A-350Zh (5V61) missiles) being towed through Red Square, 7th November 1967.

The massive GR-1 rocket system was used as the impressive parade final in the late 1960s. The system was known by the US and NATO as "SS-X-10 Scrag". (US DoD)

7th November 1967 – 50th Anniversary of the Great October Socialist Revolution

On 7th November 1967, the Soviet Union had reached its first half-century anniversary. The 50th Anniversary of the October Revolution parade celebrating a half-century of the Soviet Union and its armed forces, historical and modern, was thereby as might be expected another large-scale occasion, as had been the Victory Parade of May 1965. Being a major anniversary event, November 1967 included significant parade debuts, particularly in the realm of rocket technology. The parade was for the first time transmitted in colour on Soviet television. But there was apparently no means to record and store the live transmissions, so no archive of the original parade as shown live on Soviet television remains, with only the traditional record-to-film cameras capturing the events of the day for posterity.

The 7th November 1967 Anniversary parade was as in May reviewed by the Defence Minister, Marshal of the Soviet Union Andrey A. Grechko, with the parade commander being the 1st Deputy Commander of the Moscow Military District (MVO), Colonel General Evgeny F. Ivanovsky. The commanders by tradition met in the centre of Red Square in their ZiL-111V cabriolet parade cars.

The marching displays began with military units dressed in uniforms from the earliest days of the Revolutionary Red Army and the period of

The 7th November 1967 parade was the 50th Anniversary of the Great October Socialist Revolution and as such was a major event with many new weapons making their public debut. 2P24 SPU vehicles for the 2K11 "Krug" SAM system are followed through Red Square by ATS-59 artillery tractors.

The BMP mechanised infantry combat vehicle made its public debut in November 1967. These vehicles are making final practicing runs at the old Central Airfield at Khodynka, still in their operational unit markings. (RGAKFD)

the Russian Civil War when the Red Army came to prominence, Soviet naval "matros" forces from the time of the Battle for Odessa, and military commissars dressed in their leather coats. The parade included "tachanki" machine gun carts each drawn by four white horses, with two 7.62mm PM-1910 "Maxim" water cooled machine guns mounted on each cart, and with the crews also dressed in revolutionary era uniforms. Horse-drawn 122mm M-1902/30 howitzers were paraded in columns of four, with each howitzer drawn by a team of horses, followed by more revolutionary era artillery.

The vehicular parade began with a display of nine reproduction "Izhorsky-FIAT" armoured cars, which were less than accurately built on modern 4x2 GAZ-52/53 chassis, albeit with genuine 7.62mm PM-1910 "Maxim" machine guns in the turrets. The anniversary parade was also significant in that it introduced a number of new weapons systems for the benefit of domestic and foreign press consumption.

The modern part of the parade began with drummers of the Moscow Military Music School, staff of the "M.V. Frunze" Military Academy, the "V.I. Lenin" Military-Political Academy, the "F. Eh. Dzerzhinsky" and "V.V. Kuibyshev" Military Engineering academies, the "R.Ya. Malinovsky" Armoured Forces Academy, the "N.E. Zhukovsky" Air Force Engineering Academy, cadets of the Leningrad "M.V. Frunze" Higher Naval College, the Moscow Higher Border Guards

ZSU-23-4V air defence vehicles parked on Gorky Street awaiting parade start orders.

Early production BMPs making their Red Square parade debut, 7th November 1967. (Tank Museum 2472/B6)

Command College, marines, troops of the "F.Eh. Dzherzhinsky" division, cadets of the Moscow and Kalinin Suvorov academies, and cadets from the Moscow Higher All-Arms Command School of the Upper Soviet of the RSFSR.

The mechanised part of the parade was led by the Guards Red Banner, Order of Suvorov, "M.I. Kalinin" Tamanskaya Motorised Rifle Division, which had been awarded the Guards title based on its wartime service, beginning at Smolensk and Kursk, followed by the similarly titled Guards Kantemirovskaya Tank Division featuring the heavier armoured vehicles. The vehicular section of the parade directly following the historical section began with GAZ-69s as column lead vehicles, followed by BRDM based 2P32 launch vehicles which fired the 3M11 "Fleyta" rocket for the 2K8 "Falanga" (NATO: Swatter) ATGM system and 9P110 launch vehicles which fired the 9M14 "Malyutka" rocket for the 9K11 (NATO: Sagger) ATGM systems, all in columns of four.

Wheeled BTRs of the Tamanskaya Motorised Rifle Division (MRD) were represented by the BTR-60PA with an armoured roof and 12.7mm DShKM heavy machine gun pintle-mounted for parade purposes in place of the standard 7.62mm SGMB weapon, directly followed by the later and definitive BTR-60PB with its turret mounted 14.5mm KPVT heavy machine gun, two successive generations of the design paraded together, also in columns of four.

The wheeled BTRs were immediately followed by the public debut of an entirely new military vehicle type, the BMP mechanised infantry combat vehicle (MICV), with columns of early production BMPs of the 339th Guards Motorised Rifle Regiment being followed directly onto Red Square by its direct predecessor, the final production BTR-50PK with overhead armour. The BMP would rapidly replace the BTR-50 tracked APC as an armoured vehicle type in the Soviet Army, albeit the BTR-50PK was nevertheless displayed on Red Square alongside the BMP until November 1974. The BMP changed the concept of mechanised infantry operation on the battlefield, delivering infantry into combat as with traditional tracked APCs,

The T-62 main battle tank (MBT) was the default Soviet tank paraded on Red Square from its debut in 1965 until 1974.

or "battlefield taxis", but with the infantry in the BMP able to operate their personal weapons from within the vehicle without disembarking, while the BMP, armed with a 73mm 2A28 "Grom" low-pressure gun and 9M14M "Malyutka" (NATO: AT-3 Sagger) ATGM system could provide covering fire to infantry located within the vehicle or deployed. Further, the combined weapons allowed the BMP, an infantry combat vehicle, to defeat enemy armour including tanks. As such the BMP was when introduced a formidable vehicle, and a game-changer on the world stage. For good measure, the BMP carried an "Igla" (NATO: SA-7 Grail) portable SAM system that could be fired from the open infantry hatches on the rear deck of the vehicle. NATO observers initially recorded the BMP as a new type of APC, but in fact the vehicle was entirely more complex, a new vehicle type, the Mechanized Infantry Combat Vehicle (MICV). It was during the 1973 Arab-Israeli "Yom Kippur" War that the features of the BMP were first demonstrated to the outside world.

There was a large VDV airborne forces contingent on Red Square in November 1967. The VDV airborne forces display began with GAZ-69s in VDV airborne forces markings, with two crew and six seated VDV airborne infantry in the rear of each vehicle, followed by GAZ-66B 4x4 trucks, the lightweight VDV forces version of the standard GAZ-66. The latter was demonstrated towing both the 140mm RPU-14 towed MRS and the rarely seen 85mm SD-44 auxiliary propelled gun. The SD-44 was an innovative weapon, mounting a GAZ M-72 motorcycle engine on one carriage trail, which allowed the weapon to travel under its own power over short distances without the necessity of a tow vehicle. The SU-85 (ASU-85) airborne self-propelled gun culminated the VDV airborne forces contingent of the display.

The airborne vehicles were followed by T-62 tanks of the Guards Kantemirovskaya Tank Division, which had made their public debut in May. The newly unveiled T-62s were paraded through Red Square only five years after the parade debut of the T-55. The T-62 was more of a revolutionary than evolutionary tank design, armed with the

ZSU-23-4V air defence vehicles parade through Red Square, 7th November 1967. The ZSU-23-4 with its radar guided quadruple 23mm 2A7 cannon installation was lethal to low flying aircraft. (Mikhail Baryatinsky)

The GAZ-66B was a lightened version of the standard GAZ-66 4x4 general service truck, developed for the Soviet VDV airborne forces. These GAZ-66B vehicles are towing RPU-14 towed rocket launchers and 85mm SD-44 auxiliary propelled guns.

2P32 launch vehicles for the 2K8 "Falanga" ATGM system parade through Red Square, 7th November 1967. (RGAKFD).

new 115mm U-5TS (2A20) "Molot" (Hammer) smoothbore tank gun, which fired cumulative and HE-Frag rounds, but for which the 3BM series sub-calibre armour-piercing fin-stabilised discarding sabot (APFSDS) round had also been developed. The T-62 would two years later be deployed in combat with Soviet forces on the Chinese border during an engagement on Soviet held Damansky Island at the confluence of the Ussuri and Amur rivers in Eastern Siberia before being exported to the Middle East.

Tactical "OTR" rockets in November 1967 consisted of the 2P16 "Luna" on its tracked chassis displayed together with the new 9P113 "Luna-M" mounted on the wheeled ZiL-135 chassis, which would remain a parade regular until the very last Soviet era military parade in November 1990. There was a similar generation change with the larger OTR rockets, with four 2P19 SPU vehicles for the R-17 (8K14) rocket on a modified ISU-152K chassis, and two later 9P117M SPU vehicles on their wheeled MAZ-543A chassis, displayed together. The 9P117M was the wheeled SPU replacement for the tracked 2P19, in both cases for

ZiL-157KV 6x6 tractor trucks towing V-300 rockets for the S-25 "Berkut" SAM system through Red Square, 7th November 1967.

the 9K72 "Elbrus" rocket system. These OTR vehicles were followed by the 2P30 SPU vehicle for the contentious 2K17 coastal defence cruise missile system mounted on its ZiL-135K 8x8 chassis.

The artillery component of the November 1967 parade included another rare public appearance of the original ATS-59 medium tracked artillery tractor with its diminutive cab, towing the 130mm M-46 field gun, directly followed by the already long-serving AT-T heavy tracked tractor towing the 180mm S-23 field gun. The 9K51 (BM-21) "Grad" MRS mounted on the Ural-375D chassis also had its public debut, replacing several earlier generation multiple rocket systems.

Per tradition since the end of the 1950s, air defence systems including anti-aircraft missiles followed the towed artillery onto Red Square. Air defence vehicles paraded in November 1967 included the ZSU-57-2 and the ZSU-23-4V variant of the new ZSU-23-4 "Shilka". The ZSU-23-4, based on the GM-575 tracked chassis and armed with four radar controlled 23mm 2A7 machine guns would also subsequently show its effectiveness during the 1973 "Yom Kippur" Arab-Israeli war.

The short-range air defence vehicles were followed by the SAM missile systems. Self-propelled systems included the 2P25 SPU vehicle for the 2K12 "Kub", which was rather more vaguely described by Soviet commentators at the time as: *"a self-propelled air defence systems with three rockets"*. The 2K12 "Kub" (NATO: SA-6 Gainful) SAM system was able to destroy air targets at low and medium altitude. The 2K12 had been accepted for service the previous year, and was taken into operational service with Soviet Army ground forces in 1967. The 2P25 SPU vehicle was displayed on Red Square in November 1967 with the 3M9 missiles in travel lock position facing rearwards rather than in the firing position. The 2P24 SPU vehicle for the 2K11 "Krug" (NATO: SA-4 Ganef) SAM system was also displayed in November 1967.

Static launched systems followed in the guise of twelve S-75 (NATO: SA-2 Guideline) and eight S-25 (NATO: SA-1 Guild) rockets towed on their transport trailers by ZiL-157Vs, accompanied by the ZiL-157 PR-14 TZM vehicle mounting two S-125M "Neva-M" (NATO: SA-3 Goa) rockets. The long-range "Izdeliye-400" "Dal" followed, towed on its semi-trailer by the Ural-375S. The long-range "Dal" SAM system and its 5V11 rocket was always somewhat of an enigmatic weapon for foreign observers, resembling the significantly

THE SOVIET ARMY ON PARADE 1946-91

The Izdeliye-400 "Dal" long-range SAM never entered service, but was nevertheless regularly paraded on Red Square until 1968.

The A-350Zh/A-35 anti-ballistic missile system towed through Red Square from the 1960s played a major role in starting negotiations between the US and the Soviet Union on strategic arms limitation.

smaller S-75 "Dvina" but being a two stage, multi-channel guidance long range rocket designed to engage targets at an altitude of up to 30km and with a range of over 150km. It was developed and tested in the early to mid 1960s, but never entered service, which only became known in later years..

Strategic rockets followed the earlier appearance of the A-350Zh. AT-T and MAZ-537V tractors towing R-13 (D-6) and R-29 submarine launched MRBM rockets respectively were followed by four 9P120 (NATO: SS-12 Scaleboard) Front level tactical rockets on their MAZ-543A chassis, two second prototype 8U253 (15U59) TU / SPU vehicles for the RT-15 MRBM together with The RT-15 rockets displayed separately to the TU / SPU vehicles, towed by MAZ-537V wheeled tractor vehicles.

Four 9P120 SPU vehicles for the 9K76 "Temp-S" (NATO: SS-12 Scaleboard) rocket also passed through Red Square on 7th November 1967. The system was classified as tactical Front level rocket that had a range of 800-900km, close to that of the earlier R-5M, which was the first strategic rocket displayed on Red Square precisely one decade earlier. The 9P120 SPU vehicle was based on the chassis of the 8x8 MAZ-543A with twin control cabs.

In accordance with Red Square tradition since the end of the 1950s, the November 1967 Red Square parade culminated with a display of particularly large and powerful strategic rocket systems. Naval rockets included the R-13 (D-6) SLBM towed by the AT-T tracked artillery tractor, and the R-29 SLBM towed by the MAZ-537V. Two 8U253 (15U59) SPU vehicles for the RT-15 strategic rocket were paraded through the

The 15U51 SPU vehicle for the RT-20P - being the first land mobile ICBM - represented a major change in Soviet strategic capability. Deployment of the 15P699 system was however refused by the RVSN (Strategic Rocket Forces) due to logistics complexities with the mix of solid and liquid fuel stages.

square, directly followed by two trailer mounted RT-15 rockets towed by AT-T tracked tractors. Other strategic rockets included R-14U (8K65U) silo mounted ICBM rockets towed by 8x8 MAZ-535A wheeled tractors and two MAZ-535A vehicles towing RT-2 ICBM rockets. Two A-350Zh rockets for the A-35 (NATO: ABM-1 Galosh) anti-ballistic missile (ABM) system followed, towed by MAZ-537V 8x8 tractor vehicle and 4x4 powered trailer combinations, the commonly paraded anti-ballistic missile system being the first "10x10" vehicle paraded on Red Square.

As in recent years, the final weapons to pass through the square were two R-26 ICBMs towed by MAZ-535A 8x8 tractors, two tracked land mobile RT-20P (15P699) ICBM SPU vehicles, and finally two R-36 and two GR-1 ICBMs, also both towed by MAZ-535A series tractors.

The RT-15 MRBM as again shown on 7th November 1967 was displayed at the same parade together with the similarly mobile RT-20P ICBM. The larger, road mobile RT-20P was considered a major threat due to its mobility and redeployment capability, however the system was in 1967 not quite the threat as presented on Red Square. There were significant logistical issues with the launch site fuelling of the dual-fuel rocket system, and the Soviet Strategic Rocket Forces (RVSN) were not ready to accept the RT-20P, as it remained complex to bring into launch position and also to maintain. Further development and operational trials were approved, but in 1967 the fate of the RT-20P was uncertain.

The impressive R-14U (8K65U) rockets were towed through Red Square on their two-axle transport trailers by the MAZ-535A, followed by the huge R-26 (8K66) towed by the MAZ-537V on its massive three-axle semi-trailer. Finally, the Soviet Union displayed two giant R-36 (8K67) (NATO: SS-9 Scarp) ICBMs. Whereas the RT-20P was experimental at the time of its parade appearances, and subsequently not adopted for service, the R-36 was very much current, and could deliver a 20Mt warhead to a range of 10,000km, which was to NATO, the US capital of Washington included, a real and present danger. Two massive R-36 rockets were towed through Red Square on their transport trailers by MAZ-535A wheeled 8x8 tractors. In later years the R-36M (NATO: SS-18 Satan) would also be introduced, and there was frequent conflation in NATO reporting of these rocket systems, the true Soviet designation for which appeared only in later years. The parade final consisted of two RT-20P ICBMs, two MAZ-535A 8x8 tractors towing the RT-2 ICBM, two RT-20P land mobile ICBMs, two MAZ-537Vs towing R-36 ICBM rockets with a range of 10,000km, and finally, culminating the parade,

MAZ-537V tractor trucks (specifically the MAZ-537G version) with a modified Chelyabinsk ChMZAP trailer, towing RT-15 MRBM rockets through Red Square, 7th November 1967. (Aleksandr Koshavtsev)

two MAZ-535A towing massive GR-1 (8K713) ICBMs on their exceptionally long twin-axle trailers.

The increasing deployment of long-range strategic rockets in the 1960s, coupled with deployment of the A-350Zh rocket for the A-35 ABM system had meantime brought about a political reaction in the United States which was now in no doubt that the latest generations of Soviet rockets being deployed had the range to strike the United States in addition to Europe. This, combined with the understood Soviet deployment of the defensive A-350Zh rocket for the A-35 anti-ballistic missile system around Moscow, led US President Lyndon B. Johnson to in January 1967 call for strategic arms limitation talks with the Soviet Union, the SALT acronym becoming synonymous with the thawing of Soviet-American relations from the late 1960s. Soviet Premier Aleksey Kosygin met with President Johnson in Washington in January 1967.

The 7th November 1967 military parade in Frunze (today Bishkek) in the Soviet Republic of Kyrgyzstan included this unusual combination of ATS-59S (Izdeliye-667) tracked semi-trailer tractors towing the S-75 "Dvina" SAM system.

A BRDM reconnaissance vehicle leads columns of BTR-60PB wheeled APCs near the Zimny Dvorets (Winter Palace) in Leningrad for the 7th November 1967 parade.

1968

The year 1968 started quietly in the Soviet Union, but would become dominated by events in Czechoslovakia late in the year, which began with major reforms related to trade unions, the free press and freedom of speech introduced from January under the new communist leader Alexander Dubček. The momentum would build, resulting later in the year in what would become known as the "Prague Spring". The United States was in 1968 meantime pre-occupied with ongoing events in Vietnam where American combat troops deployed in the country had reached a peak number of 568,000 and with the decisive North Vietnamese "Tet" Offensive beginning at the end of January.

Domestically, the Soviet Union again had its own internal troubles. In April 1968, there was serious rioting involving Crimean Tatars in the Soviet republic of Uzbekistan, the same Tatars that had been exiled from Crimea by the Soviet NKVD in April 1944 due to alleged collaboration with the Germans during the Second World War. The Tatars were rehabilitated politically in 1967, but their original home territories remained occupied by ethnic Russians and Ukrainians.

On 1st July 1968, the Non-Proliferation Treaty on nuclear weapons was signed between the Soviet Union and the United States, with further meetings that would subsequently lead to the Strategic Arms Limitation Treaty (SALT) talks. At a strategic level, all appeared well between the superpowers. In May however, the Warsaw Pact staged military manoeuvres close to the Czechoslovakian border. At a local European level, the tanks were about to roll again.

By the time of the 7th November 1968 parade much had happened in Europe, and the parade was held against a background of the events that had transpired in Eastern Europe in the preceding weeks. The 7th November 1968 parade was held a matter of weeks after 200,000 Soviet and Warsaw Pact troops from Bulgaria, East Germany, Hungary and Poland had invaded Czechoslovakia, supported by 2,000 tanks which had on the night of 20th August 1968 moved into Czechoslovakia, putting an end to liberalization reforms in the country. The Soviet tanks, including the later production T-10M heavy tank, which had never been displayed on Red Square, were not engaged in direct combat, but their very presence ensured that local resistance was minimised. The bloodshed was limited compared with Hungary in 1956, but approximately 76 people were killed during the fighting. In the aftermath of the invasion, Alexander Dubček was replaced in Czechoslovakia by the more compliant Gustaf Husak. By prior standards Dubček's subsequent treatment was however relatively benign - he was made Ambassador to Turkey and then further demoted to running a forestry organisation rather than being executed, as had happened to the renegade leadership in Hungary the previous decade. The forthcoming Brezhnev Doctrine again tightened up Soviet control of Eastern Europe however, which soon brought protests from the more troublesome allied states of Albania and Yugoslavia.

At a strategic level, the relationship between the Soviet Union and the United States was by 1968 again evolving, due to the introduction of intercontinental range ballistic missiles (ICBMs) with multiple independently targetable re-entry vehicle (MIRV) warheads. This made the counting of actual individual warhead deployment capability more difficult to determine from a treaty perspective, and the interception of incoming warheads more difficult to guarantee, such that the anti-ballistic missile (ABM) element of the negotiations became more acute.

1st May 1968

The 1st May 1968 military parade taken by Soviet Defence Minister Andrey Grechko and commanded by General Lieutenant E. F. Ivanovsky was the last 1st May Red Square parade that would include a military element. The parade included staff and students of the various military academies such as the "N.E. Zhukovsky" Air Force Engineering Academy and the "F.Eh. Dzherzhinsky" Military Engineering Academy to name but two of many, joined per tradition by marching ranks from the Moscow Garrison (MVO).

Leonid Brezhnev stood as Soviet Premier on the Lenin Mausoleum and reviewed the parade columns, accompanied by other Soviet ministers and dignitaries, but without the attendance of Soviet hero of space exploration Yuri Gagarin, who had on 27th March 1968 been killed in an air crash when piloting a MiG-15 fighter aircraft during a routine training flight.

The mechanised section of the May 1968 parade began with columns of BRDM based 9P110 ATGM vehicles, mounting six 9M14 "Malyutka" rockets of the 9K11 (NATO: Sagger A) ATGM system. 2P32 ATGM vehicles for the 2K8 "Falanga" system firing the 3M11 "Fleyta" (NATO: AT-2 Swatter A) ATGM were also on parade, followed by GAZ-69s with VDV personnel. The T-62 MBT was the only tank type on display, and would remain so until tanks were temporarily removed from Red Square parades after 1974.

OTR tactical rockets were represented by the 2P19 SPU vehicle with the R-17 rocket of the 9K72 (NATO: Scud-B) followed by the system that would ultimately replace it, the 9P117 SPU vehicle for the same 9K72 "Elbrus" (NATO: Scud B) based on the wheeled 8x8 MAZ-543 chassis. May 1968 was the last public showing of the 2P30 SPU vehicle for the 2K17 coastal defence cruise missile system firing the FKR-2/4K95 (S-5) cruise missile. The 9K51 (BM-21) "Grad" based on the 6x6 Ural-375D chassis was now the default multiple rocket system displayed on Red Square, and would remain so until long after the of the break-up of the Soviet Union.

Air defence was represented by the ZSU-23-4V, the self-propelled 2P24 SPU vehicle for the 2K11 "Krug" SAM and the 2P25 SPU for the 2K12 "Kub" SAM system. These were served by the long-serving and ubiquitous S-75 (NATO: SA-2 Guideline) towed by the ZiL-157V, and the PR-14 TZM vehicle for the "Neva" (NATO: SA-3 Goa) SAM mounted on the ZiL-157 chassis and finally the long-range "Dal" SAM system, which never entered operational service, again towed by the 6x6 Ural-375S.

GAZ-69As in naval markings led AT-T tracked and MAZ-537V 8x8 wheeled tractors towing the R-13 (D-6) and R-29 submarine launched ballistic rockets (SLBMs) respectively, with two A-350Zh ABM rockets being towed as usual by MAZ-537Vs with their powered trailers. Strategic rocket systems were also represented by MAZ-535A 8x8 tractors towing the 4,500-5,500km range R-14U ICBM that was considerably larger in diameter than the outgoing R-12. The parade concluded per late 1960s tradition with two R-36 and finally two GR-1 (8K713) ICBM rockets being towed through Red Square.

The military element of the 1st May parades was cancelled after the 1st May 1968 parade, and henceforth the Soviet Union would hold only a single military parade annually on Red Square, on 7th November, with the only additional military parades during the Soviet era being the Victory in Europe parades held on 9th May 1985 and 9th May 1990. Many reasons have been cited for this sudden change in tradition. Militarily the country was at its peak, and had effectively demonstrated during the 1960s its capability to retaliate from a position of parity or even arguable nuclear strength. With an element of parity between the superpowers, there were however other domestic priorities to attend to in a country that was entering a period of political and economic stagnation.

An SU-85 (ASU-85) returning from Red Square along the Kremlevskaya Naberezhnaya (Kremlin Embankment), photographed from the opposite embankment - the location of the former British Embassy. (Tank Museum TM2467/E4)

The 130mm M-46 field was towed through Red Square by several tracked tractors over the years, including the AT-S, later ATS-59 and finally the ATS-59G.

The SU-85 (ASU-85) airborne self-propelled gun remained a Red Square parade regular until replaced by the BMD from 1974. These vehicles are assembling in front of the Bolshoi Theatre. (Krasnaya Zvezda)

7th November 1968 – 51st Anniversary of the Great October Socialist Revolution

The 7th November military parade was received by the Soviet Defence Minister, Marshal of the Soviet Union Andrey Grechko, with the parade commander being General Lieutenant E.F. Ivanovsky, both standing in ZiL-111V parade limousines, which met per parade tradition in the centre of Red Square.

The 7th November military parade demonstrated as always the latest in Soviet military technology on Red Square for domestic and international public consumption, as tanks of the Kantemirovskaya Tank Division and armoured vehicles of the Tamanskaya Motorised Rifle Division paraded through the square. Only three months earlier, previous and current generation Soviet tanks and other armour, including the T-34-85, ISU-152 and the elusive T-10M had been operationally deployed against a Warsaw Pact country, as had the current

BMP MICVs parade through Red Square, 7th November 1968. Early production BMP vehicles had a distinctly shorter bow, later lengthened to improve amphibious stability.

T-62, ASU-85 and other vehicles which were also still displayed on Red Square.

The November 1968 parade began with GAZ-69 lead vehicles followed by BRDM based 2P32 and 9P110 ATGM vehicles. BTR-60PA and BTR-60PB variants were paraded together on Red Square as in the previous year, again representing two generations of vehicle design at the same parade. The T-62 MBT was again the only tank type displayed on Red Square in 1968, and would remain so until 1974.

Air defence was represented by the ZSU-57-2 and ZSU-23-4V local air defence systems, and the 2P24 and 2P25 SPU launcher vehicles for the 2K11 "Krug" (NATO: SA-4 Ganef) and 2P25 SPU (NATO: SA-6 Gainful) SAM systems respectively, followed by the static launched S-125 (NATO: SA-3 Goa) mounted on the PR-14 TZM vehicle based on the ZiL157 chassis.

Airborne forces were represented by the SU-85 (ASU-85), which had long-since replaced the lighter ASU-57 vehicle on Red Square parades, while the Soviet Navy was represented by four door GAZ-69As in naval markings which acted as parade lead vehicles for the R-13 (D-6) and R-29 SLBMs towed by AT-T tracked and MAZ-537V wheeled tractors respectively. The 2P30 SPU vehicle for the 2K17 coastal defence cruise missile system completed the display of naval and coastal defence rocket systems.

As was standard practice in the 1960s, land based strategic rocket systems completed the November 1968 parade. RT-15 tracked MRBM and RT-20P tracked ICBM vehicles were complemented by the two RT-2 ICBMs towed by MAZ-535A 8x8 tractors on their three-axle transport trailers. The parade as in November 1967 ended with two MAZ-535A tractors towing R-36 ICBMs and two MAZ-535A towing the massive GR-1 (8K713) ICBMs through Red Square.

BTR-50PK tracked APCs pass through Red Square, 7th November 1968. The new BMP displayed concurrently, and the changes in mechanised warfare that resulted from its introduction, would quickly render the BTR-50 obsolescent.

The base model BRDM-2 was never displayed on Moscow's Red Square. This BRDM-2 is on parade in Kiev, where tyres were painted with white bands for ceremonial purposes.

The PR-14A TZM vehicle, mounted on the ZiL-157 6x6 chassis, was a transporter-reload vehicle for the V-600 (5V24) rockets of the S-125 "Neva" static launched SAM system.

The 2P24 launch vehicle for the 2K11 "Krug" SAM system was based on the Obiekt-123 chassis, related to that used by the later 2S3 self-propelled howitzer and the GMZ minelayer.

1969

At the beginning of 1969, Soviet relations with the United States, where Richard Nixon had been inaugurated as the President of the United States of America on 20th January, were largely benign, while for the Soviet Union it was declining political relations with China that would cause greatest concern during the year. Relationships between the Soviet Union and the United States had improved somewhat after Khrushchev's forced retirement in 1964, but disputes over territory on the Sino-Soviet border, which long pre-dated the formation of the Soviet Union, would come to a head in 1969 as the Chinese government itself went through rapid changes.

Tensions between the Soviet Union and China had been brewing since 1968, and the Soviet Union had in recent months moved considerable forces, including short-range missile systems to strategic points along the extensive border with China. The tension turned to fighting in March 1969, with a direct clash between Soviet border guards and troops of the Chinese People's Liberation Army (PLA) over the control of Damansky Island (later known by the Chinese as Zhenbao Island) at the confluence of the Russian Amur and Ussuri rivers. During the engagement, 58 Soviet soldiers were killed, including the commanding colonel. One of four T-62 tanks used in the engagement was also lost in action after being hit by a rocket-propelled grenade (RPG) round on the frozen river. The T-62 had never been exported and was at the time considered secret Soviet technology, with a smoothbore 115mm U-5TS tank gun firing APFSDS* round with a central 40mm hardened core. The Soviet border forces that had deployed the T-62 were unable to recover the tank, which apparently broke through the ice and sank, with the prevailing account being that Chinese divers recovered the tank at night. The tank lost during the incident can be seen on display today at the Chinese Military Museum in Beijing.

The T-62 MBT, only unveiled on Red Square in 1965, had entered combat against China rather than in Europe, just as the T-18 (MS-1) tank had first entered combat against the Chinese in 1929 rather than in Europe.

The Damansky Island incident was the most serious of several border clashes in the far eastern region from March to September 1969 in an area that remained contested for many decades. An agreement on the border in the region near Khabarovsk would be signed between the contestant countries only on 14th October 2004. There were further serious clashes with China in the early autumn of 1969, this time on an extensive area (52,000 km²) of Soviet controlled land in the Pamir Mountains on the border between the Soviet Republic of Tajikistan and China's Xinjiang region, the border of which had originally been agreed between the Russian Empire and the Qing Dynasty in 1892. A series of clashes on this part of the Sino-Soviet border escalated to the point where both countries considered a nuclear exchange as imminent. On 28th August 1969, China was formally warned that war was a likely consequence to its territorial ambitions, and was also advised that the Soviet Union would not hesitate to go nuclear as a defence measure. As with the crisis in Cuba earlier in the decade, the threat of a major nuclear exchange led to direct behind the scenes dialogue, which included Soviet Prime Minister Kosygin visiting Beijing on 11th September on his return from Ho Chi Minh's funeral in Vietnam. The Soviet and Chinese ambassadors were returned to their respective foreign postings, and talks resumed in October as China meantime went through the Cultural Revolution, as a consequence of which its current or future intent became difficult to quantify for the Soviet Union and Western powers alike. Thirty years later, in 1999, the now independent country of Tajikistan ceded 1,000 km² of land in the Pamir Mountains

*APFSDS - Amour Piercing Fin Stabilized Discarding Sabot.

to the People's Republic of China, and China relinquished its long held claims over 28,000 km² of territory located in Tajikistan, ending an outstanding dispute along the "Silk Roads" which had lasted some 130 years, long pre-dating the Russian Revolution and the appearance of the Soviet Union. The international situation with China was clearly fraught in 1969, but was also accompanied by domestic dissent during the year, predominantly within the Soviet southern republics, with riots in Tashkent, the capital city of Soviet Uzbekistan, which also had to be put down by the Soviet Army.

7th November 1969 - 52nd Anniversary of the Great October Socialist Revolution

The November 1969 Red Square parade was accompanied by particularly heavy early winter snowfalls, with all vehicles on parade being covered in snow. Per Soviet norms, the November 1969 parade taken by Defence Minister Grechko began with marching columns consisting of the staff and students of the various military academies such as cadets of the Upper Council of the RSFSR and the "V.V. Kuibyshev" Military Engineering Academy to name but two of many, together with military personnel from all the arms of the Soviet armed forces.

The November 1969 parade was a repeat of the November 1968 parade, with parade stand-

The final and definitive series production variant of the BTR-60 series was the BTR-60PB, mounting a turret with a 14.5mm KPVT heavy machine gun and co-axial 7.62mm PKT weapon.

ard display vehicles such as the BRDM armoured reconnaissance vehicle and its 2P32 and 9P110 ATGM versions, the default BTR-60PB wheeled "bronetransporter" with turret mounted 14.5mm KPVT main armament, the airborne forces SU-85 (ASU-85) and the T-62 MBT. The air defence element was also unchanged, with the ZiL-157V towing S-25 and S-75 SAM systems on their respective PR-3 and PR-11 series TZM transport/reload trailers. Two generations of what was known in the West as the "Scud-B" OTR tactical rocket were again displayed together on Red Square, namely the tracked 2P19 SPU vehicle for the 9K72 OTR and the later wheeled 9P117M SPU vehicle for the same system based on the wheeled MAZ-543A 8x8 chassis that would ultimately replace it in service.

The last Red Square parade of the 1960s ended as had the first parade of the decade, with a finale consisting of long-range strategic rockets for which the parades had become famous during the decade as these rockets had become ever larger, powerful and with significantly increased range. At end of the November 1969 parade, the usual strategic rockets were displayed; namely the tracked mobile RT-20P, followed by MAZ-537V wheeled tractors towing R-29 SLBMs and finally the R-26 (8K66) and R-36 (8K67) ICBMs, towed by MAZ-535A and MAZ-537V wheeled tractors, with the R-36 covered in snow being the last rocket system paraded through Red Square in November 1969.

More strategically significant in November 1969 than the parade of Soviet military hardware on Red Square were the diplomatic preparations being made behind the scenes for continuation of the SALT agreements. On 17th November, exactly ten days after the November Red Square parade in Moscow, Soviet Premier Leonid Brezhnev and American President Richard Nixon met in Helsinki to continue the SALT agreement talks begun by their respective predecessors in January 1967. The negotiations would continue until signed in 1972, however the last months of the 1960s were enveloped by the warm winds of rapprochement and détente between the superpowers that had at the beginning of the same decade come as close as the world had ever seen to nuclear war.

The 9P110 was the final ATGM version of the original BRDM armoured reconnaissance vehicle. The vehicle mounted six 9M14M "Malyutka" missiles under a lightly armoured retractable roof. (Mikhail Baryatinsky)

The SU-85 (ASU-85) mounted the 85mm D-70 gun, which provided Soviet VDV forces with significant mobile, albeit air-landed rather than parachute deployed, anti-tank capability.

The 9P113 SPU vehicle for the 9K52 "Luna-M" (NATO: FROG-7) OTR system was one of the most enduring of Red Square parade participants, being, regularly paraded from the mid 1960s until the end of the 1980s.

As in all years, military parades were held in other cities around the Soviet Union. These 9P110 ATGM vehicles on the BRDM chassis are returning from a parade in Kiev. (Steven J. Zaloga)

The PR-14A TZM vehicle for the S-125 "Neva" SAM system was based on the ZiL-157 chassis during the 1960s. The "Neva" system was named after the River Neva in Leningrad, as it was a development of a naval missile system.

9P113 SPU vehicles for the 9K52 "Luna-M" OTR rocket system traverse Red Square during the 60th Anniversary of the Great October Socialist Revolution on 7th November 1977.

The 1970s

The 1970s were, if not entirely a period of détente, then certainly a period of greatly reduced tension in contrast with the preceding decade. While the "shakhmaty" (chess) of international politics took its course, there were no immediate threats of direct conflict between the superpowers during the decade. This was in large part due to the superpowers having effectively reached nuclear parity, or the capability for "Mutually Assured Destruction" as occasionally referred to in popular parlance; with the superpowers both grudgingly acknowledging a situation of being in "check" and with neither superpower being close to "check mate" or likely to be so in the foreseeable future.

For the United States at the beginning of the 1970s, a nuclear standoff with the Soviet Union was not uppermost in the public psyche. At the beginning of the decade the United States continued to be preoccupied with the deteriorating situation in the war in Vietnam, which was deeply unpopular at home and had proven such a debilitating war that all thoughts of combatting the Soviet threat of world communism had been shelved for the interim. In 1972, the Soviet Union finally signed the SALT-1 agreement, which had been in negotiation since early 1967, and the superpower tensions of the 1960s were declining. The threat of international superpower conflict and Armageddon of the 1960s was in the early 1970s replaced by a series of small and not so small scale proxy wars in the Middle East, the most significant in military technology terms being the October 1973 "Yom Kippur" war which saw Syria and Egypt with a cameo role from Iraq being again decisively defeated by Israel in combat in the Egyptian Sinai and the Syrian Golan Heights. The short but decisive war was significant in that it provided a proxy for evaluating the military technology of the respective superpower blocs. Israel was armed almost exclusively with American and British tanks and other military technology, while Soviet client states Egypt and Syria were almost exclusively Soviet supplied. The war not only provided a "hot" scenario for equipment evaluation but also allowed for American and Soviet evaluation of captured tanks and armoured vehicles squirrelled out of the region back to Aberdeen, Maryland and to Kubinka in the Moscow Oblast respectively.

The period of general détente between the superpowers in the 1970s would come to an end in 1979. The Soviet invasion of Afghanistan in that year, at a time when the United States was preoccupied with events in Iran, would result in a return to a more direct form of proxy-war. It was not until the beginning of the following decade however that the United States would actively increase its campaign of interference against Soviet military operations in Afghanistan.

The Soviet military parades held on Red Square in the 1970s to a significant extent reflected the changing political situation, with direct conflict between the superpowers not regarded as likely. The parades were in consequence significantly different in character to those of the preceding decade. The Khrushchev years of demonstrations of massed military might, in particular new generations of MRBM and ICBM missile technology were replaced by smaller demonstrations of military "tekhnika", which subsequent to the November 1974 parade were also devoid of intercontinental rocket systems. Tanks were also briefly removed from the parades mid-decade, with the new developments premiered on Red Square annually being limited primarily to new generations of secondary armoured vehicles and air defence missile technology. The mid 1970s parades were "passive" or "defensive" inasmuch as any military parade can be so designated.

The 1970s was also significant in that two branches of the Soviet Army saw significant technical developments debuted on Red Square. The 1970s witnessed the belated introduction of tracked artillery systems into Soviet Army service. The 2S1 "Gvozdika" and 2S3 "Akatsiya" self-propelled howitzers were demonstrated on Red Square in Moscow, however other members of the GRAU "2S" family developed over a long period in the 1960s were paraded only in regional cities. The decade was also significant for the introduction of the BMD-1 airborne mechanised infantry combat vehicle, the VDV airborne forces now having their own purpose designed equivalent to the ground forces BMP-1.

On 9th May 1970, in commemoration of the 25th Anniversary of Victory in Europe, the traffic lights in Moscow were all switched to red for one minute, but there was no anniversary Victory Parade as there had been in May 1965.

1970

The Soviet Union was relatively devoid of significant events in 1970, and internationally focus remained on conflicts in the Middle East and Asia Pacific. In Eastern Europe however, there were small political tremors that would be a warning for the future. During the year, there were strikes in the Polish shipyards at Gdansk, led by a young and charismatic trade union leader, Lech Wałęsa. The seemingly local events in Poland would prove to be particularly significant in the eventual downfall of the Soviet Union, being the proverbial first crack in the dam wall.

R-36 (8K67) ICBMs and their MAZ-535A tractor vehicles await parade start orders on a particularly snowy November parade.

9P120 SPU vehicles for the 9K76 "Temp-S" (NATO: SS-12 Scaleboard) Front level rocket system await the same parade.

7th November 1970 – 53rd Anniversary of the Great October Socialist Revolution

The 7th November 1970 military parade was as in 1969 held against a backdrop of a particularly heavy snowstorm that blanketed the cobbles on Red Square, covering all the vehicles on display as they crossed Red Square and the spectators watching from either side of the Lenin Mausoleum in equal measure. The parade taken by Soviet Defence Minister Grechko included staff of the "M.V. Frunze" Military Academy, the "V.V. Kuibyshev" Military Engineering Academy and marching troops of the Moscow Garrison (MVO) and other forces, followed after a short break by mechanised units of the Tamanskaya Motor Rifle Division beginning the mechanised section of the parade.

The BTR-50PK tracked APC remained on display in 1970 alongside the newly introduced BMP MICV, both vehicles displayed in columns four vehicles wide, representing two distinct generations of mechanised infantry vehicles. The SU-85 (ASU-85) remained the airborne forces armoured vehicle on display, while there were no changes in air defence systems, with the ZiL-157V continuing in service on Red Square as the tractor vehicle for the S-25 and S-75 SAM systems mounted on their respective PR-3 and PR-11 series TZM semi-trailers.

The 2P19 and earlier 2P16 tactical OTR rocket SPU vehicles were from the end of the 1960s now replaced by the wheeled 9P113 SPU vehicle for the 9K52 "Luna-M" (NATO: FROG-7) and 9P117M SPU vehicle for the 9K72 "Elbrus" (NATO: Scud-B) on their respective BAZ and MAZ 8x8 chassis. Other parade standards such as the A-35 "Aldan" (NATO: ABM-1 Galosh) anti-ballistic missile system and the R-36 (8K67) and GR-1 (8K713) ICBMs remained on display as since the late 1960s.

Although the public focus was always on Red Square parades during the Cold War, Soviet tanks were also paraded throughout the Soviet Union and in Warsaw Pact states. In 1970, T-62 MBTs and other vehicles were for-instance paraded through the centre of Magdeburg in East Germany (GDR/DDR) on 18th October 1970 following manoeuvres in the area.

The second variant of the RT-15 SPU vehicle, the 8U253 (15U59), differed from the original version as paraded, and as evaluated in operational trials. Note the modified cab arrangement compared to the vehicle displayed in 1965-66.

MAZ-535A 8x8 tractors towing R-36 ICBM's across Red Square during the wintry 7th November 1970 parade.

The 15U51 SPU vehicle for the RT-20P land mobile ICBM – also known by the system designation 15P699 - was regularly displayed on Red Square from 1965 until 1972.

The trailer mounted RT-2 (8K98) ICBM, known by the US and NATO as SS-13 "Savage", was the basis for the shorter range RT-15, and the precursor to the post-Soviet RT-2PM "Topol" road-mobile ICBM.

A 9P120 SPU vehicle for the 9K76 "Temp-S" returns from the 7th November parade in 1970.

A-35 (NATO: ABM-1 Galosh) ABM systems parked on Manezhnaya Square facing the Moscow Hotel prior to the snowy 7th November 1970 Red Square parade. (RAI Novosti)

1971

From a Soviet perspective, 1971 was again a relatively quiet year, with negotiations between the superpowers that would lead to a major breakthrough in the reduction of nuclear armaments in the following years. The main focus of the United States remained meantime the war in Vietnam, from which American President Nixon continued to withdraw conscripted and disillusioned American forces, with the number remaining in country dropping to 196,700 by the end of the year, less than half of peak deployment.

7th November 1971 - 54th Anniversary of the Great October Socialist Revolution

The 7th November 1971 parade continued the line-up of the late 1960s parades, with no revelations. From 1971, the earlier ZiL-111V cabriolet was replaced by the ZiL-117V as the limousine transport for the parade commanders. The marching parade included cadets of the "S.M. Kirov" Caspian Higher Naval Technical College, the Moscow Higher Border Guards Command School and other military academies. The parade standards of previous years were in evidence, with the BTR-50PK and BMP-1, the SU-85 (ASU-85), AT-T tracked tractors towing the (still misreported in Western press) 180mm S-23 gun, the 9P113 SPU vehicle for the 9K52 "Luna-M" (NATO: FROG-7) and the 9P117M SPU vehicle for the 8K72 (NATO: Scud B) OTR system, the tracked self-propelled RT-15 (8U253) and RT-20P (15U51), four R-29 SLBMs towed by

The ZiL-117V cabriolet parade limousine was by 1971 the default vehicle for the traditional meeting of the Defence Minister and Parade Commander. The poster in the background is for the 24th Party Conference of the CPSU.

MAZ-537Vs and four 9P120 SPU vehicles for the "Temp-S" (NATO: SS-12 Scaleboard) Front level rocket system. The parade concluded with two trailer mounted silo-launched R-36 (8K67) rockets followed by two trailer mounted GR-1 (8K713) ICBMs as the parade finale, both rocket types towed by the MAZ-535A. The GR-1 rocket was remarkable in many respects, for its sheer size, the fact that it was towed backwards through Red Square as otherwise the excessive length of tow bar required would make it unstable, and for the belatedly understood fact that the "Global-Rocket-1" never once left the ground, the project having been cancelled before the prototype rockets first appeared on Red Square. At a more subtle level, 1971 was the last year that the 6x6 ZiL-157 series was on display as the tractor and TZM vehicle for air defence missile systems, being replaced from the following year by the modernised ZiL-131, which had entered production a decade previously.

SU-85 (ASU-85) VDV airborne forces self-propelled guns returning to base in via Krymsky Val and across the Krymsky Bridge, 7th November 1971.

BRDM based 9P110 ATGM vehicles on the same run back to base at Khodynka via the Krymsky Val and the Sadovaya Koltso (Garden Ring) circular road, 7th November 1971.

1972

On 22nd May 1972, the American President Richard Nixon visited Moscow; the first time a serving American president had done so. His mission was superpower bi-lateral nuclear weapons reduction. Four days later, on 26th May 1972, Soviet Premier Leonid Brezhnev and American President Richard Nixon signed the interim Strategic Arms Limitation Talks Agreement (SALT-1) and the associated ABM Treaty in Moscow, heralding a new era of strategic arms cooperation, with the long ongoing process of retreating from the nuclear brink formalised between the two superpowers. The agreement froze the number of land based strategic ballistic missile launchers at existing levels and limited further land based ICBM deployment. It also restricted new submarine-launched ballistic missile (SLBM) systems to the direct replacement of older, decommissioned types. The United States and NATO agreed to limit their respective naval fleets to 50 nuclear capable submarines each with a total limit of 800 SLBM warheads between them. The treaty was ratified by the US government on 3rd August 1972, ushering in a period of international détente between the Cold War superpowers.

7th November 1972 – 55th Anniversary of the Great October Socialist Revolution

The 1972 November parade was a double anniversary, the 55th Anniversary of the Great October Socialist Revolution and also the 100th military parade to be staged on Red Square. The parade, undertaken during a light snowstorm, was taken by Marshal of the Soviet Union Andrey Grechko, who would remain Defence Minister until April 1976, with the parade being commanded by the recently appointed Moscow Military District (MVO) commander, General-Colonel Vladimir Leonidovich Govorov.

The opening marching parade consisted of columns from cadets of the Moscow Higher Border Guards Command School, staff of the Armoured Command (ABTU) school, "Nakhimov" Academy students and "Suvorov" cadets.

As per tradition, the Guards Tamanskaya Motorized Rifle Division (MRD) opened the procession of wheeled armoured vehicles and BTR mechanised columns of what was in comparison with previous years a relatively lightweight parade. The year 1972 was the last parade appearance of the GAZ-69 as a parade column lead vehicle, the GAZ-69 being replaced on Red Square by the UAZ-469B from 1973, and was also the last appearance of the original BRDM in 2P32 and 9P110 ATGM vehicle configuration. The BTR-60PA and BTR-60PB were also displayed together with the latter variant following the former, again an outgoing and incoming generation change paraded on the square. The BMP-1 MICV that had operationally begun to replace the BTR-50PK tracked APC was similarly displayed together with the earlier and outgoing vehicle on Red Square. GAZ-69 light vehicles were also paraded in VDV airborne forces configuration followed by the final appearance of the original SU-85 (ASU-85) before it was replaced by the modified SU-85M (ASU-85M). The armoured element of the parade was represented by T-62 tanks of the

Kantemirovskaya Tank Division, still in the original production version as paraded in 1965, moving through the square in columns of four.

November 1972 was the public debut of the enigmatic ATS-59G tracked medium artillery tractor, which made its debut appearance towing the 130mm M-46 field gun, now in its third decade of parade appearances on Red Square, followed by the 9K51 (BM-21) MRS mounted on the 6x6 Ural-375D chassis as the default MRS on display.

Air defence PVO vehicles included the modernised ZSU-23-4M version of the "Shilka" short range air defence system unveiled on Red Square in 1967, the 2P24 SPU vehicle for the ZRK 2K11 "Krug" and the newer 2P25 "Kub" SAM system, with the rockets of the latter being in the stowed transport position during the 1972 parade. The S-25 "Berkut" and S-75 "Dvina" (now modernised in service as the S-75M3 "Volkhov") SAM systems remained on parade, but with the ZiL-157V series being replaced from November 1972 by the ZiL-131V as tractor vehicle, with the ZiL-131 now also being used as the PR-14M TZM vehicle for the S-125M "Neva-M" SAM system.

OTR tactical and Front level rockets were in November 1972 represented by eight 9P113 SPU vehicles for the 9K52 "Luna-M", eight 9P117M SPU vehicles for the 9K72 "Elbrus" and four 9P120 "Temp-S" rocket systems.

The MAZ-535A and MAZ-537V series 8x8 tractors continued to tow MRBM, ICBM and SLBM rockets through Red Square, with the self-propelled and autonomous RT-15 and RT-20P strategic rockets also still on display in 1972. Two A-350Zh rockets for the A-35 anti-ballistic missile system were demonstrated as they had been since the mid 1960s, joined by the parade debut of two trailer mounted RT-2 (8K98) ICBMs towed by the MAZ-535A. Two silo mounted

9P120 SPU vehicles for the 9K76 "Temp-S" Front level rocket system parade through Red Square, 7th November 1973. The "Temp-S" Front level rocket had a range of 800-900km.

cylindrical UR-100 ICBMs were also towed through Red Square in their transport containers by MAZ-537Vs in the very early 1970s, their cylindrical containers giving little clue as to their content. The parade finale consisted of two R-36 (8K67) ICBM systems, with the R-36 providing the parade finale in 1972, having replaced the impressive but never-operational GR-1 (8K713) in that role on Red Square.

The Moscow Red Square parades were throughout the era of the Soviet Union only the most public of military parades that were held in many cities of the Soviet Union, with the parades in other cities often featuring different weapons from those paraded on Red Square. The November parade in Leningrad in 1972 now included some of the weapon systems which by 1972 were no longer seen on Red Square, including the Izdeliye-400 "Dal" long-range SAM system and the R-12 (8K63) strategic rocket which had been replaced by the R-14 (8K65) on Red Square in the mid 1960s.

On the political front, with the interim SALT (SALT-1) agreement signed, negotiations began at the end of 1972 on the SALT-2 agreements, which would continue through the decade until finally being signed off in 1979.

The ATS-59G medium tracked artillery tractor made its public debut on 7th November 1977, replacing the short-lived ATS-59. (Steven J. Zaloga)

From 1972, the ZiL-157V was replaced by the ZiL-131V in the role of tractor vehicle for the S-25 "Berkut" (seen here) and the S-75 "Dvina" SAM systems on their respective TZM semi-trailers.

1973

In 1973, the focus of world attention from a military perspective was again on the Middle East, in particular the October "Yom Kippur" war between Israel and its Arab adversaries. The United States meantime was embroiled in the domestic "Watergate" scandal that had begun the previous year, and the ongoing war in Vietnam as the United States moved towards completing its withdrawal of American forces from the country.

Meanwhile, in Afghanistan, which had been relatively stable under a constitutional monarchy since the 1930s, a prolonged period of severe droughts and food shortages exacerbated by administrative corruption led to a coup d'état in 1973, with the last king of Afghanistan being overthrown by his cousin Mohammed Daoud Khan. At the time this was, as with the internal situation in Cuba as it had developed in the 1950s, largely an irrelevance to the superpowers. But not for the first or last time in history the situation in the Central Asian country would become a military quagmire for world powers that sent armies to the chaotic and deeply tribal country with the aim of importing foreign ideals of order and democracy.

7th November 1973 – 56th Anniversary of the Great October Socialist Revolution

The 7th November 1973 Red Square parade was again a relatively lightweight event. With Soviet Premier Brezhnev looking on from the Lenin Mausoleum review stand, Defence Minister Marshal of the Soviet Union Andrey A. Grechko took the parade, now standing in the back of a ZiL-117V cabriolet parade car.

The parade, conducted on a wet and rainy Moscow morning, began with a march past of drummers, then the staff of the "M.V. Frunze" Military Academy, the "V.I. Lenin" Military Political Academy, the "F. Eh. Dzerzhinsky" Military Engineering Academy, the "R Ya. Malinovsky" Armoured Forces Academy, the "V.V. Kuibyshev" Military Engineering Academy, the "S.K. Timoshenko" Chemical Defence Academy, the "Yu. A. Gagarin" VVS (Soviet Air Force) Academy, the "N.E. Zhukovsky" Air Force Engineering Academy, and many other military training institutions. The parade was also attended by cadets of the Kiev Naval Academy, a Guards VDV regiment, the Moscow Border Guards Academy, by a regiment of VMF naval infantry, and cadets from the Moscow and Kalinin "Suvorov" schools.

The mechanised parade was as always undertaken by tanks and armoured vehicles of the Kantemirovskaya Tank Division and the Tamanskaya Motorised Rifle Division. A subtle change was that the venerable GAZ-69 (actually UAZ-69) that had led the parade columns for two decades was now replaced by the new UAZ-469B, which would serve even longer than the two decades that the GAZ-69 had performed the role on Red Square.

The BTR-50PK tracked APC remained on display alongside the revolutionary BMP as late as 1974, by which time the BMP (BMP-1) was the standard service infantry fighting vehicle in the Soviet Army and had even been exported to the Middle East.

The large display of VDV airborne forces heavy support equipment included the SU-85 (ASU-85), now modernised as the SU-85M (ASU-85M), with a 12.7mm DShKM anti-aircraft machine gun mounted on the fixed superstructure roof. The Kantemirovskaya Tank Division continued to parade T-62 tanks, now the T-62 M-1972 production variant, also armed with a 12.7mm DShKM anti-aircraft machine gun and referred to at the time in Western countries as the T-62A. In both cases, the air defence machine gun had been added for local air defence in response to the developing threat of attack helicopters armed with anti-tank rocket systems.

Artillery weapons included the high velocity smoothbore 100mm MT-12 (2A29) "Rapira" anti-tank gun, towed through Red Square by the ZiL-131 6x6 truck, and the venerable 9K51 (BM-21) "Grad" MRS mounted on the 6x6 Ural-375D chassis.

Air defence vehicles included the modernised ZSU-23-4M air defence system, the 2P24 SPU vehicle for the 2K11 "Krug" and the 2P25 SPU vehicle for the 2K12 "Kub" missile systems, with the latter again in stowed position in 1973. Static launch site SAM systems were represented by the ZiL-131V towing the S-25 "Berkut" and the S-75 (S-75M3 "Volkov" as in service) SAMs on their respective PR-3 and PR-11 series trailers.

Intercontinental strategic missiles displayed on Red Square again included two UR-100 silo-launched ICBMs that had been seen the previous year, which together with the A-350Zh rockets for the A-35 ABM system were perhaps the most disguised of all rockets ever displayed on Red Square, the cylindrical transport-installation (TU) containers giving no clue whatsoever as to their actual appearance.

OTR systems were represented by eight 9P113 "Luna-M" and eight 9P117M "Elbrus" SPU vehicles, followed by four 9P120 SPU vehicles for the 9K76 "Temp-S" (NATO: SS-12 Scaleboard) system. The display of strategic rockets was as for 1972, including MAZ-537 tractors towing R-13 (D-6) and R-29 SLBM rockets, the aforementioned A-35 (NATO: ABM-1) anti-ballistic missile system, two RT-2 ICBM rockets towed by the MAZ-535A and the two UR-100 silo-launched ICBMs. The parade finale was again two R-36 ICBMs towed by MAZ-535A 8x8 tractors.

The T-62 MBT as demonstrated from November 1973 was the "M-1972" version with a 12.7mm DShKM anti-aircraft machine gun. The retrofit, designated T-62A for many years in the West, was primarily for defence against ground-attack helicopters.

While Soviet military technology was being displayed on Red Square in November 1973, Soviet built tanks and other military equipment had been used in the recent October 1973 Arab-Israeli "Yom Kippur" War, the latest of several wars in the Middle East. The Soviet T-54, T-55 and T-62 had been used in combat against Israeli armour provided by the United States and Great Britain, and much technical evaluation of captured military technology was as a result undertaken by the respective superpowers. From a military test ground perspective, the short 1973 "Yom Kippur" conflict was another useful proxy war for the superpowers to evaluate the performance of their respective military technologies, albeit on the understanding that the exported equipment, crew training and ammunition types were not necessarily directly comparable to that of the originators of the technology. Most of the Soviet origin equipment secreted out of the Middle East was procured via Israel and exported primarily to the United States for evaluation, though the Soviet Union also inherited some American and British tanks from the same conflict. Some of these tanks can now be seen in museum collections in Great Britain, Israel, the United States and even within the Kubinka collection near Moscow in the Russian Federation.

The silo-launched UR-100 (8K84) (NATO: SS-11 Sego) was the last new ICBM design to be paraded on Red Square before all strategic weapons were removed from display after November 1974.

1974

1974 was another benign year in superpower relationships. Domestically, Soviet emigration policy was eased, which allowed many Soviet nationals, in particular those with Jewish roots, to emigrate to Europe, Israel and the United States, and with the country receiving favoured trade status as a direct consequence of these relaxations in policy.

The United States at the time remained almost exclusively preoccupied externally with the declining combat situation in Vietnam, while domestically President Nixon on 9th August 1974 resigned as a result of the ongoing Watergate scandal, which had been plaguing American politics since 1972.

7th November 1974 – 57th Anniversary of the Great October Socialist Revolution

The weather was overcast and it was raining heavily as the 7th November 1974 Red Square parade began in 1974, watched from the review stand by Soviet Premier Leonid Brezhnev and senior government and military figures. The parade was again taken by the Defence Minister Marshal of the Soviet Union Andrey A. Grechko, with the parade commander being General-Colonel V.L. Govorov, both standing in the rear of their respective ZiL-117V cabriolet limousines.

Per standard tradition, the Kantemirovskaya Tank Division and Tamanskaya Motorized Rifle Division in the name of M.I. Kalinin provided the tanks and infantry related armoured vehicles respectively. UAZ-469B light vehicles again acted as parade column lead vehicles, having the previous year replaced the GAZ-69 that had performed the role on Red Square for the previous two decades.

The BRDM-2 9P122 (NATO: Sagger) and 9P124 (NATO: Swatter) were both demonstrated on 7th November 1974, with 21 of each vehicle, followed by columns of 21 BTR-60PA and 21 BTR-60PB wheeled APCs, two generations of the BTR-60 still displayed together long after the latter had replaced the former in production. The outgoing BTR-50PK tracked APC and its ultimate replacement the BMP-1 MICV also continued to be displayed together as in 1973. Although the anti-tank variants of the BRDM-2 were displayed on Red Square, the base model BRDM-2 reconnaissance vehicle was never demonstrated in public in Moscow.

Airborne forces vehicles followed, the parade staple SU-85 (ASU-85), again in modernised SU-85M (ASU-85M) configuration, being joined in November 1974 by the parade debut of the airborne forces equivalent of the BMP, the BMD (Boevaya Mashina Desanta) airborne armoured vehicle. The BMD (later re-designated BMD-1) was a highly mobile VDV airborne forces equivalent of the ground forces BMP-1; smaller, lighter and with less desant infantry crew, but with the same turret and 73mm 2A28 "Grom" low-pressure gun as its larger ground forces sibling. In 1974, the VDV desant crews in the final vehicle row were armed with "Igla" (NATO: SA-7 Grail) hand held air defence rocket systems. Five years later, BMD airborne vehicles would lead the attack on the presidential palace of the newly installed Afghan President Hafizullah Amin in Kabul on the first day of what would become the ten year long Soviet war in Afghanistan. The BMD-1 was followed on to Red Square in November 1974 by the aforementioned later SU-85M (ASU-85M), modified with 12.7mm DShKM anti-aircraft machine gun mounted on the roof, reflecting the increase in air defence requirements for AFVs against new attack helicopter developments as described earlier.

The T-62 main battle tanks followed; now the later "M-1972" or "T-62A" as described by the United States and NATO countries at the time, with two turret cupolas and mounting a 12.7mm DShKM heavy anti-aircraft machine gun for the same reasons as the SU-85M (ASU-85M). In the background, discreetly located around the entrances to Red Square were IS-2T armoured recovery vehicles based on converted IS-2M heavy tanks with their turrets removed and the turret race plated over.

The 2P25 SPU vehicle for the 2K12 "Kub", with the 3M9 rockets located in the forward "launch" rather than transit position, and the 2P24 SPU vehicle for the 2K11 "Krug" were displayed together. The ZiL-131V 6x6 tractor vehicle was now used to tow the S-25 "Berkut" and S-75 "Dvina" (and now operationally "Volkhov") SAM systems, still on display in 1974 having had their public debut at the end of the 1950s (S-75) and at the beginning of the 1960s (S-25). The ZiL-131 based PR-14M TZM vehicle for the S-125 was also displayed, with all the vehicles displaying bold red stars on the cab doors.

The ATS-59G tracked tractor was again paraded in 1974 towing the 130mm M-46 field gun. The ATS-59G was a return to the full crew cab arrangement of the earlier AT-S, as what had proven to be the interim ATS-59G with its small cab without crew seats had proven unsatisfactory in operational service..

From 1974, there was a major shift in emphasis during Red Square parades, with less armoured

Modernised T-62 "M-1972" main battle tanks pass through Red Square, 7th November 1974. Photographer - Boris Volovenko

and more secondary vehicles being demonstrated on Red Square. ZiL-131 6x6 general service trucks towed the 122mm D-30 towed howitzer in a rare appearance of a long in service standard artillery piece. The early 1970s were the swansong years of Soviet towed artillery on Red Square, as the 2S1 and 2S3 (2S3M) self-propelled systems as demonstrated on Red Square later in the decade (and the 2S4, 2S5 and 2S7 which were never displayed in Moscow) began to complement and slowly replace towed systems in Soviet Army service. The 122mm D-30 was a particularly versatile design, with three trail legs which each swung out at 120°, with the gun carriage then raised allowing the weapon to rotate through 360°. The 122mm D-30 was also unusual in that it featured a tow hook located under the muzzle brake, and was thereby towed muzzle first behind the ZiL-131 tractor vehicle through Red Square. The towed artillery was followed by columns of the now parade standard 9K51 (BM-21) "Grad" MRS, mounted on the Ural-375D chassis.

Two generations of OTR rockets, with eight 9P113 "Luna-M" (NATO: FROG-7) vehicles being followed by eight 9P117M SPU vehicles for the 8K72 "Elbrus" (NATO: Scud-B). Two R-29 SLBMs were towed by MAZ-537V tractors, which were also used as usual as the tow vehicle for the two A-350Zh rockets for the A-35 "Aldan" (NATO: ABM-1 Galosh) anti-ballistic missile system. Four 9P120 "Temp-S" (NATO: SS-12 Scaleboard) Front level rockets followed, mounted on the MAZ-543A chassis, followed directly by two MAZ-537V 8x8 wheeled tractors towing two huge UR-100 ICBM rockets within their transport containers on their specialised three-axle semi-trailers, followed by two MAZ-535A tractors

The BRDM-2 based 9P124 launch vehicle for the 2K8M "Falanga-M" ATGM replaced the earlier 2K8 "Falanga" ATGM system on the original BRDM based 2P32 chassis. The 9P124 had an engagement range of 4,000m. (Mikhail Baryatinsky)

towing two RT-2 rockets on their own specialised trailers. The parade ended with two MAZ-535A 8x8 tractors towing massive R-36 8K67 (NATO: SS-9 Scarp) ICBMs on their two axle transport trailers. These R-36 ICBMs were to be the last silo-launched intercontinental ballistic missiles to ever pass through Red Square in the time of the Soviet Union.

The 7th November 1974 parade was the last "full scale" parade during which the Soviet Union would display strategic land and VMF naval (submarine) based ICBMs on Red Square. The parades of 1975 and 1976 would feature only light and secondary vehicles, with no tanks or heavy armour on display. The country was entering yet another era of détente with the United States and

The BMD airborne combat vehicle made its public debut appearance on 7th November 1974, providing VDV airborne forces with their own equivalent to the ground forces BMP first shown on Red Square in 1967.

The BMD mounted the same turret with 73mm 2A28 "Grom" low-pressure gun and 9M14 "Malyutka" ATGM as the ground forces BMP in a more diminutive and parachute-deployable vehicle.

NATO, which would in the years ahead lead to a series of strategic armament reduction treaties. The Cold War was thawing, the Soviet Union was beginning to stagnate politically and economically, and the Soviet reality was that it could not continue to compete economically with the US in the "arms race" in which the Soviet Union had demonstrated technical equivalence. That equivalence had been achieved however at the expense of a state almost entirely dedicated to military prowess to the detriment of social development for the population.* Strategic rockets would be absent on Red Square from 1975 until the unexpected appearance of the RT-2PM "Topol" ICBM during the last Soviet military parade on 7th November 1990.

SU-85M (ASU-85M) airborne self-propelled guns parade through Red Square on 7th November 1974. The modernised version also mounted a 12.7mm DShKM anti-aircraft machine gun. (Mikhail Baryatinsky)

2P24 launch vehicles for the 2K11 "Krug" mobile SAM system during the same November 1974 parade.

---

* The Soviet Union was a highly militarised society, but defence procurement then as now was directly with the military equipment manufacturers. The provision of education, secure employment, social housing, medical care and basic essentials was a foundation block of the Soviet State, and though there were few luxuries, the standard of living for the majority compared not unfavourably with many "first world" countries.

1975

1975 was another year in which the relative positions of the superpowers entered a period of what would in the post-Soviet era be termed "reset". The United States administration remained almost exclusively focused in 1975 on events in Asia Pacific. The rebel movement started by Ho Chi Minh when rebuffed by the French government in Paris in 1946 had morphed into the battle hardened North Vietnamese Army (NVA), which was by 1975 the fifth largest in the world and would early in 1975 capture Saigon, decisively ending the Vietnam War. For several years after the end of the war in Vietnam, the United States would enter a period of strategic reflection, not quite to the isolationist levels of before World War Two, but certainly more domestically orientated. The Soviet military parades of the 1970s were, as if a mirror reflection, from 1975 relatively benign, reflecting the lessening of superpower tensions at a strategic level.

*"A Soviet military parade is an impressive spectacle. Masses of men and equipment are displayed in these demonstrations of military might"**

7th November 1975 - 58th Anniversary of the Great October Socialist Revolution

In 1975 the Soviet Union celebrated 30 years of Victory in the Second World War, with the November parade also being the 103rd military parade held on Red Square. In contrast with the previous Victory in Europe (VE Day) decade anniversary in 1965 and the later one in 1985 there was no military VE Day parade with a mechanised component held in May 1975. The November parade was also limited compared to earlier parades, with no tanks or other heavy armour present, and no strategic weapons on display. The parade was also the last taken by Defence Minister Marshal Andrey Grechko after ten years in the role, as he would die in service the following April.

The mechanised part of the parade was as usual opened by the Tamanskaya Motorized Rifle Division, followed by other mechanised troops. By contrast with the last military parade in November 1974, the 1975 parade was one of the lowest key parades of the Cold War, with light armoured vehicles, no tanks or other heavy armour. Artillery towed by ZiL-131 trucks replaced tanks, and there were no surprises, with the OTR tactical rocket vehicles having the longest offensive range during a Red Square parade devoid of strategic rocket systems. The parade was also relatively short. The new SAM systems which debuted in 1975 provided a significant improvement in air

* Introduction to FM30-40 Handbook on Soviet Ground Forces. HQ Department of the (US) Army, 30th June 1975.

defence capability for mechanised forces however, with the debut of both the 9K31 "Strela-1" based on the BRDM-2 chassis and the 9K33 "Osa" system with its associated tracking and engagement radar systems mounted on the BAZ-5937 amphibious chassis.

The 1975 parade began with UAZ-469B lead vehicles, followed by BRDM-2 based 9P122 launch vehicles for the 9M14M "Malyutka" (NATO: AT-3 Sagger) replacing the original BRDM based 9P110. Columns of BTR-60PB "bronetransporters" were directly followed by ZiL-131 6x6 general service trucks paraded with troops, and towing 122mm D-30 howitzers and a 100mm MT-12 anti-tank guns. There were no tanks, no BMP-1 infantry combat vehicles and no BMD-1 VDV airborne forces vehicles after the cameo appearance of the latter in November 1974. The November 1975 parade did however include the public debut of new Soviet air defence systems, namely the BRDM-2 mounted 9P31 launch vehicle for the 9K31 "Strela-1" (NATO: SA-9 Gaskin), and the original pre-series and initial 9A33B production series SPU launch vehicles for the short-range 9K33 "Osa" (NATO: SA-8 "Gecko") SAM system mounted on the BAZ-5937 6x6 amphibious chassis.* The initial 9A33B SPU vehicle for the ZRK 9K33 "Osa" system was armed with four 9M33 rockets on an open mounting. The "Osa" SAM system was in continuous development at the time, and the vehicles initially paraded in November 1975 were a mix of pre-series and early series production 9A33B "Osa" SPU vehicles, with the four earlier vehicles with their distinctive cropped bow on the BAZ-5937 chassis displayed in the final row behind the two rows of modified "Osa" production vehicles. The final row of early development prototypes would quickly be replaced by the standard production variant, which would subsequently be displayed annually until the "Osa" was replaced on Red Square by the later 9A33BM3 SPU vehicle for the 9K33M3 "Osa-AKM", which mounted six rockets located within their TPK containers, the latter appearing on Red Square from 1982. The new "Osa" systems were followed by the long-known SAMs, the PR-14M TZM for the S-125M "Neva-M" mounted on the

The 9A33B launch and guidance vehicle for the 9K33 "Osa" mobile SAM system made its public debut on Red Square on 7th November 1975. The "Osa" system, based on the amphibious BAZ-5937 chassis, was presented in two variants during the same parade.

---

* Two variants of the original 9A33B SPU vehicle for the 9K33 "Osa" SAM system were displayed on Red Square in November 1975. A single 9A33BM SPU vehicle for the modified "Osa-A" was built and used for development trials, ultimately resulting in the 9A33BM2 SPU vehicle for the "Osa-AK" with six containerised rockets.

The final row of four 9A33B launch and guidance vehicles for the 9K33 "Osa" SAM system displayed in 1975 were early trials vehicles with a distinctive blunt nose to the BAZ-5937 chassis.

The BRDM-2 based 9P124 launch vehicle for the 2K8M ATGM vehicle was a modernisation of the BRDM based 2P32 launch vehicle for the earlier 2K8 system. (Steven J. Zaloga)

ZiL-131, and ZiL-131V tractors towing the S-25 "Berkut" and S-75 "Dvina/Volkhov" SAM systems on their respective PR series semi-trailers.

In what was at the time standard configuration for completing a parade, the finale consisted of eight 9P113 "Luna-M" (NATO: FROG-7) and four 9P117M "Elbrus" (NATO: Scud-B) OTRs, with the rear-guard of the foreshortened parade being taken up by four 9P120 (9K76) "Temp-S" (NATO: SS-12 Scaleboard) Front level rockets, reduced from six on earlier parades. There were no strategic weapons displayed on Red Square in 1975, nor would there be until November 1990.

The relatively low key display on Red Square in 1975 was noted by the American military attachés responsible for reporting back on such events, but in April of 1975 the United Sates had lost Saigon to the advancing troops of the People's Army of Vietnam and the Viet-Cong, with Soviet design origin Chinese T-59 tanks crashing through the US Embassy gates on 30th April. The decade-long Vietnam war had cost the lives of 58,220 American servicemen and women, the majority of whom had been conscripted for service, and the war weary public mood in the United States was such that relationships between the United States and the Soviet Union would be benign for the rest of the decade. At the end of which decade the Soviet Union embarked on its own version of America's Vietnam in a country with its own historical past of proving impossible for foreign powers, colonial or otherwise, to control - Afghanistan.

A 9P124 ATGM vehicle for the 2K8M "Falanga-M" ATGM system returns from the November 1974 Red Square parade. (Steven J. Zaloga)

1976

1976 was another uneventful year in the Soviet Union and on the world stage. Domestically in the Soviet Union, the KamAZ truck plant was completed that year in Naberezhny Chelny, in the Soviet semi-autonomous Republic of Tatarstan. Work had begun on building the plant in 1969, and the project was significant in that it involved several major multi-national technology transfers. The American companies Ford and Mack had originally considered direct involvement, but were stopped by US export control regulations, albeit an American company collaborated in the construction of the giant foundries. The French company Renault worked on designing and installing the engine plant and on diesel engine development, while other multinational companies such as the German company Liebherr also worked on the project. The KamAZ plant was to the Soviet Union of 1976 what the GAZ plant had been in 1932 - a massive ground-up truck plant construction project using the latest in foreign technology and design expertise, despite the political differences between the countries concerned. The KamAZ plant began with the production of diesel engined 6x4 KamAZ-5320 and 6x6 KamAZ-4310 vehicles, with a large part of production going to the Soviet Army. The KamAZ plant is today a major manufacturer of many military vehicle types for the modern Russian Army, now also including wheeled armoured vehicles and strategic load carriers.

7th November 1976 - 59th Anniversary of the Great October Socialist Revolution

The Red Square parade of 7th November 1976, the 104th to be held on the square, was one of the shortest of all post-war Soviet Army Red Square parades, being of barely 30 minutes duration. As with the previous year, it was also a demonstration of primarily defensive weapons, devoid of tanks or strategic weapons, the parades of 1975 and 1976 being in stark contrast to the strategic Soviet parades of the late 1960s and early 1970s.

The parade was taken by Marshal of the Soviet Union Dmitry F. Ustinov, who had taken the position of Defence Minister on 30th July after the death of Marshal Grechko in April. Marshal Ustinov would remain in place as defence Minister until December 1984. The parade began with drummers of the Moscow Military Music School, followed by the usual extensive list of parade participants. These included students of the "M.V. Frunze" Military Academy, the "V.I. Lenin" Military-Political Academy, the "F. Eh Dzerzhinsky" Military Engineering Academy, and the Tank Forces Academy named after Marshal of the Soviet Union R. Ya. Malinovsky. These marching units were followed by students of the "V.V. Kuibyshev" Military Engineering Academy, the Chemical Defence Academy named after Marshal of the Soviet Union S.K. Timoshenko, the "Yu. A. Gagarin" Air Force Academy, the "N.E. Zhukovsky" Air Force Engineering Academy and many other academies and military units. There were border guards units, naval infantry, the "F.E. Dzerzhinsky" military division, Moscow and Kalinin Suvorov academies, the Leningrad Naval Academy and many other participants too many to list.

The military equipment display was as in 1975 again primarily a "defensive" parade, being a mix of secondary armoured vehicles and air defence weapons, but lacking the main battle tanks and heavier weapons which had been a feature of parades until November 1974. The mechanised section of the parade opened as usual with BTR-60PB armoured personnel carriers of the Tamanskaya Motorized Rifle Division named after M.I. Kalinin, followed by artillery, air defence and tactical level missiles. All vehicles were painted green with Guards symbols as appropriate to the units represented.

The parade procession was per standard Soviet 1970s norms, with UAZ-469B column lead vehicles being followed by the BRDM mounted 9P122 ATGM vehicle, the BTR-60PB, ZiL-131 6x6 trucks towing the 122mm D-30 towed dual purpose gun and the 9K51 (BM-21) "Grad" multiple rocket launcher on the 6x6 Ural-375D chassis. As in 1975, there were no tanks, and no BMP ground forces or BMD airborne forces infantry combat vehicles. Air defence included the BRDM-2 mounted 9P31 SPU vehicle for the 9K31 "Strela-1" (NATO: SA-9 Gaskin) and the 9A33B SPU vehicle for the 9K33 "Osa", both of which had their parade debut the previous year, followed by the parade standard ZiL-131 PR-14M TZM for the S-125M "Neva-M" SAM, and the S-25 and S-75 SAM systems towed by the ZiL-131V on their respective TZM semi-trailers. The parade concluded with the 9P113 "Luna-M" (NATO: FROG-7) and 9P117M (9K72) (NATO: Scud-B) OTR systems and finally the 9P120 "Temp-S" (NATO: SS-12 Scaleboard) as the longest-range rocket system finalising the parade.

The 2P25 launch vehicle for the 2K12 "Kub" (Cube) SAM mobile system was displayed on Red Square annually from 1965-1977, and on an irregular basis in the 1980s. (Mikhail Baryatinsky)

9P113 SPU vehicles for the 9K52 "Luna-M" (NATO: FROG-7) OTR during final parade practice.

The BRDM-2 based 9P31 launch vehicle for the 9K31 "Strela-1" SAM system made its public debut on Red Square on 7th November 1975, but was regularly displayed only for a few years. (Mikhail Baryatinsky)

1977

Although again a relatively quiet year in the Soviet Union, across the State's southern borders there were riots in the Afghan capital Kabul in September against the leadership of Mohammed Daoud Kahn, who had taken control from his cousin in a coup d'état in 1973. The Soviet Union observed these events with significant concern in that any instability in Afghanistan could easily spread Islamic fundamentalism across the borders into the largely Muslim populated southern republics of the Soviet Union. The increasing instability in Afghanistan was in 1977 a foreign matter for observation. By 1979 it would become both a domestic Soviet matter, and an international concern. Meantime, as the relatively neutral period of détente in the mid 1970s made way for another spike in superpower tensions, the Soviet Union deployed the RSD-10 "Pioner" (NATO: SS-20 Saber) MRBM in Eastern Europe, while the United States deployed cruise missiles at Greenham Common near Newbury in Great Britain, and deployed both cruise missiles and Pershing strategic rockets in West Germany.

7th November 1977 – 60th Anniversary of the Great October Socialist Revolution

By November 1977 the Soviet Premier Leonid. I. Brezhnev had been formally elected as President under a change in the Soviet constitution. Brezhnev and Aleksey N. Kosygin stood on the review stand with other members of the Soviet government and the armed forces, as the parade commenced on a particularly snowy Moscow November morning. As Soviet Premier Leonid Brezhnev stood on the parade podium reviewing the parade below, he looked frail and unwell.

The 7th November 1977 parade on Red Square commemorated the 60th Anniversary of the Great October Socialist Revolution, and being a decade anniversary it was significantly larger than previous years, with some 336 military vehicles traversing Red Square on the day. The parade, once again taken by Marshal of the Soviet Union Dmitry F. Ustinov, also marked the return of tanks and other armoured vehicles to Red Square after two year absence, and the public debut of the T-72 main battle tank, with 46 new T-72 tanks traversing the square in columns of four. The T-72 MBT series had made its public debut on Red Square in November 1977, a decade after the T-62 had done so in 1965.

The parade began with the musicians of Moscow Military Music School as the year before, and featured the same line-up of marching units, with the armoured vehicles provided per tradition by the Kantemirovskya Tank Division and the Tamanskaya Motorized Rifle Division. All vehicles were in 1977 again painted drab green with guards symbols painted on most divisional vehicles.

The November 1977 parade began with the public parade debut of columns of 9P148 ATGM vehicles on the BRDM-2 chassis. The parade also included the BTR-60PB, now without the earlier BTR-60PA, and the BMP-1, still in the original format introduced a decade previously, followed by the parade debut of the MT-LB multipurpose tracked vehicle towing the 100mm MT-12 (2A29) anti-tank gun and the new "2S" series of self-propelled guns. The GRAU "2S" series of self-propelled artillery vehicles were all named after flowers. The 2S1 "Gvozdika" (Carnation) and the 2S3 "Akatsiya" (Acacia) self-propelled howitzers represented the self-propelled artillery on display, together with the older 9K51 "Grad" MRS. The parade debut of the 2S3 (2S3M) was as with the 2S1 several years after it had entered service with the Soviet Army. In the case of the 2S1 it was also but a cameo appearance, the 2S3 being one of many vehicles which over the years appeared on Red Square only to then disappear and return to Red Square as a regular participant only years later. The D-30 howitzer was in 1977 towed through Red Square by the ZiL-131.

The BMP-1 and BMD-1 reappeared at the November 1977 parade having been missing for two years. The BMP-1 had been a parade regular since 1967 before disappearing after the 1974 November parade, while the equivalent BMD-1 VDV airborne forces vehicle had made its parade debut in November 1974 and then disappeared before reappearing in 1977. Western intelligence manuals often showed the BMD-1 as having made its public debut in 1977, but it had in fact made a cameo appearance on Red Square in 1974 before becoming a parade regular from 1977.

Air defence vehicles on display again included the new BRDM-2 mounted 9P31 SPU vehicle for the 9K31 "Strela-1" (NATO: SA-9 Gaskin), the S-125M "Neva-M" SAM (NATO: SA-3 Goa) on the PR-14M TZM vehicle with two reload rockets mounted on the ZiL-131 truck chassis, and the S-25 and S-75 SAM systems towed by the ZiL-13V on their respective TZM semi-trailers. Other air defence vehicles represented were the now long-since parade regular 2P24 SPU vehicle for the 2K11 "Krug" (NATO: SA-4 Ganef) SAM system, and the 2P25 SPU vehicle for the 2K12 "Kub" (NATO: SA-6 Gainful) with the 3M9 rockets in the forward firing position rather than stowed as at other parades. The 9K33 "Osa" SAM system was again displayed, but with the early pre-production SPU vehicles with the distinctive blunt nose now replaced by the standard

After a hiatus of two years, tanks returned to Red Square in November 1977 in the form of the T-72 main battle tank. The original T-72 (Obiekt-172M) was later replaced on Red Square by the T-72A and T-72B modifications.

The Red Square public debut of the BMD was in November 1974, with the vehicle thereafter returning to Red Square only in November 1977. (TASS)

The BMD, later re-designated BMD-1, was a powerfully armed VDV airborne forces multi-role combat vehicle, seen here making a return appearance on Red Square in 1977.

early 9A33B SPU chassis vehicle for the 9K33 "Osa" (NATO: SA-8 Gecko) SAM system as introduced the previous year. The 9K33 underwent significant technical changes over a short time period, such that the vehicles displayed on Red square had been replaced in testing and service by newer versions even before they first appeared on Red Square. The venerable ZSU-23-4M was again displayed, replacing the earlier production models that had been displayed on Red Square since the late 1960s.

Culminating what was very much another "defensive" parade, the final vehicles displayed on Red Square in November 1977 were the 9P113 and 9P117M SPU vehicles for the "Luna-M" and "Elbrus" OTR systems, followed by four MAZ-543A mounted 9P120 "Temp-S" rocket systems, the Front level weapons completing the parade.

9P31 launch vehicles for the 9K31 "Strela-1" SAM system traversing Red Square, 7th November 1977.

The 9P148 ATGM vehicle made its public debut on 7th November 1977, mounting five launch tubes for the 9K113 "Konkurs" ATGM.

The launch assembly for the five 9K113 "Konkurs" ATGMs was retracted through a hatch in the hull roof for reloading. (Steven J. Zaloga)

The T-72 would be displayed on Red Square from 1977 until the final Soviet era parade in 1990, during which time several upgrades and versions were shown.

The early production T-72 (Obiekt-172M) "Ural" as first displayed on Red Square was fitted with a TPD2-49 coincidence rangefinder in the turret roof, with an L2AG infrared searchlight on the right of the gun and with no side skirts fitted.

The 2S1 self-propelled howitzer also had its Red Square public debut on 7th November 1977. The "2S" series of self-propelled weapons had been developed from the early 1960s and were gradually introduced from the early 1970s.

The 2S1 was related to the MT-LB tracked multi-role artillery tractor chassis. It was fully amphibious, using its tracks for directing water through channels fitted to the track guards (stowed on the turret rear of this vehicle) to provide propulsion.

The 2S3 (2S3M) self-propelled howitzer made its public debut in November 1977 but then re-appeared only in the early 1980s. The original 2S3 had already been modified in production as the 2S3M with improved ammunition handling and complement before the new vehicle type made its debut Red Square appearance.

1978

The mid 1970s remained a particularly benign period of the Cold War from an international perspective, but internally the Soviet Union was beginning to suffer economic stagnation. Throughout the 1960s, economic growth had been in the region of 5% per annum, but by the late 1970s this had dropped to 1-2% and increased bureaucracy was also taking its toll. Events outwith the Soviet Union were also about to greatly increase the financial burdens on the country. On 26th April 1978, the Afghan capital Kabul was seized in the "Saur Revolution" - a communist military coup - with the incumbent President Daoud Khan being executed. The People's Democratic Party of Afghanistan had seized power, and on 1st May the country was renamed the Democratic Republic of Afghanistan, but was now a country again at war within itself.

As a result of the "Saur Revolution", Nur Muhammed Taraki became the first communist leader of Afghanistan. After considerable and not particularly amiable negotiation considering the violent change of government, Afghanistan signed a 20 year Treaty of Friendship with the Soviet Union on 5th December 1978. Soviet financial, educational and humanitarian aid followed. Nur Muhammed Taraki would later ask for military aid from Aleksey Kosygin as Chairman of the Soviet Council of Ministers, which was refused on the basis that the Soviet Union did not want to get militarily involved in the volatile situation in the country which was not in of itself a direct concern of the Soviet Union. Brezhnev was then approached in his capacity as General Secretary of the CPSU, and provided the same answer. For the moment, Afghanistan remained a domestic problem, but in a not so distant country, located on the southern borders of the Soviet Union where the religious basis of the indigenous population, including elements of fanaticism, mirrored that latent in the Soviet southern republics.

7th November 1978 - 61st Anniversary of the Great October Socialist Revolution

The 7th November 1978 Red Square parade commemorated the 61st Anniversary of the Great October Socialist Revolution and was the 106th military parade to be held on Red Square. The parade was taken by Defence Minister Marshal of the Soviet Union Dmitry F. Ustinov, and as per tradition began with marching columns. There were "Suvorovtsi" - students of the Suvorov Military Academy, the Moscow All-Arms Academy, the Moscow "Mossoviet" Border Guards Command School, and marching columns from the Soviet Army, the Soviet Air Force and the Soviet Navy, VDV airborne forces, the "Dzerzhinsky" Division and many other military and training units that made up the marching element of all Soviet military parades.

The military "tekhnika" or equipment part of the parade began with armoured columns of the Guards Tamanskaya Motorized Rifle Division named after M.I. Kalinin, with each section of the parade led by UAZ-469B light vehicles. The primary armoured vehicles displayed were the now ubiquitous 9P148 ATGM system on the BRDM-2 chassis, the BTR-60PB, BMP-1, and the T-72 MBT.

The vehicles displayed in 1978 featured a mix of parade markings, with most, such as the 9P113 "Luna-M", ZiL-131 based PR-14M TZM

The 9K51 "Grad" MRS was a regular Red Square parade participant from the mid 1960s until the last Soviet era parade in November 1990. The "Grad" MRS was originally mounted on the 6x6 Ural-375D chassis, being latterly re-mounted on the Ural-4320 chassis with a diesel engine.

The 2S1 "Gvozdika" (Carnation) self-propelled howitzer was regularly paraded across the Soviet Union from 1977, and in many former Soviet cities well into the 21st Century.

transloader for the S-125 SAM and the BAZ-5937 based 9K33 "Osa" SPU vehicle featuring a single red star, others such as the ZiL-131V tractor vehicles with their S-25 "Berkut" and S-75 "Dvina/Volkhov" rockets in tow featuring Guards symbols.

Artillery included the 2S1 "Gvozdika", ZiL-131 6x6 trucks towing the 122mm D-30 howitzer, the 9K51 "Grad" MRS mounted on the Ural-375D chassis, and MT-LB multiple purpose tracked vehicles towing the 100mm MT-12 (2A29) anti-tank gun. The 2S3 "Akatsiya" self-propelled howitzer which had made its public debut in 1977 was however conspicuous by its subsequent absence. The 2S3 (2S3M) would make other cameo appearances but would not become a parade regular until after 1984.

PVO air defence forces equipment displayed in 1978 included twelve BRDM-2 mounted 9A31 SPU vehicles for the 9K31 "Strela-1" SAM system, twelve S-125M "Neva-M" PR-14M TZM vehicles based on the ZiL-131 and twelve each of the S-25 and S-75 SAM systems towed by ZiL-131V tractor vehicles. The 9K33 "Osa" (NATO: SA-8 Gecko) SAM system was again displayed, mounted on the original BAZ-5937 based 9A33B SPU vehicle mounting the four original 9M33 rockets in an open configuration.

The parade concluded with the late 1970s staple display of 9P113 "Luna-M" and the 9P117M "Elbrus" OTR tactical rocket systems in the era of "defensive" Red Square parades devoid of long-range strategic rocket systems.

1979

The year 1979 was another watershed year for Soviet-American relations, but not for the first or last time it was events in Asia and Asia Pacific and the Middle East rather than Europe that held the attention of the superpowers. The year began with unrelated events in disparate regions of the world that would draw the superpowers into renewed tension on the world stage. On 7th January, the North Vietnamese Army (NVA) liberated Phnom Penh in Cambodia from the Khmer Rouge. One week later, on 15th January 1979, the "Sino-Soviet Treaty of Friendship, Alliance and Mutual Assistance" signed between the Soviet Union and China in 1950 expired. That day, China sent 80,000 troops accompanied by over 300 tanks into North Vietnam from which the United States had departed four years prior, and the violence and instability in the region entered a new phase.

The Chinese had again risen as the decisive military force in the Asia Pacific region. In the Middle East, Mohammad Reza Pahlavi, the Shah of Iran, who had ruled with the support of the United States and other Western powers* would be forced to leave the country forever, ushering in a new and very different regime. While the United States and other countries adjusted to the developing form of government in Iran that was antagonistic to those same Western powers, events continued to unfold in Afghanistan that would have a direct bearing on the Soviet Union and its armed forces. After the Herat uprising in March 1979, during which elements of the Afghan Army mutinied and in a week of blood letting Soviet civilians based in the city were murdered, President Taraki of Afghanistan on 20th March requested military assistance from the Soviet Premier (General Secretary of the CPSU and Chairman of the Presidium of the Supreme Soviet) Brezhnev in the form of direct military intervention into the country by Soviet troops. Brezhnev refused on the basis that the presence of Soviet troops would exacerbate the situation largely of Taraki's making in Afghanistan and in the near abroad for both Taraki and the Soviet Union.

Meantime in the United States, President Carter on 3rd July signed a directive providing secret aid to the Afghan opposition, on the advice of his National Security Advisor Zbigniew Brzezinski. It was hoped that the provision of aid to the Afghan opposition (against President Taraki of Afghanistan) would prompt a Soviet military incursion into Afghanistan, drawing the Soviet Union into a war similar to that in Vietnam from which the United States had only recently extracted itself. This overly provocative if not unusual action was in part an effort to keep the Soviet Union preoccupied while the United States was at the time contemplating war with Iran to the south, with the entirely Western backed Shah of Iran having left the country permanently on 7th January, the same day the NVA had liberated Phnom Penh in Cambodia.

The turmoil in Afghanistan meantime continued to grow. On 11th September 1979, President Taraki of Afghanistan returned to the country from meetings in not so nearby Cuba. He was met and arrested at Kabul airport by his cousin Hafizullah Amin, a graduate of Columbia University in the United States, in another Afghan military coup that would again overthrow the existing regime, with Amin becoming the Afghan General Secretary on 16th September 1979. The now deposed President Taraki was murdered on Amin's orders on 8th October. The Soviet Union had no direct interest in involvement in Afghanistan, military or otherwise, but it had more than passing interest in stability there. The ethnic make-up of the Soviet Union's southern republics was such that instability - government by tribalism - in Afghanistan could rapidly move north, destabilising the southern republics of the Soviet Union. By the end of the year, and with great reluctance on the part of Brezhnev and the Soviet government, Soviet troops had been committed to Afghanistan in response to the deteriorating situation there.

---
* Mohammad Reza Pahlavi had taken control of Iran in 1953 in a coup d'etat arranged by Great Britain and the US as "Operation Boot" and "Operation Ajax" respectively.

While events in Iran and Afghanistan continued to unfold during 1979, superpower relations had remained overall more positive until the end of the decade and the beginning of the Soviet war in Afghanistan. The defining moment in these improving steadily relationships was the SALT-2 agreement on nuclear weapons limitations signed on 18th June 1979 in Vienna by Soviet Premier Leonid Brezhnev and American President James (Jimmy) Carter. The treaty limited each signatory to a maximum of 2,250 nuclear delivery vehicles (warheads). At a strategic level, the superpowers were in a state of balance. By the end of 1979, the declining situation in Afghanistan would lead to a regression towards superpower conflict by proxy in the ever-troubled country, albeit American efforts were initially tempered by the surprise speed of Soviet consolidation in Afghanistan, and by greater overall concerns in the United States at the time with regard to events in Iran.

7th November 1979 – 62nd Anniversary of the Great October Socialist Revolution

The 62nd "October Revolution" Anniversary parade was reviewed by Defence Minister of the USSR, Marshal Dmitry F. Ustinov, with the parade commander being army General Vladimir L. Govorov. Soviet Premier Brezhnev observed the parade from the review stand above the Lenin Mausoleum, looking visibly ill. The parade was conducted during a typical light snowstorm of early winter, with the vehicles that had been parked up before the parade being covered in a light dusting of snow as they appeared on Red Square.

The marching parade began per tradition with students of the "M.V. Frunze" Academy and the "F. Eh. Dzerzhinsky" Military Engineering

A significant number of Soviet military vehicles were never displayed on Red Square. The SU-122-54 tank destroyer, of which only 77 were built, served in secrecy, but decommissioned vehicles converted to TOP armoured recovery vehicles were used on standby at Red Square parades in the 1980s. It was the "parade appearance" of the converted TOP vehicles that confirmed the existence of the enigmatic SU-122-54 tank destroyer.

Academy, the Tank Forces Academy named after Marshal of the Soviet Union R. Ya. Malinovsky, the "V.V. Kuibyshev" Military Engineering Academy, the Military Academy of Chemical Defence named after Marshal S.K. Timoshenko, the "Yu. A. Gagarin" Air Force Academy, the "N.E. Zhukovsky" Air Force Engineering Academy and units representing all of the armed forces of the Soviet Union. There were cadets of the Higher Naval Forces College in the name of A.S. Popov, a regiment of naval infantry from the Black Sea Fleet, and students of the Moscow All-Arms Academy of the Verkhnogo Soviet (Upper Council) of the RSFSR, and many other units on parade.

The mechanised part of the parade consisted of armoured vehicles belonging to the Tamanskaya Motorised Rifle Division named after M. I. Kalinin, and T-72s of the Kantemirovskaya Tank Division, and as always a mix of ground and air defence artillery and missile systems. Columns

The appearance of decommissioned SU-122-54 tank destroyers reconfigured as TOP parade recovery vehicles was the first public acknowledgement that the SU-122-54 had ever existed.

Soviet Army and local military parades were also held in Warsaw Pact countries during the 1980s, such as these (GDR /DDR) service T-72M (Obiekt-172M) main battle tanks on parade in East Germany. (Yuri Pasholok)

of BRDM-2 based 9P148 anti-tank missile vehicles began the parade, followed by the BTR-60PB and BMP-1 infantry combat vehicles. These were directly followed by the airborne BMD-1 (still with the original "Malyutka" ATGM) and by the T-72 main battle tanks, all covered in snow, with UAZ-469B light vehicles leading the individual columns.

The 1979 parade had a relatively rare display of towed artillery, with twelve MT-LB multi-purpose tracked vehicles towing 100mm MT-12 (2A29) "Rapira" smoothbore anti-tank guns, and ZiL-131 trucks towing the D-30 howitzer following the 2S1 self-propelled howitzers on to Red Square, and the now parade standard 9K51 (BM-21) "Grad" MRS mounted on the Ural-375D chassis. The 2S3 "Akatsiya" was however absent having made its debut appearance in November 1977.

Air defence was unchanged. The 9K33 "Osa" (NATO: Gecko) SAM system with its 5km altitude and 10km range engagement envelope was still displayed in its original 9A33B SPU vehicle configuration with four open mounted 9M33 rockets. Twelve S-25 "Berkut" and twelve S-75 "Dvina" (later "Volkhov") SAM rockets were towed on their semi-trailers by ZiL-131V tractor vehicles, together with the ZiL-131 based PR-14M TZM trans-loader vehicle for the S-125M "Neva-M" SAM.

The parade culminated by late 1970s tradition with a display of limited range OTR tactical rockets, consisting in 1977 of six 9P113 "Luna-M" SPU vehicles followed directly by the parade finale display of four 9P117M SPU vehicles for the "Elbrus" (NATO: Scud B) tactical rocket system, followed by three rearguard UAZ-469Bs in what was a Red Square parade of "defensive" weapons.

The last weeks of the 1970s were eventful for the Soviet Union, due to the series of events that had been unfolding in Afghanistan in the last two years of the decade, the repercussions of which would reverberate through to the present day. In September 1979, Nur Muhammed Taraki had been overthrown as leader in Afghanistan by Hafizullah Amin, who had proven less than stable and rather more friendly to the United States mission in Afghanistan than the Soviet Union considered healthy. The United States was as related having its own difficulties in Iran, and the Middle East was yet again becoming unstable, which from a Soviet perspective was a major concern. This was not least because the Soviet Republics on the southern border of the Soviet empire at the time lacked a comprehensive strategic air defence system, whereby any American or NATO move in countries such as Afghanistan could from a Soviet viewpoint leave the soft underbelly of the Soviet Union critically exposed to any potential attack through such "aligned" countries.

Changes in government, and an increasingly unstable regime in Afghanistan (with Hafizullah

Some significant weapons systems never appeared on Red Square. The RSD-10 "Pioner" (NATO: SS-20 Saber) was accepted for service on 11th March 1976 and was deployed from 1977 to 1983. The early 15U106 SPU vehicle was based on the MAZ-547V chassis.

Though it began to enter service from 1977, the RSD-10 "Pioner" was never paraded on Red Square before being decommissioned in accordance with the INF Treaty on intermediate-range nuclear weapons. The later 15U106 SPU vehicle was based on the MAZ-7916 chassis with larger cabs.

Amin being in Soviet eyes the governing factor in this situation) was causing wider instability that was endangering the southern flank of the Soviet Union. The Politburo agonized in December 1979 as to whether a Soviet military intervention could be avoided, knowing that the existing situation could potentially de-stabilise the Islamic Soviet southern republics, thereby weakening the Soviet Union's southern border. Direct action by the Soviet Union would inevitably lead to American support for anti-Soviet adversaries in the region. The murder of Soviet civilians in Afghanistan was however the final straw that led to Soviet Premier Leonid Brezhnev reluctantly agreeing in December 1979 to a military solution to a problem that the Soviet Union would have preferred not to have engaged with. The Soviet Chief of the General Staff, General Ogarkov, a highly qualified engineer by education, was opposed to the potential deployment of a "limited contingent" of up to 80,000 troops in Afghanistan, on the basis that such a small (by Soviet standards) number of conventional troops could never hope to operate effectively in such a large and mountainous country with limited road infrastructure. He was over-ruled by the Defence Minister, Dmitry Ustinov, a career politician and civilian, who had no such doubts. The result was that the socialist Soviet Union was forced to invade a formerly non-communist country to overthrow its new communist leaning but troublesome leadership, which was potentially undermining the southern republics of the Soviet Union. The subject of Afghanistan was from a Soviet perspective defence of the realm rather than manoeuvring on political system preferences.

On 24th December 1979, advance elements of the Soviet 40th Army invaded Afghanistan. Airborne forces, consisting of three VDV airborne divisions totalling 24,000 men and supported by BMD-1 airborne vehicles seized the Tark Tajberg palace in Kabul, deposed and executed the troublesome president Hafizullah Amin and installed a more compliant regime in Kabul, in a prelude to what would become a decade long war in the country. The main armoured elements of the Soviet 40th Army, spearheaded by the 285th Regiment, crossed the Amu-Darya river from Termez in southern Uzbekistan, the 24th Guards crossed near Kushka, while the 234th Regiment crossed into Afghanistan over a narrow pass in the Pamir mountains. Amin was assassinated by Soviet Spetznaz troops on 27th December 1979 during "Operation Shturm-333" (Storm-333). The Soviet explanation for the invasion was the not unreasonable concern that events in Afghanistan would lead to the growth in Islamic fundamentalism in the predominantly Muslim southern republics of the Soviet Union. While the United States was and would increasingly be a proxy opponent of the Soviet Union in the war in Afghanistan, the American government was at the time of the Soviet invasion effectively being forced to face down the very same issue that year in the country on Afghanistan's western border.

The détente of the 1970s had gradually eroded from the very beginning of the decade, but there was nevertheless no return to the strategic level nuclear annihilation rhetoric of the early 1960s as the Mutually Assured Destruction (MAD) concept remained as 1980 approached as valid as it had been in 1970.

The United States was meantime more concerned with and focused on the situation in Iran, and was initially taken by surprise by the Soviet intervention in Afghanistan. The British and Amercian backed Shah of Iran had fled his country at the beginning of the year and by November 1979 as the Red Square parade was underway in Moscow, he was in a hospital in the United States receiving medical treatment, much to the chagrin of Ayatollah Khomeini in Iran. The following week, as American - Iranian relations spiralled ever downward, the United States on 12th November 1979 began its embargo on Iranian crude exports, having only four days before the Soviet incursion into Afghanistan itself considered a direct military attack on Iran's offshore islands. For the moment, the United States was not considering the Soviet situation in Afghanistan particularly closely, as it had more immediate issues to resolve. A few months later, as the Soviet campaign in Afghanistan was underway, the devastating Iran-Iraq war broke out.

The Soviet 40th Army, the tank element of which was later predominantly based on T-62 MBTs, would be engaged in combat operations in Afghanistan for almost a decade. During that time 1,340 tanks were damaged in combat, most of which were returned to service, with approximately 385 tanks destroyed beyond repair. The Soviet War in Afghanistan would continue under the successive leadership of Brezhnev, Chernenko, Andropov and finally Gorbachov, the latter being Soviet Premier when the war was concluded. The war in Afghanistan, which was deeply unpopular with the Soviet population, particularly the families of those soldiers sent to the seemingly ungovernable country which even the once mighty British Empire had failed to bring to order, cost the lives of approximately 15,000 Soviet servicemen and women. The combat experience in the mountainous country, fighting an insurgent rather than a conventional military opponent, would directly lead to the modification of several military vehicle types that would subsequently be displayed on Red Square.

The 2S6 "Tunguska" self-propelled air defence system was also not displayed on Red Square in the late 1980s, though at the time entering Soviet Army service. These 2S6 vehicles are on display in Samara on 9th May 1995. The vehicle would be seen on parade in Moscow only in 2008. (Mikhail Baryatinsky)

2S5 self-propelled howitzers on display in Samara in 1995. The 152mm calibre 2S5 is one of several GRAU "2S" series self-propelled weapons never displayed on Red Square, but seen in other regional cities. (Mikhail Baryatinsky)

The T-72 main battle tank was demonstrated on Red Square from 1977 until the last Soviet era parade in November 1990. During these years the original T-72 was replaced by the T-72A seen here and finally the T-72B. (TASS)

The 1980s

The Soviet Union began the 1980s with the country deeply involved in a war in Afghanistan that would also develop into a proxy-war with the United States, the latter backing the local Afghan "Mujahidin". The Soviet Army quickly secured the major cities and supply routes in Afghanistan, and even from the viewpoint of United States military analysts, Afghanistan for the Soviet Union looked in 1980 like a mission accomplished. The decade began with an ineffectual boycott of the Moscow Olympics by some countries in 1980 related directly to the December 1979 invasion of Afghanistan, followed by American President Ronald Reagan introducing a new era of American military defence spending after his appointment to office in January 1981. During the forthcoming decade the United States spent an inordinate amount of effort in supporting the "Mujahidin" against the Soviet Army in Afghanistan, but otherwise it was a relatively benign "business as usual" between the superpowers in the 1980s, albeit with the Cold War becoming somewhat frostier in the 1980s than it had been in the previous decade.* The incoming American President Ronald Reagan, who would serve from January 1981 until 1989, was opposed in principle to the SALT-2 agreement as signed by his predecessor President Carter in 1979, but agreed to abide by the treaty (never ratified by the US) as it had been signed until its expiry date on 31st December 1985.

There were some changes in the configuration of Red Square military parades during these years, but the era of strategic rockets crossing the square directly outside the Kremlin walls had died out in the mid 1970s, and contemporary Soviet strategic missile systems such as the 5,000km range RSD-10 "Pioner" (NATO: SS-20 Saber) MRBM which would have culminated parades in the previous decade were conspicuous by their absence. The military parades of the 1980s were less overt as a statement of Soviet military capacity, reflecting that the Cold War was in decline, and being replaced by a period of superpower détente. With the SALT-1 and SALT-2 nuclear treaties in place, attention in the 1980s turned towards the Intermediate Range Nuclear Forces (INF) Treaty which would be signed between the Soviet Union and the United States in 1987, and which would see the elimination of several of the Soviet Union's mobile strategic rocket systems, including the RSD-10 "Pioner" MRBM which was never in consequence paraded on Red Square. Soviet military parades were devoid of strategic medium and long-range rocket systems in the 1980s, continuing the largely defensive displays of the late 1970s. The majority of Soviet military parades in the 1980s culminated with 9P113 "Luna-M" (NATO: FROG-7) and finally with 9P117M (NATO: SS-1 Scud B) OTR systems taking up the parade rear-guard, with the 9P120 (9K76) "Temp-S" (NATO: SS-12 Scaleboard) vehicle being displayed for the last time in a cameo appearance in November 1985.

---

* Zbigniew Brzezinski, the former National Security Advisor to President Carter in his memoirs described the Soviet invasion of Afghanistan as the "Afghan Trap". He also admitted that the CIA began training the Mujahidin in July 1979, six months before the Soviet intervention into the country.

The 1980s were also largely devoid of new vehicle debuts on Red Square. The BTR-70 wheeled APC made its first public appearance on Red Square in 1980, but the majority of new vehicles were otherwise minor modifications of existing designs, the main exception being the introduction of new airborne vehicles such as the 2S9 "Nona-S" airborne SPM and the BTR-D airborne APC.

Not widely known at the time, either at home in the Soviet Union or abroad, the 1980s was also the decade when the US and the Soviet Union again came close to nuclear war based on a series of unrelated events which were misinterpreted by the ailing Soviet leadership. President Ronald Reagan had made it clear on coming to office in January 1981 that he would increase the US defence budget exponentially, which was duly carried through, and would also develop the Strategic Defence Initiative (SDI) effectively taking the nuclear "arms race", at least theoretically, into space. A single event occurred in November 1983, which was effectively more dangerous than the Cuban Missile Crisis in the autumn of 1962, but it was not until many years later that details of the incident entered the public domain.

The reality of the 1980s extra-planetary spike in the "arms race" was that in the 1980s the technical capability of even the United States trailed behind the Hollywood based aspirations of its president. However the perceived increased threat to the Soviet Union, coupled with an unstable period of Soviet leadership due to a very human combination of age and ill health, led to a period of retrenchment, while the costs of the Cold War simultaneously increased exponentially on both sides of the Atlantic, and the Soviet Union was meantime losing the economic ability to compete financially with the United States. The election of a relatively young (by most recent Soviet standards) Mikhail Gorbachov as Soviet Premier in March 1985 would signal yet another new era in Soviet politics, and ironically under the leadership of a young and energetic leader, the era of terminal decline for the Soviet Union. The Soviet Union would decline rapidly under Gorbachov, as the former centrally controlled State checks and balances began to be disregarded.

Meanwhile, the populations of some Eastern European countries, particularly Poland and Yugoslavia were experiencing a period of significant austerity for much of the decade. The origins of these financial difficulties were in no small part related to over-borrowing from Western banks in the 1970s and difficulty in repaying the higher rates of interest now being charged on these loans in the 1980s. This would lead to popular discontent and open protest aimed at the current system, and the Soviet Union, rather than at the Western banks and the financial beneficiaries of the Eastern European debt situation. Regardless of origin, the pressures for autonomy began to build in the 1980s, with Poland at the forefront, and these demands for change would also cross the border into the Soviet Union.

1980

The Soviet collective memory of the 1980s was dominated by the war in Afghanistan and a psychological hardening of attitudes after the Moscow Olympics. The war in Afghanistan had initially been a strategic success for the Soviet Union, but as with the United States in Vietnam the war quickly turned to one of attrition. By October 1980 as many as 900,000 Afghan refugees had relocated into neighbouring Pakistan which would in turn become a staging ground for Mujahidin attacks in the region. Meanwhile in the United States, the right-wing Republican Party candidate Ronald Reagan was on 4th November elected President of the United States. Reagan's viewpoint towards the Soviet Union was far less accommodating than that of his predecessor President James (Jimmy)

Carter. The Chairman of the Council of Ministers Alexsey Kosygin, one of the stalwarts of late Soviet era diplomacy alongside Brezhnev died in 1980 and was replaced by Nikolai Tikhonov, with Brezhnev himself dying in November 1982. The Soviet "Old Guard" was literally dying out, and the late 1970s had been the calm before the next storm in Soviet relations with the United States and its Western affiliates.

7th November 1980 - 63rd Anniversary of the Great October Socialist Revolution

The 7th November 1980 Red Square parade was set against the background of the Soviet Union having endured its first year of war in Afghanistan. The Soviet military contingent in Afghanistan had by the end of 1980 made significant progress in consolidating its position militarily in the country, and the United States did not at the time see great merit in getting more deeply involved with supporting opposition causes, not least because the country was preoccupied with troubles in the Middle East centred around Iran following the US Embassy hostage crisis which had started on 4th November 1979 and would continue into early 1981. The difficulties that the Soviet Union would later face in tribal led Afghanistan were in 1980 still in the future, and in November 1980 the Soviet Union seemed firmly in control of the situation in the country. The 1980 summer Moscow Olympic Games had been boycotted by the United States and several other countries as a direct diplomatic response to the Soviet invasion of Afghanistan, but the overall impact of the gesture

The BTR-70 had its public debut during the 7th November 1980 Red Square parade. (TASS)

The BTR-70 featured a reconfigured hull, now with small access doors between the second and third axles. The engine and transmission arrangement was also modified, but the vehicle retained the turret and armament of the BTR-60.

politics had been minimal. The Soviet intervention in Afghanistan would however set the scene for Soviet-American relationships for the majority of the 1980s.

The 63rd Anniversary parade of the Great October Socialist Revolution as held on 7th November 1980 was commanded by the Soviet Defence Minister, Marshal of the Soviet Union Dmitry F. Ustinov, with Leonid Brezhnev on the Lenin Mausoleum review stand. With light snow falling on the square, the parade contained few major surprises, and this pattern would continue throughout the last decade of the Soviet Union. The parade began as usual with a meeting of the parade commanders, standing in ZiL-117V open cabriolet parade cars, with the military vehicle columns led by UAZ-469B light vehicles as had been the case since 1973.

The parade began with drummers and cymbalists, followed by students of the Black Sea Fleet Academy named after N.S. Nakhimovsky, columns of VDV airborne forces, naval infantry, and students of the Moscow "Mossoviet" Higher Border Guards Command School amongst many others. There were marching columns of infantry from the "Dzerzhinsky" Division, the Moscow and Kalinin "Suvorov" cadets, the Leningrad "Nakhimovsky" Naval Academy, and the All-Arms Command School of the Verkhnogo Sovieta (Upper Council) of the RSFSR and all the regular and reserve service of the Soviet Army, Soviet Navy and Soviet Air Force, border guards and other military and paramilitary units.

The mechanised part of the parade was as always led by armoured vehicles of the 2nd Guards Tamanskaya Motorised Rifle Division named after Kalinin, with tanks of the 4th Kantemirovskaya Tank Division, accompanied as always by VDV airborne forces, towed artillery, and finally OTR rockets. The military vehicles on parade in 1980 were painted in standard green with white parade markings, with Guards markings where appropriate to the military units on parade.

The parade was led by columns of BRDM-2 based 9P148 ATGM vehicles, followed by BMP-1 and BMD-1 infantry combat vehicles presenting Soviet Army ground and airborne forces respectively. The venerable BTR-60 series which had been paraded in consecutive P, PA and PB variants on Red Square since 1961 was from 1980 replaced by the BTR-70, which made its public debut on 7th November 1980. T-72 main battle tanks of the Kantemirovskaya Tank Division were displayed, followed by artillery including the 100mm MT-12 (2A29) smoothbore anti-tank gun towed by the MT-LB multi-purpose armoured vehicle and the 2S1 self-propelled howitzer. The 2S1 self-propelled howitzers were followed directly by ZiL-131 6x6 trucks towing the 122mm D-30 howitzer, a display of mixed towed and mechanised self-propelled artillery in the same parade at a time when the GRAU designation "2S" series of self-propelled artillery was entering service in the Soviet Army in significant numbers.

In general the Red Square parade line-up would change little during the 1980s. The 2P24 tracked launch vehicle for the 2K11 "Krug" SAM system made its last public appearance in 1980, paraded alongside the early production 9A33B SPU vehicle for the 9K33 "Osa" SAM on its wheeled BAZ-5937 chassis (i.e. still the original version with four rockets on open launcher mountings). A further modified version of the system was accepted into service with PVO forces of the Soviet Army in 1980 as the 9K33M3 "Osa-AKM" and would appear on Red Square from 1982.

The ZiL-131 had long replaced the earlier production ZiL-157 as a general transport and semi-trailer tractor vehicle on Red Square displays, with the 1980 parade including the ZiL-131 based PR-14M TZM vehicle for the S-125 "Neva-M" and as the ZiL-131V tractor vehicle for the S-25 and S-75 surface-to-air missile systems. The long-serving Ural-375D continued on parade as the base chassis for the 9K51 (BM-21) MRS. The final rocket systems paraded in 1980 were four 9P113 "Luna-M" (NATO: FROG-7) and four 9P117M SPU vehicles for the 9K72 "Elbrus" (NATO: Scud-B), with the longer range 9P120 "Temp-S" SPU vehicles no longer being displayed. As such the 1980 parade continued the benign "defensive" status of all Soviet parades since 1974.

Meantime, one of the stalwart countries of the Warsaw Pact, Poland, was suffering austerity in part related to the increasing cost of servicing Western bank loans taken out in the 1970s. A strike at the Lenin Shipyards in Gdansk had in August 1980 been resolved by the leadership of the new workers Trade Union "Solidarity", led by a charismatic orator, Lech Wałęsa. This seemingly localised event in Poland would be followed by increasing instability in the country and the ultimate imposition of martial law, followed by calls for free elections and independence. The event was the first crack in a post-war political structure and system of government and military security that had remained stable for almost four decades. The strike was effectively the first organised demand during the 1980s for change in the prevailing system, and ultimately independence, that would in the decade ahead spread throughout the countries of the Warsaw Pact, into the Soviet Republics and into the heart of the Soviet Union itself.

The 9P148 ATGM vehicle based on the BRDM-2 chassis mounted a retractable launcher fitted with five transport/launch containers for the 9K113 "Konkurs" ATGM. (Steven J. Zaloga)

1981

1981 was another quiet year domestically for the Soviet Union, with the primary international focus being on the ongoing war in Afghanistan. The 1981 Soviet Census showed however that the Russian national indigenous population had dropped from 55% of the Soviet total in 1959 to 52% in 1979. This in of itself was not a hugely significant drop over two decades, but it reflected a pattern of which Khrushchev had been well aware when handing Crimea to Ukraine in 1954 as a bolster to "solidarity" between the core Soviet bloc members - the Russian RSFSR and the Soviet Republics of Ukraine and Belorussia. Family size was decreasing in these core Soviet countries, as it was in Europe, but in the southern Soviet Republics such as Kyrgyzstan, Tajikistan and Uzbekistan the population was increasingly exponentially. This was partly as a result of the provision of better medical services and consequent child survival rates due to these and other support services in the less developed and infinitely poorer Soviet Republics. The Soviet Union was by 1981 very cognisant of a demographic clock that was also ticking in other regions of the world. The approaching collapse of the Soviet Union was in part related to the inability of the central Soviet bloc countries to finance and feed a growing population in the southern republics that were in economic terms largely unproductive. When the Soviet Union collapsed a decade later, vast numbers of people from these newly independent republics, having gained full autonomy to govern themselves, actually left their home countries to seek employment, and often safety, in the Russian Federation they had petitioned hard to be independent from. Independence from the Soviet Union would bring personal responsibility for those individual governments, but as is often the case, the more educated and motivated native citizens of these countries needed to emigrate to find stable employment, education and a future for themselves and their families after independence.

By the time of the 7th November 1981 Red Square parade, relationships between the Soviet Union and the United States had changed significantly since the previous November, and not for the better. On 20th January 1981, the former Hollywood actor Ronald Reagan had taken office as President of the United States, replacing James (Jimmy) Carter. Reagan was far more militaristic than President Carter had been with regard to the Soviet Union, ushering in a period of significant increases in defence spending and new technology developments, some largely imaginary, with which the Soviet Union would have difficulty competing economically. Reagan made it clear from the outset that he did not believe in the Mutually Assured Destruction (MAD) nuclear stalemate principle which had held the superpowers in check since 1949, and that Carter's pragmatic "live and let live" attitude to relationships with the Soviet Union was at an end. He authorised a massive State spending program on military technology, which included conventional weapons and the development of the Strategic Defence Initiative (SDI), that would later become known as "Star Wars", involving potential laser technology anti-missile systems being located in space. President Reagan made good on his plans, increasing US defence spending 50% (to 7% of national GDP) during his first term in office, and by re-introducing projects such as the strategic B1 bomber that had earlier been scrapped by President Carter. The nuclear-armed Pershing-II ballistic missile was also prepared for deployment in Europe. All of this would be achieved at the expense of increasing the US national debt, which rose from $1 trillion to $4 trillion during the decade, while domestic welfare programmes were cut back. The Soviet Union was during the 1980s also beginning to suffer from the financial strains of trying to compete militarily with the United States; however with the customary benefit of hindsight the latter country was not in of itself in a great financial position to be upping the stakes in the game of international poker. But at the time the Soviet Union had no way to know for sure that their bluff was being called. The Cold War was in the 1980s fought as a proxy war, primarily in Afghanistan, while not for the first or last time in the century between the Russian Revolution in 1917 and the present day the real war was conducted on the economic front.

The inauguration of Ronald Reagan resulted in a new chill being introduced into what had in recent years been a tepid Cold War. After the new stance again brought the nuclear superpowers to the brink of war in 1983, that policy would be significantly re-thought by Reagan, and a fresh period of conciliation would emerge, with nuclear arms reduction becoming the main theme later in the decade. The Soviet Union continued to play chess, while the United States continued to play poker.

In May of 1981, General Secretary Leonid Brezhnev met with KGB Chairman Yuri Andropov and the Soviet leadership in a closed session to review the deteriorating relationship with the United States, and hence NATO, since the inauguration of Reagan as President of the United States in January. The subject of the meeting was American preparations for potential nuclear war with the Soviet Union. As a direct result of the meeting, the GRU (Soviet military intelligence) was tasked with exponentially increasing all intelligence gathering in order to ascertain the likelihood and timing of such a nuclear attack. The intelligence gathering operation was designated "Operation RYaN" (Raketnoe Yadernoe Napadeniye - Nuclear Missile Attack). In November 1983 the results of this intelligence gathering operation, linked to a series of misinterpreted events would again bring the world to the brink of nuclear war.

The 1981 year ended with a footnote that would be indicative of the trouble fermenting in the years ahead. On 13th December, due to increased civil disorder in Poland, the communist government under Prime Minister Wojciech Jaruzelski was given permission by Moscow to establish martial law in Poland, and outlaw the "Solidarity" union that had grown in strength and influence after the strikes in the Gdansk shipyards. Post-war Eastern European history was repeating, now in Poland rather than Hungary or Czechoslovakia, but the result would be different from either 1956 or 1968.

7th November 1981 – 64th Anniversary of the Great October Socialist Revolution

The 7th November 1981 parade, the 109th military parade on Red Square, was taken by Marshal of the Soviet Union Dmitry. F. Ustinov, with the parade commander being the MVO commander, General Petr G. Lushev. The venerable hand-built ZiL-117V cabriolet parade cars used by parade commanders for many years were from 1981 replaced by the equally hand-built ZiL-41044 cabriolet version of the ZiL-4104 limousine.

The parade line up repeated that of November 1980. The military academies that formed a major part of the all-arms parade were as always well represented, including the Military Academy in the name of M.V. Frunze, the Military-Political Academy in the name of Lenin, the Military Engineering Academy in the name of F. Eh. Dzerzhinsky and the Military Academy of Armoured Forces named after Marshal of the Soviet Union R. Ya.

Malinovsky. There were representatives of the Air Force Academy named after Yu. A. Gagarin, and the Air Force Engineering Academy named after N.E. Zhukovsky, the Military Engineering Academy in the name of V.V. Kuibyshev, and the Military Chemical Defence Academy named after Marshal of the Soviet Union S.K. Timoshenko. Cadets of the Leningrad Higher Naval Engineering Academy named after F. Ye. Dzerzhinsky were paraded, as were VDV airborne forces, and cadets of the Moscow Higher Border Troops Academy, amongst many others.

The mechanised parade line-up was almost identical to 1980. Columns of UAZ-469B light vehicles were followed by 9P148 anti-tank missile launcher vehicles based on the BRDM-2 chassis. The latest generation BTR-70 wheeled APC which had debuted in 1980 was again on display, as was the original BMP-1, still armed with the 73mm 2A28 "Grom" low pressure gun and "Malyutka" ATGM system, followed directly by the airborne BMD-1, also still in its original configuration with the same turret armament as the BMP-1. The T-72 tanks on display were now the T-72A modification, the most obvious change being the new main gun sighting, repositioned 902 series "Tucha"* smoke dischargers and the fitment of side skirts protecting the running gear. The tanks were followed directly by ground artillery systems. The ubiquitous but rarely seen MT-LB tracked multi-purpose vehicle towed the 100mm MT-12 (2A29) "Rapira" anti-tank gun, followed by the tracked self-propelled 2S1 and 2S3M, the latter having made its parade debut as a cameo appearance in 1977. The 2K51 (BM-21) "Grad" MRS followed, mounted on the Ural-375D 6x6 truck chassis. Air defence consisted of the original 9A33B SPU vehicle for the "Osa" with its four 9M33 rockets mounted in an open configuration, followed by ZiL-131 S-125M "Neva-M" PR-14M TZM vehicles, but no S-25 or S-75 SAM systems in 1981. The parade concluded with the 9P113 "Luna-M" on its BAZ-135 8x8 chassis (NATO: FROG-7) - now in service for nearly two decades - and the 9P117M SPU vehicle for the 9K72 "Elbrus" (NATO: Scud-B) on the MAZ-543A 8x8 chassis as the most formidable OTR system on display.

A BTR-70 returns from the November 1981 parade. The BTR-70 was a relatively short-lived Red Square parade participant, being replaced by the BTR-80 in 1987.

* The 902 "Tucha" was a standardised smoke discharger system developed for use on main battle tanks, BMPs and BTRs. It was built in 902A, 902B, 902V and 902G variants. The system had a range of 300m.

1982

On 10th November 1982, Soviet Premier Brezhnev, who had led the country for eighteen years during the apex of the Soviet Union's military strength and internal stability and prosperity died at the age of 75, and was replaced by KGB chief Yuri Andropov, who became General Secretary of the CPSU on 12th November. The Soviet Union was about to undergo a period of rapid changes in leadership which would greatly weaken the Soviet State.

7th November 1982 - 65th Anniversary of the Great October Socialist Revolution

The 7th November 1982 parade, the 110th military parade on Red Square, was as in 1981 taken by Soviet Defence Minister Dmitry Ustinov, with the parade commander again being General Petr Lushev. The 7th November 1982 military parade was the last to be presided over by Leonid Brezhnev as Soviet Premier. Visibly ill as he reviewed the parade, Brezhnev died only three days later. The Soviet Premier who had presided over the Soviet Union for 18 years was gone, and was replaced in the role of General Secretary of the CPSU on 10th November 1982 by Yuri Andropov, who was himself already 69 years old and also in poor health. His credentials were however impeccable. He had formerly been head of the KGB, being the first ex chief of the State security service to be elected to

The T-72A, introduced from 1980, introduced many improvements, including reconfigured sighting, 902 series "Tucha" smoke dischargers and standard side skirts.

the position of Soviet Premier. He had little foreign international experience, though what experience he had was more than appropriate. His only foray abroad had been in 1956, when he had visited Hungary in the company of Soviet troops that had at his instigation entered the country to crush the Hungarian uprising. Although Andropov proved an able caretaker Soviet Premier, his health failed within months of him taking office, and he spent much of 1983 in Kuntsevo hospital on the western outskirts of Moscow. As rapid changes of elderly leadership ensued, the Soviet Union was entering a period of instability, and terminal decline.

The parade line up for November 1982 almost exactly repeated that of 1981, with as always a few subtle changes such as the Red Square parade debut of the modernized BMP-2, replacing the original BMP-1 after a period of 15 years, and also the debut of the newer 9A33BM3 SPU vehicle for the 9K33M3 "Osa-AKM" (NATO: SA-8 Gecko) version of the BAZ-5937 based short-range SAM system, now mounting six containerised rather than four open-mounted 9M33 series rockets.* The BTR-70 remained the standard wheeled APC, the T-72A the only MBT on display, with the MT-LB the tracked multipurpose vehicle towing the 100mm MT-12 (2A29) anti-tank gun. The ZiL-131V 6x6 tractor towed the S-25 and S-75 SAM rockets. As in recent years, the 9P117 (9P117M) SPU vehicle for the 9K72 "Elbrus" OTR was the most powerful rocket system on display.

The BMP-2 made its Red Square public debut appearance in November 1982, replacing the original BMP (BMP-1), that had been a parade regular since 1967.

* The original 9K33 "Osa" SAM system was followed in production by the 9K33M2 "Osa-AK" and associated 9A33BM2 SPU vehicle, now mounting six containerised rockets. This was rapidly superseded by the 9K33M3 "Osa-AKM" and associated 9A33BM3 SPU vehicle. The latter SPU vehicle featured updated electronics and was externally indistinguishable from the 9A33BM2.

The modernised 9A33BM3 "Osa-AKM" version of the original 9K33 "Osa" also made its parade debut appearance in November 1982.

The BTR-70 was replaced by the BTR-80 on Moscow's Red Square from 1987, but remained on parade in other cities for many years thereafter. These BTR-70s are on parade in Riga, Latvia on 7th November 1990. (TASS).

1983

In February 1983 Soviet Premier Andropov became chronically ill, and was admitted to Kuntsevo hospital on a near permanent basis. His poor health and relative isolation were not conducive to strong leadership, but there were no alternative candidates with both the required experience and the general good health able to take over the reigns of leadership. Meantime, in the United States, President Ronald Reagan in March 1983 declared the Soviet leadership: *"the focus of evil in the modern world."*, an accolade which has been given to several other inconvenient countries in the years since that time. He then on 23rd March also announced the Strategic Defence Initiative (SDI) popularly known as the "Star Wars" program, which would theoretically cancel out the potential of Mutually Assured Destruction (MAD) that had hitherto held the superpowers in a state of check and balance. After the period of détente in the 1970s, a decade during which the Soviet Union had first reduced its display of strategic nuclear rockets on Red Square and then eliminated them altogether, the United States in the early 1980s was viewed by the Kremlin as once again newly aggressive.

At the very time that the United States under Reagan was reasserting its military might and had begun, theoretically at least, developing viable space weapons that the Soviet Union did not have the financial resources to compete with on yet another "front", the country was facing a perceived military crisis. In an effort to forestall further pressures on defence expenditures, Andropov in August 1983 announced that the country was stopping the development of space-based weapons. Meanwhile, the GRU intelligence gathering operation authorised by Soviet Premier Brezhnev in May 1981 when Andropov was the head of the KGB confirmed in 1983 an increasing number of activities deemed a threat to the Soviet Union. These activities were not always directly related to the Soviet Union, and in some cases not at all related, but it was the task of the GRU to determine and analyse all threats to the State, so as to allow a military response as required, and that is what almost transpired as events combined to reach a crisis point in November 1983.

7th November 1983 – 66th Anniversary of the Great October Socialist Revolution

The 7th November military parade, the 111th military parade on Red Square was considered at the time both domestically and internationally as simply another annual parade of Soviet military might. In retrospect, and with the benefit of information released since the break up of the Soviet Union from both Russian and NATO country sources, the Cold War almost turned hot the same week, while people around the world were oblivious to the events that had unfolded, which did not enter the public domain at the time, or for many years thereafter. The majority of the world's population has remained oblivious of the events to the present day.

The 7th November 1983 military parade, by contrast with events unfolding in Europe and Soviet leadership preparations in response to these events, remained a positively low-key event. The parade, as usual taken by Soviet Defence Minister Marshal Dmitry Ustinov, began with UAZ-469Bs leading 9P148 ATGM vehicles per 1980s tradition, with the modernised T-72A remaining the primary Soviet main battle tank on display even though the T-80 MBT was long in service. Despite its widespread use in the Soviet Army, the MT-LB was rarely seen, but was paraded on Red Square in the early 1980s towing the 100mm MT-12 (2A29) "Rapira" anti-tank gun. November 1983 was also the parade debut of the BMD-1P modernisation of the original BMD airborne combat vehicle, which had been introduced on Red Square in 1974, now armed with a 9P135M launcher for the "Konkurs" ATGM replacing the 1960's era "Malyutka". Other parade standards such as the 2S1 self-propelled howitzer and the 9K33M3 "Oka-AKM" SAM system were displayed, with the parade finale being the 9P117M SPU vehicle for the 9K72 "Elbrus" tactical rocket as the longest-range weapon on display.

It was however occurrences transpiring far from Red Square that were of more military importance in November 1983. A series of unrelated events had led up to the situation as it unfolded in November, just as the parade preparations

T-72A main battle tanks move down Gorky Street towards Red Square for the 7th November 1983 Red Square parade.

were underway in Moscow. Talks on MRBM and SRBM deployment in Europe were suspended by the USSR in November 1983 as relations with the US deteriorated, but the situation was far more serious than the postponing of meetings on nuclear weapons.

In March 1983, American President Ronald Reagan had as noted begun the American "Star Wars" Strategic Defence Initiative (SDI). This was a new military angle on the space race whereby a system of ground and space based weapons would provide a missile defence shield, effectively negating the "Mutually Assured Destruction" (MAD) concept which had held the superpowers in check since the Soviet Union caught up with the United States by exploding its first atomic weapon in 1949. Nearly a decade after the events of 1983, the United States would admit that the programme was technically unfeasible without a minimum further decade of development, but by then the Soviet Union that it was aimed against had ceased to exist. The program was formally scrapped in 1993, two years after the dissolution of the Soviet Union which had in the meantime accelerated its own "Buran" programme as a direct Soviet response to the US "Challenger" space shuttle programme. Though the military aspects of this programme remain classified to the present time, one of the principal aims of the Soviet program during the 1980s was the delivery of weapons into space that were capable of intercepting and destroying the mythical laser weapons that the United States planned to deploy there as part of President Reagan's SDI program. The American threat was almost pure Hollywood - the program was perhaps not incidentally named after the 1977 Sci-fi film - but the development cost of finding an antidote was for the Soviet Union very much reality. It was the escalating costs of military programmes such as "Buran" that would lead to the Soviet Union finally accepting that it could, or should, not continue to compete economically with American military developments, real or imaginary.

Since March 1983, the Soviet leadership had acknowledged their new position of being: "the *focus of evil in the modern world.*" as announced by President Reagan as he had ramped up US military spending, and unveiled the SDI "Star Wars" program. The Soviet Union had as noted earlier accordingly increased GRU intelligence gathering

The modernised BMD-1P made its public debut appearance on 7th November 1983.

initiated with "Operation RYaN" two years earlier. It was well understood by the Soviet leadership that the rhetoric coming from the United States, coupled with increased military expenditure, required the Soviet Union to respond as appropriate to new superpower hostilities that the previous decade had already seemed to be in the past.

The political situation was worsened by an incident on 1st September 1983 that seems familiar with regard to the recent history of modern Russian relationships with the United States and some countries in Europe and elsewhere. On that date, Flight KL-007, a civilian South Korean Airlines Boeing 747 aircraft en-route from New York to Seoul via Anchorage, drifted several hundred kilometres north of its intended course, taking it first over Soviet Kamchatka and then Sakhalin Island. The aircraft was shot down by a Soviet fighter and crashed into the sea near the unpopulated Moneron Island west of Sakhalin, with the loss of 269 passengers and crew, including a serving US congressman, Larry McDonald.

The exact circumstances as to why the aircraft was so far off course and the reasoning for it being shot down are not clearly defined from published information. A United States Air Force RC-135 reconnaissance aircraft was also in the area at the time but it remains unknown if the civilian aircraft was misidentified as the latter. Soviet divers found only limited wreckage and no identifiable human remains, but did manage to recover the flight cockpit voice recorders, the contents of which were released in 1992, showing that whatever the circumstances, the KL-007 pilots were relaxed and unaware of both their errant flight path and their impending predicament. The facts of the KL-007 tragedy have never been categorically established, however President Reagan lost no time in denouncing the shooting down of KL-007 as a terrorist act, and with that the already difficult relations between the Soviet Union and the United States deteriorated further. The downing of Flight KL-007 was however just the beginning, as within weeks, a series of unfortunate and unrelated events would come together culminating in a potential nuclear war scenario.

A single incident, and a single decision by a Soviet officer in September 1983 averted the potential for a nuclear war as relations between the Soviet Union and the United States continued to deteriorate. That month, a new Soviet satellite based early warning system detected the "launch" of five American "Minuteman" ICBMs, to which the doctrinal Soviet response was "launch on warning". The satellite had actually detected a rare alignment of sunlight on cloud cover over the

The modernised 9A33BM3 "Osa-AKM" launch vehicle version of the original 9K33 "Osa" system mounted six transport/launch containers in lieu of the four open mountings of the earlier version. The "Osa" system was in constant development in the 1970s and 1980s with the launch vehicle variants being designated 9A33, 9A33A, 9A33B, 9A33BM2 and 9A33BM3.

American "Minuteman" base, which had triggered the false warning. The duty officer that day was Colonel Stanislav Petrov, who rather than blindly following protocol reasoned that the newly commissioned system had known "bugs" which could account for false reports, and further reasoned that an all-out attack would not be confined to the launch of five rockets only. Colonel Petrov held his nerve and waited 23 minutes until ground based "Over The Horizon" radar failed to pick up the "incoming" rockets, proving the alarm to have been entirely false. Had Petrov directly followed protocol then the Soviet Union would have launched a "counter-strike" and World War Three might have occurred due to a technology glitch. The incident passed, but the level of increased international tension nevertheless continued to escalate. Colonel Petrov was reprimanded for his "insubordination", doubtless by relieved senior officers, but would continue his career, retiring with the rank of Lieutenant-Colonel. He died in Moscow in May 2017 at the age of 77. His personal experience and seasoned military judgement literally saved the day for both superpowers, though the fact that he had highlighted problems in the new missile detection systems caused him difficulty with senior officers responsible for those glitches. This individual publicised story where many others have doubtless yet to surface provides in retrospect a clear demonstration that during the Cold War the professional military personnel on both sides of the political divide were just that - professionals.*

As the terminally ill Andropov lay in his hospital bed at Kuntsevo west of Moscow, other events conspired to convince some of the Soviet leadership that war might be imminent. On becoming Soviet Premier, Andropov in answer to President Reagan's threatening rhetoric and exponentially increased budgets had, in addition to the ongoing GRU "Operation RYaN", also tasked his former KGB associates to be watchful for any change in regular military activity or communications that might signal a potential direct attack on the Soviet Union. Having been tasked with increasing vigilance, the information incoming from various military and State intelligence sources showed that there was indeed greatly increased military activity by the United States. The assumption was that this was related to the Soviet Union, and an element of paranoia took hold, doubtless not assisted by Andropov's relatively isolated hospital environment.

The BMP-1 retained the original 73mm 2A28 "Grom" main armament, but now mounted a 9P135M launcher for the 9K113 "Konkurs" ATGM system in lieu of the earlier 9M14 "Malyutka" rocket mounted over the barrel. (Mikhail Baryatinsky)

* The Man Who Saved the World. Gwynne Dyer. SME Bratislava September 2017.

Only a matter of weeks after the KL-007 incident, intelligence was in October 1983 received by the Kremlin that the United States military was being mobilised for foreign operations. This was entirely factual, but the conclusions reached by the Soviet leadership were erroneous. The US mobilisation and increased SigInt (signals intelligence) traffic was related to the Middle East - specifically Lebanon, where American peacekeeper forces had been stationed since the war there in 1982, and with the global communications actually being primarily related to a terrorist attack on the American marine base in Beirut on 23rd October. Two days later, on 25th October, American marines invaded the British Commonwealth island of Grenada in the Caribbean. The armed forces of the United States were on high alert worldwide, and SigInt traffic was correspondingly intense, but for Soviet purposes what was particularly worrying was the communication intensity between the United States and Great Britain. For the Soviet leadership, the logical conclusion was that the United States was conferring with its NATO allies and that the Soviet Union may be under threat. As President Reagan himself later admitted, some of the communications traffic from the United Kingdom was his close friend British Prime Minister Margaret Thatcher giving him a verbal "hand-bagging" for invading a British Commonwealth country without a "by your leave" from the British government.* The Soviet leadership however, by adding recent events to those of the entire year, felt the threat was very much related to the Soviet Union.

The rapidly worsening relationship between the United States and the Soviet Union came to a head in November. The bi-annual NATO exercise "Able-Archer" held in Germany in November 1983 included a SigInt scenario whereby the role-play called for a potential launch of tactical nuclear weapons by NATO, a de-facto planned defence response to an inability to hold back a Soviet armoured thrust with conventional forces for more than a few days known to all who served in NATO forces. The culmination of this series of unrelated events would come to pass the day after the 7th November 1983 Red Square military parade in Moscow.

On 8th November 1983, having increased the NATO threat status from DEFCON-5 to DEFCON-1 a SigInt role-play during Exercise "Able Archer" requested permission to launch a tactical nuclear strike against Soviet forces in Europe. This end-game but entirely role play communication was intercepted by the GRU, and relayed directly to Andropov, who by this time had the launch codes for the Soviet Union's nuclear arsenal by his bedside. The Soviet RVSN (Strategic Rocket Forces) stood the country's nuclear resources ready for immediate retaliation. Nuclear submarines deployed under the Arctic ice and close to the American coast were alerted to prepare for a potential "hot launch" of their weapons systems, land mobile RSD-10 "Pioner" (NATO: SS-20 Saber) ICBM rockets were deployed and dispersed, silo mounted rockets readied for launch and Soviet aircraft in East Germany and Poland were armed with nuclear weapons as they stood on runways with their engines idling, ready for immediate take-off.

What thoughts may have gone through Andropov's mind as he sat in his hospital room at Kuntsevo on 8th November are hard to imagine. As far as can be ascertained, pragmatic advice was provided by the Soviet military hierarchy and the Soviet intelligence services, and although the Soviet Union was primed to respond, no response was required. The NATO exercise was what it claimed to be, a training exercise, and the Soviet armed forces, in particular the RVSN strategic rocket forces were stood down. Such an absurd situation may seem with retrospect even more "Hollywood" than President Reagan's SDI "Star Wars" program, but archives released by the American CIA, British SIS and even the Soviet GRU indicate that 8th November 1983 could have been the day that World War Three began. Unlike the Cuban Missile Crisis, the events of late 1983 were for many years kept secret by both superpowers and their NATO and Warsaw Pact partners.

---
* One US strategic concern regarding Grenada was apparently the extension of the runway at the country's main airport, whereby the Soviet Union could potentially land strategic bombers in the country.

1984

The chronically ill Andropov died on 9th February 1984, and four days later was replaced by Konstantin Chernenko who was at the time also terminally ill, and would in turn remain in office for just over a year before dying in March 1985. In stark contrast to the stable Brezhnev years, the Soviet Union was going through a period of rapid changes of leadership, with the associated instability and uncertainty that these changes brought. The new era Soviet "defensive" parades of the 1980s continued apace in 1984, and on the surface all remained as before, but there were major problems developing in the Soviet economy. One indicator is that while Soviet mineral resource (primarily oil and gas) exports were 18% of total exports in 1972, this figure had by 1984 risen to 54%. The country was becoming more and more dependent on raw material exports, while the export of manufactured goods was stalling.

By November 1984, Soviet-American relations had undergone yet another "reset" as a result of both governments having understood the potential results of sabre-rattling coupled with the misinterpretation of world events at political levels the previous year. The critical situation that had developed in the autumn of 1983 had resulted in further intense communications between Europe (in particular Great Britain led by Margaret Thatcher) and the United States. The communications were now however with regard to the urgent need to repair relations with the Soviet Union, ensuring better and more open communications, and thereby ensuring that a situation could not escalate towards potential nuclear war based on "pilot error" as had occurred in the autumn of 1983. Having realised how close the world had come to nuclear war based on mistrust and misunderstanding, President Reagan and the US government from January 1984 began developing a more conciliatory relationship with the Soviet Union in the manner that President John F.

The final version of the T-72A displayed on Red Square in 1984 and 1985 featured many detail changes including additional combination armour/radiation lining on the turret roof, and modified OPVT wading system stowage. This final version was displayed only in 1984 and 1985 before being replaced by the T-72B.

Kennedy had undertaken after the Cuban Missile Crisis before his assassination in November 1963. A few weeks after the November 1984 parade, the rising star of the Politburo, Mikhail Gorbachov, on 10th December 1984, launched reforms in the Soviet Union under the banners of "Perestroika" (Rebuilding) and "Glasnost" (Openness). By the time of the next military parade on Red Square in May 1985, Gorbachov would be the Soviet Premier.

7th November 1984 – 67th Anniversary of the Great October Socialist Revolution

The military parade on 7th November 1984 celebrating the 67th Anniversary of the October Revolution was a relatively lightweight line-up, perhaps reflecting a conciliatory tone after the near disaster at the time of the 7th November parade the previous November. The duties of taking the parade were undertaken by Marshal Sergey L. Sokolov in lieu of Defence Minister Dmitry Ustinov as the latter, having taken the Red Square parades since 1976, was at the time seriously ill. The parade commander in 1984 was the MVO commander Petr Georgevich Lushev.

The usual marching columns including all of the service arms and cadets from the military schools and academies such as the "Kalinin" Naval Academy were per tradition followed by the mechanised parade.

The parade began with UAZ-469B lead vehicles, now over a decade in service, followed by the BRDM-2 based 9P148 ATGM systems and directly thereafer by columns of BTR-70 wheeled APCs. The modernised BMP-2 had since November 1982 now replaced the BMP-1 that had been a parade regular on Red Square since 1967. The

MT-LB universal tracked tractors towing 100mm MT-12 anti-tank guns through Red Square, 7th November 1984. (TASS)

BMD-1 had meantime been replaced since the previous November by the modernised BMD-1P, fitted with a 9P135M launcher for the 9K113 "Konkurs" ATGM. The late production model of the T-72A MBT followed, now with additional combination armour/radiation lining on the turret, representing the most modern armour on display. The MT-LB towed the 100mm MT-12 (2A29) anti-tank gun, with tracked 2S1 and 2S3M self-propelled artillery pieces being followed by the 9K51 (BM-21) "Grad" MRS. Air defence consisted as usual of the ZiL-131 based PR-14M TZM with the S-125M "Neva-M" SAM, the ZiL-131V towing the S-25 and the ZiL-131V with PR-11 series trailer as now used with the S-75M3 "Volkhov" version of the original S-75 "Dvina" as late as mid 1980s. The later 9K33M3 "Osa-AKM" version of the wheeled air defence system was also displayed. As was standard in the 1980s, the 1984 parade culminated with four 9P117M (NATO: SS-1 Scud-B) SPU vehicle for the relatively short-range 9K72 "Elbrus" tactical OTR system.

ZiL-131 PR-14M TZM vehicles for the S-125 "Neva" SAM system traverse Red Square on 7th November 1984. The TZM vehicle transported two reload rockets for the static launchers. (TASS)

The BMP-2 featured a reconfigured hull, new side skirts providing better buoyancy in water, and a new turret mounting a 30mm 2A42 automatic cannon and 9P135M launcher for the 9K113 "Konkurs" ATGM system.

A final production model T-72A with additional turret radiation lining moving along the Prechistenskaya Embankment on the post-parade return run to Khodynka. The "House on the River" in the background is well known to all Muscovites with knowledge of Soviet history.

The two man turret and high fire-angle capable 30mm 2A42 automatic cannon was introduced on the BMP-2 as a direct result of Soviet combat experience in the war in Afghanistan. The 9P135M launch/control system for the 9K113 "Konkurs" ATGM also extended the anti-tank capability of the BMP series.
(Mikhail Baryatinsky)

The 9P113 "Luna-M" (NATO: FROG-7) was a parade regular on Red Square for two decades. The base BAZ-135LM chassis was designed by ZiL in Moscow but built at BAZ in Bryansk. The BAZ-135LM chassis was complex, powered by two ZiL-375 engines driving the roadwheels via two transmissions providing redundancy in the event of damage.

1985

The year 1985 was the 40th Anniversary of Victory over Germany and its Axis allies in Europe, and the year began with yet another change of Soviet leader. On 10th March Konstantin Chernenko died, and was immediately replaced by Mikhail Gorbachov as General Secretary of the CPSU. Within a month of taking office, Gorbachov on 8th April announced the first unilateral Soviet initiative, a temporary freeze on intermediate range (MRBM) nuclear rocket deployment in Europe. While the Strategic Defence Initiative was being promoted in the United States, the largely fabricated science of which would have a debilitating effect on the Soviet Union, President Reagan, cognisant of how close the countries had come to nuclear war began taking history lessons on the Soviet Union; and even took to watching old Soviet films to try and better understand "the Soviets" and their mindset. The situation in 1984 was effectively a repeat of that immediately after the Cuban Missile Crisis in 1962, when the realities of having narrowly avoided nuclear conflict led to a less charged and more cooperative atmosphere between the superpowers. In Geneva on 20th November, the Soviet Union was nevertheless unable to convince the United States to officially drop the SDI "Star Wars" programme.

Domestically, the human and political cost of the Soviet incursion into Afghanistan continued to take its effect on the national psyche, as had the Vietnam experience for the United States in the previous decade. The Soviet government was by

On 9th May 1985, the Soviet Union commemorated the 40th Anniversary of Victory in Europe with a major display on Red Square and in other cities of the Soviet Union.

1985 evaluating solutions that would allow the Soviet Army to withdraw from the deeply tribal country that no outside nation had ever found a "solution" for in any century, including the British at the height of the days of the British Empire.

The Soviet Defence Minister at both the May and November 1985 Victory Day and annual 7th November parades was Sergey L. Sokolov, who had become Defence Minister on 22nd December 1984 on the death two days earlier of Marshal Ustinov who had fulfilled the role of Soviet Defence Minister since 1976. Marshal Sokolov had a long and particularly varied military career, having fought against the Japanese at Lake Khasan in 1938, in World War Two and later in Afghanistan, being awarded the status of Hero of the Soviet Union in 1980. His exemplary career would be abruptly terminated two years later by the actions of a 19-year-old German civilian light aircraft pilot.

The Soviet Union underwent another rapid change of leadership in 1985. Chernenko was on 11th March replaced by Mikhail Gorbachov, who became the new General Secretary of the Communist Party of the Soviet Union (CPSU). Though it was not known at the time, he would also be the last Soviet Premier. The country under Gorbachov would undergo a period of massive political and economic change that would six years later conclude with the dissolution of the Soviet Union. In the intervening years the principles of "Glasnost" and "Perestroika" as launched in December 1984 were rolled out, with the Soviet Union gradually moving away from its own separatist communist history to become a proactive member of the world community. The military parades continued however, with there being two such parades in 1985, the first on 9th May commemorating the 40th Anniversary of Victory in Europe, and the second per tradition celebrating the Russian Revolution of 1917.

9th May 1985 Victory Day Parade

On 9th May 1985 the Soviet Union commemorated the 40th Anniversary of Victory in Europe (VE day, commemorated in the Soviet Union and post-Soviet countries on 9th May rather than the previous day as commemorated in Europe). Mikhail Gorbachov stood on the Lenin Mausoleum in unseasonably warm temperatures approaching 40°C, together with other government and military officials, and was joined by his wife Raisa and his daughter Irina, in what was seen at the time as a change from the more austere leadership of the Soviet past. The 9th May 1985 military parade was significantly larger than the 7th November 1984 parade the preceding year, with a flypast also being organised at the Tushino airfield in north-west Moscow, to which foreign dignitaries and the press were not invited.

The 9th May parade was taken by the Defence Minister, Marshal of the Soviet Union Sergey L. Sokolov, with the parade commander again being General-Colonel Petr G. Lushev standing in their respective ZiL-41044 parade limousines. The parade began with marching World War Two veterans, accompanied by the standards from the ten wartime Fronts, with the parade including foreign contingents from Warsaw Pact countries including Poland and Czechoslovakia. The parade was also attended by the British Ambassador to Russia, Iain Sutherland, but was not attended by officials from the United States and Germany due to an ongoing boycott of Soviet activities by NATO countries as a result of the 1979 Soviet intervention in Afghanistan. Soviet Premier Gorbachov delivered the keynote speech, with Marshal Sergey Sokolov the Soviet Defence Minister addressing what was seen as a deliberate underplaying by the West of the role of Soviet forces in defeating Nazi Germany in World War Two. Within the background of the politics of the day, and despite the American boycott of the parade, the occasion was also used to award Everell Harriman, the American wartime Ambassador to the Soviet Union and Special Envoy to Europe, with the Soviet Order of the Great Patriotic War. This was in recognition of his wartime services in ensuring cooperation between the Soviet Union and its wartime American ally during the war, in particular his coordination of the Lend-Lease program.

The marching parade on 9th May 1985 consisted of representatives of the Military Forces Academy of the USSR, higher military academies, airborne forces, border guards, naval infantry, "Suvorov" and "Dzerzhinsky" academy cadets. The tanks and other armoured vehicles on display belonged by tradition to the Guards Tamanskaya Motorised Rifle Division (in the name of M.I. Kalinin) and the Kantemirovskaya Tank Division (in the name of Yu. V. Andropov) together with VDV airborne forces, PVO air defence vehicles per parade standard and a display of Operativno-Takticheskye Rakety (OTR) or tactical rockets.

With the anniversary being a major "decade" jubilee event, the parade on Red Square included for the first time restored wartime era armour

A T-64B-1 moving down Gorky Street towards Red Square, 9th May 1985. The T-64 was known as the "Gvozd" (nail). (Mikhail Baryatinsky)

A 9P148 ATGM vehicle also moving down Gorky Street towards Red square, 9th May 1985. (Mikhail Baryatinsky)

On 9th May 1985, historical T-34-85 medium tanks and SU-100 self-propelled guns were both displayed on Red Square. These SU-100s have 1960s upgrades including new wheels, lights and a transfer pump box behind the commander's cupola.

A T-34-85 moving past Mayakovsky Square en-route to Red Square for the 9th May 1985 Victory Parade. The tank has 1960s upgrades including new wheels, lights and a new transfer pump storage box.

making a re-appearance on the cobbles of Red Square. The parade was led by twenty T-34-85 tanks followed immediately by a similar number of SU-100 self-propelled guns manoeuvring in formation onto Red Square, following three lead UAZ-469Bs with crews in World War Two era uniforms. The wartime vehicles led the armoured contingent of the historical parade.

The T-34-85s and SU-100s had been rebuilt at the Lvov (today Lviv) Tank Repair Plant in Ukraine especially for the parade, with both the T-34-85 and the SU-100 having 1960s tank repair plant upgrades. All displayed Guards symbols and rumbled through Red Square followed by massed columns of ZiL-157 trucks representing World War Two vehicles. ZiL-157 trucks towed wartime 76.2mm ZiS-3 anti-tank guns, 122mm M-1938 (M-30) howitzers and there were wartime BM-13 "Katyusha" rocket launchers mounted on 1960s era ZiL-157 6x6 chassis. The BM-13 had original- ly been mounted on the ZiS-6 and then latterly standardised on the Lend-Lease Studebaker US6 (as the BM-13N), before being remounted on the ZiS-151 post-war. More ZiL-157s towing 37mm M-1939 anti-aircraft guns followed, with current production Ural-4320 trucks towing wartime 85mm M-1939 anti-aircraft guns culminating the historical section of the parade.

The modern vehicle contingent was headed by three UAZ-469B vehicles, followed by the BRDM-2 based 9P148 ATGM vehicle as the lead contingent of the modern parade section. BTR-70 wheeled APCs were followed by the new BMP-2, and the BMD-1P airborne infantry combat vehicle, both now mounting the 9P135M "Konkurs" ATGM launcher, followed by the contemporary tanks.

Modern armour was again represented in the form of the T-72A MBT, since 1984 seen on Red Square fitted with a combination armour/

T-64B-1 tanks parade through Red Square, 9th May 1985, the sole cameo appearance of the tank on Red Square.

BMP-2 MICVs parade through Red Square, 9th May 1985. (TASS)

radiation liner on the turret roof, followed by the singular Red Square parade cameo appearance of the enigmatic T-64 main battle tank (MBT) in the form of 20 T-64B-1 "Gvozd" (Nail) MBTs in what was the only public Red Square parade appearance of the T-64 MBT series. The T-64 had served with Soviet GSFG forces in East Germany but had never been further distributed, such that the T-64 and its development principles remained unclear almost until the tank had begun to leave Soviet service, to be replaced by the T-80 MBT. The T-64 never saw operational combat service during its Soviet Army service life, only to become the principle tank type used by the Ukrainian Army in the conflict in Eastern Ukraine in 2014.

Two new airborne forces vehicles also had their public debut on 9th May 1985. The BTR-D was a tracked airborne forces armoured personnel carrier based on a stretched BMD chassis, while the 2S9 "Nona-S" was a self-propelled close support vehicle armed with a 120mm 2A51 low-pressure gun/mortar. The VDV airborne forces 2S9 and the ground forces 2S1 and 2S3M self-propelled howitzers directly followed the T-64B1

The BTR-D made its public debut on Red Square during the 40th Anniversary of the Great Patriotic War Victory Parade held on 9th May 1985. The BTR-D was a purpose designed VDV airborne forces tracked APC based on an extended BMD chassis. (TASS)

This T-34-85 parading through Nizhny Tagil on 9th May 1985 is today plinth mounted outside the Uralvagonzavod (UVZ) plant in Nizhny Tagil.

9K51 (BM-21) "Grad" MRS on parade in Minsk, the capital of the Soviet Belorussian Republic.

The MT-LB based 9K35 "Strela-10" SAM system made its Red Square debut on 9th May 1985.

MBTs, the 2S9s being presented with the other self-propelled artillery rather than as part of the airborne vehicles contingent.

The 9K51 (BM-21) "Grad" on the Ural-375D chassis was in May 1985 followed by the debut appearance of the new and rarely seen 6x6 KrAZ-260 general service truck, intended to replace the venerable KrAZ-255B, towing the new 152mm 2A36 "Hyacinth-B" gun-howitzer with its unusual twin axle gun carriage.

The ground artillery was followed by air defence systems, beginning with twelve MT-LB based 9A34 SPU* vehicles for the 9K35 "Strela-10" SAM and twelve 2P25 SPU vehicles for the 2K12 "Kub" (NATO: SA-6 Gainful), with the rockets deployed facing forward in the launch rather than the transit position, followed by the later 9K33M3 "Osa-AKM" with six containerized 9M33M3 rockets, the venerable ZiL-131 PR-14M TZM mounting the S-125 and ZiL-131V towing the S-25 on a PR-3M trailer. The latter had outlived the S-75 (still best known in the West by its NATO designation "SA-2 Guideline"), which had been replaced by the mobile ZRK vehicles on display.

9P117M SPU vehicles for the 9K72 "Elbrus" OTR system, designated SS-1 "Scud-B" by the US and NATO.

* The 9K35 "Strela-10SV" SAM system featured two near identical SPU vehicles, the 9A-34 and the 9A35, the latter fitted with additional passive radar sensors

A KrAZ-260 towing the 152mm 2A36 field gun returns from Red Square, 9th May 1985 after the public debut of both the truck and the towed artillery piece.

A BTR-70 returning to the Khodynka staging area along the Sadovaya Koltso ring road. (Mikhail Baryatinsky)

The 9th May 1985 parade also saw the public debut of the new 9P129 SPU vehicle for the "Tochka" (Point) OTR (NATO: SS-21 Scarab), with four vehicles being demonstrated on Red Square during the May parade. These were followed by the older 9P113 "Luna-M" OTR vehicles, with six MAZ-543 based 9P117M SPU vehicles for the 9K72 OTR system, with their R-17 "Elbrus" rockets (best known internationally by its NATO designation "Scud-B") completing the parade, with five UAZ-469Bs forming the parade rearguard. TOP ARV vehicles, converted from the highly secretive SU-122-54 "Istribitel Tank" or tank destroyer were discreetly located around the edges of Red Square to cover for any unfortunate breakdowns.

The same day, Victory Parades were held in other cities, with the local parade in the Siberian city of Nizhny Tagil, home of the wartime Plant №183 that built the T-34-85, commemorating the day by parading the 35,000th T-34 to be produced through the city centre. Other Soviet Republics including Ukraine also celebrated the same 40th Anniversary with large military parades, often as per tradition involving tanks and vehicles quite dissimilar to those paraded on Moscow's Red Square.

A 2P25 launch vehicle for the 2K12 "Kub" SAM system returning from the 9th May 1985 Red Square parade. The 3M9 rockets are in the firing position.

An SU-100 with 1960s upgrades returning from the 9th May 1985 parade.

The secretive T-64, the T-64B-1 modification of which had its public debut on Red Square on 9th May 1985 remained an enigmatic tank many years after it entered service with the Soviet Army. (Mikhail Baryatinsky)

A T-64B-1 returning from the Red Square parade of 9th May 1985.

The cameo appearance of the T-64B-1 on Red Square in 1985 was the sole public appearance of the tank.

7th November 1985 – 68th Anniversary of the Great October Socialist Revolution

The second Red Square parade of 1985 was on 7th November, in celebration of the 68th Anniversary of the Great October Revolution, being also the 114th military parade to be held on Red Square. The parade was taken as in May by the Defence Minister, Marshal of the Soviet Union Sergey L. Sokolov, with the November parade commander being the MVO commander General-Colonel Vladimir Mikhailovich Arkhipov. The parade began as usual with the staff of the various military academies, followed by UAZ-469B vehicles leading the mechanised parade led by columns of BRDM-2 based 9P148 ATGM vehicles followed by BTR-70 wheeled APCs. The BMP-2 and BMD-1P followed, representing ground forces and airborne MICVs, before the display of T-72A tanks of the 4th Guards Kantemirovskaya Tank Division. Airborne forces 2S9 "Nona-S" artillery vehicles led the ground forces 2S1, 2S3M artillery and 9K51 (BM-21) "Grad" rocket artillery systems, the latter still mounted on the Ural-375D chassis dating from the early 1960s. Air defence was represented by the 9K35 "Strela-10" SAM system mounted on the tracked MT-LB chassis, followed by the BAZ-5937 mounted 9K33M3 "Osa-AKM" SAM system and the ZiL-131V tractor truck with the venerable S-25, now almost completing its third decade of appearances on Red Square. The S-75 surface to air missile, which had become famous in May 1960 over the skies of Siberia was after a quarter of a century of stellar Red Square parade service now retired. As was the norm in the 1980s, the parade ended with a display of tactical (OTR) rockets, with six each of the 9P129 "Tochka", 9P113 "Luna-M" and the 9P117M "Elbrus" SPU vehicles on display.

Newly unveiled 9K35 "Strela-10" and 9K33M3 "Osa-AKM" SAM systems bracket the late 1960s era 2K12 "Kub" SAM system on Red Square.

Though it entered service in the early 1970s, the 2S3M became a regular Red Square participant only in the 1980s.

An overhead view of the 2S9 "Nona-S" VDV airborne forces self-propelled close support weapon. The 2S9 was developed on the extended BTR-D chassis.

A 2S3M self-propelled howitzer returning from Red Square.

The BTR-D, with a vehicle crew of three and nine VDV "desantniki" paratroopers. The BTR-D was the first purpose-designed VDV airborne forces tracked APC, based on an extended BMD-1 chassis.

A 9A34 SPU vehicle for the 9K35 "Strela-10" SAM systems returns from Red Square. The operator's window is clearly seen below the transport/launch containers in this view.

A rear view of the same 9A34 launch vehicle for the 9K35 SAM system, which used both 9A34 and 9A35 launch vehicles.

A side view of the 2S9 "Nona" self-propelled airborne forces artillery support vehicle on its extended BMD chassis.

A 2S9 "Nona" vehicle returning from Red Square. The low-pressure gun-mortar features a particularly high fire-angle.

1986

There was a considerable improvement in Soviet - American working relations in the year between the November 1985 and November 1986 Moscow military parades, particularly with regard to nuclear arms reduction talks. Immediately after the November 1985 parade, Soviet Premier Mikhail Gorbachov and President Reagan of the United States on 19th November 1985 held their first summit on nuclear arms reduction in Geneva, Switzerland. By diplomatic standards these talks proceeded with breakneck speed, and the second such summit was held in Reykjavik, Iceland immediately before the November 1986 Red Square parade. On 19th February the "Mir" (Peace) space station launched into orbit heralding a new era of cooperation between the superpowers in space. The major notable Soviet event of 1986 was on 26th April, when the nuclear reactor located at Chernobyl near Pripyat in Ukraine on the southern border of the Soviet Belorussian Republic suffered a catastrophic accident and meltdown, resulting in nuclear fallout over much of the Soviet Union and Europe. The incident was unrelated to the Soviet military other than that a large number of military personnel and specialist equipment was sent to the scene, but the Chernobyl incident was a significant blow to Soviet prestige.

7th November 1986 – 69th Anniversary of the Great October Socialist Revolution

After the massive 9th May 1985 Victory Day commemoration, standard parades resumed on Red Square in November 1986, the 115th military parade on Red Square. The 1986 parade was taken by the 1st Deputy Defence Minister Petr G. Lushev, in lieu of Sergey Sokolov, with the parade again commanded by the MVO commander, Vladimir M. Arkhipov.

UAZ-469B parade lead vehicles led columns of 9P148 ATGM vehicles directly followed by BTR-70 wheeled APCs, all Kantemirovskaya and Tamanskaya division vehicles in 1986 being painted in green with Guards symbols; with other secondary vehicles on parade featuring a red star. BMP-2 infantry and BMD-1P airborne combat vehicles followed, in standard formations of one lead and twenty "line" vehicles, followed by the Red Square parade debut of the upgraded T-72B MBT, the most noticeable feature of which was its additional frontal turret armour, the T-72B MBT being humorously described by US and NATO intelligence as the new "Super Dolly Parton" modification of the tank, after the well-endowed American Country and Western singer.

Self-propelled artillery was represented by the airborne 2S9 "Nona-S" leading the ground forces 2S1 and 2S3M and the 9K51 "Grad" MRS - still mounted on the original Ural-375D chassis.

The air defence vehicles contingent of the November 1986 parade was considerable, with the venerable ZiL-131V towing the S-25 "Berkut" SAM on its PR-3 series TZM semi-trailer and the S-125 "Neva-M" PR-14M TZM vehicle on parade mounted on its ZiL-131 chassis, though with the S-75 series of SAM systems no longer present. The older SAM systems were joined by the MT-LB based 9A34M SPU vehicles for the 9K35M "Strela-10M" SAM system, and the 9K33M3 "Osa-AKM" SAM system with its six container mounted rockets based on the BAZ-5937 amphibious 9A33BM3 SPU vehicle chassis.

The parade finale in 1986 consisted of tactical OTR rockets being represented by the 9P129 "Tochka" (NATO: SS-21 Scarab) OTR on the amphibious BAZ-5921 chassis, replacing the long-serving 9P113 "Luna-M", followed directly by six 9P117M SPU vehicles for the 9K72 "Elbrus" OTR.

The T-72B replaced the T-72A on Red Square from 1986. The increased turret frontal armour was the most evident feature of the new T-72B variant.

A 2S1 self-propelled howitzer returning from Red Square. (Mikhail Baryatinsky)

A 9P129 SPU vehicle for the 9K79 "Tochka" OTR returning from Red Square, 7th November 1986. (Mikhail Baryatinsky)

A ZiL-131V towing a V-300 rocket for the S-25 "Berkut" SAM system crosses the bridge on Krymsky Val returning from Red Square. (Mikhail Baryatinsky)

A 9A33BM3 launch vehicle for the 9K33M3 "Osa-AKM" SAM system on the return run from Red Square. The "Osa" system was modernised several times during its service life, and the designations remain conflated even in original sources.

A later production BTR-70 returns from Red Square. The modified model (sometimes designated BTR-70M) featured a new BPU-1 turret module and BTR-80 wheels.

BTR-70s parade through Leningrad on 7th November 1986. (TASS)

1987

The year 1987 began with Soviet Premier Gorbachov officially declaring on 27th January, that the country was undergoing a period of continued economic stagnation, a public admission that all was not well with the Soviet State. At a strategic military level, the Soviet news agency TASS on 15th April reported the Soviet unilateral proposal to remove all land based SRBMs and MRBMs from Europe, leading to the Soviet Union and the United States agreeing to scrap intermediate range nuclear missiles (MRBMs).*

An unprecedented event occurred on Red Square on 28th May 1987, when a small Cessna 172 plane piloted by a 19-year-old German national by the name of Mathius Rust landed on the square, having flown across Soviet airspace from Helsinki. The curious incident though perhaps amusing for some, led to sweeping changes in the Soviet military hierarchy. The Defence Minister, Sergey Leonidovich Sokolov, whose impeccable service record has been related earlier, was fired, as was the Chief Marshal of Aviation Aleksandr Koldunov who was commander of the Air Defence Forces. Koldunov had been awarded the sta-

---
* The Intermediate Range Nuclear Forces (INF) Treaty was signed by Soviet General Secretary Mikhail Gorbachov and US President Ronald Reagan on 8th December 1987.

tus of Hero of the Soviet Union in 1948 for his wartime service as a fighter pilot, having been the 8th ranking ace in the 1941-45 "Great Patriotic War". As the Red Square aircraft incident faded into history, the storm clouds were however now gathering on the Soviet Union's western borders. As preparations were underway for the 70th Anniversary of the Great October Socialist Revolution in November 1987, political movements were underway in the Baltic Republics, with agitation for autonomy having begun in Estonia in June of that year.

7th November 1987 - 70th Anniversary of the Great October Socialist Revolution

The 7th November 1987 military parade, being exactly 70 years since the Great October Socialist Revolution of 1917, was a major anniversary. Consequently, the parade taken by the new Defence Minister Dmitry Timofeevich Yazov and commanded by the MVO Commander Vladimir M. Arkhipov, began with infantry in revolutionary era military costumes, followed by similarly attired cavalry on a mix of white and brown horses, and horse drawn "tachanki" - revolutionary period machine gun carts. The historic display was followed by marching infantry in period "Great Patriotic War" costume; some armed with wartime PPSh sub-machine guns, followed by naval forces and marines in period uniforms. The historic parade was followed by the traditional

The BTR-D was the first purpose-designed Soviet VDV airborne forces APC. Note the 7.62mm PKT machine guns and the AGS-17 grenade launcher.

display of military technology, beginning with the 1980s parade default 9P148 ATGM vehicle, mounted on the BRDM-2 chassis, which began the armoured section of Red Square parades for almost the entire decade. Soviet Defence Minister Dmitry Yazov, who had taken his position on 30th May 1987, would take all the remaining Soviet era Red Square parades, retiring during the 1991 attempted "Putsch"or coup d'etat on 23rd August 1991 as Soviet tanks were being deployed in Moscow, but not for ceremonial purposes.

The BTR-80 wheeled armoured personnel carrier made its public debut on Red Square in 1987, replacing the BTR-70 that had made its own debut on Red Square only seven years before. The BTR-80 as with the BTR-70 retained the turret and armament from the BTR-60PB, but had a modified hull with double clamshell doors between the second and third axles for easier crew egress, and major changes to the vehicle mechanicals. Due to the collapse of the Soviet Union, the BTR-80 would remain in service far longer than any of its predecessors, the current production BTR-82 series being a minor modernisation of the original design now in service for over 30 years.

BMP-2 MICVs of the Tamanskaya Motorised Rifle Division were followed by a large number of Soviet VDV airborne forces vehicles, represented by the modified BMD-1P, with the original 9M14M "Malyutka" ATGM launch rail of the earlier production BMD-1 now replaced by a turret mounting for the 9P135M ATGM launcher. The BTR-D tracked APC was again displayed, as was the 2S9 "Nona-S" self-propelled artillery support vehicle, the Soviet VDV airborne forces by the mid 1980s having a significant range of specialised armoured vehicles available to them. The 2S9 led the ground forces 2S1 and 2S3M self-propelled howitzers onto Red Square rather than being demonstrated with the other VDV airborne forces vehicles.

T-72B tanks of the Kantemirovskaya Tank Division were paraded in 1987; having recently replaced the T-72A, followed by the usual collection of tracked and wheeled artillery systems, the 2S1 and 2S3M self-propelled howitzers, and

The T-72B featured increased turret frontal armour, hence the humorous "Dolly Parton" nomenclature adopted by the US and disseminated through NATO. (P. Kazachkov)

the 9K51 (BM-21) "Grad" MRS, still mounted on the venerable Ural-375D 6x6 truck for parade purposes though the modernised Ural-4320 was in standard Soviet Army service.

The November 1987 parade included some relatively rare appearances, such as the new KrAZ-260, first demonstrated in May 1985, again towing the 152mm 2A36 field gun on its twin axle gun carriage, which had its Red Square public debut in 1985. The KrAZ-260 was the long-overdue replacement for the venerable KrAZ-255B, the family lineage of which dated back to the YaAZ-214 of the early 1950s. The KrAZ-260 began to enter service with the Soviet Army in moderate numbers at the end of the 1980s, but being built at Kremenchug in Ukraine, the vehicle was not required by the post-Soviet Russian Army. The KrAZ-260 was subsequently developed in Ukraine into the KrAZ-6322.

Air defence vehicles displayed on 7th November consisted of the 9A34M SPU vehicle for the 9K35M "Strela-10M" (Strela-10MSV) SAM based on the MT-LB chassis and the 9K33M3 "Osa-AKM" (NATO: SA-8 Gecko), and the S-125 (NATO: SA-3 Goa) TZM vehicle based on the ZiL-131 chassis.

The parade finale as in all 1980s parades was represented by the 9P129 SPU vehicle for the 9K79 "Tochka" OTR, the 9P113 "Luna-M" on its BAZ-135 chassis, designated by NATO as the "FROG-7", with the parade being concluded by six 9P117M "Elbrus" (NATO: Scud B) launch vehicles.

The 70th Anniversary of the Great October Socialist Revolution parade held in November 1987 was conducted immediately before the third and final Intermediate-range Nuclear Forces (INF) reduction summit with the United States, held in Washington. After the tensions of the early 1960s and the temporary spike in the early 1980s, the Cold War was again thawing, and now, as appeared at the time, on a permanent basis.

Soviet Premier Mikhail Gorbachov and American President Ronald Reagan signed the INF Treaty on short and medium range nuclear missiles in Washington on 8th December 1987. The treaty, which was ratified by the US government on 27th May the following year, eliminated two types of land based rocket system, namely short range rockets with a range of 500-1,000km and intermediate range rockets with a range of 1,000-5,500km. The land mobile RSD-10 (NATO: SS-20 Saber) MRBM which had been accepted for service in 1977 was firmly within the latter bracket and was thereby scheduled for decommissioning even as it was still in the process of being operationally deployed by the Soviet Union. The RSD-10 was as a result the only road mobile Soviet strategic missile system to enter service and yet never be displayed on Red Square.

A 9P129 SPU vehicle for the 9K79 "Tochka" OTR system crosses the bridge on Krymsky Val near Gorky Park on the return leg from Red Square. (Mikhail Baryatinsky)

The BTR-80 replaced the BTR-70 on Red Square from 1987. The BTR-80 featured a modified hull with full "clamshell" doors providing greatly improved egress from the vehicle.

A 2S3M "Akatsiya" self-propelled howitzer turns post-parade onto the "Sadovaya Koltso" (Garden Ring) ring road returning to the Khodynka staging area.

A 2S1 "Gvozdika" self-propelled howitzer, armed with the 122mm 2A31 (D-32) howitzer derived from the towed 122mm D-30. (P. Kazachkov)

The 2S9 "Nona" self-propelled gun-mortar mounted a 120mm 2A51 low-pressure gun with a maximum elevation of 80°. It was first deployed operationally with the Soviet Army in Afghanistan. (P. Kazachkov)

1988

In the winter of 1987-88, ethnic conflicts had developed between Armenian and Azeri nationals in the region of Nagorny Karabakh within the Soviet Republic of Azerbaijan. As the Soviet State had become less oppressive in enforcing the Soviet centralised system of government, so the various nationalities within the Soviet Union began to fight among themselves to assert their ethic and religious differences, a pattern that would develop as the Soviet grip loosened. A sign of the rapidly developing changes was the passing of new laws on 2nd January 1988, during the traditional New Year and Orthodox Christmas holiday period in the country, allowing Soviet citizens to travel to the countries of the Warsaw Pact without obtaining (exit) travel visas.

After nine years of war in Afghanistan, Soviet forces began to withdraw from the country on 15th May, with approximately half of all Soviet forces having been withdrawn by August. The United States continued to supply the Mujahidin with weapons and training however, and Pakistan continued to allow operations to be continued across its borders, and the internal situation in Afghanistan deteriorated rapidly as Soviet forces departed. The Mujahidin continued to attack withdrawing Soviet troops, as their predecessors had attacked the British Kabul Garrison under the command of Major General Sir William Elphinstone as it retreated from Kabul to Jalalabad in 1842, murdering some 4,500 soldiers and 12,000 civilian men, women and children with equal atrocity. Without Soviet support, the Soviet trained Afghan Army fought a losing battle against the Mujahidin, which latterly morphed into the Taliban, and the vacuum created duly sucked in British, American and many other foreign forces in a country which was more enlightened, "democratic" and contemporary in 1842 , the early 1930s, or under Soviet rule in the 1970s than it is today.

As Soviet forces were beginning to withdraw from Afghanistan, American President Ronald Reagan arrived in Moscow for meetings with Premier Gorbachov and the Soviet government on a variety of issues. In the new spirit of multilateral cooperation with the Soviet Union, Reagan declared at the end of May 1988 that Moscow was no longer the capital of the "Evil Empire", doubtless to the relief of native Muscovites. The relationship between the Soviet Union and the United States, and thereby NATO, was at its most constructive point since the beginning of the Cold War despite the proxy-war that had been fought in Afghanistan between the superpowers. While the Soviet Union and the United States had reached accommodation on the nuclear front, events were however unfolding in Europe that would rapidly escalate change in the status quo which had held in Europe since the end of World War Two.

On 1st October 1988 Mikhail Gorbachov replaced Andrey Gromyko as Chairman of the Presidium of the Supreme Soviet in addition to the role of General Secretary of the CPSU, a post Gorbachov had held since 1985. One of his announcements was the unveiling of "Perestroika", or rebuilding, of the State structure as originally proposed in December 1984. Three years later that process of "Perestroika" had resulted in the structure being demolished altogether.

The year ended with another major change in the Soviet Union's relations with Europe and NATO, when on 7th December Mikhail Gorbachov advised the UN General Assembly that the Soviet Union intended to withdraw all Soviet tank divisions from the territory of its Warsaw Pact allies, primarily located in Czechoslovakia, East Germany, and Hungary. The Soviet military withdrawal from Eastern Europe was underway. Gorbachov expressed a clear Soviet expectation that NATO would not attempt to fill the resultant vacuum, and the question of NATO potential expansion would be expressed even more strongly by the Soviet Union with regard to the imminent reunification of Germany. In the years after the fall of the Soviet Union, those "goodwill" expectations proved to be entirely unfounded.

7th November 1988 - 71st Anniversary of the Great October Socialist Revolution

The 1988 November parade was another of those occasional bright and frosty early November parades that were accompanied by the light snows of early winter. The 1988 Red Square parade was taken by Soviet Defence Minister Dmitry Yazov, and commanded by the MVO Commander General Konstantin A. Kochetov. The majority of vehicles were painted in overall green with a red star, and with Guards symbols where appropriate to the 4th Guards Kantemirovskaya and 2nd Guards Tamanskaya divisions that provided as always the majority of armoured vehicles on display.

The mechanised part of the 1988 parade began as with all parades since 1976 with UAZ-469B vehicles leading BRDM-2 based 9P148 ATGM vehicles, as had now been tradition for several years, followed by the wheeled BTR-80 and tracked BMP-2 for the Tamanskaya Motor-

A ZiL-131 PR-14M TZM (trans-loader) vehicle, mounting two 5V24 (V-600) rockets for the S-125 "Neva" SAM system. The ZiL-131 replaced the earlier ZiL-157 in the trans-loader vehicle role.

During the 1980s TOP parade support vehicles were placed around the Red Square parades for emergency recovery if required.

ised Rifle and Kantemirovskaya Tank Division forces respectively. The wheeled vehicles were followed by the VDV airborne forces BMD-1P and by the modernised T-72B MBT unveiled on Red Square in 1986. As was often standard for Red Square parades, the VDV airborne forces 2S9 "Nona-S" and ground forces 2S1 and 2S3M tracked artillery pieces were displayed together grouped as self-propelled artillery systems rather than the 2S9 being displayed together with other airborne forces vehicles. The 9K51 (BM-21) "Grad" MRS was displayed, still mounted on the venerable Ural-375D 6x6 truck chassis with its original V-8 petrol engine, although the diesel engine Ural-4320 was then in series production and Soviet Army service.

There were no surprises with regard to the air defence vehicles on display. The MT-LB based 9A34M SPU vehicles for the 9K35M "Strela-10M" SAM were followed by the later 9K33M3 "Osa-AKM", and the ZiL-131 PR-14M TZM for the S-125 "Neva" (NATO: SA-3 Goa) SAM system, but the older S-25 (NATO: SA-1 Guild) and S-75 (NATO: SA-2 Guideline) were no longer present. The parade finished with 9P129 "Tochka" OTR rocket system SPU vehicles followed by six 9P113 "Luna-M" (NATO: FROG-7) SPU vehicles on their BAZ-135 chassis, and finally six 9P117M "Elbrus" (NATO: Scud-B) OTR systems based on the MAZ-543M. With the 9P120 "Temp-S" (NATO: SS-12 Scaleboard) no longer on display, the parades of the late 1980s were limited to tactical battlefield weapons as the longest-range projection of military might, and were thereby as in the mid 1970s largely parades of defensive rather than offensive weaponry.

Meantime, far from Red Square, as the Soviet Union edged towards its end of days, events began to unfold in the Soviet Republics that would define the following decade. On 16th November 1988, the Estonian SSR declared sovereignty from Moscow. A military response was entirely expected from the Kremlin, as history had shown, but there was no military intervention in 1988 as a result of the announcement, and "negotiations" remained at a diplomatic level. Lithuania and Latvia would follow suit in March and May 1990 respectively, but with a very different outcome.

Troubles for the Soviet Union were not confined to the Baltic Republics. In the Southern Republics of the Soviet State, fighting had broken out in 1988 in Nagorno-Karabakh, which had been a region within Azerbaijan since 1923, and conflict there would continue sporadically until 1994. Other similar regional conflicts began to erupt as the central control that had kept political and often tribal factions in place for years in the immense territory of the Soviet Union began to be loosened and Soviet States and individual regions began to push for independence.

Parades were held in many Soviet cities annually though the Red Square parades were obviously the best covered by the press. This ZiS-131 based 9P138 launcher vehicle for the 9K55 "Grad-1" or "Prima" MRS is preparing for a parade in Sevastopol in 1988. The 36 barrel "low profile" MRS was originally developed to potentially replace the 9K51 "Grad" and entered service in 1974, but had restricted distribution such as to the Soviet naval infantry as seen here. Approximately 500 were built in the mid 1970s.

1989

The year 1989 began with George H. W. Bush being inaugurated on 20th January as President of the United States. A month later, on 15th February, the Soviet Union announced that the withdrawal of Soviet forces from Afghanistan begun in 15th May the previous year was now complete. The last contingents of the 40th Army commanded by Colonel-General Boris Gromov and under the direction of General of the Army Valentin Varennikov had on 15th February crossed over the "Bridge of Friendship" back into the Soviet Union at Termez in southern Uzbekistan. The Afghan Mujahidin would ultimately take Kabul, and from the chaos of renewed civil war the Taliban would emerge. The Soviet southern borders were secured, but in 1989 there were riots between rival factions in the Soviet Republics of Georgia, Kazakhstan, Uzbekistan and Tajikistan that all required direct military intervention, and Gorbachov as Chairman of the Supreme Soviet was forced to announce on State television that the stability of the Soviet State was under threat. In July 1989 there were ethnic clashes between Abkhaz and Georgian nationals in the coastal town of Sukhumi in the quasi-independent Soviet Republic of Abkhazia, with similar disturbances between Uzbeks and Meshketian Turks in Uzbekistan. The nationalistic drive emerging in some of the Southern Republics of the Soviet Union was paralleled by ethnic tensions now that the centralised Soviet State was less strong, or perhaps less ruthless than in earlier years. Meanwhile in Eastern Europe, all was also far from well within the Warsaw Pact from a Soviet perspective. Lech Wałęsa, the leader of the "Solidarity" union in Poland, which had masterminded the Lenin Shipyard strike in Gdansk precisely nine years earlier, formed the Solidarity Party into a democratic coalition government in Poland in August 1989. The Lithuanian Communist Party had meantime declared its independence from the Soviet Communist Party and the three Baltic countries staged a human chain, the "Baltic Way", to commemorate the 50th Anniversary of the Soviet-German Molotov-Ribbentrop Pact of August 1939.

1989 was also a year of political change and revolutions in Eastern Europe. There were significant political upheavals in Bulgaria, Czechoslovakia, East Germany, Hungary, Poland and Romania, which coincided with the withdrawal of Soviet troops from these countries. The Soviet Union began the removal of these Soviet troops from Eastern Europe in 1989 in accordance with the official announcement made by Defence Minister Dmitry Yazov with regard to "demilitarisation of international relations". This was as much a cost saving exercise as political good will, and the vacuum was soon filled. In 1989, the 25th and 32nd Tank Divisions were to be removed from the Group of Soviet Forces Germany located in East Germany, and the 13th Tank Division and other units from the Central Group of Forces located in Czechoslovakia and Hungary. A tank regiment and other units were also to be removed from the Northern Group of Forces located in Poland. In 1990 the 7th Guards Tank Division and the 12th Guards Tank Division and VDV airborne forces would also leave East Germany. Soviet troops began withdrawing from Hungary on 26th April concurrently with the drive for political freedom in that country. Ironically, as the Soviet Union was releasing its grip on Eastern Europe and a wave of political changes swept the former Warsaw Pact countries, conflicts in the Soviet Republics also began to grow in scale. The Soviet Union was not alone with regard to significant changes in its political operating environment - on 4th June the world also witnessed a political shift in China heralded by the events on Tiananmen Square.

On 7th November 1989, the communist government of East Germany resigned. Two days later, on 9th November, the checkpoints between East and West Germany were opened, and the Berlin Wall metaphorically fell. From 10th November the best known symbol of the Cold War began to be demolished, with many sections of wall being taken as souvenirs.

On 2nd December, Gorbachov and Bush met for two days of talks on the historic island of Malta, which had been deliberately chosen as a neutral location far from the recent events in Eastern Europe. The meeting was cordial, and statements made afterwards by both participating parties suggested that the Cold War was coming to an end. Three days later, on 5th December, rioters in Dresden in East Germany stormed the local offices of the

The BTR-80 replaced the BTR-70 on Red Square parades from 1987, but remained on parade in other cities such as Leningrad and Kiev for much longer.

feared Stasi secret police before moving on to the local headquarters of the Soviet KGB. An officer approached the gate from within the latter building and calmly advised the crowds not to force entry as the guards were armed and would use their weapons if necessary. He then called the local Soviet Army tank unit to dispatch protection for the KGB offices that were effectively under siege. The KGB officer was told that nothing could be done without instruction from Moscow and that unfortunately for those concerned "Moscow is silent". That response doubtless remained in the mind of the young KGB officer as a decade later he on 31st December 1999 assumed the role of Acting President of the Russian Federation on the resignation of then President Boris Yeltsin. Vladimir Putin was on 7th May 2000 confirmed as President of the Russian Federation.

The year ended with continued disintegration of the Soviet-centric power base in Eastern Europe, with riots in Romania and the overthrow of the Ceaușescu regime. Gorbachov had considered the Romanian regime excessively restrictive even by the standards of Soviet history, and had advised Nicolae Ceaușescu to be less tyrannical towards his people, but the advice from the Soviet government was ignored. Riots in Bucharest turned to a coup d'état, with the Romanian military siding with the civil population. Ceaușescu and his wife were arrested, tried and subsequently executed by Romanian airborne forces on 25th December at a military base near Bucharest - an imperative demanded by the Romanian Army in return for their support of the new Romanian National Democratic Front. After the execution of the Ceaușescus the death penalty was subsequently abolished in Romania. The lesson that any regime can be overthrown if the population are sufficiently angry was however understood in the Soviet Union at a time when nations in Western Europe could talk of democracy with some aura of authority.

The 7th November Red Square parade was then held against a backdrop of major changes in Europe. Only two days after the parade the Berlin Wall fell, and Europe would enter a new phase whereby the traditional Warsaw Pact allies would one by one begin to drift away from the centralised power bloc that had ruled the region for nearly four decades. The Warsaw Pact was beginning to disintegrate abroad, and there were regional conflicts and demands for independence arising at home in the Soviet Union.

Some vehicles were never paraded on Red Square. The enigmatic SU-122-54 tank destroyer served in very small numbers (only 77 were built) and was almost unknown during the Cold War with the exception of this image. The TOP ARV conversion would however subsequently appear at Red Square parades. (Steven J. Zaloga)

7th November 1989 – 72nd Anniversary of the Great October Socialist Revolution

The 7th November 1989 military parade on Red Square was again taken by Defence Minister Marshal of the Soviet Union Dmitry Yazov, as Mikhail Gorbachov and the Soviet elite looked on from the Lenin Mausoleum review stand. Although it was not known at the time, the 7th November 1989 parade would be the penultimate 7th November military parade on Red Square. The parade was led by the marching band of the Moscow Military Music School, which had been a regular parade participant since 1940. Participants from the usual "Dzerzhinsky", "Frunze" and "Kuibyshev" military academies marched past the Lenin Mausoleum, together with parade default representation from the Soviet Navy, Air Force, Soviet marines and other uniformed branches of the Soviet armed services.

The mechanised section of the parade was an almost exact replica of the previous year, with only minor technical developments. The BTR-80

Although the SU-122-54 was never paraded on Red Square, the TOP parade support vehicles used in the 1980s and as late as 1995 were converted from decommissioned SU-122-54 vehicles.

The 9K51 (BM-21) "Grad" was originally mounted on the Ural-375D 6x6 chassis. Though replaced in service by the diesel engine Ural-4320, the original version was not replaced on Red Square parades until after 1987. This later production vehicle is on parade in Kiev.

The modified BMD-1P, with a 9P135M launch/guidance system for the "Konkurs" ATGM replaced the original BMD-1 on Red Square parades from 1983. These BMD-1P vehicles are on parade in Kiev, 7th November 1989.

The BMD-1P modernised the long-range ATGM capability of the VDV airborne forces BMD-1 in line with the ground forces BMP-2, as seen here in Kiev, 7th November 1989.

A Soviet Army BMP-2 followed by a BMD-1P, Kiev, 7th November 1989. The BMP-2 featured a new two-man turret armed with a 30mm 2A42 automatic cannon, a 9P135M launcher/guidance system. The side skirts were modified and filled with polyurethane foam for added buoyancy.

and BMP-2 represented armoured infantry transport for motorised rifle and tank divisions respectively, followed by the final parade appearance of the original BMD-1 (BMD-1P) series airborne combat vehicle. T-72B tanks of the 4th Guards Kantemirovskaya Tank Division represented the heavy armour, followed by the 2S9 "Nona" VDV airborne forces and 2S1 ground forces tracked artillery pieces displayed together, but there was again no appearance of the 2S3M self-propelled howitzer which had been sporadically displayed on Red Square. The 9K51 (BM-21) "Grad" MRS was now finally demonstrated mounted on the concurrent diesel engined Ural-4320 chassis rather than the earlier petrol engined Ural-375D, which had been introduced into service in the early 1960s. The air defence section of the parade was relatively short, with MT-LB mounted 9K35M "Strela-10M" SAM systems followed by the BAZ-5937 mounted 9K33M3 "Oka-AKM" SAM system.

Defence industry conversion was a theme of the parade commentary. While much effort was being expended on converting military enterprises to civil production, the commentary at the parade made it clear that conversion would not be at the expense of a reduction in military defence capability. The parade finale consisted as in recent years of six 9P129 "Tochka", six 9P113 "Luna-M" and finally six 9P117M "Elbrus" SPU vehicles for the 9K79, 9K52 and 9K72 OTR tactical rockets respectively. As the vehicles completed the 7th November parade the accompanying commentary was that "Perestroika" nevertheless needed such weapons for State protection, albeit the rockets were far less powerful than the medium and long-range strategic rockets displayed on Red Square before 1974.

Not participating in the parade but parked strategically at either end of Red Square and in the surrounding streets were the now standard TOP armoured recovery vehicles. These ARV vehicles were converted specifically for potential recovery operations during parades. Their origins were however particularly interesting, as they were converted from the highly enigmatic SU-122-54 (Obiekt-600) tank destroyer, which was one of the most secretive of all Soviet armoured vehicles. The SU-122-54 was deployed with the Soviet Army in small numbers during the 1950s and early 1960s and had served in almost complete secrecy. The TOP ARV conversions seen in the background of Red Square parades in the 1980s served as the only indicator that the gun-armed armoured vehicle on which they were based had ever existed, but for a single publically released image of a bogged down SU-122-54 in service in the 1960s.

The 5P85S SPU vehicle for the S-300P (NATO: SA-10 Grumble) SAM system made its debut Red Square appearance in 1990, but would not be seen again in Moscow until May 1995.

Year 1990-91

The 1990s was a decade of major change, which began with the political unrest in the southern republics of the Soviet Union gathering in intensity. The Soviet Army was in January 1990 forced to intervene in inter-ethnic fighting in Baku, the capital of Soviet Azerbaijan, and the following month there were more inter-ethnic clashes in the Soviet Republics of Uzbekistan and Tajikistan. On 15th March 1990, Mikhail Gorbachov became President of the Soviet Union. In September 1990, East Germany left the Warsaw Pact in preparation for its unification with West Germany, and would be followed within weeks by Czechoslovakia, Hungary and Poland. By the end of 1990, the Warsaw Pact was crumbling, as was its central support infrastructure in the Soviet Union.

In direct contrast with the previous seven decades, the decade that followed 1990 would be entirely devoid of military parades involving armoured vehicles and other heavy military equipment on Red Square. The last two Soviet era military parades were held in May and November 1990, after which the only military parade involving military vehicles or "tekhnika" held in Moscow during the decade was on 9th May 1995, with this parade being held on Moscow's Kutuzovsky Prospekt, rather than Red Square. Parades were however held in other cities of the new Russian Federation, and in some of the republics of the former Soviet Union.

There were two military parades held in Moscow in 1990, the first on 9th May celebrating the 45th Anniversary of Victory in Europe, the second being the annual 7th November Red Square parade. The latter, held against a background of heavy snow, would also turn out to be the last Soviet era military parade celebrating the Great October Socialist Revolution. Due to a worsening political situation, there was no military parade held in November 1991, and the following month the Soviet Union was dissolved. There followed a political and financially tumultuous time in the early 1990s, as the Russian Federation moved away from seventy years of a State planned economy and the financial, employment and security certainties that had accompanied that system evaporated. The Russian Federation, being the administrative cornerstone of the former Soviet Union, managed to cope with independence better than the other former Soviet Republics, of which only those with oil and gas reserves fared well in the initial post-Soviet era. The new freedoms in former Soviet Republics brought direct conflict in the 1990s, with a civil war in Tajikistan which began in 1992 and lasted as late as 1997 in some areas, and the first of two brutal wars in the Russian semi-autonomous republic of Chechnya, together with several other conflicts on a more limited scale in other former republics and regions.

The 1990s was meantime in Moscow effectively a decade without major military parades, with the exception of the aforementioned 50th Anniversary of Victory in Europe Day parade on 9th May 1995 held on Kutuzovsky Prospekt in western Moscow. Tanks and other armoured vehicles would nevertheless be observed in Moscow in 1991 and 1993, but in each case these were deployed on the streets as a result of civil and political unrest, the deployments being far from ceremonial in nature. As the stability of the Soviet Union evaporated, it was replaced by the uncertainties of the post-war 1990s, which for many ordinary citizens included loss of professional employment, security, status and life savings, which for many, particularly the older generation, installed a yearning for the stability of the old Soviet Union.

1990

The year 1990 was eventful in the Soviet Union, and a prelude to an even more eventful following year. On 15th March 1990, Mikhail Gorbachov became President of the Soviet Union, a role he would hold until he himself formally dissolved the Soviet State on 25th December 1991. There would be two major military parades on Red Square in 1990. The first, held on 9th May, commemorated the 45th Anniversary of Victory in Europe in 1945. The second, held as usual on 7th November, would be the last Soviet era military parade ever held on Red Square.

The year began with Soviet troops being deployed in Azerbaijan in January after a pogrom against Armenians in the Soviet Republic, in what was a continuation of what became known as the Nagorno-Karabakh conflict. As the situation on the Soviet Union's southern borders deteriorated, the situation in the Baltic Republics also began to decline. After Lithuania declared independ-

The final weapons system to be paraded through Red Square during the last Soviet era Red Square parade was the 11,000km range RT-2PM "Topol" ICBM. The 15U168 SPU vehicle was based on the MAZ-7917 chassis.

ence from the Soviet Union on 11th March 1990, Soviet Premier Gorbachov sanctioned an economic blockade of the country, while on 4th May Latvia declared independence from the Soviet Union. The 9th May 1990 Victory Parade was held against a backdrop of the rapid disintegration of the Soviet Union and a political system that had survived seven decades, but was now in its swansong months. Meanwhile, meetings were held in February 1990 between the Federal German government in Bonn and the American government in Washington. The subject was the future of a unified Germany and its military as an independent entity, or within NATO, for presentation to Soviet Premier Mikhail Gorbachov. American President George H.W. Bush wanted a "Special Military Status" within NATO for the new, united Germany. In return for the Soviet Union agreeing to the reunification of Germany, Soviet Premier Gorbachov requested guarantees that that there would be no expansion of NATO into those countries formerly under the direct Soviet sphere of influence.

The weeks leading up to the 7th November parade were equally eventful. East Germany formally left the Warsaw Pact in September in preparation for its unification with West Germany, and would be followed within weeks by Czechoslovakia, Hungary and Poland. East and West Germany were re-unified as a single state on 3rd October. Amid the rapid disintegration of the Soviet Union and its former Warsaw Pact allies as a political and military bloc, Soviet Premier Mikhail Gorbachov was on 15th October awarded the Nobel Prize for his work on Soviet internal reforms and in reducing Cold War tensions.

9th May 1990 Victory Day Parade

The end of the Second World War in Europe, signed in the early hours of 9th May 1945 according to Moscow time, had been commemorated twenty years later, on 9th May 1965 by a major anniversary military parade. The 40th Anniversary was accordingly commemorated with a major parade on 9th May 1985, with the next planned centenary date expected to be the major 50th Anniversary on 9th May 1995. The Soviet Union was in 1990 however beginning to disintegrate, and perhaps acknowledging that there might not be another occasion to do so, the decision was taken to hold a Victory Parade in 1990 in commemoration of the 45th Anniversary of the end of the Second World War in Europe. The parade was duly held on Red Square on 9th May 1990, with the armoured element led by rebuilt T-34-85 medium tanks of wartime vintage.

The Defence Minister, Dmitry Timofeevich Yazov took the parade from his ZiL-41044 cabriolet limousine as Soviet Premier Mikhail Gorbachov observed from the traditional observation stand on the Lenin Mausoleum. The parade commander was Colonel-General Nikolai Vasilevich Kalinin, who had formerly been commander of the Soviet VDV airborne forces before taking the position of MVO commander in 1989.

Repeating the format of the 40th Anniversary parade in 1985, the 1990 parade also included a major historical element, beginning with infantry and marines in wartime uniform. The armoured element began with a parade of 21 rebuilt T-34-85s, painted in Second World War markings and with common wartime slogans such as "Boevaya Podruga" (combat girlfriend) painted on their turrets. A single T-34-85 led a row of three tanks, which was immediately followed by another lead tank ahead of sixteen T-34-85 tanks - apparently replicating the parade formation of the original Victory Parade in June 1945. In contrast with the last historic parade in May 1985, there were no SU-100s displayed in 1990.

The restored T-34-85s were followed by UAZ-469B vehicles with troops in wartime uniform, 16

2S3M self-propelled howitzers parade through Red Square on 9th May 1990, painted as with all participating vehicles in field camouflage rather than parade markings.

early 1960s vintage ZiL-157s with troops dressed in "Great Patriotic War" era uniforms, and more ZiL-157s towing wartime 76.2mm M-1942 (ZiS-3) dual-purpose guns.

Modern armour followed the historical introduction, with the military vehicles on parade in May 1990 being painted in a three-colour camouflage paint scheme. BTR-80 wheeled armoured personnel carriers led the armoured section of the parade, having since 1987 replaced the BTR-70, which had been the short-lived parade standard wheeled APC on Red Square only since 1980. The new BTR-80s were followed by 16 ZiL-131s towing wartime 122mm M-1938 (M-30) howitzers, and more ZiL-157s mounting the famous BM-13MNN "Katyusha" MRS, ZiL-131s with wartime 37mm M-1939 anti-aircraft guns, and Ural-4320 6x6 all-terrain trucks towing wartime 85mm M-1939 anti-aircraft guns taking up the rear-guard of the wartime section of the parade.

As was often the case in Red Square parades, two successive generations of vehicle, incoming and outgoing, were paraded together in May 1990. The BMP-2 paraded through Red Square immediately followed by its production replacement, the new BMP-3, which made its first public appearance at the 9th May 1990 parade. A total of 25 BMP-3s were paraded through Red Square with a further ten vehicles distributed along the parade route as reserve vehicles. The BMP-3 did not appear during the following November parade, and would not be seen again on Red Square until 2008, nearly two decades later.

The tank contingent at the 9th May 1990 parade consisted of the T-72B and T-80UD MBTs of the Tamanskaya and Kantemirovskaya divisions, followed by the 2S1, 2S3M and airborne 2S9 self-propelled artillery pieces. The modernised BMD-2 VDV airborne forces vehicle also had its parade debut in May 1990 as the production replacement for the venerable BMD-1, which had first debuted on Red Square in 1974. The BMD-2 featured a new enlarged turret armed with a 30mm 2A42 cannon, replicating the modernisation of the original ground forces BMP-1 to BMP-2 specification.

The rocket artillery was as always paraded immediately following the armoured section of the parade, with 9K51 (BM-21) "Grad" MRS, now mounted on the modernised and diesel engined Ural-4320 chassis, and with the parade debut of the larger and already long-serving 9K57 (BM-27) "Uragan" and its 9P140 launcher vehicle mounted on the BAZ-135LMP chassis, which had also been in Soviet Army service for nearly 30 years. The large number of military trucks evident included the new KrAZ-260 produced at Kremenchug in Ukraine as a replacement for the

9P129 SPU vehicles for the 9K79 "Tochka" tactical rocket (OTR) system parade through Red Square in May 1990; followed by 9P117M SPU vehicles for the 9K72 "Elbrus" OTR.

The BMP-2 was in May 1990 paraded together with its designated replacement, the BMP-3, but the BMP-3 was not subsequently paraded in November, and would not be seen again on Red Square until 2008. (Mikhail Baryatinsky)

venerable KrAZ-255B heavy all-terrain load carrier, towing the new 152mm 2A36 field gun.

The ground artillery was followed by the usual ubiquitous display of surface to air missile systems. The tracked MT-LB based 9K35M 'Strela-10M" - sometimes designated Strela-10SV (Sukhoputnye Voiska - Ground Forces) and later production 9K33M3 "Osa-AKM" mounted on the amphibious BAZ-5937 chassis were followed by the parade debut of the S-300 SAM system, with the 9P85S SPU vehicles based on the 8x8 MAZ-543M chassis.

By standard tradition since the early 1970s, the May 1990 parade concluded with a display of OTR tactical rocket systems, with no long-range strategic nuclear delivery weapons on display. The long-serving 9P113 "Luna-M" (9K52) (NATO: FROG-7) SPU vehicle mounted on its 8x8 BAZ-135 chassis was followed by six 9P129 "Tochka" (9K79) (NATO: SS-21) launcher vehicles, with the parade finale consisting of six 9P117M SPU vehicles for the 9K72 "Elbrus" (NATO: Scud B) OTR system.

The historic element of the 9th May 1990 Victory Parade included the wartime BM-13 "Katyusha" MRS mounted on the 1960s era ZiL-157 chassis as the BM-13NMM (2B7R).

As with all armoured vehicles paraded on 9th May 1990, this BTR-80 is painted in a three-colour field camouflage colour scheme.

This view of a BTR-80 during the 9th May 1990 Red Square parade clearly shows the defining features of the final Soviet era wheeled APC, namely the clamshell side doors and significantly modified engine deck.

The 9P140 launcher vehicle for the 220mm calibre 9K57 "Uragan" (Hurricane) MRS also had its Red Square public debut on 9th May 1990.

The new 9K57 "Uragan" MRS was mounted on the complex 8x8 BAZ (ZiL)-135LMP all-terrain chassis, which had been developed at ZiL three decades earlier.

The 5P85S SPU vehicle for the S-300P SAM system also made its Red Square public debut on 9th May 1990. Several versions of the S-300 system were produced, mounted on trailer, wheeled and tracked chassis, but only the wheeled MAZ-543M based S-300P versions were ever displayed on Red Square.

7th November 1990 – 73rd Anniversary of the Great October Socialist Revolution

The 7th November 1990 parade on Red Square commemorated the 73rd Anniversary of the Great October Socialist Revolution. It was to be the last-ever Soviet era Red Square military parade, though that may not have been clear to the population at large at the time. Demolition of the Berlin Wall had begun in June 1990. East Germany had left the Warsaw Pact in September 1990, and had on 3rd October reunited with West Germany, and the withdrawal of 380,000 Soviet troops from Germany was ongoing. By the time of the November 1990 parade, Czechoslovakia, Hungary and Poland had also all left the Warsaw Pact.

The November parade was as in May taken by Defence Minister Marshal of the Soviet Union Dmitry T. Yazov, with the parade commander being the commander of the Moscow Garrison (MVO) Colonel-General Nikolai Vasilevich Kalinin. Soviet President Mikhail Sergeevich Gorbachov stood on the Lenin Mausoleum review stand in his dual role of General Secretary of the TsK KPSS (the Central Committee of the Communist Party of the Soviet Union or CPSU) and Soviet Premier, together with the usual assembly of ministerial figureheads. The 7th November 1990 parade as presided over by Soviet Premier Mikhail Gorbachov would be the last Soviet military parade to be held on Red Square.

The parade was conducted in light snow with banners expressing "Perestroika". In somewhat direct contrast to the reformist words on the banners, the military parade culminated in the reap-

The BMD-2 airborne combat vehicle made it public debut on 7th November 1990. The 30mm 2A42 automatic cannon and 9P135M "Konkurs" ATGM launch system provided the BMD-2 with the same firepower as the ground forces BMP-2. (TASS)

pearance of intercontinental range strategic nuclear weapons on Red Square as a reminder to the West that the country remained one of the world's two superpowers, just in case the "Perestroika" did not take hold. In the eventuality, the rebuilding of "Perestroika" would sweep the Soviet Union from existence and the Soviet Premier would latterly take up residence in Surrey, England, operating a charitable foundation based in California.

Soviet Premier Mikhail Gorbachov personally made the speech from the Lenin Mausoleum, which was in of itself ominous, in that the only other time the Soviet Premier had directly made the commemorative speech was on 7th November 1941 when Stalin addressed the assembled parade as the country was fighting for its very survival. The situation was in 1990 not dissimilar, though the threat in 1990 was from within; the Warsaw Pact had disintegrated, and the Soviet Union itself was imploding as the armoured vehicles by tradition traversed Red Square on 7th November 1990.

The marching columns consisted of the usual mix of infantry from the Moscow Garrison (MVO), representatives of the various branches of the armed forces and cadets from military academies, followed by armoured columns and other heavy equipment. The tanks and armoured vehicles of the Kantemirovskaya Tank Division and Tamanskaya Motorized Rifle Division entered Red Square from their traditional staging point on Gorky Street, the PVO (air defence) and rocket systems from Manezhnaya Square, with the VDV airborne vehicles entering Red Square from the direction of Okhotny Ryad.

All of the vehicles paraded through Red Square as the first snow flurries of winter fell on the carefully formed cobbles were as in May again painted in three-colour camouflage. The parade was a balance of all current military technology as perhaps befitting a final "full" parade of Soviet military might, with the vehicles for the last time in history entering Red Square in four columns, two either side of the Lenin Museum. The rebuilding of the arched wall Voskresensky Gate across one

The RT-2PM "Topol" (NATO: SS-25 Sickle) ICBM made its public debut on 7th November 1990, the first appearance of such a long-range strategic rocket since 1974. The six RT-2PM "Topol" ICBMs on their 15U168 SPU vehicles based on the MAZ-7917 chassis were the very last weapon systems to parade through Red Square during the Soviet era. (TASS)

of the entrances to Red Square the following year would ensure that even as the military parades were restarted many years later, they could never again be on the massed scale of Soviet era parades.

The November 1990 parade replicated the May parade with the notable absence of the historical element, and the 9P113 and 9P117M OTR systems for the 9K52 and 9K72 OTR systems which had been parade staples for 25 years, but with the significant reintroduction of intercontinental missiles after an absence of 15 years. The parade was as usual led by UAZ-469B light vehicles, followed by 21 BTR-80 wheeled APCs of the Guards Tamanskaya Motor Rifle Division directly followed by 21 tracked BMP-2 infantry vehicles. The BMP-3s paraded for the first time in May were nowhere to be seen, with the BMP-2s being in November followed directly by 25 VDV airborne forces BMD-2 tracked airborne vehicles that had their parade debut in May 1990. Tanks then entered the square in the form of 25 late model T-72B tanks of the 2nd Guards Tamanskaya Motor Rifle Division and 25 T-80UD MBTs of the 4th Guards Kantemirovskaya Tank Division.

Self-propelled artillery was represented in the form of twelve VDV airborne forces 2S9 "Nona-S" artillery support vehicles which led 12 2S1 "Gvozdika" 122mm and 12 2S3M "Akatsiya" 152mm tracked howitzers, followed by twelve Ural-4320 mounted 9K51 (BM-21) "Grad" and twelve 9K57 (BM-27) "Uragan" multiple rocket systems mounted on the BAZ-135LMP chassis. Air defence vehicles were demonstrated in the form of twelve of the later BAZ-5937 based

The T-80UD MBT was paraded on Red Square in May and November 1990 together with the T-72B. The diesel engine powered T-80UD as displayed on Red Square was built in Kharkov. The T-80U was built in Leningrad and Omsk. (Mikhail Baryatinsky)

9K33M3 "Osa-AKM" (NATO: SA-8 Gecko) and MAZ-543M based 9P85S SPU vehicles of the S-300 (S-300P) system. The end of the parade was however the defining differentiator from the preceding May parade. Six BAZ-5921 mounted 9P129 (9K79) "Tochka" (NATO: SS-21 Scarab) vehicles were displayed as in May, now having replaced the venerable BAZ-135 mounted 9P113 "Luna-M" on Red Square after a quarter of a century of regular appearances. These OTR vehicles were however followed by what might be described depending on one's viewpoint as either the swansong of the Soviet Union's military displays on Red Square, or the sting in the Soviet Union's tail.

Medium and long range strategic rockets had not been demonstrated on Red Square since 1974, and the first truly road mobile medium range ballistic missile, the RSD-10 "Pioner" (NATO: SS-20 Saber) mounted on the MAZ-547A chassis was never displayed in public before being eliminated from service and decommissioned during the final years of the Soviet Union in accordance with the 1987 INF agreement. However, a far more fearsome mobile strategic rocket made its public debut at the very end of the very last Soviet parade held on 7th November 1990. The highlight of the November 1990 parade was undoubtedly the debut of the RT-2PM "Topol" ICBM mounted on its 14x12 MAZ-7917 based 15U168 SPU vehicle, six RT-2 PM (RS-12M) "Topol" (NATO: SS-25 Sickle) ICBMs forming the rear-guard of the last Soviet era military parade ever held in Red Square. The "Topol" missiles had a range of 11,000km which gave the ability to strike locations in the heartland of the United States when launched from locations in European Russia - a metaphorical "parting shot" from the Soviet Union, indicating that although it was in its swansong months, the strategic military power of the State remained very much intact.

The 7th November 1990 parade was the last Red Square military parade held in the era of the Soviet Union. There would be no military parade held in November 1991, and the following month the Soviet State would cease to exist. The era of Soviet military parades on Red Square was at an end.

The T-72B was the final version of the T-72 MBT displayed on Red Square during the Soviet era. The significantly increased turret frontal armour is evident in this view.

1991

The disintegration of the Soviet Union that had begun with the Estonian Soviet Socialist Republic (SSR) declaring State sovereignty from Moscow on 16th November 1988 had by the end of 1990 led to similar demands for independence in the Lithuanian and Latvian SSRs, and ethnic clashes in Nagorno-Karabakh, Georgia, Kazakhstan, Uzbekistan and Tajikistan. The Warsaw Pact was disbanding, Germany had re-united and the troublesome "Solidarity" union leader and reformer Lech Wałęsa had in December 1990 become President of Poland. The established order in the Soviet Union and its post-war allied Warsaw Pact states was rapidly disintegrating. Within months, the Soviet Union would collapse, and for several years thereafter all thoughts of military parades were secondary to pressures of individual and State economic survival.

The Soviet collapse of 1991 was sudden, but the decline had been gradual. The military parades of the late 1960s had been the epitome of Soviet military might on public display, but the Soviet State had thereafter begun to stagnate both politically and economically as it struggled to compete with the West economically in the latter stages of the Cold War "arms race". The combined costs of major developments such as the decade-long war in Afghanistan and demands for autonomy within the Warsaw Pact countries starting with Poland had also begun to take their toll on the Moscow based government that was central to the Soviet empire.

The Estonian SSR, which had declared State sovereignty from Moscow on 16th November 1988, had been renamed the Republic of Estonia on 8th August 1990. The Lithuanian SSR had in January 1991 attempted the same reformation, which resulted in Premier Gorbachov on 8th January sending the elite Soviet "Alfa" anti-terrorist group and the 76th VDV Airborne Division to Lithuania. Over the three days 11-13th January the attempt at independence was militarily crushed

Soviet T-72BV tanks in Vilnius during the "January Events" of 11-13 January 1991, which were a foretaste of events later in the year in Moscow.

by Soviet armour, this time of the airborne variety. The situation facing Gorbachov in 1991 was reminiscent of that facing Khrushchev in 1956, and Brezhnev in 1968, except that it was now the republics of the Soviet Union that were breaking away rather than allied Warsaw Pact members. In 1991 the Soviet Premier himself would come under direct threat.

The Soviet Union did not receive the level of criticism that might have been the expected norm during the final months of Cold War as it was sending troops into Lithuania. The Soviet military operation in Lithuania received news coverage, but the focus of the United States and many other countries was at the time otherwise diverted in the Middle East. As the Soviet Union fought a rear-guard action in the Baltic Republics, a coalition of 35 nations was preparing to invade Iraq in response to Saddam Hussein's invasion of Kuwait, of which he had advised the United States beforehand, and for which action he believed he had received tacit acceptance if not approval. Days after Soviet airborne forces armour had been deployed in Lithuania, Western coalition armoured forces were deployed in Iraq in what would later be called the (first) Gulf War.

The Warsaw Pact was formally disbanded in Prague on 1st July 1991 by the Czech President Václav Havel, thus ending an enduring military cooperation that had started six years after the formation of NATO and which had lasted for thirty-six years.

The following month, hard-line communists within the CPSU in August 1991 staged a coup d'état in Moscow, while Gorbachov was in Crimea on vacation - the August "Putsch". On 19th August Gorbachov after an unsuccessful "interview" at Foros in Crimea was confined under house arrest at his dacha and his communications cut by the KGB, all of whose personnel were returned to duty from vacation. As news of Gorbachov's "kidnap" spread, there were widespread public protests in Moscow and Leningrad. The army was deployed on the streets of Moscow, but the civilian protesters responded with Molotov cocktail petrol bombs, with the news coverage worldwide showing burning BMPs in central Moscow surrounded by rioters. The Soviet Army refused to support the coup attempt beyond immediate direct action required to maintain order, and an impasse was reached.

Without the support of the Soviet Army, the

Though the last Soviet Red Square parade was in November 1990, tanks would be seen on the streets of Moscow in August 1991, and again in early October 1993. On both occasions this would be as a result of major political upheavals rather than deployment for ceremonial purposes.

T-80UD tanks parked on Vasilevsky Spusk, the cobbled exit ramp used by vehicles leaving Red Square parades for decades. On this occasion, the tanks are parked up following the attempted coup d'état of August 1991.

coup attempt rapidly lost momentum, and Gorbachov regained full control of the government within days, with the assistance of his political rival Boris Yeltsin, famously pictured standing on a tank belonging to the Tamanskaya Motorised Rifle Division outside the State Parliament building. The coup collapsed on 23rd August, the day following Gorbachov's return to Moscow by his captors. There were major changes in the structure of the armed forces during such a period of massive upheaval and uncertainty, and the same day Marshal of the Soviet Union Dmitry Yazov was replaced by Marshal of Aviation Yevgenny Shaposhnikov.

During the week of the attempted coup d'état in the Soviet Union, Estonia and Latvia had however declared independence, on 20th and 21st August respectively. The day after the coup collapsed, Ukraine on 24th August also declared independence. Belorussia declared independence on the 25th, Moldova on the 27th, and Kyrgyzstan and Uzbekistan on the 31st August, with Tajikistan and Kazakhstan following suit on 9th and 16th September respectively. The Soviet Union was in a state of collapse.

By the end of the week of the coup attempt, it was clear that the Soviet Union could not con-

Soviet Militia on the Krymsky Bridge near Gorky Park in August 1991 as the Soviet Union was in its swansong months of existence.

Crowds mingle with T-72B tanks and BMP-1 MICVs of the 2nd Guards Tamanskaya MRD after the failed attempted coup d'état of August 1991.

A column of T-80 tanks moving along the Sadovaya Koltso (Garden Ring) second Moscow ring road after the events of August 1991.

tinue as it had in the past, with dissent in the former Warsaw Pact countries, in the Soviet Republics, and in the Soviet capital, Moscow. The coup attempt had been foiled, but it was clear others would follow, and the crushing of the August "Putsch" had boosted the presence of Boris Yeltsin as a new and powerful character in Soviet politics.

The street fighting in Moscow in the latter days of August 1991 was brief, but the direct clashes between the State and the civil population was the fledgling Russian Federation's first close shave with civil war. Tanks that had been traditionally paraded on Red Square had been operationally deployed on the streets of Moscow, and would be deployed once again in 1993. T-72 and T-80 MBTs of the 4th Guards Kantemirovskaya Tank Division and the 2nd Guards Tamanskaya MRD patrolled the streets of Moscow, supported by wheeled BTR-70 APCs, tracked BMP MICVs and BTR-60PU-12 communications vehicles. Soviet VDV airborne forces and their BMD armoured vehicles were also briefly deployed in several areas of the city. Subsequent to the events in Moscow, Marshal of the Soviet Union Dmitry Yazov was on 23rd August 1991 replaced in his po-

BMD-1 and BTR-D VDV airborne forces vehicles parked on Kalinin Prospekt (renamed Novy Arbat in 1994) in central Moscow, during the attempted coup d'état of August 1991.

A Russian "babushka" (grandmother) remonstrating with a T-72B MBT near the Russian Bely Dom (White House) in August 1991. The exact scene would repeat two years later, during which the building (unseen to the left of the photograph) would be destroyed by tank-gun fire.

Boris Yeltsin standing on a T-72BV tank outside the Russian Bely Dom on 22nd August 1991. The same building would be central to further events involving military intervention in October 1993. (TASS).

sition of Soviet Defence Minister by Marshal of Aviation Yevgenny Shaposhnikov. The last Soviet Defence Minister, who would remain in the position until 21st December 1991, would not oversee any military parades on Red Square.

Considering the overall events of 1991, and the recent attempt at a coup d'état in August with the Soviet Army requiring to be deployed on the streets of Moscow, the decision was taken in the circumstances not to hold a 7th November military parade in 1991. The following month, on 25th December 1991, Mikhail Gorbachov signed the declaration dissolving the Soviet Union. That evening, the Soviet flag was lowered from the Kremlin roof for the last time and with the Supreme Soviet ratification of the declaration on 26th December, the Soviet Union was no more. On paper, the Soviet Union was abolished at midnight on 31st December 1991, but it had already ceased to exist with the declarations of independence made by the other republics including the "core" republics of Belorussia and Ukraine in the recent autumn. With the formal dissolution of the Soviet Union, the fledgling Russian Federation was now again approximately the size it had been at the time of the original pre-revolutionary Russian Empire. The founding State of the Soviet Union entered a period of sustained economic crisis and for several years all considerations of military parades were abandoned as the Russian Federation adjusted to the severe difficulties of the initial post-Soviet years, at both a State and an individual level. The end of socialism would bring unemployment, instability, depopulation of rural centres as the population drifted to the cities to seek employment, and social devastation caused by the collapse of the system which had provided stability for several decades, all of which was achieved under the brief premiership of Mikhail Gorbachov.

For the remainder of the 1990s, there were no military parades involving heavy "tekhnika" held in Moscow's Red Square, with the only parade involving tanks and heavy weapons being held on 9th May 1995 on Kutuzovsky Prospekt to the west of the city centre in celebration of the 50th Anniversary of Victory in Europe. Military parades continued to be held occasionally in other Russian cities however, and also in some former Soviet States such as Ukraine which continued to hold parades in major cities including Kiev and Kharkov, but now on the 24th August celebrating Ukrainian Independence Day rather than on 7th November as in Soviet times. These parades were not however on the scale of Soviet era parades and did not have the attention that had been afforded the Red Square parades, which had been the signature display of Soviet military might throughout the Cold War.

Epilogue

As 1992 dawned, the Russian Federation was entering a new phase of development, as were the former states that had been integral to the history of the Soviet Union. The country switched from seven decades of "Soviet socialism" to free-market "capitalism" almost overnight, Western businesses and financial companies flooded into the country, and the Russian Federation quickly entered the world business community. American and other foreign businessmen in Siberian "banyas" learned from their affable hosts the devastating statistics of the Eastern Front in World War Two, and admitted with good grace that what they had been taught in school had not given the complete story. Russian hosts in turn thanked their American, British and Canadian guests for Lend-Lease assistance during the Second World War, and toasts were drunk to international cooperation, beautiful women, families and peace in our time. American companies sold equipment to the new Russian Federation, European companies set up vehicle and other manufacturing plants, Russian built rockets were (and still are) used to put American satellites into space, while aircraft engines and other advanced engineering components were built for export in the same cities that had previously specialised in military manufacture for the Soviet State.

The biggest surprise for "Westerners" based in and travelling to the Russian Federation in those immediate post-Soviet days, was that the Russians they dealt with had far more in common with them than they had differences. Many of those foreign businessmen working in the Russian Federation in the 1990s were former military personnel - Americans that had served in Vietnam, and British with service in Northern Ireland and Iraq. Many Russians meantime had relatively recent combat experience in Afghanistan. The differences in history, culture, and individual politics were of no consequence when seated round the table with former "adversaries". Why there ever should have been a Cold War conflict between Russians and Americans in particular, who were so similar in outlook and character despite very different cultural upbringings, was a constant theme of discussion as individuals met and got to know each other, and their respective families and children.

The history of World War One, the Russian Revolution and subsequent Russian "civil" war, "Operation Barbarossa" and World War Two, and the Cold War flashpoints in Europe and by proxy around the world were now all a closed chapter in a darker time in history. The emergent superpowers of the late 20th Century had closed out their differences and moved forward in a spirit of peace and cooperation as the century came to a close. The world was now looking at a brighter future, based on trade and commerce with the Russian Federation and the countries of the former Soviet Union rather than the threat of superpower conflict over competing ideologies, whether real or inflated for military budgeting purposes. For those who lived through those years in the Russian Federation in the 1990s, whether Russian national or foreign expatriate, it was inconceivable that the world could or would slide backwards so dramatically. The Cold War was over. Or so it had seemed at the time.

> *"Us, and them.*
> *And after all we're only ordinary men.*
> *Me, and you.*
> *God only knows it's not what we would choose to do.*
> *"Forward" he cried from the rear*
> *and the front rank died.*
> *And the General sat and the lines on the map*
> *moved from side to side."*
>
> "Us and Them". Lyrics © Roger Waters*

---

* With personal thanks to Roger for kind permission to use his lyrics from "Dark Side of the Moon"

"Tekhnika" Paraded on Red Square
1946-91

The "tekhnika" or military equipment described below is divided into the equipment types as demonstrated on Red Square from the end of World War Two until the breakup of the Soviet Union in 1991. The equipment within each section is as far as possible grouped chronologically according to its original appearance on Red Square rather than alphabetically, as this provides a better historical context, albeit with a bit of searching required within a section to find a particular vehicle or equipment type.

BRDM

BRDM 2P27

BRDM 2P32

BRDM 9P110

BRDM-2

BRDM-2 9P122 (9P133)

Armoured Cars

BRDM

The BRDM was the first purpose designed amphibious "Bronirovanaya Dozornaya Mashina" (Armoured Patrol Vehicle) to be series manufactured for the post-war Soviet Army. Designed by the V.A. Dedkov design bureau as the GAZ-40P (Plavayushy - amphibious), the BRDM armoured car was accepted for service with the Soviet Army in 1958. The first production batch of vehicles featured an open roof, but the majority were fitted with an armoured roof with hatches. The BRDM featured four retractable chain driven aviation type auxiliary wheels to prevent the vehicle bottoming out on rough ground. The BRDM was used for conventional reconnaissance and as a chemical survey (RKh) vehicle. The base vehicle had a crew of two and was armed with a pintle-mounted 7.62mm SGMB or later PKT machine gun. The 5.6 metric tonne combat weight vehicle was powered by a GAZ-40P petrol engine developing 93hp, providing a maximum road speed of 80-90km/h and a road range of 500km. Water speed was 9km/h. After replacement by the later BRDM-2, the BRDM was latterly also referred to as the BRDM-1 to distinguish it from the later model.

BRDM 2P27, 2P32 and 9P110 ATGM Vehicles

With the introduction of anti-tank guided missile (ATGM) systems, the BRDM was also used as a launch platform for three subsequent generations of ATGM system. The earliest 2P27 consisted of a BRDM mounting the 2K16 system and firing the 3M6 "Schmel" (NATO: AT-1 Snapper) ATGM. The later 2P32 launch vehicle introduced into service in 1960 mounted the 3M11 "Fleyta" rocket of the 2K8 "Falanga" (NATO: AT-2 Swatter A) ATGM on the same original BRDM chassis. The final ATGM launch vehicle mounted on the original BRDM was the 9P110 introduced in 1963, firing the 9M14 "Malyutka" (NATO: AT-3 Sagger A) ATGM rocket of the 9K11 system. The 9P110 vehicle mounted six rockets under a retractable roof, with a total complement of 14 rockets. It was later replaced by the 9K11M system mounted on the BRDM-2 based 9P122 ATGM vehicle.

BRDM-2

The BRDM-2 was developed from 1962 as the Izdeliye-41 (Article-41) by a team led by the engineer V.K. Rubtsov at the V.A. Dedkov SKB at GAZ as the earlier BRDM (BRDM-1) was entering service with the Soviet Army. It was accepted for service in 1962 as a replacement for the relatively short-lived BRDM (BRDM-1) and was in series production from December 1964 until 1989. The BRDM-2 was armed with a turret-mounted 14.5mm KPVT heavy machine gun and co-axial 7.62mm PKT machine gun, unified with that mounted on the BTR-60PB, providing considerably improved firepower in comparison with the original BRDM (BRDM-1). Approximately 19,000 BRDM-2s were built in total, of which 50% were specialised variants. The vehicle was powered by a GAZ-41 V-8 petrol engine developing 140hp, providing similar performance to the earlier BRDM (BRDM-1). The BRDM-2 retained the chain driven auxiliary wheels of the earlier vehicle. The BRDM-2 was also widely used in the Soviet Army as a reconnaissance vehicle and a platform for ATGM systems. It was exported to more than 50 countries.

BRDM-2 9P122 (9P133) ATGM Vehicle

The 9P122 launcher vehicle for the 9K11M ATGM system was developed in 1967-68. The vehicle was armed with six 9M14M "Malyutka-M" ATGMs developed at the KBM Bureau at Kolomna, mounted under a hydraulically retractable roof. The missiles were originally known by NATO as the "AT-3 Sagger-A", the same designation as applied to the earlier BRDM mounted vehicle. The missiles had an effective anti-tank range of 500-3,000m and could penetrate 410mm of vertical armour plate, giving the relatively small and lightweight vehicle considerable anti-tank capability. The missiles could be fired remotely from outwith the vehicle by means of a control box, providing long-range overwatch defence for Soviet tank and motorised rifle divisions. The 9P122 had the same 14 rocket complement as the earlier BRDM based vehicle. The 9P122 was paraded on Red Square from 1973. From 1969, the original 9P122 began to be replaced by the modified 9P133 vehicle firing the 9M14P "Malyutka-P" ATGM of the 9K11P system with second generation infrared Semi-Active Command Line of Sight (SACLOS) guidance, with better first hit probability and improved minimum range. The system was further upgraded in 1977, firing the improved 9M14P2 "Malyutka-P2" missile with infrared SACLOS guidance. The 9P133 (NATO: AT-3 Sagger B) was a later modification of the BRDM-2 vehicle mounted system with modified ATGM rockets and improved rocket fire control systems.

BRDM-2 9P124 (9P137) ATGM Vehicle

The relatively rarely seen 9P124 version of the BRDM-2 was also developed from 1967, and was first seen in public on Red Square in 1973. The system mounted four 9M17M "Falanga-M" (NATO: AT-2 Swatter B) missiles of the 2K8M "Falanga-M" system under a retractable overhead roof that looked almost identical to the 9P122. The system was a long-range over watch role ATGM however, while the less capable but simpler and cheaper 9P122 was the more widely deployed system. Four missiles were mounted in the launcher, with another four stored within the hull. The 9M17M "Skorpion-P" rocket could defeat 560mm of vertical armour, had a maximum range of 3,500m and was provided with infrared SACLOS missile guidance. The 9P137 (NATO: AT-2 Swatter C) entered service in 1974.

BRDM-2 9P148 ATGM Vehicle

The 9P148 was the ultimate universal replacement for the 9P122/9P133 and 9P124/9P137 ATGM systems. The vehicle began to enter service in 1974 but was first seen in public on Red Square on 7th November 1979. The 9P148 mounted a retractable multiple 9P135 launcher for the 9K113 (NATO: AT-5 Spandrel) system, firing the 9M113 Konkurs missile, developed at the KBP bureau in Tula, of which 14 were carried within the vehicle - five mounted ready to fire and the remainder within the armoured hull. The missile could penetrate 600mm of vertical armour plate and had a greater operating range of 75-4,000m. The missile also travelled at a faster rate of 208m/s, which reduced flight time to target and thereby its vulnerability to countermeasures.

The five-rail launch system mounted the 9M113 "Konkurs" missiles in their individual launch tubes, with the launcher being rotated through 90° and retracted into the vehicle hull for reloading. The system could also fire the smaller 9M111 "Fagot" missile. The SACLOS guided ATGM was operated by means of an electro-optical sight mounted on the right side of the fighting compartment roof.

BRDM-2 9K31 Strela-1 SAM System

The 9K31 "Strela-1" (NATO: SA-9 Gaskin) SAM was the first new Soviet wheeled SPADS to enter service with the Soviet Army since the 14.5mm KPVT armed BTR-40A and BTR-152A of the 1950s. The system fired the 9M31 missile developed from 1960 at the Nudelman OKB in Moscow in conjunction with several other design bureaus, with the 9P31 launch vehicle being built in Saratov. The 9K31 was in development for a decade before service acceptance with the Soviet Army and Soviet Naval Infantry forces in 1968.

Each Soviet tank regiment and motorised rifle regiment was provided with two anti-aircraft battalions, one of which had two sections equipped with two 9K31 systems, the other provided with the ZSU-23-4 SPADS. The systems were used in combination; the former located 500-2,500m behind the latter, forming a comprehensive defence shield. The original 9P31 launch system vehicle had an engagement range of 4,200m and an altitude ceiling of 3,500m. It was updated from 1970 as the 9P31M, firing the "Strela-1M" missile, with improved lock-on capability and firing altitude of 3,500m and range of up to 8,000m. Subsequent upgrades were the 9P-31M2, 9P-31MR and 9P-31R, firing the improved "Strela-1M2", "Strela-1MR" and "Strela-1R" missiles. The system was replaced in the 1980s by the ZRK "Strela-10", mounted on the tracked MT-LB chassis.

BRDM-2 9P124 (9P137)

BRDM-2 9P148

9P31 (9K31 "Strela-1")

9P31 (9K31 "Strela-1")

Wheeled BTRs

BTR-40

BTR-152

BTR-60P

BTR-60PA

BTR-60PB

BTR-40

Developed as the Obiekt-141, the BTR-40 was the Soviet Union's first post-war wheeled scout car and APC (BTR in Russian). The vehicle was accepted into Soviet Army service in 1950 and remained in series production at GAZ until 1960. The BTR-40 was based on the 4x4 GAZ-63 truck chassis and was used in a variety of models and roles. Variants included the BTR-40A, BTR-40B and the BTR-40K with overhead armour. There were various specialised versions, including anti-aircraft versions, Kh chemical reconnaissance and ZhD rail scout modifications. The BTR-40 was used as both a scout vehicle and light (small) BTR, being complemented in the latter role by the larger BTR-152. The original open-roofed BTR-40 was armed with a single pintle-mounted 7.62mm SGMB machine gun. The later BTR-40B variant, introduced in 1958, had an all welded hull and an armoured roof. A SPADS variant, the BTR-40A, was armed with a tandem 14.5mm ZTPU-2 machine gun installation. Despite the BTR-40 being a standard vehicle used in large numbers by the Soviet Army, it was never paraded on Red Square.

BTR-152

The BTR-152 was the first Soviet designed wheeled APC to enter series production. Developed as the Obiekt-140, based on a modified 6x6 ZiS-151 chassis, the prototype ZiS-152 was accepted for service as the BTR-152 in accordance with a Resolution of the SM SSSR dated 24th March 1950. Though basically an armoured truck with 6-13mm armour, the BTR-152 gave the post-war Soviet Army the type of armoured infantry vehicle it had lacked during World War Two. The BTR-152 remained in series production from 1950 to 1962, with 12,421 vehicles built in several modifications. Originally designed to transport a Soviet infantry section and to tow anti-tank weapons, the original BTR-152 was updated as the BTR-152V - the first wheeled APC in the world with a central tyre pressure regulation (CTPRS) system, the V1 with internal air lines for the CTPRS, and the later V2 and V3 as the ZiS-151 chassis was replaced by the modernised ZiL-157 chassis. The final production model was the BTR-152K with overhead armour. Command vehicles were also built on the BTR-152, designated BTR-152I (BTR-152U in the West).

The original BTR-152 was an open vehicle, with a crew of 2+17, a full Soviet infantry section, armed with a pintle-mounted 7.62mm SGMB machine gun and powered by a ZiS-123 engine developing 110hp, providing a maximum road speed of 70km/h and a range of 780km. Subsequent versions of the vehicle were based on the later ZiL-157 chassis and mechanical components, with the final production model BTR-152K having overhead armour. The BTR-152 was a standard Red Square parade participant in the 1950s. The vehicle remained in service with DOSAAF reserve training units into the 1970s

BTR-60

The BTR-60 (GAZ-49) series was developed in late 1950s by the GAZ design bureau under the direction of V.A. Dedkov, and was accepted for service with the Soviet Army on 13th November 1959 in accordance with Ministry of Defence Order №202. The original production model BTR-60P (Plavayushy - amphibious) was an open roofed vehicle with a crew of 2+14 and a pintle-mounted 7.62mm SGMB machine gun as main armament. The original open BTR-60P was from 1963 replaced by the BTR-60PA (GAZ-49A - known in the West as the BTR-60PK) with overhead armour, and a reduced crew of 2+12, and ultimately with the definitive BTR-60PB variant, which was accepted for service in 1964, armed with a turret mounted 14.5mm KPVT and co-axial 7.62mm PKT machine gun. The BTR-60PB had a crew of 2+8 (a half infantry section).

The early BTR-60P and BTR-60PA were powered by twin GAZ-40 petrol engines developing 90hp each, latterly replaced on the BTR-60PB by twin GAZ-49 petrol engines, in all cases giving a typical maximum speed of 80km/h and a road range of 500km. Water speed was 10km/h. The final BTR-60PB was in production from 1966 to 1976, serving as the main wheeled

APC during the Soviet war in Afghanistan. Several specialised command and communications versions were built on the chassis, such as the R-145BM radio station.

BTR-70

The BTR-70 was developed in 1971 at the GAZ SKB under chief designer Igor S. Mukhin on the basis of the BTR-60PB and via the GAZ-50 prototype. The new vehicle was accepted for service with the Soviet Army on 21st August 1972 in accordance with Ministry of Defence Order №141. The BTR-70 was a major change in design from the earlier BTR-60PB, with a modified hull with half-doors in the sides between the second and third road wheels, providing an element of cover under combat conditions for egressing "desantniki". The turret mounted 14.5mm KPVT and 7.62mm PKT co-axial armament was retained from the BTR-60PB. The crew was now reduced to 3+7 but with far better vehicle ergonomics hence fighting capability. The 11,500kg combat weight vehicle had a road speed of up to 80km/h and a range of 450-500km. The BTR-70 had its Red Square parade debut in November 1980.

The BTR-70 was originally powered by twin GAZ-49B engines developing 115hp each, later replaced by ZMZ-4905 V-8 engines each developing 120hp, for a total of 240hp. Although at 11.5-12.0 metric tonnes the BTR-70 was slightly heavier than its predecessor, road and water performance was identical, with range extended to a maximum 600km. The BTR-70 was produced at GAZ from 1976 until 1981, and thereafter at the affiliated Arzamasky Zavod Avtomobilnikh Zapchasty (Arzamas) plant. Production was on a smaller scale than the preceding BTR-60 or the following BTR-80. The BTR-70 was paraded on Red Square until replaced by the BTR-80 in November 1987.

BTR-80

The BTR-80 appeared in the late 1980s, replacing the BTR-70. The BTR-80 (known also by the manufacturer's designation GAZ-5903) had an enlarged hull relative to the BTR-70, with full height "clamshell" exit doors between the second and third axles providing better egress than with the preceeding BTR-70. The first series production vehicle was completed on 24th February 1984. The BTR-80 retained the same turret and 14.5mm KPVT and co-axial 7.62mm PKT armament arrangement introduced on the BTR-60PB and continued through the BTR-70, albeit with an improved 1P3-2 sight. The vehicle had a crew of 3+7.

Due to the break-up of the Soviet Union, the BTR-80 remained in production and service for more than two decades largely without modification, and remains the principle wheeled BTR in Russian Army service today. The BTR-80 has seen active service with Russian Army and MVD forces in many local conflicts including the two wars in Chechnya, in Ingushetia, Dagestan and more recently during the short Russo-Georgian war in Southern Ossetia in August 2008. It has also seen considerable service abroad with UN contingents such as KFOR. The BTR-80 has now been in service longer than any previous Russian wheeled APC, having been developed taking into consideration service experience with the earlier BTR-60 and BTR-70 series. The 13.6 metric tonne BTR-80 was originally powered by a single KamAZ-7403 V-8 turbo-diesel engine developing 260hp, giving a 90km/h road speed and 600km road range. From 1993, following a fire at the KamAZ engine plant, the BTR-80 has also been fitted with a YaMZ-238M2 diesel engine developing 240hp. Final production BTR-80s have a maximum road speed of 90km/h, with a road range of 600km and an amphibious speed of 10km/h.

BTR-60PB

BTR-70

BTR-70

BTR-80

Tracked APCs

BTR-50PK

MT-LB

BTR-50

The BTR-50 tracked APC was accepted for service with the Soviet Army in 1954 and was series produced from 1954 until as late as 1974. The initial production model was the BTR-50P, armed with a pintle-mounted 7.62mm SGMB machine gun. The BTR-50PA was armed with a 14.5mm KPVT. The BTR-50P had a crew of two and could transport 20 "desant" infantry. The later BTR-50PK featured overhead armour. The BTR-50 had a maximum road speed of 44km/h and a range of approximately 250km. The BTR-50 series was fully amphibious, with a water speed of 10km/h. It was a standard participant in Red Square parades from the mid 1950s until the early 1970s.

MT-LB

The MT-LB multi-purpose armoured vehicle was developed at the KB of the Kharkov Tractor Plant (KhTZ) under the project designation Izdeliye-6 from 1959, and was accepted for service with the Soviet Army on 25th December 1964. The primary role of the MT-LB was as a tracked artillery tractor that could tow ordnance weighing up to 6,500kg together with the gun crew (crew 2+11) and ammunition complement of up to 2,500kg under armour into combat zones. It was also used as a tracked APC and as an SPU vehicle for the ZRK "Strela-10" SAM system. The MT-LB chassis was also used for the MT-LBu series of "1V" command vehicles. The MT-LB was most commonly used to tow the 100mm MT-12 "Rapira" anti-tank gun, though it was also used to tow other light and medium artillery. The MT-LB had a maximum road speed of 62km/h and a range of 500km.

Mechanized Infantry Combat Vehicles (MICVs)

BMP-1

BMP-1

BMP-1

The BMP (Boevaya Mashina Pekhoti - Infantry Fighting Vehicle, known in the West as the MICV) was developed at the Chelyabinsk Tractor Plant (ChTZ) under the direction of Pavel. P. Isakov. It was taken into service with the Soviet Army in accordance with a Resolution of the SM SSSR dated 14th April 1966. The BMP had its public debut at the 7th November 1967 November parade. The BMP was an entirely new concept, developed as the Obiekt-765 at ChTZ in Chelyabinsk. The fully amphibious vehicle did not just deliver desant infantry into combat as with a conventional APC; rather the infantry could egress the vehicle or engage enemy positions from within the protective armour of the vehicle as circumstances dictated. The armour was designed to provide protection from 7.62mm small arms fire at 50 metres. The 12.6 metric tonne BMP (later produced as the BMP-1) also featured an entirely new level of armament for an infantry combat vehicle. The turret was armed with a 73mm 2A28 "Grom" low pressure gun, and also mounted a new ATGM above the main gun barrel, the 9M14 "Malyutka" (NATO: AT-3 "Sagger", capable of engaging MBTs at 1,000m, allowing the vehicle to engage and destroy all encountered targets including tanks. The BMP had a maximum road speed of 60km/hour, good all-terrain capability and was fully amphibious, with the tracks providing propulsion in water at 7km/hour.

The 7th November 1967 parade included the public debut of the BMP-1. The BMP was a ground-breaking new concept; a tracked vehicle that could deliver infantry in the manner of tracked APCs such as the BTR-50, British FV432 and US M113, but was powerfully armed with a combination of 73mm 2A28 low pressure gun and "Malyutka" guided anti-tank missile. The armament allowed the BMP to provide protective fire against infantry, but more importantly, the BMP could also engage and defeat armour including tanks.

The later BMP-1P (Obiekt-765Sp4) mounted the 9P135M ATGM launcher which fired the 9M113 "Konkurs" and smaller 9M111 "Fagot" ATGMs.

BMP-2

The BMP-1 was replaced by the BMP-2, which featured improved armour and a new two-man turret armed with a 30mm 2A42 cannon, and also fired the 9M113M "Konkurs" ATGM. Developed from 1974 via the Obiekt-675 prototype, and based on direct experience from the war in Afghanistan, the BMP-2 entered service with the Soviet Army in 1980. The BMP-2 was originally powered by a UTD-20 engine developing 300hp, and had a maximum road speed of 65km/h, and a range of 600km. The vehicle was amphibious at 7km/h.

BMP-3

The BMP-3 made its public debut at the 9th May 1990 Red Square parade, subsequently appearing on parade on Kutuzovsky Prospekt in the west of Moscow on 9th May 1995, and thereafter re-appearing on Red Square only on 9th May 2008 as military parades were restarted on Moscow's Red Square. The BMP-3 is a complete redesign of the original BMP concept, with an enlarged hull and a new turret mounting a 100mm 2A70 and 30mm 2A72 cannon, with the engine moved from the rear of the vehicle to provide better crew access and protection, and a much enlarged and ergonomically more efficient fighting compartment.

BMP-2

BMP-3

Main Battle Tanks

T-54

The T-54 MBT together with the later T-55 perhaps epitomised Soviet armoured might during the Cold War - the default "Soviet" tank. The T-54 was developed from the interim T-44 by the KB at Plant №183 (Nizhny Tagil). It was in series production from 1947 until 1959 at three plants, namely Plant №183 (Nizhny Tagil), Plant №174 (Omsk) and Plant №75 (Kharkov), with approximately 16,665 tanks built overall in several base modifications. Later modifications included the T-54A, T-54B, and T-54M. Variants included the SU-122-54 tank destroyer, the ZSU-57-2 SPAAG and the MTU-1 (MTU-12) bridgelayer.

The T-54 tank was the staple Soviet MBT during the 1950s and was widely exported in later years. The T-54A was also licence manufactured in Czechoslovakia, Poland and China.

The T-54 had its parade debut on 7th November 1957 concurrently with the parade debut (and only appearance) of the Soviet T-10 heavy tank. It was paraded until the early 1960s, when it was replaced by the T-55 and rapidly thereafter the T-62.

T-55

The T-55 was developed as the Obiekt-155 by the KB at Plant №183 (Nizhny Tagil) as a major redesign of the T-54B. It was accepted for service with the Soviet Army on 8th May 1958, confirmed by the Soviet Ministry of Defence on 24th May 1958. The tank had its parade debut on 7th November 1962, only five years after the earlier T-54 had made its own parade debut on Red Square. The T-55 resembled the T-54B but was a significant modification of the earlier tank. The T-55 was armed with the 100mm D-10T2S tank gun, with a new V-55 engine developing 580hp and myriad other changes.

The T-55 was produced from 1958 until 1983 at the same three plants that manufactured the T-54, namely Plant №183 (Nizhny Tagil), Plant №174 (Omsk) and Plant №75 (Kharkov), with approximately 23,000 Soviet origin tanks built in several modifications including the main T-55, T-55A and T-55M production variants.

The base model T-55 was followed by the T-55A, T-55M / T-55AM and other variants. The T-54 series was produced until as late as 1983 for export. The T-55 tank was, together with the T-54, the best-known default

T-54

T-54B

T-55

T-55

T-62

T-62 M-1972

T-64B

T-64B-1

Soviet tank of the Cold War period. The tank was as with the T-54 licence produced in Poland and Czechoslovakia.

T-62

The T-62 was developed by the KB at Plant №183 (UVZ) at Nizhny Tagil from 1958. For reasons largely related to rivalry between design bureaus and manufacturing plants, the tank was accepted into service as an MBT with long-range overwatch capability, effectively a tank destroyer in the genre of the SU-122-54. The T-62 was armed with a 115mm U-5TS (2A20) "Molot" (hammer) smoothbore gun firing fin-stabilized 3BM series APFSDS sub-calibre ammunition in addition to conventional rounds. The tank was powered by a V-55 (later V-55V) engine developing 580hp.

The T-62 was accepted for service in August 1961 and was series produced from 1st July 1962 until 1975, during which time approximately 20,000 T-62 tanks were built. The tank had its Red Square public debut in November 1965.

The T-62 was used extensively in the Soviet Army. Subsequent to an early variant having been captured by the Chinese Army after being destroyed near Damansky Island at the Amur-Ussuri river confluence near Khabarovsk during fighting on the Sino-Soviet border in 1969, the tank was also released for export relatively early in its production life.

T-64

The T-64 was perhaps the most enigmatic of all post-war Soviet tanks. Development work began as early as 1953, with the design being developed via the Obiekt-430 prototype of 1956 and the later Obiekt-432 prototype, on which work began in 1960. The T-64 was the high-technology, high risk design path alternative to the conventional low risk T-72, ultimately fitted with the same 125mm armament with autoloader (reducing the tank crew to three) but with a horizontally opposed piston 5-TDF diesel engine developing 700hp, which was relatively quiet in service and gave the T-64 a 61km/h maximum road speed and 600km range, but with high levels of maintenance requirements. The T-64 was developed at the KB60 design bureau within Plant №75, the Kharkov Morozov (KhBM) tank plant in Kharkov, Ukraine under the direction of A.A. Morozov.

The first series production batch of T-64 tanks, armed with a 115mm U-5TS (2A20) tank gun were built from October 1963 at the Kharkov Malyshev Plant where it was designed. The T-64 was accepted into service with the Soviet Army as the T-64 MBT on 30th December 1966. The first T-64 tanks were deployed with the 41st Guards Tank Division located near Kharkov, and thereby tested close to home.

The later T-64A was taken into service with the Soviet Army in May 1968, armed with the 125mm 2A46-1 tank gun. The T-64B was introduced in parallel, with later versions, the T-64BV and T-64BV-1 featuring "Kontakt" ERA armour. The T-64 remained in series production for the Soviet Army until 1987, with production being restarted in Ukraine as the T-64BM after the collapse of the Soviet Union.

The T-64 had served with Soviet GSFG forces in East Germany but had never been further distributed, such that the T-64 and its development principles remained unclear almost until the tank had left Soviet service, replaced by the T-80 MBT. The T-64B-1 variant was accepted for service in January 1985, and was the first (and only) T-64 tank type to be paraded on Red Square, four months later, during the 40th Anniversary of VE day on 9th May 1985. The T-64 appeared on Red Square as the tank was effectively leaving service after a 25 year long production run, the tank's belated public debut being in stark contract to most tanks and AFVs which were displayed on Red Square soon after they entered service with the Soviet Army.

The T-64 had served with Soviet GSFG forces in East Germany but had never been further disseminated, such that the T-64 and its development principles remained unclear almost until the tank had left Soviet service, replaced by the T-80 MBT. The T-64 never saw combat during its Soviet Army service life, but in 2014, 23 years after the break-up of the Soviet Union, the T-64 entered combat in large numbers in service with the Ukrainian Army as war raged across Eastern Ukraine.

T-72

Development of the T-72 began at the KB of Plant №183 (UVZ) in Nizhny Tagil in 1963, via a series of prototypes tested from 1967, with the Obiekt-172 being tested for service in February 1971. Redesign work resulted in the Obiekt-172M, with an Establishment Lot of 15 tanks being built for evaluation by the Soviet Army in 1971. The Obiekt-172M was accepted for service with the Soviet Army as the T-72 "Ural" MBT by a Resolution of the TsK KPSS i SM SSSR dated 7th November 1973. A further Establishment Lot of 30 tanks was built in 1973, with T-72 series production commencing at UVZ in 1974. The 44.5 metric tonne T-72 was powered by a diesel engine developing 840hp, which gave the tank a maximum road speed of 60km/h, and a range of 500km.

The T-72 MBT was armed with the 125mm 2A46, fitted an autoloader, thereby reducing the crew to three as with the T-64. The T-72 tank had its public debut on Red Square in November 1977. The modified T-72A (Obiekt-172A) entered service with the Soviet Army in 1979 and was seen on Red Square from 1981. From 1984, the T-72A was displayed with additional armour lining on the turret roof. The modified T-72B (Obiekt-184) was accepted for service with the Soviet Army by a Resolution of the TsK KPSS i SM SSSR dated 27th October 1984, and introduced into service in 1985, appearing on Red Square from the following year. The T-72B-1 featured additional armour on the hull and turret front. The T-72M and M1 models were built for export from 1980 and 1982 respectively. The T-72 was licence manufactured in Czechoslovakia and Poland. The T-72 was paraded on Red Square during the late 1970s and early 1980s in T-72, T-72A and later T-72B modifications.

In April 1989, the T-72B was deployed on the streets of Tibilisi, Georgia. T-72A and T-72B tanks were deployed on the streets of Moscow during the attempted coup in August 1991, in Azerbaijan in May 1992, and in Nagorno-Karabakh in August 1992. In May 1992, T-72s of the 201st MRD were deployed in Dushanbe, Tajikistan at the beginning of what would become a five-year long civil war in the country. The T-72A saw action in Chechnya in December 1994, for the duration of the first Chechen war and during the five-day war between Georgia and Yuzhno Ossetia in 2008.

The T-72S, the export configuration version of the T-72B, fitted with ERA, was displayed on Moscow's Kutuzovsky Prospekt during the 9th May 1995 Victory Day celebrations. The T-72 series would make a comeback on Red Square in a modernized form in 2017 as the T-72BM3.

T-80

The T-80 MBT was developed at the SKB-2 at LKZ in Leningrad from 1968 and was accepted into service with the Soviet Army on 6th August 1976. It was series produced at LKZ (Leningrad) from 1976 to 1990, with later production also being introduced from 1985 at OZTM (Omsk) and at KhZTM (Kharkov). The T-80 MBT was the first series production MBT to be fitted with a GTD gas turbine engine. The T-80, which was initially armed with the 125mm 2A46-1 tank gun, was modified several times during its production life, with variants including the T-80B (Obiekt-219R) introduced in 1978, armed with the 2A46-2 gun, 1A33 fire control system and powered by the GTD-1000TF engine uprated to 1,100hp, the T-80U (Obiekt-219AS) introduced in 1984, armed with the 2A46M-1 gun and powered by the GTD-1250 engine developing 1,250hp, the T-80BV introduced in 1985 with ERA armour, the 1A33-1 fire control system and other changes, the T-80UD (Obiekt-478B) introduced at KhBM in Kharkov in 1987 and powered by a 6TD diesel engine developing 1,000hp, and the later T-80UM.

The T-80 (T-80UD) had its public debut on Red Square in the very twilight years of the Soviet Union, being paraded on Red Square in May and November 1990 and at a single post-Soviet Victory Parade held in Moscow in May 1995. The T-80 was however evident on the streets of Moscow in 1991 and on a larger scale in 1993, and not for ceremonial reasons. During the latter constitutional crisis, T-80 tanks were moved into Moscow to put down a rebellion, and in 1993 fired live rounds into the Russian Parliament Building, the Russian "White House".

T-72

T-72A

T-72B

T-80U

T-80UD

THE SOVIET ARMY ON PARADE 1946-91

Heavy Tanks

T-10

The T-10 heavy tank was the last of the famous Iosef Stalin or IS line of Soviet heavy tanks, and also the last Soviet heavy tank to be series manufactured. The T-10 made a single appearance on Red Square in November 1957. The T-10B as paraded once only on Red Square on 7th November 1957 was already being replaced by the radically modernised T-10M at the time the "older" variant (by two years only) was being demonstrated on Red Square. By the time of the T-10s introduction, the heavy tank concept was becoming redundant due to the development of Main Battle Tanks (MBTs) and also the introduction of Anti-Tank Guided Missile (ATGM) systems. The T-10 would be the last Soviet production heavy tank design, and thereby the last Soviet heavy tank to be paraded on Red Square.

T-10

Self-Propelled Artillery

SU-76

The SU-76 self-propelled gun was developed in late 1942 by the N.A. Astrov design bureau as a close-support weapon for infantry and tank formations, mating the 76.2mm M-1942 (ZiS-3) dual purpose gun with a modified T-70 light tank chassis. The early SU-76 (SU-12) entered production in January 1943, but was quickly replaced by the modified SU-76M (SU-15) with a less capricious tandem engine layout and other modifications. The SU-76 was produced at Plant №38 (Kirov), Plant №40 (Moscow) and GAZ in Gorky. The SU-76 series was second only to the T-34 in terms of armoured vehicle production output in World War Two. The SU-76M featured in the very early post-war parades on Red Square.

SU-76M

SU-100

SU-100

The SU-100 was a development of the earlier SU-85 based on the original T-34 chassis. Introduced into production in September 1944, its formation into combat units was delayed until November when sufficient supplies of newly developed ammunition were made available for the 100mm D-10S armament that was developed from a naval weapon. The SU-100 proved an efficient tank-killer in the final months of the Second World War. It served with the Soviet Army in a reserve capacity into the 1960s and was manufactured under licence in Czechoslovakia post-war as the SD-100.

ISU-122

ISU-122

The late wartime ISU-122 continued in service with the post-war Soviet Army for several years, but the T-54 MBT armed with a 100mm D-10T tank gun provided almost the same level of armour penetration, such that the ISU-122 was quickly relegated to reserve status, with many ISU-122s later being converted to ISU-T ARVs. The ISU-122 was apparently demonstrated on Red Square in 1946, but thereafter only the ISU-152 was regularly displayed.

ISU-152

ISU-152

The wartime ISU-152 continued to serve with the Soviet Army in the immediate post war years as a heavy support assault gun, but as with the ISU-122 the ISU-152 was quickly relegated to reserve status. The ISU-152 was paraded on Red Square until the end of the 1940s.

2S1 Gvozdika

The 2S1 "Gvozdika" (Carnation) SPH was the first of the GRAU designation "2S" series of tracked artillery vehicles, which were developed in the 1960s but introduced into service in the 1970s. The 2S1 SPH was developed in accordance with a Resolution of the TsK i SM SSSR №609-201 dated 4th July 1967, which authorised full-scale development of the "2S" series of self-propelled artillery. The GRAU "2S" series, all named after flowers, included the 2S1 "Gvozdika", the 2S2 "Fialka", the 2S3 "Akatsiya" and the 2S4 "Tulipan". The 2S1 was developed on the Izdeliye-10 (MT-LBuSh) chassis as a long-overdue self-propelled replacement for the towed 122mm M-1938 (M-30) and the more recent 122mm D-30 in Soviet Army motorised rifle regiments. The 2S1 was taken into service with the Soviet Army in accordance with a Resolution of the TsK KPSS i SM SSSR dated 14th September 1970.

The 2S1 chassis was built at KhTZ in Kharkov based on components of the MT-L and MT-LB chassis. The 122mm 2A31 (D-32) howitzer armament was developed by OKB-9 (the Petrov design bureau) at Uralmash with the YaMZ-238N engine developing 300hp built at Yaroslavl.

Maximum range was 15.3km with conventional ammunition or 21.9km using rocket-assisted projectiles. The 15.7 tonne combat weight 2S1 had a road speed of 61.5km/h. The 2S1 was fully amphibious with a water speed of 4.5km/h. The 2S1 was allocated to Divisional artillery regiments and Regimental artillery battalions.

2S3 Akatsiya

The 2S3 "Akatsiya" (Acacia) SPH was also developed at Uraltransmash in accordance with a Resolution of the TsK i SM SSSR №609-201 dated 4th July 1967 authorising the "2S" series of self-propelled guns. The 2S3 (Obiekt-303) was based on the same universal chassis as also used for the 2K11 "Krug" medium range SAM system, and powered by a V-59-4 V-12 engine developing 520hp. Designed as a self-propelled replacement for the towed 152mm ML-20, D-1 and D-20 howitzers, the 2S3 was accepted for service in December 1971.

The 2S3 was armed with the 152mm 2A33 (D-22) howitzer, developed at OKB-9 in Perm on the basis of the towed 152mm D-20. Maximum range was 17.3-20km depending on ammunition type with a maximum rate of fire of three rounds/minute. The vehicle had a road speed of 60km/h and a range of 500km.

The original 2S3 was modernised in 1975 as the 2S3M, with a new 12 round ammunition carousel system for the 2A33M gun, increased ammunition complement (40 to 46 rounds), modified ammunition loading hatches and new ammunition types. The return rollers were also repositioned. The 2S3M was subsequently modified from 1987 as the 2S3M1, with a new 1P-5 sight, 1V116 command and control system and additional ammunition types, and finally as the 2S3M2. The 2S3 was replaced by the 2S19 "Msta-S" after the fall of the Soviet Union.

The 2S3 had its Red Square parade debut cameo appearance in November 1977, but was not regularly displayed until 1981, with the later 2S3M having entered series production two years before the earlier 2S3 was first displayed on Red Square. Although the 2S3 was a relatively common parade participant, the other land forces GRAU designation "2S" series, namely the 2S4, 2S5 and 2S7 were never paraded on Red Square, although they did appear at parades in other Soviet cities before 1991 and also in the post-Soviet era.

2S1 "Gvozdika"

2S3 "Akatsiya"

BM-8

BM-13

BM-31

Multiple Rocket Systems (MRS)

BM-8

The 82mm BM-8 MRS* was mounted on the ZiS-6 6x4 truck at the outbreak of World War Two, and also on the T-60 tank chassis. It was latterly mounted on the Lend-Lease Studebaker US6 chassis, and was in this configuration displayed during the 1945 Victory Parade in Moscow.

BM-13

The 132mm BM-13 was the default wartime Soviet "Katyusha" multiple rocket system. It was mounted on the ZiS-6 and later the STZ-5 tracked artillery tractor and a variety of Lend-Lease chassis before being standardised on the Studebaker US-6 chassis as the BM-13N. It was the latter version that was displayed on Red Square during the Victory Parade in 1945. The GAU (GRAU) designation for the later BM-13M/MM was 2B6/2B6R, and the BM-13NM/NMM was the 2B7/2B7R.

BM-31

The wartime BM-31 MRS, firing the 300mm M-31

---

* BM - Boevaya Mashina - Combat Machine. e.g. BM-13-16 - Combat machine, 13cm (132mm) - 16 round.

BM-14

RPU-14

BM-24 (2B3)

BM-24T

BMD-20 (8U33)

rocket was from 1944 standardised on the US6 Studebaker chassis, with 1,800 systems built in the final months of the war, of which 100 were lost in combat. Post-war the BM-31 was initially mounted on the ZiS-150 4x2 truck for parade purposes, and as standard on the 6x6 ZiS-151 chassis. The BM-31 was as with the wartime BM-8 and BM-13 quickly replaced post-war by modernised systems.

BM-14

The 140mm BM-14 (Boevaya Mashina 140mm) MRS was developed at NII-1 (rocket) and SKB-1 (launch system) bureaus from 1948 as a development of the wartime 132mm BM-13 MRS. The BM-14 MRS was accepted for service with the Soviet Army in 1952 and was built in several mobile configurations. The 16 round smoothbore tube launched BM-14 was initially mounted on the 6x6 ZiS-151 chassis as the BM-14-16 (8U32) with a limited number later mounted on the ZiL-157 as the BM-14M (2B2) and even the ZiL-131 as the BM-14MM (2B2R). The 16 round BM-14-16 was displayed on Red Square in 1950s and 1960s, initially mounted on the ZiS-151 chassis and latterly on the ZiL-157 chassis. The system fired M-14-OF high-explosive fragmentation rockets to a range of 10km, with a salvo reload time of 2-3 minutes. The RPU-14 (originally designated as the RPU-65 by NATO) was a towed version for use by VDV airborne forces. The ZiS-151 based BM-14 was displayed on Red Square in the 1950s and early 1960s.

RPU-14 (8U38)

The sixteen barrel 140mm RPU-14 (8U38) was a lightweight towed version of the 10km range BM-14 MRS specifically developed for VDV airborne forces, with which it entered service in 1957. The RPU-14 was a reconfigured 16 round launcher mounted on the carriage of the 85mm D-44 gun. The weapon fired the same ammunition and had the same characteristics as the vehicle mounted BM-14-16. Designed for towing behind a lightened airborne version of the GAZ-66 4x4 truck, the RPU-14 was intended to provide MRS artillery support for otherwise lightly armed Soviet VDV airborne forces.

BM-24 (2B3)

The twelve round frame-launched 240mm BM-24 MRS was introduced into service with the Soviet Army in the 1950s, mounted on the ZiS-151 6x6 truck. The system consists of a tubular frame launcher with two rows of six launch frames, firing HE-Frag and other rockets to a range of 11km. The BM-24 was subsequently mounted on the modernised ZiL-157 6x6 truck, and was ultimately replaced by the later BM-21 and BM-27 systems. The GRAU designation for the BM-24 was 2B3.

BM-24T

The twelve round BM-24T 240mm tube-launcher MRS was a derivative of the BM-24 mounted on the AT-S tracked tractor, which was for a number of years used for the provision of artillery support in Soviet tank and motorised rifle divisions. The vehicle was shown on Red Square at the end of the 1950s but was quickly removed from service.

BMD-20 (8U33)

The BMD-20 (GRAU: 8U33) MRS was developed at the NII-1 institute under the direction of V.P. Barmin. The four round frame launched 200mm (201mm) system firing the MD-20F rocket entered service in 1952, based on the 6x6 ZiS-151 chassis. The system had a range of 18.8km. The launch vehicle had the GRAU designation 8U33.

The BMD-20 was displayed on Red Square in 1950s and 1960s, initially mounted on the ZiS-151 chassis and latterly on the ZiL-157. The 4 round MRS which had a range of 18.8km, was also known as the BM-20-4.

9K51 (BM-21) Grad

The 40 round 122mm 9K51 (BM-21) or 2B5 "Grad" (hail) MRS was developed at the NII-147 "Splav" design bureau in Tula from 1960 under the direction of A.N. Ganichev to replace the BM-14 as a divisional multiple rocket system. The 9K51 "Grad" launcher was developed at SKB-203 in Sverdlovsk and the rockets designed at NII-6 in Moscow. The "Grad" system was accepted for service with the Soviet Army by a Resolution of the TsK KPSS i SM SSSR dated 28th March 1963 as a replacement for the earlier BM-14. The system, firing the 9M22 HE-Frag rocket as standard, was mounted on the then newly developed Ural-375D 6x6 all-terrain heavy load carrier that entered production in 1964. The "Grad" system was allocated to divisional artillery regiments in battalions of eighteen launchers, and also in motorised rifle divisions, which had a battery of six BM-21s. The BM-21 fired M-210F HE-Frag, incendiary and chemical rockets with a maximum range of 20.8km, with a full salvo launched in 20 seconds and a reload time of 7 minutes. The 9M22U "Grad" launcher unit was originally based on the 6x6 Ural-375D that could travel at 75km/h and had a road range of up to 500km. The 9K51 was from the mid 1980s mounted on the diesel-engined Ural-4320 with better fuel economy and an increased range of 750km, which remains in service with the modern Russian Army today. The 9K51 "Grad" was the default Soviet Army MRS of the Cold War era, and remains in service to the present day, being the largest production MRS in Soviet and now Russian history, with over 7,500 systems built between 1964 and 1988. The system has also been widely exported.

9K57 (BM-27) Uragan

The 16 round 220mm 9K57 "Uragan" (Hurricane) MRS was developed at NII-147 "Splav", and was accepted for service with the Soviet Army in 1975 based on the chassis of the 8x8 BAZ-135LMP chassis, with the launcher vehicle designated 9P140. The 9K57 was assigned to the rocket launcher battalions of tank divisions and motorised rifle divisions, and also combined arms artillery brigades.

The launcher has two rows of six launch tubes with a row of four mounted on top. A dedicated 9T452 TZM reload vehicle mounted on the same BAZ chassis could reload the system in five minutes. The 9P140 launcher fires HE-Frag, chemical and cassette sub-munition rockets to a maximum range of 31km to 40km with a minimum range of 8.5km. A full salvo could be fired in 20 seconds, with reload taking 15 minutes.

The 9P140 launch vehicle was mounted on the BAZ-135 (BAZ-135LMP) 8x8 all-terrain load carrier chassis designed at ZiL in Moscow but with series production of the chassis undertaken in Bryansk, hence the BAZ designation. The vehicle is powered by dual ZiL-375 180hp petrol engines and with duplex transmissions, allowing the vehicle to operate with one power system or wheels damaged. Road speed is 75km/h and road range 500km. The 9K57 MRS was from 1979 deployed with the Soviet Army in Afghanistan and had its parade debut on Red Square in May 1990.

9K51 (BM-21) Grad

9K57 (BM-27) Uragan

Towed Artillery

57mm S-60 USV Anti-Aircraft Gun

The 57mm S-60 (52-P-281) was developed as a collaborative effort between Plant №4, Plant №88 and NII-58 from 1945 under the direction of V.G. Grabin. The weapon, which was used in conjunction with PUAZO off-carriage fire control guidance, had an altitude ceiling of 4,000m and a range of 6,000m, with a rate of fire of 12 rounds/minute. A dual version of the weapon, the S-68, was installed in the ZSU-57-2 self-propelled anti-aircraft system. The weapon could also be used in a ground support role.

100mm M-1949 (KS-19) Anti-Aircraft Gun

The 100mm M1949 (KS-19) anti-aircraft gun was developed as a replacement for the earlier 85mm M-1939 and M-1944 weapons, with improved capability against modern aircraft including jet-engined fighters. The 100mm KS-19 had an altitude ceiling of 11-12km, a range of 21km and a rate of fire of 14-15 rounder per minute.

76.2mm M-1942 (ZiS-3) Dual-Purpose Gun

The wartime 76.2mm M-1942 (ZiS-3) dual-purpose gun was not originally intended as an anti-tank gun but had proven highly effective in that role during World War Two. The weapon remained in service in the immediate post-war years, and was towed through Red Square by the BTR-152 wheeled APC when it was introduced at the beginning of the 1950s.

85mm D-44 Divisional Gun and 85mm D-48 Anti-Tank Guns

The 85mm D-44 Divisional Gun and related 85mm

57mm S-60 USV Anti-Aircraft Gun

100mm M-1949 (KS-19) Anti-Aircraft Gun

76.2mm M-1942 (ZiS-3) Dual Purpose Gun

85mm D-44 Divisional Gun

85mm SD-44 Divisional Gun

100mm BS-3 Dual-Purpose Gun

100mm T-12 Anti-Tank Gun

122mm D-30 Field Howitzer

130mm M-46 Field Gun

D-48 anti-tank gun were used in the post-war era as replacements for the 76.2mm ZiS-3 and also to an extent the 100mm BS-3 dual-purpose gun. The 85mm D-44 gun was developed at the OKB of Plant № 9, with approximately 13,000 built between 1945 and 1953. The weapon had a maximum range of 15.8km and a rate of fire of 20-25 rounds/minute. The 85mm D-48 was a later variant developed as an anti-tank gun, which in contrast with the D-44 with its double baffle muzzle brake was fitted with a multiple baffle type.

85mm SD-44 Divisional and Anti-Tank Gun

The 85mm SD-44 was a specialised auxiliary propelled version of the 85mm D-44 weapon developed from 1948 at the OKB of Plant №9 for use by Soviet VDV airborne forces to augment airborne bridgehead artillery and anti-tank capability. Built at Plant №9 from 1954-1957, the weapon was powered by an M-72 motorcycle engine developing 18hp, mounted on one of the gun trails, allowing all-terrain travel at up to 25km/h over short distances, though the theoretical range was 220km if required. A total of 704 SD-44s were built, 116 new build, 438 rebuilt from the standard D-44 and 150 fitted with night vision equipment.

100mm BS-3 Dual-Purpose Gun

The 100mm M-1944 (BS-3) dual-purpose gun was introduced into service with the Red Army in 1944 and continued in service with the post-war Soviet Army into the 1960s. It was replaced in Soviet Army service by the smaller calibre 85mm D-44 field and D-48 anti-tank guns.

100mm T-12 (2A19) Anti-Tank Gun

The 100mm T-12 (2A19) anti-tank gun was the first Soviet smoothbore anti-tank gun, entering service with the Soviet Army in 1961 and series manufactured from 1961-1970, with 10,918 such weapons being built. The weapon fired a range of ammunition including armour-piercing fin stabilised discarding sabot (APFSDS) sub-calibre anti-tank rounds, with a maximum practical range of 3,000m and a sustained rate of fire of 10-12 rounds/minute. The T-12 could penetrate 230mm of armour at 500m, 215mm at 1,000m and 180mm at 2,000m. The weapon remained in service with anti-tank units of tank and motorised rifle regiments until the end of the 1980s.

100mm MT-12 (2A29) Anti-Tank Gun

The 100mm MT-12 (2A29) "Rapira" anti-tank gun was introduced into Soviet Army service in 1972 as a modification of the previous generation 100mm T-12. The smoothbore weapon, which as with its predecessor fired sub-calibre APFSDS ammunition that could now penetrate 600mm of vertical armour plate, had a rate of fire of up 6-14 rounds/minute and a maximum theoretical range of 4,000m. The weapon was also known as the T-12A.

122mm D-30 Field Howitzer

The 122mm D-30 (2A18) field howitzer was developed at the beginning of the 1960s by the F.F. Petrov design bureau at Artillery Plant №9 in Sverdlovsk as a versatile replacement for the 122mm M-1938 (M-30) howitzer. The distinctive weapon employed a three-leg gun carriage and with a firing jack mechanism which raised the gun carriage off the ground, thereby providing a highly stable firing platform which also allowed the weapon to be swung through 360°, providing a useful ground support and if required anti-tank capability in addition to the primary artillery role. The 122mm D-30, with its distinctive multiple-baffle muzzle brake, fired case-type separate loading HE-Frag, smoke and specialist ammunition, with a maximum range of 15.3km and 21km respectively and a rate of fire of 6-8 rounds/minute. The weapon also fired a HEAT-FS round which could penetrate 460mm of vertical conventional armour. The 122mm D-30 was issued to Soviet tank divisions on a scale of two battalions of 18 guns each, for 36 per division. The weapon was subsequently modified for use in the 2S1 self-propelled howitzer. In contrast with most Soviet artillery, the 122mm D-30 was towed muzzle first by a mounting located under the muzzle with all trails locked together facing forward. The weapon was later modified as the 122mm D-30A (2A18M).

130mm M-46 Field Gun

The 130mm M-1953 (M-46) field gun was first seen at the 1st May parade in 1954. The weapon was deployed within artillery regiments at Army level, with two battalions, each with eighteen 130mm M-46 field guns, formed into three batteries. Artillery divisions also each had two regiments with fifty-four 130mm M-46 weapons each. The barrel was withdrawn out of battery lock for transport. The weapon fired separate-loading HE-Frag and other artillery rounds with a significant maximum range of 27.2km. The weapon had a rate of fire of 8 rounds/minute and fired armour piercing tracer rounds that could penetrate 230mm of vertical armour plate giving a secondary anti-tank capability. A rocket-assisted projectile (RAP) was introduced for the weapon in the late 1960s.

152mm D-1 Howitzer

The 152mm M-1943 (D-1) howitzer was developed under the direction of F.F. Petrov as a replacement for the wartime 122mm M-1938 (M-30) and 152mm M-1938 (M-10) howitzers. The weapon, which resembled the wartime weapons had a distinctive double baffle muzzle brake, had a maximum range of 12.4km and a rate of fire of 3-4 rounds/minute.

152mm 2A36 Field Gun

The 152mm 2A36 "Hyacinth-B" towed gun was developed at the SKB in Perm from 1968 and accepted for service with the Soviet Army in 1979. The gun, with its distinctive four-wheel gun carriage had a range of 28.5km with HE-Frag ammunition, increasing to 30km with the use of rocket-assisted projectiles, and a rate of fire of 6 rounds/minute. The weapon was demonstrated on Red Square in the mid 1980s, towed by the new KrAZ-260 6x6 truck, which but for the dissolution of the Soviet Union would have replaced the KrAZ-255 series in Soviet Army service. The 152mm 2A37 modification of the weapon was mounted in the 2S5 "Tuilpan" self-propelled gun. The 152mm 2A36, which featured an unusual twin axle gun carriage, is one of those weapons that disappeared from Red Square parades as quickly as it had appeared.

180mm S-23 Heavy Gun

The enigmatic 180mm S-23 long-range gun made its public debut on Red Square in 1955 towed by the AT-T heavy tractor, the first seven examples having been built at the Barrikady Plant the same year. The weapon was designed as a wheeled replacement for the wartime 152mm Br-2 and 203mm B-4 tracked heavy artillery pieces allocated to the RVGK strategic command reserve. The (naval) origins and even the designation of the gun were a mystery to Western observers, it being known by NATO for years as the 203mm M-1955 based on its predecessor's calibre and year of parade debut appearance. What was known however was that the 180mm S-23 could out-range almost all contemporary NATO towed and self-propelled artillery. The weapon fired separate-loading ammunition with variable bag charges, including OF-43 HE-Frag, G-572 concrete-piercing and a 0.2Kt tactical nuclear warhead. Ranges varied according to ammunition type to a maximum 30.4km, or 43.8km when using a later rocket-assisted projectile (RAP). The weapon was towed through Red Square by the AT-T tractor with the 8.8 metre length barrel withdrawn out of battery lock for transport purposes.

160mm M-160 Mortar

The 160mm M-1943 mortar was introduced into service at the end of World War Two, and remained in service in the 1950s and 1960s. It had a range of 5.1km and a maximum rate of fire of 3 rounds/minute. Almost identical in appearance to the larger 240mm M-240 mortar, the modified 160mm M-1953 version (also known post-war as the M-160) could be distinguished by its original use of GAZ-AA perforated road wheels.

240mm M-240 Mortar

The towed M-240mm mortar was accepted for service in 1950 and was occasionally paraded on Red Square in the 1950s. The M-240 could fire a 131kg HE-Frag round to a range of 9.7km, and also had the capability to fire the 3BV4 nuclear round. The ordnance from the M-240 was also used for the 2S4 "Tuilpan" self-propelled mortar introduced the following decade, which was never paraded on Red Square.

152mm D-1 Howitzer

152mm 2A36 Hyacith-B Field Gun

180mm S-23 Heavy Gun

160mm M-160 Mortar

240mm M-240 Mortar

Self-Propelled Air Defence Systems (SPADS)

ZSU-37

ZSU-57-2

ZSU-23-4V

ZSU-23-4M

ZSU-37

The first Soviet light tracked anti-aircraft system to be series produced, albeit in small numbers, was the ZSU-37, based on a modified SU-76 self-propelled gun chassis and armed with the 37mm M-1939 (61-K) anti-aircraft gun. The ZSU-37-2 was built at Plant №40 in Mytischi from February 1945 but did not see active service in World War Two. Only a small pre-production batch of 12-16 vehicles was completed in 1945, with the ZSU-37 being displayed on Red Square in September and November 1946.

ZSU-57-2

The ZSU-57 was developed at NII-58 under the direction of V.G. Grabin from 1946, with the first prototype completed in 1953. The vehicle was accepted for service in September 1955 and had its parade debut on 1st May 1957, remaining a parade standard for the following decade. The system was designed to provide low-level air defence for Soviet tank and motorised rifle divisions, with an effective altitude ceiling of 4,000m and a range of 6,000m. The ZSU-57-2 was based on a significantly modified and lightened T-54 chassis with one wheel pair omitted. It mounted a large open turret armed with a twin 57mm S-68 gun installation, modified from the towed 57mm S-60. The ZSU-57-2 had a secondary ground support role, for which armour piercing rounds were provided, though it was primarily an air defence system. The ZSU-57-2 was displayed on Red Square until the mid 1960s and was replaced in service by the ZSU-23-4.

ZSU-23-4 (2A6)

The ZSU-23-4 close-range SPADS was approved for development as a replacement for the ZSU-57-2 by a Resolution of the SM SSSR dated 17th April 1957 and was accepted for service with the Soviet Army in the autumn of 1962. The ZSU-23-4 (GRAU designation 2A6) began to enter service with operational Soviet Army units from 1965 replacing the ZSU-57-2 as a local air defence weapon for tank and motorised rifle regiments. The quadruple mount 23mm 2A7 automatic cannon armed vehicle added an entirely new level of air defence capability to the recently introduced ZSU-57-2. The vehicle was paraded on Red Square from 7th November 1965. The ZSU-23-4 was armed with four 23mm 2A7 machine guns from the towed ZU-23, with an on-board radar system. It could engage aircraft flying at up to 450km/h with a vertical range of 2,000m and a horizontal range of 2,500m. With a combined burst rate of fire of 3,400rpm, the vehicle provided devastating firepower, against low flying targets, as was demonstrated when it was first deployed in the Middle East. The vehicle has a crew of four. The GM-575 chassis developed at OKB-40 at Mytischi under the direction of N.A. Astrov is powered by a 6 cylinder diesel engine developing 280hp and providing the 19 metric tonne combat weight vehicle with a maximum road speed of 50km/h and a range of 450km. The original ZSU-23-4 was later modified, with the main Soviet era production variants being the V (1968-69), V1 (1970-71), M1 (1971-72), M2 (1978-79) and M3 (1977-78).

Airborne Vehicles

The VDV (Soviet airborne forces) began to display equipment on Red Square in the immediate post war period, beginning with ZiS-150 4x2 transport trucks with VDV troops aboard, followed soon thereafter by a series of revelations of particularly specialised airborne vehicles. The diminutive ASU-57 self-propelled gun was the first such revelation, followed soon thereafter by the SU-85 (known by NATO and Western forces as the ASU-85), then the BMD airborne MICV, followed successively by the BMD-2, BMD-3 and from 2008 the BMD-4.

ASU-57

The ASU-57 was an air portable and parachute deployable airborne assault gun for supporting VDV airborne forces. It was developed from 1948-50 by the SKB-40 team at the MMZ plant in Mytischi in northern Moscow as the Obiekt-572 under the designer N.A. Astrov who had developed several small and light tank designs including the T-38, the T-40 and the T-60. The diminutive ASU-57 was accepted for service in accordance with Resolution SM SSSR №3541-1648ss, entering service with Soviet VDV airborne forces in 1951. The vehicle had its parade debut on 1st May 1957.

The original production model was armed with a 57mm Ch-51 gun with a distinctive multi-baffle muzzle brake, which was from 1955 replaced in production by the 57mm Ch-51M with a conventional double baffle type. The lightly armoured 3.35 metric tonne vehicle was transported in and parachute dropped from the An-8 and An-12 transport aircraft. The ASU-57 was powered by a 4 cylinder GAZ M-20E petrol engine, providing a 45km/h road speed and a range of 250km. The ASU-57 was a regular participant at Red Square parades during the late 1950s.

SU-85 (ASU-85)

The N.A. Astrov bureau designed SU-85 was as with the ASU-57 developed at the SKB-40 design bureau at the MMZ plant at Mytischi in the northern suburbs of Moscow, as the Obiekt-573. The SU-85 was developed in order to provide Soviet VDV airborne forces with a fully armoured vehicle with better anti-tank capability than the diminutive ASU-57. The SU-85 was developed as a ground and VDV forces vehicle, hence the designation SU-85 rather than ASU-85 is used in most Soviet records. The vehicle was armed with the 85mm D-70 (2A15) gun and co-axial 7.62mm SGMT machine gun. The fully enclosed, better-armed and armoured SU-85 (ASU-85) was significantly larger than the ASU-57. It was therefore air transported and landed in the An-12, and later An-22 and Il-76 transport aircraft rather than being parachute dropped (though early trials considered this and it could be dropped on a P-16 platform if required). The ASU-85 was tested for service from 1954 and accepted for service with the Soviet VDV airborne forces on 6th August 1958. Each Soviet airborne division was ultimately provided with 31 SU-85s. The SU-85 had a relatively short production life, being produced at MMZ from 1958 to 1964 (some sources state 1959-1967). The vehicle could travel at 45km/h and had a range of 360km. The later ASU-85M, which had its parade debut on 7th November 1973, mounted a 12.7mm DShKM anti-aircraft machine gun.

BMD (BMD-1)

The BMD airborne fighting vehicle was developed as the Obiekt-915 at the KB of the Volgograd Tractor Plant (VgTZ - the former STZ plant famous for wartime T-34 production) from 1965 under the direction of chief design engineer Igor V. Gavalov. It was accepted for service in 1969, soon after the ground forces BMP, but made its Red Square parade debut only on 7th November 1974. At the time of its introduction the BMD was as revolutionary as the BMP ground forces infantry fighting vehicle introduced a decade earlier representing a new concept in airborne vehicles, capable of transporting five "desant" infantry into combat and providing defensive fire against targets including tanks. The BMD was the first series production airborne combat vehicle that allowed the crew to fight from within the vehicle or dismount as required, with the BMD providing significant protection to airborne

ASU-57

ASU-57

SU-85 (ASU-85)

SU-85 (ASU-85)

BMD-1

BMD-1

BMD-1

BMD-1P

BTR-D

BMD-2

2S9 "Nona-S" Self-Propelled Gun-Mortar

infantry on the ground. The BMD (later re-designated BMD-1 to distinguish it from the later BMD-2) mounted the same armament as the BMP, namely a 73mm 2A28 "Grom" low pressure gun, co-axial and additional 7.62mm PKT machine guns, and a 9M14M "Malyutka" ATGM system for engaging armour significantly heavier than the BMD itself, including tanks. The later BMD-1P, which had its parade debut on 7th November 1987 replaced the "Malyutka" with the later 9P135M ATGM launcher. Maximum road speed was 62km/h and road range 500km. The vehicle had a water speed of 10km/h. The BMD was designed to be air-dropped from the An-12B transport aircraft, from which it could be dropped by conventional parachute or PRS parachute drop systems using rocket retro-braking on landing, which reduced the parachute system weight from 2 metric tonnes to under 1 metric tonne. The later An-22 and Il-76 transport aircraft greatly increased VDV forces airlift capability. On 27th December 1979, BMDs air-landed at Kabul airport supported the VDV airborne forces assault on the palace of Hafizullah Amin at the start of the decade-long Soviet war in Afghanistan.

BMD-1P

The modernized BMD-1P was accepted for service in 1978 and had its public debut on Red Square in November 1983. The vehicle had mechanical improvements, and an increased 60km/h road speed, but most noticeably the original 9M14 "Malyutka" ATGM installation was replaced by a 9P135M ATGM launcher for the 9M113 "Konkurs" and 9M111 "Fagot" ATGMs.

BTR-D

The BTR-D was a tracked airborne APC variant of the BMD-1, developed in the 1970s and accepted for service with the Soviet Army in 1974. It had its Red Square public debut on 9th May 1985.

The turretless BTR-D, which was 483mm longer than the BMD-1, was used for airborne APC, command and communication vehicle roles and could if required transport a "desant" crew of 10 or a load of 1,400kg. Armament originally consisted of two 7.62mm PKT machine guns and a 30mm AGS-17 "Plamya" grenade launcher. The BTR-D was from 1979 also fitted with the 9P135M/M1 ATGM launcher system for the 9M113 "Konkurs" and 9M111 "Fagot" missiles as the BTR-RD "Robot". Field modifications included the mounting of the 23mm ZU-23 anti-aircraft machine gun. The BTR-D had a maximum road speed of 62km/h, a range of 500km and a water speed of 10km/h.

BMD-2

The BMD-2 was developed from 1983 at the KB of VgTZ in Volgograd under the direction of A.V. Shabalin as a modification of the BMD-1. The BMD-2 mounted a new turret with upgraded armament, consisting of a 30mm 2A42 automatic cannon with co-axial 7.62mm and additional PKT machine guns and a 9P135M launcher firing the 9M113 "Konkurs" or 9M111 "Fagot" ATGMs, in line with modification of the original ground forces BMP-1 as the BMP-2. The BMD-2 had a crew of 2+5 and a combat weight of 8,200kg. The 5D-20 6 cylinder engine, developing 240hp provided a maximum road speed of 61km/h and a range of 500km. The vehicle had a water speed of 10km/h. The BMD-2 had its Red Square parade debut on 9th May 1990.

2S9 "Nona-S"

The 120mm 2S9 Samokhodnoe Orudye (Obiekt-926) "Nona-S" self-propelled airborne close-support vehicle was developed as a close-support artillery vehicle for VDV airborne forces. The vehicle mounts the 120mm 2A51 low-pressure gun-mortar developed in the 1970s on the lengthened BTR-D chassis for close support of VDV airborne forces. The 2S9 served with the Soviet Army in Afghanistan. The turret mounted 120mm "Nona" mortar has a maximum elevation of 80°, a rate of fire of 10 rounds/minute and a range of 7-9km depending on the ammunition type used, or 13km with RAP rounds. The 8.5 metric tonne 2S9, which has a crew of four, is powered by a 5D20 diesel engine developing 240hp and providing a maximum road speed of 60km/h and a range of 500km. The vehicle is amphibious with a water speed of 10km/h. The vehicle had its Red Square public debut on 9th May 1985.

Surface to Air Missile (SAM) Systems

SAM systems have been perhaps the most consistent type of Soviet military hardware demonstrated on Red Square, with the ZRK S-25 (NATO: SA-1 Guild), ZRK S-75 (NATO: SA-2 Guideline) and ZRK S-125 (NATO: SA-3 Goa) being the most regular of all parade participants. The S-25 (NATO: SA-1 Guild) was initially towed through Red Square by the ZiS-121B tractor, later replaced in the role by the ZiL-157K/KV and latterly by the ZiL-131V. By contrast, some SAM systems such as the 9K81 S-300V tracked version of the S-300, known in the West as the SA-12 "Gladiator/Giant" were never displayed on Red Square even though their publicity value might have been greater than the wheeled versions.

ZRK S-25 "Berkut"

The S-25 (Systema-25 or 205) "Berkut" (NATO: SA-1 Guild) SAM system, firing the V-300 rocket developed at NPO "Almaz", was designed as a static launched rocket system to be deployed around the Soviet capital city Moscow. The system was installed in a circle known as the "betony krug" or "concrete ring", built specifically for servicing the launch sites for the "205" or S-25 SAM system, consisting of 56 launch sites, each with 60 rockets and with each site capable of engaging 20 targets simultaneously. A total of 1,800 S-25 SAM systems were built from 1957-1987.

The S-25 "Berkut" was accepted into service with PVO forces of the Soviet Army service in accordance with a Resolution of the TsK KPSS i SM SSSR dated 7th May 1955, and first displayed on Red Square on 7th November 1960. It was a regular feature of Red Square military parades for many years thereafter. The system, on its PR-3 series transport / rocket fuel trailer was originally displayed on a PR-3 single-axle trailer towed by the ZiS-121B tractor version of the ZiS-151, later replaced by the PR-3M/M3 TZM trailer towed by a ZiL-157V tractor truck, and latterly the PR-7 and PR-8 towed by the ZiL-157K, KV and ZiL-131V 6x6 tractor vehicles.

The enigmatic S-25 was statically deployed in a defensive ring of static launch stand (pad) sites around Moscow to protect the capital. The system was the first Soviet rocket developed specifically for the defence of "krupnikh obiektov" or major sites - i.e. Moscow. The rocket had a maximum altitude of 20-27km (later 30km), a range of 35km (later 43km), and could engage aircraft travelling at up to 1,250-1,500km/h, giving it significant defensive capability.

The initial Izdeliye-206 version of the V-300 rocket was developed from 1951, followed by the Izdeliye-207 and 208 in 1952. Testing was particularly swift, conducted in 1953-54, with service acceptance in 1955 as the "205". The rocket remained enigmatic to Western observers for many years.

ZRK S-75 "Dvina", "Desna", Volkhov"

The medium-range S-75 "Dvina" SAM (NATO: SA-2 Guideline) was developed at NPO "Almaz" in accordance with Resolution №2838-1201 dated 20th November 1953 and was taken into service with Soviet PVO ground forces in 1962. With its 35-45km range and 30km altitude ceiling, the S-75 was a game-changing weapon, becoming famous when on 1st May 1960 it downed the American CIA pilot Francis Gary Powers in his U-2A reconnaissance aircraft over Sverdlovsk, as the 1st May parade on Red Square was about to begin.

The S-75 system and its V-750 rocket were widely deployed in the Soviet Union and the Warsaw Pact, with several generations of system and rocket updates over the years, with later versions of the system later designated "Desna" and "Volkhov". The S-75 was also widely exported, participating in most significant wars of the 1960s and 1970s, the S-75 being the most widely deployed SAM system in history. Various versions of the S-75 SAM were towed through Red Square over the years, originally on the PR-11A semi-trailer TZM by the ZiS-121B (ZiL-151V) 6x6 tractor truck, and latterly by the ZiL-157V, KV (PR-11B trailer) and later ZiL-131V PR-11 series tractor-trailer TZM combinations.

ZRK S-125 "Neva" (4K90)

The two stage short-range solid fuelled 4K90 S-125 "Neva" (NATO: SA-3 Goa) was developed in the late 1950s and taken into service with Soviet PVO forces in

ZRK S-25 "Berkut"

ZRK S-25 "Berkut"

ZRK S-75 "Dvina"

ZRK S-75 "Dvina" TZM

ZRK S-125 "Neva"

ZRK S-125 "Neva" TZM

ZRK S-200 "Angara"

ZRK Izdeliye-400 "Dal"

ZRK 2K11 "Krug"

ZRK 2K12 "Kub"

ZRK 2K12 "Kub"

1961. In Soviet service the system, which had a range of 25km and an altitude ceiling of 12km, was generally mounted on tandem static launchers. The S-125 and its 5V24 (later 5V27) or V-600 rocket was also deployed widely within the Warsaw Pact, where it was often mounted on quad static mountings, and was widely exported. PR-14 series TZM reload vehicles mounting two reload rockets were displayed during Red Square parades, displayed from the late 1960s into the 1980s, initially mounted on the ZiL-157 chassis, and latterly on the ZiL-131 chassis. The system was a development of a naval air defence rocket, hence it being named after the Russian river.

ZRK S-200 "Angara"

The S-200 "Angara" (NATO:SA-5 Gammon), was never displayed on Red Square. The Izdeliye-400 "Dal" and S-25 "Berkur" were however at various times misidentified as the S-200, the technical characteristics of which remained opaque until after the dissolution of the Soviet Union. Though never displayed in Moscow, the system was displayed in other cities including Kiev and Kharkov in Ukraine.

ZRK Izdeliye-400 "Dal"

With the S-25 "Berkur" ("205") having been accepted for service and being deployed in a circle of static launch sites around Moscow, work began at OKB-301 in cooperation with several other institutes on a planned multi-channel guidance long-range rocket. Development was approved in accordance with Resolution SM SSSR №602-369 dated 24th March 1955.

The system, later known by the OKB-301 designation Izdeliye-400 (Article-400), was tested as a "dalnego deistviya" or long-range static lunched anti-aircraft rocket system, from which it took its short form designation "Dal". The system, which had a projected range of 160-180km, with an ability to hit targets travelling at 1,500-3,000km/h at altitudes of 5-30km, was originally developed by the Soviet designer S.A. Lavochkin, who died during initial polygon testing in July 1960, with his work being taken over by M.M. Pashinin. A large number of test launches were undertaken in 1960-63, but after Lavochkin's death financing for the project was reduced and work gradually prioritised on the smaller and less ambitious S-200.

The "Dal" and its two stage 5V11 rocket was for many years was not well understood by Western observers, not least as the rocket resembled the infinitely smaller S-75 "Dvina". The Izdeliye-400 was for display purposes towed through Red Square on a single-axle PR-41A TZM semi-trailer originally towed by the 4x4 MAZ-502V and later by the 6x6 Ural-375S. The system was frequently misidentified by NATO as the S-200 (NATO: SA-5 Griffon).

ZRK 2K11 "Krug" (2P24 SPU Vehicle)

The 2K11 "Krug" SAM system was developed under the direction of L.V. Luliev at OKB-8 at Sverdlovsk (latterly the Antei design bureau) from 1958-60 in accordance with a Resolution of the TsK KPSS i SM SSSR dated 15th February 1958. Development was under the overall direction of NII-20 GKOT and its chief designer V.P. Efremov.

The 2K11 SAM system was accepted for service with the Soviet Army in accordance with a Resolution of the TsK KPSS i SM SSSR dated 26th November 1964, and entered service with PVO units of the Soviet Army the following year. The system originally had an engagement ceiling of 3-24km and a range of 11-45km. The 3M8 rocket suffered some delays in final testing, such that the 2K11 system entered service later than the static/moveable pad launched S-75 which took precedence while the more versatile tracked mobile 2K11 was perfected.*

The 2P24 TEL vehicle was mounted on the new Obiekt-123 tracked chassis. The 2K11 system entered service in 1965 but early production vehicles were first paraded in 1964. The 2K11 was in 1967 modernised as the 2K11A "Krug-A", with the low-altitude engagement height reduced to 250m. In 1971, the 2K11 "Krug-M" was introduced, with an altitude ceiling of 24.5km and a range of 50km, and immediately followed by the 2K11M1 "Krug-M1".

ZRK 2K12 "Kub" (2P25 SPU Vehicle)

The 2K12 "Kub" ZRK and its 2P25 SPU vehicle firing the 3M9 rocket were developed in accordance with a Resolution of the SM SSSR, №817-839 dated 18th July 1958. The system was accepted into service with the Soviet Army in 1966 and taken into service in 1967.

---

* The V-755 (3M8) rocket of the 2K11 system was a development of the V-750 "Volkov" rocket of the static launched S-75 SAM system

The rocket system was developed at the NII-3 institute under the direction of B.V. Orlov and OKB-15 GKAT under the direction of chief designer V.V. Tikhominov, with the 2P25 SPU vehicle developed under the direction of A.I. Yashin. The 2K12 "Kub" system was series produced at the Ulyanovsk Mechanical Plant on the GM-578 chassis built at MMZ in Mytischi in Moscow where it had also been designed within OKB-40 at the plant under the direction of N.A. Astrov. The 1S91 radar vehicle was also based on the GM-568 chassis. The system began to be produced in the early 1960s but was formally accepted for service in 1967. The 3M9 rocket of the 2K12 "Kub" system had an altitude and range envelope of 14km and 24km respectively. The SPU vehicle could travel at 44km/h and had a road range of 300km. The "Kub" ZRK was subsequently modernised as the 2K12M "Kub-M, the "2K12M1 "Kub-M1" (1973), and the 2K12M2 and later 2K12M3 with the SPU vehicles designated 2P25M, M1, M2 and M3 respectively. The system was exported, particularly to the Middle East where it was used during the wars of 1967-73. In Soviet Army service, the 2K12 "Kub" system was replaced by the 9K37 "Buk" SAM system.

ZRK 9K31 "Strela-1" 9P31 SPU Vehicle

The BRDM-2 mounted 9K31 "Strela-1" (NATO: SA-9 Gaskin) was developed over nearly a decade in accordance with a Resolution of the TsK KPSS i SM SSSR №946-398 dated 25th August 1960. After successful trials it was accepted for service with the Soviet Army on 25th April 1968, but it would be several years before it was seen on Red Square. The systems was designated 9K31, firing the 9M31 rocket, with the SPU vehicle designated 9P31. Four 9P31 launcher vehicles were co-located with the ZSU-23-4 in the anti-aircraft battery of Soviet tank and motorised rifle regiments.

ZRK 9K33 "Osa" and 9K33M3 "Osa-AKM" SAM Systems

The 9K33 "Osa" (NATO: SA-8 Gecko) mobile short range-range SAM was developed by the Antei and Fakel design bureaus in response to a Resolution dated 27th October 1960, with the original "Osa" being accepted for service by a Resolution of the SM SSSR dated 4th October 1971.

The "Osa" was in constant development, such that the modified 9K33M2 "Osa-AK" was accepted for Soviet Army service in 1973, with the first vehicles taken into service with Soviet ground forces in 1975, but with the earlier 9K33 "Osa" variant displayed on Red Square that November. The original version had an altitude ceiling of 0.2-5km, and a range of 1.6-10km.

The "Osa" system SPU vehicle was mounted together with its associated acquisition radar on a new purpose designed 6x6 amphibious BAZ-5937 6x6 chassis, with the 9T217 TZM reload vehicle based on the related BAZ-5939 chassis. The original "Osa" or "Osa-A" SPU vehicle taken into service on 4th October 1971 mounted four 9M33 rockets in an open configuration was designated 9A33 (9A33B as it entered service). The original system was rapidly modernised as the 9K33M2 "Osa-AK", and later as the 9K33M3 "Osa-AKM". The "Osa-AK" modification firing the later 9M33M2 rocket was tested in 1974, before the original 9K33 and its 9A33B SPU vehicle had its public debut on Red Square the following year. The 9K33M2 "Osa-AK" was taken into service with the Soviet Army in 1975.

The 6x6 amphibious SPU vehicle was developed from the very late 1960s and built at the BAZ plant in Bryansk from the mid 1970s in parallel with the BAZ-5921/5922 chassis used for the "Tochka" OTR. The BAZ-5937/5939 was powered by a 6 cylinder engine developing 300hp, giving the vehicle a road speed of 60km/h and an amphibious speed of 8km/h.

Development of the 9K33 system was rapid and constantly evolving. The original 9A33 launch vehicle for the 9K33 "Osa" system was modernised as the 9A33BM ("Osa-A") developed as a single vehicle in 1973 before being modified as the 9A33BM2 SPU vehicle for the 9K33M2 "Osa-AK". The modernised "Osa-AKM" (9K33M3) and associated 9A33BM3 SPU vehicle firing the 9M33M3 rocket was accepted into service with Soviet ground forces in 1980 and displayed on Red Square from 1982. The 9K33M3 system had an altitude ceiling of 12km and a range of 15km. The "Osa-AKM" was still on parade in 2017 in some Russian cities.

As noted, the original "Osa" SPU vehicle was updated several times during service, with subsequent variants designated 9A33BM2, 9A33BM3, with rockets accordingly designated 9M33M1,M2 and M3. *

ZRK 9K31 "Strela-1"

ZRK 9K31 "Strela-1"

ZRK 9K33 "Osa"

ZRK 9K33M3 "Osa-AKM"

ZRK 9K33M3 "Osa-AKM"

BAZ-5937 chassis ("Osa" SPU vehicles)

* The 9A33B vehicles for the 9K33 "Osa" SAM system displayed from 1975 were effectively development prototypes. The later 9K33M2 "Osa-AK" and modernised 9K33M3 "Osa-AKM" with upgraded control systems and electronics were indistinguishable externally.

ZRK 9K35 "Strela-10"

ZRK S-300 (S-300P)

The data on the "Osa" SAM system are conflated even in Russian original sources, largely due to the rapid development of the system in various guises. Per official Soviet GRAU classification, the 9A33B was the SPU vehicle for the original "Osa" SAM prototype, subsequently modified as the 9A33BM for the "Osa-A", the 9A33BM2 for the "Osa-AK" and finally the 9A33BM3 for the "Osa-AKM".

9K35 "Strela-10"

Design work on the 9K35 "Strela-10" (NATO: SA-13 Gopher) began in accordance with a Resolution of the TsK KPSS i SM SSSR dated 24th July 1969, with a remit to develop a short range SAM system for the protection of Soviet tank and motorised rifle divisions against helicopters and low flying aircraft. The MT-LB mounted 9K35 "Strela-10" firing the 9M37 rocket was introduced into service with the Soviet Army in 1976. There were two distinct "BM" SPU vehicles, the 9A34 and the 9A35, which operated in conjunction with the 9V839 radar and 9V915 technical support vehicles. The 9M37 rockets could engage airborne targets to a maximum altitude of 3,500m and to a range of 5,000m.

The original 9K35 "Strela-10" was later modernized as the 9K35M "Strela-10M", firing the 9M37M rocket and with the SPU vehicles designated 9A34M and 9A35M, which was taken into service in 1979, as the 9K35M2 "Strela-10M2" with improvements in engagement targeting and accuracy, and finally as the 9K35M3 "Strela-10M3". The system is sometimes designated "Strela-10SV" (Sukhuputnye Voiska - ground forces).

S-300 (S-300P)

The S-300 (NATO: SA-10 Grumble) system, mounted on its MAZ-534M 9P85S launch vehicle made its public debut on Red Square in 1990, and would be a parade regular from 2008.

Strategic Artillery Systems

2A3 "Kondensator"

2A3 "Kondensator"

2B1 "Oka"

The first Soviet attempts at strategic weapons capable of delivering chemical and nuclear warheads were conventional, with munitions being developed for heavy artillery such as the 240mm M-240 heavy mortar and the 203mm B-4M heavy howitzer. In the late 1950s, the Soviet Union unveiled two enormous strategic weapons, both mounted on tracked tank chassis, the 2A3 "Kondensator" and the 2B1 "Oka". Four of each built and trundled through Red Square at the end of the 1950s. Although impressive parade pieces, these vehicles had been technically overtaken by rapidly emerging rocket technology even as they were being designed. Similar systems such as the "0842" (S-103) were developed on paper but never saw the light of day. The next-generation, rocket based technology replacements for the 2A3 and 2B1, the "Filin" and "Mars" rockets (both designated "FROG" by NATO) were already paraded alongside these huge weapons as they made their parade debut by 1957.

2A3 "Kondensator" Strategic Self-Propelled Gun

The 2A3 "Kondensator" (Kondensator-2P) 406mm self-propelled gun was developed as a strategic artillery piece capable of delivering a 570kg nuclear projectile to a range of 25.6km. The system was developed at TsAKB-34 in Leningrad from 1954, with official approval provided by a Resolution of the SM SSSR dated 18th November 1955, which also authorised development of the 2B1 strategic self-propelled mortar. Four of each of these weapons were built at LKZ in Leningrad on the Obiekt-271 chassis using components of the Obiekt-272 (T-10M) heavy tank. The vehicle had an estimated road range of 200-220km, had it been operationally deployed. The 2A3 was the Soviet Union's first attempt at a long-range strategic weapon. It was paraded on Red Square from 1957 until as late as 1963.

2B1 "Oka" Strategic Self-Propelled Mortar

The 2B1 "Oka" (also known during development as the "Transformator") was a strategic 420mm calibre self-propelled mortar developed to fulfil the same strategic requirements as the 2A3 "Kondensator". The project was initiated in December 1956, with the prototype completed in 1957. The 2B1 with its 20-metre long smoothbore mortar barrel was based on the Obiekt-273 chassis, also derived from the Obiekt-272 (T-10M) heavy tank chassis, with the 420mm mortar ordnance, which was designated 2B2, having a range of 45km. The 2B1 was paraded on Red Square concurrently with the 2A3 "Kondensator" and met an identical fate, as neither the 2A3 nor the 2B1 could pass under bridges, and both were oversize for transit by the Soviet rail system. Although highly effective parade vehicles, they were not particularly useful as operational weapons, and both systems were terminated in 1960 and replaced by rapidly emerging rocket technology which had begun to be displayed on Red Square concurrently with the 2A3 and 2B1 weapon systems.

Tactical Rockets (OTRs) (NATO: FROG and SCUD)

The first Soviet tactical rockets, known in Russian as Operation Level Tactical Rockets (OTRs) were the ZR-1 for the 2K1 "Mars" and the ZR-2 for the 2K2 "Filin" systems, both designed by the NII-I institute concurrently from 1955, and based on light and heavy tank chassis respectively. The design of Soviet land forces rockets was at an exponential rate in the late 1950s and early 1960s, such that the early systems were rapidly replaced by modernised 2K6 "Luna" and later systems based on wheeled chassis beginning with the 9K52 "Luna-M" and 9K72 "Elbrus". The early systems were referred to in NATO terminology as "FROG" (Free Rocket Over Ground) systems or as SSMs (Surface to Surface Missiles). The actual Soviet designations for these systems were clarified only after the fall of the Soviet Union. There are also some anomalies, as the YaAZ-214 truck mounted 2K5 "Korshun" (BM-25) which is usually designated as a multiple rocket launcher, in fact fired the ZR-7 rocket, which in Soviet terminology firmly placed it as a (multiple) OTR rather than a more conventional multiple rocket launcher.

2K1 Mars (2P2 SPU Vehicle)

The 2K1 "Mars" was the first operational tactical level rocket system deployed in the Soviet Union. The 2P2 "Pion" SPU vehicle for the 2K1 "Mars" OTR complex firing the ZR-1 "Sova" rocket was developed at the NII-1 Institute under the direction of N.P. Mazurov, with the prototype 2P2 SPU and 2P3 TZM vehicles developed at NII-58. The "Mars" OTR was taken into service in accordance with Resolution SM №328-199 dated 20th March 1958. 25 2P1 "Mars" SPU systems (i.e.2P2 SPU and 2P3 TZM vehicles) were built at the Barrikady Plant in Stalingrad in 1959-60 on the S-122/123A chassis, derived from the chassis used for the PT-76 amphibious light tank. The 1,760kg launch weight ZR-1 "Mars" rocket was 324mm in diameter and had a range of 17.5km. The 2K1 "Mars" rocket system had its public debut on Red Square on 7th November 1957, together with the 2K4 "Filin" rocket system. NATO designated the rocket as "FROG" or sometimes "FROG-1".

2K2 Filin (2P4 SPU Vehicle)

The 2K2 "Filin" tactical level rocket system debuted on Red Square 7th November 1957, concurrently with the lighter 2K1 "Mars" system. The 2P4 "Tuilpan" SPU vehicle was paraded until the mid 1960s. The 2K2 was originally also designated as a FROG rocket by NATO; however the 4,430kg launch weight, 612mm diameter ZR-2 "Filin" rocket was significantly larger and heavier than the ZR-1 "Mars" rocket, with a longer range of 25.7km. The 2P4 "Filin" (Obiekt-804) SPU vehicle for the tracked 2K2 system was a high-maintenance vibration prone chassis, not entirely suitable for use as a rocket SPU vehicle, hence the later move to wheeled SPU vehicles when the technology for powerful all wheel drive wheeled chassis became available.*

2K5 Korshun (2P5 SPU vehicle)

The six round 250mm 2K5 (BM-25/BMD-25) "Korshun" tactical MRS entered service with the Soviet Army in 1957 and made its public debut during the 1st May 1957 Red Square military parade in Moscow. The 2K5 "Korshun" was developed at OKB-3 NII-88 near Moscow under the direction of D. D. Sevruk in accordance with Resolution SM SSSR №2469-1022 dated 19th

2K1 "Mars" (2P2 SPU vehicle)

2K2 "Filin" (2P4 SPU vehicle)

2K2 "Filin" (2P4 SPU vehicle)

2K5 "Korshun" (2P5 SPU vehicle)

---

* The 2K2 is sometimes seen designated 2K4, but the official Soviet GRAU designation is 2K2, as the 2K4 is the GRAU designation for the "Drakon" ATGM.

2K6 "Luna" (2P16 SPU vehicle)

2K6 "Luna" (2P16 SPU vehicle)

9K52 "Luna-M" (9P113 SPU vehicle)

9K52 "Luna-M" (9P113 SPU vehicle)

8K11 (8U218 SPU vehicle)

September 1952, with the rocket launcher developed at TsKB-34 in Leningrad. The 2K5 "Korshun" (a type of eagle) fired six 250mm ZR-7 rockets from an open frame launcher to a range of 55km. Production was undertaken at the "Izhmash" plant in Izhevsk from 1957 until 1960, with a total of 1,265 systems built. The first pre-production 2P5 (BM-25) MRS vehicles were based on the YaAZ-214 chassis. Series production vehicles were from 1960 based on the KrAZ-214 chassis. At the time of service, the 2K5 was the most powerful MRS in Soviet Army service, though the ZR-7 rockets were designated as OTR rather than MRS rockets, and the system was deployed as an OTR system. The 2K5 is also known by the designation BM-25 or BMD-25.

2K6 Luna (2P16 SPU Vehicle)

The 2P16 "Luna" (Moon) was the direct Soviet equivalent to the American "Honest John" rocket system. The system was developed from 1953 at the NII-1 institute under the direction of N.P. Mazurov. The original SPU vehicle was developed at the "Barrikady" plant as the Obiekt-160, and the TZM vehicle as the Obiekt-161. The original "Luna" system, firing ZR-9 with ZN-15 He-Frag conventional warhead and ZR-10 with ZN-14 nuclear warhead rockets, and mounted on PT-76 chassis derived S-123A (SPU) and S-124A (TZM) vehicles was accepted for service in 1958 with the first ten S-123A SPU vehicles built and tested from 1959, with two systems tested on Novaya Zemlya in 1961. In service the system was latterly known as the 2P16 "Luna", and by NATO under the generic designation "FROG" with the ZR-9 rocket being "FROG-3" and the ZR-10 rocket being "FROG-5". The system was removed from service in 1982.

9K52 Luna-M (9P113 SPU Vehicle)

The 9K52 "Luna-M" SSM was the last of the "FROG" SPU vehicles as designated by NATO. The use of tracked chassis had been inevitable when the earlier rockets were developed as only such chassis provided the combination of power and all-terrain manoeuvrability required to allow the vehicles to keep pace with mechanised units. A new generation of multi-axle all-terrain wheeled vehicles developed at ZiL in Moscow and MAZ in Minsk would however provide better performance, while providing a less vibration prone chassis with reduced maintenance requirements compared with tracked vehicles. The original 9K52 system and its 9P113 SPU vehicle were accepted for service on 6th August 1964, as a modernisation of the 2K6 "Luna" system. The 9M21 rocket had a maximum range of 70km. The 9K52 "Luna-M" was authorised by a Resolution of the SM SSSR dated 20th July 1966.

The early chassis was designated 2P113, based on the ZiL-135LM chassis, later modified as the 9P113 and latterly as the 9P113M. Whereas earlier vehicles had been based on S-123/S-124 tracked chassis, the "Luna-M" (NATO: FROG-7) 9P113 SPU vehicle was based on the chassis of the 8x8 ZiL-135LM (BAZ-135LM) 8x8 vehicle. The BAZ-135 had a complex dual engine and powertrain layout, with the twin V-8 "375" engines each powering the transmission and wheels on one side of the vehicle, allowing it to operate with wheels damaged on one side of the vehicle. The vehicle was developed at ZiL but built at BAZ in Bryansk hence the BAZ designation. Final assembly of the 9P113 SPU vehicles was undertaken at the Barrikady plant in Volgograd (formerly Stalingrad) from 1964 to 1972 based on chassis supplied from Bryansk. The related TZM vehicle was designated 9T29.

8K11 R-11 (8A61) / R-11M (8K11)(8U218 SPU vehicle)

The 180km range R-11 (8A61) (NATO: SS-1 Scud-A) OTR rocket was developed at OKB-1 (NII-88) under the direction of S.P. Korolev from December 1950 and was accepted for service mounted on the 8U218 SPU chassis on 13th July 1955, with final military acceptance on 1st April 1958 as the 8K11 system. The original R-11 rocket had a conventional HE-Frag warhead. The later R-11M version, as developed for Soviet ground forces in accordance with a Resolution of the Council of Ministers dated 26th August 1954 had an RSD-4 10kT nuclear warhead. The R-11M had a launch weight of 5.5 metric tonnes.

The SPU vehicle was developed at the LKZ plant in Leningrad in 1955-56 as the Obiekt-803 under the direction of K.N. Ilin on the chassis of the ISU-152K self-propelled gun. The SPU vehicle was series produced at LKZ from 1959-62 as the 8U218. The 8K11 rocket system consisted of the R-11 conventional or R-11M nuclear rocket mounted on the 8U218 SPU vehicle. The rocket was hydraulically raised to the vertical position for firing. The 8U218 SPU launcher, which could travel at 42km/h on made roads was during its service life designated by NATO as the SS-1 Scud-A.

9K72 R-17 (8K14) (2P19 SPU vehicle)

The 8K14 rocket, also known by NATO as the original SS-1 Scud-B, was a development of the 8K11 but with a significantly increased range of 240-300km. In April 1958 an SM SSSR Resolution approved the development of the new 9K72 rocket complex firing the 8K14 (R-17) nuclear rocket, which looked similar to the R-11 but had twice the operational range. The 8K14, as with the 8K11 was provided with a 10kT nuclear warhead option. The 9K72 system consisted of the 8K14 rocket mounted on a 2P19 SPU vehicle, developed as the Obiekt-810. The 9K72 (GRAU: 2K7 "Zemlya") system was tested in 1959-61 and was accepted into service on 24th March 1962.

The SPU vehicle for the 8K14 rocket was developed at SKB-385 by a team led by V. P. Makeev within LKZ in Leningrad as the Obiekt-810, based on the ISU-152K chassis from 1958-61. The SPU vehicle entered service under the GRAU index 2P19, and remained in production until 1962, with 56 SPU vehicles being built in total. The 2P19 SPU launcher was designated as SS-1 Scud-B by NATO, the same designation used for the later wheeled SPU variant. The parade debut of the 2P19 SPU vehicle was on 7th November 1961, several months before the system was accepted for service, with four systems displayed alongside two earlier generations of OTR system.

Front Level Rockets

9K76 Temp-S (9P120 SPU Vehicle)

The original 9K71 "Temp" Front level rocket system was developed at NII-1 in response to SM SSSR Resolution №839-379 dated 21st July 1959. The 9K71 system, firing the 9M71/9M72 rocket, did not reach production, but was modified as the 9K76 which was developed by NII-1, NII-592 and NII-125 in accordance with SM SSSR Resolution №934-405 dated 5th July 1962. After

9K72 R-17 (8K14) (9P117/9P117M SPU vehicle)

The original 8K72 system was modernised at OKB-1 in 1967, with the system and its 8K14 rocket now mounted on a wheeled SPU vehicle, the 9P117, based on the chassis of the 8x8 MAZ-543A, powered by a de-rated V-12 tank engine developing 525hp providing a road speed of 60km/h. The system was accepted for service per Resolution SM SSSR №75-26 dated 27th January 1967, as a modernisation of the earlier 8K72 system with the new and now wheeled SPU vehicle designated 9P117. The system later became perhaps the most famous of all Soviet missile systems, being known by NATO and the West as the SS-1 "Scud-B". The 9K72 system, which had a maximum range of 300km was known in the Soviet Union as the "Elbrus". The original 9P117 SPU vehicle was latterly replaced by the 9P117M variant, which had a modified launcher without the auxiliary hydraulic rams on each side of the launcher frame and other changes. The 9P117 and later 9P117M were assembled at the Petropavlovsk Heavy Machine Building Plant.

9K79 Tochka (9P129 SPU Vehicle)

The 120km range 9K79 "Tochka" (Point) (NATO: SS-21 Scarab)SSM was developed as a replacement for the 9K52 "Luna-M" OTR. The original "Tochka" and its 9P129 SPU vehicle was accepted into service with the Soviet Army in 1975. The 9P129 SPU vehicle was based on the specially developed BAZ-5921 6x6 amphibious chassis, developed at the SKB at BAZ from the mid 1960s and which entered series production in 1974. The system was from 1989 modified as the 9K79-1 "Tochka-U", with the SPU vehicle designated 9P129M.

various trailer mounted PU systems were considered, the decision was made to go with a self-propelled system. The Br-278 launcher system for the 12.38m long, 1.01m diameter rocket was accordingly built at the Barrikady Plant in Stalingrad, based on the MAZ-543A chassis and powered by a powerful D12-525A diesel engine. The first prototype was completed in 1964 and the system entered series production in 1966, remain-

9K72 "Elbrus" (2P19 SPU vehicle)

9K72 "Elbrus" (9P117M SPU vehicle)

9K72 "Elbrus" (9P117M SPU vehicle)

9K79 "Tochka" (9P129 SPU vehicle)

9K76 "Temp-S" (9P120 SPU vehicle)

THE SOVIET ARMY ON PARADE 1946-91

9K76 "Temp-S"

ing in production until 1970, with the wheeled SPU vehicle being known in service as the 9P120. The 9K76 "Temp-S" system with its 9,700kg launch weight, 800-900km range 9M76/9M76B rocket was known in the West by its NATO designation "SS-12 Scaleboard". The 9P120 SPU vehicle for the 9K76 system was a regular parade participant from its parade debut in November 1967 until the mid 1980s. The similar "Oka" Army Level system, developed in the mid 1970s and firing the 9M714 rocket transported and launched from a BAZ-6944 based SPU vehicle, was never paraded on Red Square and was subsequently scrapped in accordance with INF treaty requirements on medium and short range rockets systems in Europe.

Coastal Defence Cruise Missile Systems

S-5 (2K17 system)

S-5 (2K17 system) TZM

S-5 (2K17, 4K95) Frontal Cruise Missile

The S-5 frontal cruise missile (NATO: SSC-1 Sepal/Shaddock) was a development of the naval R-5 cruise missile modified for use as a coastal defence system. The first test launch was on 21st July 1960. The system was mounted on a specialised 8x8 ZiL-135K SPU based vehicle, powered by twin ZiL-375 engines developing 180hp each. Nine ZiL-135K vehicles were built at ZiL in Moscow from 1960-62 before series production of the ZiL-135K was transferred to Bryansk vehicle plant (BAZ) in accordance with Resolution №830-354 dated 7th September 1961. The 2K17 coastal defence cruise missile system was taken into service with the Soviet Army on 30th December 1961 and given the "non secret" index 4K95, with the SPU vehicle designated 2P30. The S-5 missile cruised at 345m/s at an altitude of 400m to a range of 574km. The 2K17 (4K95) rocket system was demonstrated on Red Square throughout the 1960s, with its exact purpose only becoming clear long after its original parade appearance.

Strategic Rocket Systems – SLBM, SRBM, MRBM, ICBM, ABM

R-5M

Silo, submarine and later land mobile launched missile systems began to be demonstrated on Moscow's Red Square from the late 1950s, with the 1960s being the "missile decade" on the square. The first Soviet strategic rocket, the R-1, also known as the SA-11 or by its GRAU designation 8A11, was developed from the German A-4, better known as the V-2. The R-1 was primarily used for testing and development, and was followed by the almost identical but longer, and significantly longer range R-2. The early rockets were not however displayed on Red Square in Moscow, though they were paraded in Kiev, Ukraine on at least one occasion in the early 1950s. The first strategic rocket to be demonstrated on Red Square was the R-5M (NATO: SS-3 Shyster), which was paraded through the square for the first time on 7th November 1957, together with the first nuclear warhead delivery vehicles, the 2A3 and 2B1 tracked strategic artillery pieces which had significantly shorter range compared to the new missile technology simultaneously unveiled. The R-5M was replaced almost immediately on Red Square by the near identical R-12 such was the pace of rocket development in at the end of the 1950s.

R-5M (8K51) Pad Launched MRBM

The R-5M (NATO: SS-3 Shyster) was developed in the early 1950s and paraded through Red Square for the first time on 7th November 1957. The R-5M was a single

307

stage, 29.1 metric tonne launch weight, 1,200km range MRBM armed with a 400kT nuclear warhead. The first successful launch of the R-5M as a Soviet nuclear long-range capable rocket was conducted on 2nd February 1956 under the auspices of "Operation Baikal", with the R-5M entering service on 21st June the same year in accordance with a Resolution of the TsK KPSS i SM SSSR. The R-5M entered service in 1959 with 32 systems in service at the end of that year, increased to 60 the following year. The 20.75m long, 1.65m diameter R-5M was towed through Red Square on its transport trailer by the AT-T tracked artillery tractor. The system was quickly replaced on Red Square by the R-12 and was removed from service in 1968.

R-12/R-12U (8K63/8K63U) Pad/Silo Launched MRBM

The R-12 MRBM was developed at NII-88 in collaboration with KB №586 - later known as the "Yuzhnoe" design bureau at Dnepropetrovsk under the direction of M.K. Yankel in accordance with a Resolution of the TsK KPSS i SM dated 13th February 1953. The R-12 was also known by the GRAU designation 8K63 and by NATO as the SS-4 Sandal. The first R-12 test flight was on 22nd June 1957, with the rocket making its Red Square debut appearance in 1960. The rocket was more famous for its international debut rather than its first appearance on Red Square however. The R-12 would become perhaps the most infamous of all Soviet era strategic rockets, representing as it did the epitome of known Soviet weapons deployment at the height of the Cold War. It was not the parade debut of eight R-12 rockets towed by AT-T tracked artillery tractors across Red Square on 1st May 1960 that was the concern, rather the attempted deployment of 40 R-12 rocket systems on the island of Cuba in the following months, which had led to the Cuban Missile Crisis of September-October 1962.

Although paraded through Red Square on a trailer for display purposes, the liquid fuelled, 2,100km range R-12 was installed using an 8U210 installer and single-axle MAZ-529V tractor combination. The R-12 was 22.1m in length, 1.65m in diameter and had a launch weight of 41.7 metric tonnes, being slightly over a metre longer but otherwise almost identical to the preceding R-5M. A modified silo-launched version was accepted for service with the newly formed RVSN on 5th January 1964 as the R-12U (8K63U).

The 8K63 MRBM was produced until 1963, when it was replaced by the modified 8K63U. The systems were in service from 1960 until 1989 with the original pad launched R-12 being demonstrated on Red Square. At the time of the 1987 INF treaty on medium and short-range strategic rockets, there were 61 systems still in service, and a further 91 in strategic storage.

R-14/R-14U (8K65/8K65U) Pad/Silo Launched MRBM

The R-14 was as with the R-12 developed from 1954 by the OKB-586 (later the "Yuzhnoe" design bureau located at Dnepropetrovsk) under the direction of M.K. Yankel. The rocket entered service with the Soviet Strategic Rocket forces from 1961 and remained in service until 1987. The R-14 (NATO: SS-5 Skean) gained notoriety in 1962, being the second type of rocket that was in the process of being delivered by sea to Cuba when the Soviet vessels were intercepted by the US naval blockade of Cuba, albeit the nuclear warheads for the rockets had already been landed on the island.

The later R-14U (8K65U) silo-launched rocket was paraded through Red Square in 1964-67 by the MAZ-535A, towing a twin axle transport trailer. The R-14U (8K65U) was a significant 24.4 metres long and 2.4 metres in diameter, and had 86.3-87.0 tonne launch weight. As with the R-12, the rocket was paraded through Red Square on a transport trailer for display purposes, but was installed in silos by an 8U210P/8U224 installer towed by a single-axle MAZ-529V tractor. The R-14U had a range of 4,500-5,500km, was armed with a 1.0 Mt or 2.3Mt nuclear warhead, and had a CEP of 5.0km.

RT-15 (8K96) Land Mobile MRBM

The 15P696 mobile MRBM, also known by the GRAU index 8K96 (NATO: SS-X-14 Scamp/Scapegoat) was the first Soviet land-mobile MRBM. It was first seen on Red Square during the 1st May 1965 parade, the appearance being subsequently repeated in 1966. The system was part of an overall effort to develop mobile MRBM systems using two of the three stages of the concurrent RT-2 (8K98) ICBM.

R-12/R-12U

R-12U

R-14/R-14U

RT-15 (Obiekt-815Sp1)

RT-15 (Obiekt-815Sp1)

RT-15 (8U253/15U59)

RT-15 (Obiekt-815Sp2/8U253/15U59)

RT-20P (15U51)

RT-20P (15U51)

The RT-15 (8K96) MRBM was developed at TsKB-7 "Arsenal" under the designer P.A. Turin in accordance with Resolution TsK KPSS i SM SSSR №316-317 dated 4th April 1961. The land mobile RT-15 (8K96) MRBM was developed on the basis of the RT-2, and was significant in being the first truly self-contained land mobile MRBM system. The RT-15 (8K96) was demonstrated on Red Square 7th on November 1965 mounted on its T-10M derived SPU vehicle built at the LKZ (Kirov) plant in Leningrad.

The system and its SPU vehicle were known by various designations. The 8K96 (RT-15) rocket was mounted on the Obiekt-815Sp1 and latterly Sp2 (8U253) SPU vehicles. In parade order the original two prototypes built at LKZ in Leningrad were fitted with the fibreglass TPK transport container, the system being developed as an SPU rather than TU system at the time the original prototypes were being paraded on Red Square.

The two stage, 16 metric tonne launch weight RT-15 rocket had a range of 2,500km and was fitted with a single 0.6Mt or 1.0Mt nuclear warhead. The 11.93m long and 1.49m diameter rocket was transported within its transport-launch container on a specialized SPU chassis. The RT-15 was from 1965 displayed on Red Square concurrently with the RT-20P land mobile ICBM, with two distinct modifications of SPU vehicle being displayed in 1965-1966 and from 1967.

The RT-15 was first demonstrated on Red Square in 1965, mounted on its T-10M derived Obiekt-815Sp1 SPU vehicle for the land mobile 15P696 system, which provided fully enclosed protection for the rocket. The RT-15 rocket was 12.6m in length and 1.4m at its widest diameter, with a launch weight of 16 metric tonnes. The 15P696 SPU vehicle with rocket had a total system weight of 62 metric tonnes. It had a maximum road speed of 30km/h and a range of 2,500km.

A single regiment was to have been deployed for long-term operational trials with the Soviet Army by 1969, but although the system was further developed and was deployed for trials purposes it was subsequently scrapped in accordance with the START treaty on MRBMs. The RT-15 and the larger RT-20 represented the end of the line for tracked SPU vehicles for such systems. At the time the RT-15 was being tested, the new 8x8 MAZ-543 truck chassis was being introduced into service, originally for battlefield theatre "OTR" rockets (i.e. the 8K72 "Scud"), but larger and more powerful versions of the vehicle were subsequently developed, including the MAZ-547, MAZ-7917 and MAZ-79221, which ultimately took over the role of SPU chassis from the earlier tracked vehicles, with little loss of all-terrain performance and a less vibration prone ride.

RT-20P (8K99) Land Mobile ICBM

The RT-20P (NATO: SS-X-15 Scrooge) was first demonstrated on Red Square in 1965. The RT-20P was the first truly mobile ICBM system to be developed by the Soviet Union. Developed by the OKB-586 design bureau under the direction of M.K. Yankel in accordance with Resolution TsK KPSS i SM SSSR №316-137ss dated 4th April 1961, the two-stage rocket used a mix of solid and liquid fuel in its stage design. The large rocket was 17.8m long and 1.6m in diameter, had a launch weight of 30-30.2 tonnes and a range of 8,000 - 11,000km. The mobile system version was developed from 1964 under the designation 15P699, with the SPU vehicle designated 15U51. The land-mobile 15P699 SPU vehicle system was developed from 1964, mounted on a tracked chassis derived from a lengthened T-10M heavy tank chassis built at LKZ in Leningrad.

Technically the SPU vehicle was referred to as a TU or TUA (Transportno-Ustanovochny Agregat - Transport-Installation System) rather than an SPU vehicle, which may be due to the fact that technically the rocket was ejected from the TPK by a gas-vapour mix before "hot" launch of the first rocket stage with the rocket propelled well clear of the TPK. It was developed under the plant designation Obiekt-820 and was also known as the SM-SP20. The vehicle was provided with a hydraulic system for erecting the TPK for launch and a system for stabilising and levelling the integral launch pad. The tracked chassis (TU/SPU) weighed 78.9 metric tonnes.

In 1965 the decision was taken at the highest political level to demonstrate the TU (rather than SPU) vehicles of both the RT-15 RSD (MRBM) and RT-20P MRB (ICBM) for the benefit of the Soviet hierarchy, the Soviet Rocket Forces and the foreign press. The two newly built 15U51* (15P699) TU vehicles (effectively the prototypes) for the then under development RT-20P were thereby demonstrated on Red Square on 7th November 1965, the enigmatic rocket system being subsequently designated SS-X-15 Scrooge by NATO. Flight-testing was carried out in the summer of 1967, long after the system had been demonstrated for public consumption purposes. The RT-20P was not subsequently deployed, but formed the basis for the later RT-21 (RSD-10) "Pioner" mounted on a more versatile MAZ-547 wheeled chassis.

The RT-20P was the first truly land-mobile ICBM system, and as such represented a game-changing advance in Soviet rocket technology. The system was designated 15P099, with the SPU (TU) vehicle designated 15U51 (15P699). The RT-20P tracked SPU vehicle was derived from a lengthened T-10M heavy tank chassis with eight road wheel pairs per side and hydraulic shock absorbers. With the rocket TPK installed the vehicle had a total length of 20m.

R-26 (8K66) Silo Launched ICBM

The R-26 ICBM was developed at OKB-586 (later the Yuzhnoe KB) in Dnepropetrovsk under the direction of M.K. Yankel in accordance with a Resolution of the SM SSSR dated 23rd May 1960. The 22.38 metre long rocket, the rear section of which was 2.75m in diameter, had a launch weight of 85 metric tonnes and a range of 10,500-11,600km with options of 1.6Mt "light" and 5.0Mt "heavy" warheads according to conflicting sources. The R-26 project was abandoned in December 1961 due to issues with the fuel cell technology and officially cancelled on 9th July 1962, with design work continuing on the R-36. The abandonment of the R-26 rocket in 1962 did not detract from it being regularly paraded through Red Square on its three-axle 3-PPT-50 semi-trailer by the MAZ-537V in the mid to late 1960s, as it was a large and impressive rocket system. The R-26 was designated as the SS-8 "Sasin" by NATO, but there was initially confusion between the R-9 (8K75) and the R-26 (8K66) in NATO designations, with the actual Soviet designations becoming known only in later years. The R-26 had its Red Square parade debut on 7th November 1964.

R-36 (8K67) Silo Launched ICBM

The two-stage R-36 (8K67) ICBM was developed at OKB-586 in Dnepropetrovsk under the direction of M.K. Yankel in accordance with Resolution TsK KPSS i SM SSSR №1021-436ss dated 12th May 1962, with the system being accepted for service with the RVSN in May 1966. The nominally 11,000km range R-36 (NATO: SS-9 Scarp) finally delivered on Khrushchev's promise many years prior of developing rockets capable of striking the United States. The R-36 had its parade debut on Red Square on 7th November 1967 and was subsequently paraded through Red Square from 1967 until 1974, towed on a transport trailer behind MAZ-535A 8x8 wheeled tractor vehicles. The R-36 was an impressive rocket, being 31.7m in length and 3.0m in diameter, with a launch weight of 184 metric tonnes. The original R-36 as paraded on Red Square was later modified as the R-36M (NATO: SS-18 Satan), which version was not displayed on Red Square, though the NATO designators were conflated during the Cold War. The R-36 was originally armed with 8Mt "light" or 20Mt "heavy" warhead options, with corresponding range of 15,200km and 10,200km, through original data is considerably conflated on this. Other Russian sources state the use of 5Mt light and 10Mt heavy warhead options.

The later (developed from 1969 and in service from 1975) R-36M (GRAU 15A14) and R-36 MUTTKh (15A18) rockets had improved range and accuracy, with the final version being the R-36M2 (15A18M). All later versions were known by NATO as the SS-18 "Satan". By 1983, 308 silo-mounted R-36 MUTTKh rockets had been installed. 268 silo-mounted R-36 rockets were deployed from 1965-73, with the R-36 being paraded through Red Square on 7th November 1974; the last time a silo-launched ICBM would ever be paraded on Red Square. The R-36 was removed from service in 1978.

UR-100 (8K84) Silo Launched ICBM

The silo-launched UR-100 (Universalnaya Raketa - Universal Rocket 100) was developed at OKB-52 under the direction of V.N. Chelomey in accordance with Resolution TsK KPSS i SM SSSR №705-235ss dated 21st July 1967 as the Soviet equivalent to the U.S. "Minuteman"

R-26

R-36

R-36

UR-100

UR-100

---

* The early prototype was also refered to as 15U21

RT-2

RT-21/RSD-10 Pioner

RT-21/RSD-10 Pioner

ICBM. Development work on the rocket began in March 1963, with work on constructing the armoured launch silos for the UR-100 beginning in 1964; the first test launch of the two stage, single warhead rocket being on 19th April 1965. The 16.7m long, 2.0m diameter 42,300kg launch weight rocket could deliver a 1.1Mt nuclear warhead to a range of 10,600-11,000km (12,000km per some sources). The first three UR-100 rocket regiments were operationally deployed on 24th November 1966. The system was later modernised as the UR-100M, with a total of 990 UR-100 series rockets being built in total. The UR-100 (NATO: SS-11 Sego) was towed through Red Square by the MAZ-537V 8x8 wheeled tractor on its substantial three-axle semi-trailer. The rocket was displayed with only the rocket nose visible at the open rear of its cylindrical transport container, the rocket being towed facing backwards as with the GR-1 (8K713).

RT-2 (8K98) (RS-12) Silo Launched ICBM

The three stage RT-2 (Raketa Tverdotoplivnaya - solid fuel rocket-2) (8K98 or RS-12) ICBM was primarily developed at OKB-1 from 1961 under the direction of the rocket designer Sergei Korolev as a replacement for the R-12, and was the last of the second generation of Soviet strategic rockets. First test launched on 4th November 1966, the cold-launched RT-2 (NATO: SS-13 Savage) ICBM was the first solid fuel rocket ICBM system to be deployed by the Soviet Strategic Rocket Forces (RVSN). The systems was developed in accordance with Resolution TsK KPSS i SM №316-137ss dated 4th April 1961, the same resolution which authorized development of the RT-20P mobile ICBM. The three-stage, 51 metric tonne launch weight rocket had a range of 9,500km with its single 0.6Mt nuclear warhead, or 10,000-12,000km with a lighter 0.5Mt warhead. A 1.4Mt warhead was available, with a correspondingly reduced range of 5,000km. The RT-2 superficially resembled the RT-15 rocket but, at 21.2m long and 1.84m in maximum diameter, was significantly larger. The rocket was taken into service in 1968, but with only 60 RS-12 (15P098) systems entering service with the RVSN. A modification of the rocket undertaken from 1972 resulted in the RT-2P, which entered service in 1976, with 40 systems deployed. The original RT-2 (8K98) rocket was displayed on Red Square from 1972-1974, towed on its transport trailer by the MAZ-535A 8x8 wheeled tractor.

RT-21 / RSD-10 Pioner (15Zh45) Land Mobile MRBM

The RT-21 / RSD-10 "Pioner" (NATO: SS-20 Saber) land mobile MRBM was developed in accordance with Resolution TsK KPSS i SM SSSR №280-96ss dated 20th April 1973. Development work began at the MIT institute in Moscow on the basis of the "Temp-2S" in April 1966, with the system being tested from 1974. The 35.26 metric tonne launch weight RT-21 with its three 0.15Mt independently targetable warheads had a range of 4,500-5,000m. The 15Zh45 rocket was at 16.49m in length and 1.79m in diameter - large as well as heavy, and a special 6-axle SPU vehicle, the MAZ-547, was developed for the new mobile rocket system by the MAZ plant in Minsk. The RSD-10 "Pioner" was mounted on the specially developed 12x12 MAZ-547V chassis with the rocket located within a TPK transport-launch container. The rockets were assembled at the Votkinsk plant from 1976, with assembly of the launcher vehicles being undertaken at the Barrikady plant in Stalingrad. After initial service deployment, the original MAZ-547V 12x12 chassis used for the 15U106 SPU vehicle for the 15P645 "Pioner" was modified with an enlarged cab arrangement, the later modified chassis being designated MAZ-7916.

The 5,000km range RSD-10 as it was later designated, was accepted for service with the strategic rocket forces in accordance with SM SSSR Resolution №177-67 dated 11th March 1976, and was taken into service with Soviet strategic rocket services on 17th December 1980. Though a road-mobile system, the "Pioner" was operationally deployed from semi-permanent concrete launch sites. The original RSD-10 "Pioner" was modified in 1976 as the 15Zh53 "Pioner UTTKh" with changes to the targetable warheads and improved accuracy.

The RSD-10 "Pioner" was rapidly deployed, with 180 mobile SPU vehicles in service by 1981, rising to 300 by 1983 and 405 by 1986. The "Pioner" MRBM was short-lived however, due to being removed from service in accordance with the 1987 INF treaty relating to the deployment of medium and short-range missile systems in Europe as it was in the process of being deployed. All 405 of the 15Zh45 "Pioner" and 15Zh53 "Pioner UTTKh" rockets in service were eliminated, with the last rocket being destroyed in June 1991. Though integral to the development of Soviet land mobile MRBM and ICBM systems, the "Pioner" was never displayed on Red Square.

GR-1 (8K713) Silo Launched ICBM

The GR-1 (Globalnaya Raketa - Global Rocket -1) (GRAU: 8K713) was one of the largest - and perhaps the most misunderstood - rockets to have ever been displayed on Red Square during the 1960s and very early 1970s. The GR-1 (NATO: SS-10 Scrag) was an experimental three-stage thermo-nuclear rocket system with a theoretical range of 40,000km and capable of delivering a 2.2Mt nuclear warhead to any target worldwide. Development was sanctioned in accordance with a Resolution of the TsK KPSS i SM SSSR №1021-4360ss dated 12th May 1962; the same resolution under which the R-36 was also approved for development. The three-stage GR-1 was developed primarily at OKB-276, and was developed to prototype stage on the basis of the R-9 rocket in collaboration with SKB №3 within the OKB-1 design bureau. The 117 metric tonne launch weight rocket was intended to be launched into deep space and to re-enter the atmosphere from orbit to any required target around the world, hence the designation. The GR-1 was first demonstrated on Red Square on 1st May 1965 and was generally identified in Western intelligence documents as the SS-10 "Scrag" with an estimated range of 8,000km. In reality, the design requirement was for the time technically unfeasible, and the project was cancelled in 1964, a few months after the public debut of the prototype rocket on Red Square on 7th November 1963. The GR-1 was never actually test launched, but remained a particularly fearsome looking Red Square display rocket, two such systems being the default parade finale on Red Square for a decade, towed on their 8T139 transport trailers by MAZ-535A wheeled tractors. The GR-1 was last paraded in 1972 and it was many years later that the true identification, purpose and indeed the actual fate of the GR-1 ICBM became clear to Western observers.

RT-2PM (RS-12M) Topol (GRAU: 15Zh58) Land Mobile ICBM

The RT-2PM (RS-12M) "Topol" (NATO: SS-25 Sickle) three stage ICBM was developed by the Moscow Institute for Teplotekhnika (MIT) in accordance with a Resolution TsK KPSS i SM SSSR №668-212ss dated 19th July 1977, with the project under the direction of A.D. Nadiradze. The first test launch of the prototype "Topol" was at the Kapustin Yar polygon on 27th October 1982. The first regiment was in service by 27th May 1988, with the formal service acceptance into the RVSN rocket forces of the Soviet Army being declared on 1st December 1988. By 1st September 1990 the Soviet Union had 208 SPU vehicles in service. By the summer of 1991, 288 rockets had been deployed, rising to 340 by 1993 and 360 deployed by 1999. The number of systems deployed peaked at 369 before the system began to be replaced by the modernized RT-2PM2 "Topol-M".

The 15Zh58 "Topol" rocket, which was planned for both silo and mobile deployment, was massive, at 21.5m in length and 1.8m in diameter, with a launch weight of 45.1 metric tonnes, and armed with a 0.55Mt nuclear warhead with a maximum range of 9,400-10,000km and a CEP of 900m. The road-mobile version of the RS-12M (RT-2PM) "Topol" was initially mounted on a 7 axle MAZ-7912 based 15U128 SPU vehicle that retained the smaller cabs as used on the MAZ-543 and MAZ-547. This was later replaced with the 14x12 MAZ (MZKT) -7917 developed in the mid 1980s as the RS-12M "Topol" was entering service. The MAZ (MZKT) -7917 was largely identical to its predecessor but featured a reconfigured cab arrangement providing better crew accommodation and was one metre longer overall. The MAZ (MZKT) -7917 is powered by a V-12 diesel engine developing 710hp, which moves the 18.4m long, 3.05m wide vehicle chassis with an overall weight of 80 metric tonnes at a maximum 40km/hour, sufficient to disperse launcher vehicles over a wide area in a short time. The later MAZ-7917 based SPU vehicle as shown on Red Square in 1990 was designated 15U168.

The RS-12M (RT-2PM) "Topol" was first demonstrated on Red Square on 7th November 1990, and was the last military vehicle to parade through Moscow's Red Square on the last Soviet era military parade held

GR-1

GR-1

GR-1

RT-2PM "Topol"

RT-2PM "Topol"

A-35

A-35 TZM

A-35 TZM

on 7th November 1990, reappearing again in public on Red Square only on 9th May 2008 as the culmination of the 2008 Victory Day parade in the Russian Federation.

A-35 (A-350) Anti-Ballistic Missile System

The original "System A-35" project began with a Resolution of the SM SSSR dated 8th April 1958 regarding the development of a strategic defence rocket for protecting cites such as Moscow. The project was developed by the "Vimpel" and "Fakel" bureaus under the initial direction of chief designer G.V. Kisunko with an original intent for the system to enter service in 1964.

The A-350Zh (NATO: ABM-1 Galosh) anti-ballistic missile (ABM) was a thermo-nuclear armed weapon with a two stage ramjet principle rocket engine developed at the Grushin KB and designed for installation as a long range strategic defence system for installation around Moscow. The missile, or rather its TPK transport container, was regularly paraded through Red Square in the 1960s, towed by the 8x8 MAZ-537V tractor. The system had a projected range of 300-350km, hence the "350" designation, and a maximum altitude of 30km. The A-350Zh rocket was developed for the A-35 system in the 1960s, armed with a 3Mt thermo-nuclear warhead developed at Chelyabinsk-70. The A-35 "Aldan" project was however an ongoing development and test program that included the A-35 system with the A-350Zh (5V61) rocket, the A-35M system with the A-350R rocket and latterly the new A-135 system from 1972, with the A-35M dating to 1978 and the A-135 becoming operational from 1995. The first test launch of the A-350Zh rocket was on 24th December 1965, after the rocket (or rather its TPK container) was first demonstrated on Red Square. The A-350Zh rocket as tested from 1967-69 had a launch weight of 32.7 metric tonnes and a range of 322km. The rocket was 19.8m in length and 2.97m in diameter and as such one of the largest pieces of military hardware ever displayed on Red Square. The furst full system trials were in October 1969.

Testing of the A-35 system with the A-350Zh rocket started from 1972, with this version being displayed on Red Square. The later A-35M with the A-350R rocket was accepted for service in May 1978 but actually entered service only in December 1990 as the Soviet Union was about to disintegrate. The later developed A-135 system was accepted for service in 1995.

Transport Vehicles

GAZ-67

GAZ-69

GAZ-67 Light Vehicle

The GAZ-67 was introduced into production at GAZ in Gorky during the war as a replacement for the earlier GAZ-64, assembly of which was cut short by the need for GAZ to concentrate on other more urgent wartime production, including the T-60 tank, tank parts and mortar systems. The GAZ-67 was used in small numbers by the wartime Red Army during the last two years of the war, and was paraded on Red Square in 1945; however the majority of reconnaissance vehicles used by the Red Army were Lend-Lease supplied "Jeeps" of various types. The GAZ-67 was used as the basis for the BA-64 armoured car, also displayed on Red Square in 1945. The final production model was the GAZ-67B, on which chassis the later BA-64B armoured car was built. The GAZ-67 and GAZ-67B were used as parade column lead vehicles until replaced by the GAZ-69.

GAZ-69 Light Vehicle

The GAZ-69 general service light vehicle was introduced into service with the Soviet Army in 1952. The Soviet Army used both the two-door GAZ-69 and the four door GAZ-69A versions of the vehicle. The former was used as a general service vehicle and as a light artillery tractor; the latter was generally used for personnel transport.

The GAZ-69 was the Soviet Army's default post-war general-purpose light vehicle for two decades before being replaced by the UAZ-469B. Developed at GAZ under the direction of V.A. Grachev as a replacement for the GAZ-67, the first pre-series GAZ-69 vehicles were assembled at GAZ in 1952. Full series production began on 1st September 1953, with the vehicle having its Red Square parade debut on 7th November 1953. Production was transferred to UAZ at Ulyanovsk in 1954 with full series production beginning there in 1955. The GAZ-69 was technically thereafter the UAZ-69, but the original GAZ-69 nomenclature was retained throughout the vehicle's service life. The GAZ-69 was used in a variety of roles in the Soviet Army. On Red Square it was used as a column lead vehicle and in VDV airborne forces configuration.

UAZ-469B / 31512 Light Vehicle

The UAZ-469B was introduced into service with the Soviet Army in 1972 as a replacement for the venerable GAZ-69 series. The vehicle was in series production from 1973 until 1985 when it was replaced by the modernised UAZ-3151 series. The four door UAZ-469 "Uazik" as it was colloquially termed was a capable off-road vehicle and remains in service as the modified UAZ-31512 to the present day.

GAZ-51 4x2 Truck

The 4x2 GAZ-51 was developed at GAZ under the direction of V.A. Grachev from 1938; however series production was postponed until after the Second World War. The vehicle replaced the GAZ-AA and GAZ-MM in Soviet Army service in the 1950s. Pre-series production vehicles assembled from 1947 featured a cab of wood and steel rather than all steel construction due to a shortage of die-presses and sheet steel in the immediate post-war era. The GAZ-51 had its Red Square parade debut in May 1948, together with the ZiS-151. Full series production began in 1948, with later production vehicles featuring cabs of all steel construction. The definitive production version was the later GAZ-51A. The vehicle was used as a general service load carrier and for towing light artillery. The GAZ-51 was the largest volume production Soviet truck of all time, with 3,481,033 vehicles built from 1946-1975.

ZiS-150 4x2 Truck

The 4x2 ZiS-150 was the post-war replacement for the wartime ZiS-5/ZiS-5V, developed for use by Soviet Army "tyl" or rear services. Series production began in April 1948, with the ZiS-150 apparently making its parade debut on 1st May 1948, when it was paraded in general service (in VDV forces markings), BM-13 and BM-31 MRS versions. After military trials conducted in 1949-50, the ZiS-150, which was powered by a ZiS-120 engine developing 95hp, was accepted for service as a general-purpose load carrier and for some specialised roles in the Soviet Army. It was used briefly as chassis for the BM-8 and BM-13 MRS for Red Square parade purposes in the immediate post-war era prior to the arrival of the 6x6 ZiS-151, but this was not a standard post-war Soviet Army configuration as a 4x2 chassis was not sufficiently stable for use as an MRS launch platform. Together with the GAZ-51, the ZiS-150 was the most widely used "tyl" ostensibly road-bound rear services vehicle in the Soviet Army during the 1950s.

YaAZ-200 Truck 4x2 Truck

The prototype 4x2 YaAZ-200 was developed by the YaAZ plant in Yaroslavl in the winter of 1944-45 and demonstrated to Stalin in the Kremlin on 19th June 1945 when it was accepted for series production. The vehicle was a heavy load carrier fitted with a YaAZ-204A diesel engine developing 110hp, which could transport a 7,000kg load on roads or 5,000kg across terrain with a maximum road speed of 73km/h. The first pre-series YaAZ-200, fitted with a wooden cab, was demonstrated on Red Square on 7th November 1947. Only 54 vehicles were completed at YaAZ in 1947, increasing to 173 the following year, with production being transferred from YaAZ (sometimes YAZ) in Yaroslavl to MAZ in Minsk in 1951 in accordance with GKO Resolution N°9905 dated 26th August 1945 whereby the latter plant was to produce 25,000 MAZ-200 series vehicles as the YaAZ plant in Yaroslavl re-orientated on other production. Series production of the MAZ-200 continued as the MAZ-200 until 1965. Early production YaAZ-200 vehicles as demonstrated on Red Square featured a cab of part wooden construction, replaced from 1951 by a monocoque steel cab using press-formed stampings on later series production vehicles.

UAZ-469B/31512

GAZ-51

GAZ-51

ZiS-150

YaAZ-200

GAZ-63

MAZ-502V

GAZ-66

GAZ-66

YaAZ-210G

ZiS-151

GAZ-63 4x4 Truck

The GAZ-63 was developed at GAZ as a 4x4 all terrain version of the 4x2 GAZ-51 from which the vehicle was derived. The GAZ-63 was developed to prototype stage at GAZ under the direction of V.A. Grachev in 1940, but due to the outbreak of war, the vehicle as with the GAZ-51 entered series production and service in the immediate post-war era, from September 1948, with the first 641 vehicles completed that year. Early production vehicles as featured on Red Square from 1948 featured a cab of mixed wood and steel production, with the definitive GAZ-63A introduced in 1952 featuring an all steel cab. The GAZ-63 was used as a general service 1.5 tonne all terrain load carrier, for towing light artillery and as a platform for a myriad of specialised vehicles. A total of 474,464 GAZ-63s were built.

MAZ-502V 4x4 Tractor Truck

The MAZ-502V was a 4x4 tractor truck version of the MAZ-502A, primarily used by Soviet PVO (air defence) forces for towing surface air defence missiles on their transport trailers. The MAZ-502V entered series production in 1957 and was demonstrated on Red Square in the early 1960s towing the Izdeliye-400 "Dal" surface to air missile on its PR-41A trailer TZM system, but was also used with the S-200 (NATO: SA-5 Gammon) SAM system that was never demonstrated on Red Square. Until the introduction of the 6x6 Ural-375 series at the beginning of the 1960s, the MAZ-502V was one of the most powerful early Soviet Army all-terrain load transporters.

GAZ-66 4x4 Truck

The GAZ-66 replaced the GAZ-63 in production in 1964 and was widely used by the Soviet armed forces until after the fall of the Soviet Union. The distinctly boxy in appearance, cab over engine (COE) GAZ-66 was the standard 2,000kg all-terrain general service load carrier from its introduction into Soviet Army service the 1960s until belatedly replaced at the turn of the 21st Century by the GAZ-3308 "Sadko" and other vehicles from manufacturers including KamAZ. The GAZ-66 was powered by a ZMZ-66 V-8 petrol engine, which gave the vehicle a road speed of 90km/h. The GAZ-66 was used as a general service transport vehicles, as a light artillery tractor tow vehicle and for various specialist applications. The lightweight GAZ-66B VDV airborne forces version was paraded on Red Square from 1965-1967 towing the RPU-14 towed MRS and the 85mm SD-44 auxiliary propelled gun. 965,961 GAZ-66 vehicles of all variants were built from 1964-1999.

YaAZ-210G 6x4 Tractor Truck

The 6x4 YaAZ-210G tractor truck was used for towing artillery and trailers. The vehicle was built in ballast tractor and universal platform versions, with the former type being demonstrated on Red Square. The vehicle was powered by a 6 cylinder YaAZ-206 diesel engine developing 165hp, providing an 8,000kg load capacity and a towing capacity of 45,000kg on roads, or 25,000kg across terrain. The YaAZ-210G was produced at YaAZ in Yaroslavl from 1948, with production being transferred to Minsk in 1951, where production continued until 1958. Early YaAZ production vehicles were demonstrated on Red Square from November 1951. A later development of the YaAZ-210 series was the 6x6 YaAZ-214, which was series produced in Kremenchug, Ukraine as the KrAZ-214.

ZiS-151 6x6 Truck

The ZiS-151 6x6 truck was the first Soviet 6x6 military truck to enter series production. It was developed using technical knowledge gained from imported Lend-Lease vehicles, not least the Studebaker US6. The ZiS-151 entered service in 1948, with the Red Square parade debut being in May of that year. The ZiS-151 was used by the Soviet Army in general service and in many specialised roles during the 1950s. Due to a post-war shortage of sheet steel and die-presses, early production vehicles featured part wooden cabs, later replaced by an all-steel cab. The ZiS plant in Moscow was latterly re-designated ZiL-151 (plant in the name of Likhachev) after the death of Stalin in 1953 and the vehicles renamed accordingly. MRS variants included the 132mm BM-13NM (2B7) MRS and the 12 round 240mm BM-24 MRS introduced in 1956. The semi-trailer tractor version of the ZiS-151, designated ZiS-121B, was used to tow the S-25 "Berkut" and S-75 "Dvina" SAM systems through Red Square on their respective PR-3 and PR-11A TZM semi-trailers.

ZiL-157 6x6 Truck

The ZiL-157 6x6 general service load carrier was the production replacement for the ZiS-151, and served as a general service load carrier and in all the specialist roles for which the ZiS-151 chassis was formerly used. The ZiL-157 had single tyres on all axles, and was fitted with CTPRS as standard. The ZiL-157 gradually replaced the ZiS-151 as the standard medium all-terrain 6x6 load carrier and tractor vehicle during the 1960s. It was primarily displayed on Red Square towing the same S-25 and S-75 SAM systems, in which role the ZiL-157 replaced the ZiS-121B (ZiS-151) from the mid 1960s. Variants displayed on Red Square included:
- ZiL-121B with PR-3 (PR-3M3) trailer mounted TZM for the S-25 (S-25M) "Berkut" SAM system.
- ZiL-157 with PR-3 (PR-3M3) trailer mounted TZM for the S-25 (S-25M) "Berkut" SAM system.
- ZiL-157K with PR-11A trailer mounted TZM for the SA-75 "Dvina" SAM system.
- ZiL-157KV with PR-11AM trailer mounted TZM for the SA-75M "Volkhov" SAM system, from 1965.
- ZiL-157KV with PR-11B trailer mounted TZM for the S-75 "Dvina" SAM system.
- ZiL-157KV with PR-11BM trailer mounted TZM for the S-75 "Volkhov" SAM system.
- ZiL-157 with PR-14A (14A, 14AM, 14B) TZM for the S-125 "Neva" SAM system.

ZiL-131 6x6 Truck

The ZiL-131 gradually replaced the ZiL-157 in the 1960s, though the vehicles were for many years used in parallel. Although the ZiL-131 pre-dates the more powerful Ural-375D, the vehicle was not paraded in the 1960s when the latter vehicle was seen configured as the chassis for the 9K51 "Grad" MRS. The ZiL-131 was commonly seen on Red Square from the early 1970s, primarily as a tractor or TZM vehicle for S-25, S-75 and S-125 SAM systems, replacing the ZiL-157 in the role. The ZiL-131V was from 1972 used to tow the S-75M3 "Volkov" SAM on its PR-11 series transport trailer, while the ZiL-131 PR-14M/MA TZM vehicle was from 1967 used to transport two S-125M 5V27 "Neva-M" SAM rockets. In the early 1980s, twenty years after it had entered series production, the vehicle finally appeared in its standard general service format

towing the 122mm D-30 gun-howitzer and the MT-12 "Rapira" anti-tank gun.

YaAZ-214/KrAZ-214 6x6 Truck

The YaAZ-214 7,000kg load capacity all-terrain truck was developed at YaAZ in Yaroslavl from 1956-1959, but with the majority of series production undertaken at Kremenchug in Ukraine from 1960 as the KrAZ-214, where production continued until 1967. The YaAZ-214 was from 1959 paraded on Red Square configured as the 2P5 launcher vehicle for the 2K5 "Korshun" (BMD-25) MRS system. The later KrAZ-255B was never paraded on Red Square.

KrAZ-255B 6x6 Truck

The KrAZ-255B replaced the KrAZ-214 in production from 1967 and remained the standard Soviet Army load carrier and specialised weapons platform when the Soviet Union was dissolved in 1991. The KrAZ-255B closely resembled the earlier KrAZ-214, but had an increased 7,500kg all-terrain payload, a new and more powerful engine, and a central tyre pressure regulation system. The KrAZ-255B was never demonstrated on Red Square, though both the earlier and later generations of the vehicle were displayed for public consumption.

KrAZ-260 6x6 Truck

The KrAZ-260 was developed at KrAZ located in Kremenchug, Ukraine, in the early 1980s as a replacement for the venerable KrAZ-255B series of 6x6 all-terrain load carriers. The vehicle, which was powered by a YaMZ-238 V-8 engine developing 300hp, could transport a 9,000kg load and perform the role of wheeled artillery tractor, had its public debut on Red Square in 1985 and was seen at subsequent Red Square parades in the final years of the Soviet Union. The KrAZ-260 was beginning to replace KrAZ-255B and earlier KrAZ-214B in service with the Soviet Army when the Soviet Union was dissolved, after which the KrAZ-260 was over time replaced by domestic Russian KamAZ and Ural vehicles. In Ukraine the KrAZ-260 was later modified into the post-Soviet KrAZ-6322.

Ural-375D / Ural-4320 6x6 Truck

The 6x6, 4,000kg all-terrain load capacity Ural-375D

ZiL-157

ZiL-131

YaAZ-214 (later KrAZ-214)

KrAZ-255B

KrAZ-260

Ural-375D (9K51 "Grad" MRS)

MAZ-537V

MAZ-543A

MAZ-543M

ZiL-135K (2K17 Cruise Missile System)

M-2

was developed and built at the Ural plant in Miass which had during the Second World War built the Ural-ZiS-5V and the post-war Ural-ZiS-355 and 355M. The Ural-375D was introduced into service with the Soviet Army in 1961. The early production Ural-375 featured a canvas cab roof, but this was quickly replaced by the Ural-375D with an all steel cab. One of the most commonly observed variants of the Ural-375D was the 9K51 (BM-21) "Grad" (2B5) MRS introduced in 1964 which was regular Red Square parade participant in the 1960s and 1970s. The Ural-375S 6x6 tractor was also used to tow the Izdeliye-400 "Dal" SAM system - one of the most enigmatic surface to air missile systems of the Cold War - through Red Square. The Ural-375D was replaced in production by the Ural-4320, powered by a V-8 diesel engine, providing better a slightly increased payload and better fuel economy and range.

MAZ-535A 8x8 Tractor Truck

The MAZ plant in Minsk, Belarus manufactured the MAZ-535, MAZ-537 and later all-terrain heavy load and missile carrier vehicles used in the Soviet Army. The 8x8 MAZ-535A was used throughout the 1960s and early 1970s to tow MRBM and ICBM rockets on tow bar mounted trailers through Red Square, including the R-14 (8K65U) (NATO: SS-5 Skean) MRBM and massive rocket systems such as the R-36 (8K67) (NATO: SS-9 Scarp) and the largely theoretical GR-1 (8K713) (NATO: SS-10 Scrag) mounted on its 8T139 transport trailer.

MAZ-537V 8x8 Tractor Truck

The 8x8 MAZ-537V was used throughout the 1960s and early 1970s to tow MRBM and ICBM rockets on semi-trailers through Red Square, including the R-26 (8K66) on its three-axle semi-trailer, the silo-mounted R-36 (8K67) and the A-35 (NATO: ABM-1) anti-ballistic missile system.

MAZ-543 8x8 Truck Chassis

The 8x8 MAZ-543 series, primarily in double cab MAZ-543A and single cab MAZ-543M configuration, was the default 8x8 heavy load carrier for various Soviet-era weapons systems and only in the second decade of the 21st Century is the vehicle being very gradually replaced by other Russian vehicle types, after more than half a century of service. The vehicle was powered by a D-12-525 engine derived from that used in Soviet MBTs. The 9P117 (and later 9P117M) SPU vehicle for the 9K72 "Elbrus" (NATO: SS-1 Scud-B) and its 8K14 (R-17) rocket, the 9P120 SPU vehicle for the 9K76 "Temp-S" (NATO: SS-12 Scaleboard) and the 9A52 (and later 9A52-2) launcher for the "Smerch" MRS system were all mounted on the MAZ-543 series in the Soviet era.

ZiL-135K (2P30 TEL Vehicle)*

In the 1960s the Soviet Union developed a whole range of multi-axle all-wheel-drive vehicles for service with the Soviet Army and in civilian roles. The lead in such multi-axle vehicle development was taken by a new specialized design bureau (SKB) within the ZiL plant in Moscow. One of the first new strategic designs to reach series production had its public debut during the 7th November 1961 military parade in Moscow. The 8x8 ZiL-135K was powered by twin ZiL-375 engines developing 180hp, which gave the vehicle a 40km/h road speed and corresponding range of 500km, and was first demonstrated on Red Square configured as the 2P30 transporter-erector-launcher (TEL) vehicle for the 2K17 S-5 (4K95) coastal defence cruise missile system, with the rockets being located within their 12 metre long transport/launch containers. The role of the 2K17 coastal defence cruise missile system was for quite some time not well understood by Western intelligence, with NATO designating the system "Shaddock" and latterly "Sepal". Five of the strange looking 2P30 vehicles with their reverse inclined cab windshields were demonstrated on 7th November 1961, the first of the ZiL -135 series to be demonstrated in public. Series production of the ZiL-135 was transferred from ZiL in Moscow to BAZ in Bryansk, hence the vehicle and its various derivatives used for other weapons platforms such as the 9P113 "Luna-M" (NATO: FROG-7) OTR was later designated BAZ-135.

M-2 Medium Tracked Artillery Tractor

In 1946, the production of light artillery tractors was moved from YaAZ in Yaroslavl to MMZ in Mytischi so the YaAZ could concentrate post-war on developing new models of wheeled transport vehicles and on engine production. The M-2 (Mytischi-2) was the first post-war light and medium artillery tractor, replacing the wartime Ya-12 and its final M-12A production variant. The M-2 was designed at OKB-40 in Mytischi under

---

* The ZiL (BAZ)-135 series was also used as the SPU chassis for the 9P140 MRS and the 9P113 SPU vehicle for the 9K52 "Luna-M" OTR.

the direction of N.A. Astrov from the summer of 1946 as a major modernisation of the Yaroslavl built tractor, with an enlarged and widened load platform. Powered by a YaMZ-204B engine developing 110hp, the M-2 could tow a load of 6,000kg and transport 2,000kg of ammunition at a towing speed of up to 35km/h. The M-2 was series produced at MMZ from 1947 to 1955 and served with the Soviet Army until the mid 1960s, being used to tow artillery including the 85mm D-48 and the earlier 100mm BS-3 dual-purpose guns, the 152mm D-1 howitzer and the 57mm S-60 anti-aircraft gun.

AT-L Light Tracked Artillery Tractor (Izdeliye-5 and Izdeliye 5A)

The AT-L (Artillery Tractor - Light) medium artillery tractor was developed as a KhTZ Kharkov plant initiative designated "Izdeliye 5" under the direction of chief designer N.G. Zubarev. The original AT-L (Izdeliye-5) with six small road wheels was introduced into Soviet Army service in 1952 and was paraded on Red Square in the mid 1950s. It was latterly replaced by the modified "Izdeliye-5A", also known as the AT-LA (and known in the West as the AT-LM), with a modified cargo area, an additional 500kg load capacity and most obviously five large diameter roadwheels replacing the original design. The later variant was produced from 1957 until 1967. The AT-L in both versions was used to tow various artillery systems such as the 122mm D-74 gun, the 152mm D-20 Corps gun, 240mm M-240 heavy mortar, and medium and heavy towed anti-aircraft artillery such as the 57mm S-60 at towing speeds of up to 42km/h. The AT-L was powered by a YaMZ-204B diesel engine developing 110hp, later uprated to 135hp, providing a load capacity of 2,000kg and a towed load capacity of 6,000kg. The AT-L was officially removed from service only in 1998.

AT-P Semi-Armoured Tracked Artillery Tractor

The diminutive armoured AT-P (Artillery Tractor - Semi-Armoured) was developed at OKB-40 in Mytischi under the direction of N. Astrov. It was used by the Soviet Army as a fast artillery tractor for medium anti-tank and field artillery such as the 85mm D-48 anti-tank and 100mm BS-3 dual-purpose guns. The AT-P could tow loads of up to 3,700kg and transport 1,200kg of ammunition and could travel on roads at up to 53km/h. The AT-P was series produced at MMZ (the Mytischi Plant) in Moscow from 1954 to 1962, with the armoured hulls provided by the Vyksunsky Plant.

AT-S Medium Tracked Artillery Tractor

The limited series production AT-S (Artillery Tractor - Medium - also known as the "Izdeliye 712") medium artillery tractor was developed at ChTZ in Chelyabinsk, but series produced at the Kurgan Machine Building Plant (KMZ) from 1953 until May 1962. The AT-S, which had a distinctive tandem cab which accommodated the driver and six gun crew, with another 10 seated in the rear cargo area, could tow a load of up to 14,000kg and transport 3,000kg of ammunition at up to 35km/h. The tractor was used for towing medium and heavy artillery such as the 130mm M-46. The chassis was also used to mount the BM-24T MRS system.

ATS-59 Medium Tracked Artillery Tractor

The ATS-59 (Artillery Tractor, Medium, Model 1959) also known as the "Izdeliye 650" was developed by the SKB at the Kurgan Machine Building Plant (KMZ) in Kurgan at the end of the 1950s, and served in the Soviet Army as a tracked artillery tractor in the 1960s and 1970s. The ATS-59 was powered by a V-12 A-650 diesel engine developing 350hp, providing the 13,000kg vehicle with a maximum road speed of 39km/h. The ATS-59 could transport a 3,000kg load and tow up to 14,000kg. Though an effective artillery tractor, its small cab could only accommodate the vehicle crew, and so the later ATS-59G returned to the full cab of the earlier AT-S. The vehicle was displayed on Red Square from 1972.

ATS-59G Medium Tracked Artillery Tractor

The ATS-59G (Artillery Tractor, Medium, Model 1959, Tracked) was developed at the Kurgan Machine Building Plant (KMZ) in Kurgan in the mid 1960s, returning to the large cab arrangement of the AT-S, allowing a six man gun crew to be accommodated within the cab. The ATS-59G was powered by the same A-650 V-12 diesel engine as the earlier ATS-59, the tractor being capable of towing artillery pieces up to 14,000kg while transporting 3,000kg of ammunition in the rear

AT-L (Izdeliye 5)

AT-L (Izdeliye 5A)

AT-P

AT-S

ATS-59

ATS-59G

AT-T

AT-T

cargo area, travelling at up to 45km/h on roads. The ATS-59G was belatedly accepted into service with the Soviet Army on 28th February 1970, and had its Red Square parade debut on 7th November 1972. The tractor was used by the Soviet Army in the 1970s and 1980s to tow medium artillery and anti-aircraft weapons. Due to the Kurgan Machine Building Plant (KMZ) converting to BMP MICV production from 1966 as the ATS-59G was in development, series production of the Kurgan designed ATS-59G was later transferred to Poland, where production continued until 1989.

AT-T Heavy Tracked Artillery Tractor

The AT-T (Artillery Tractor - Heavy) was developed as the "Izdeliye-401" from 1946 at the KhTZ plant in Kharkov on the basis of the experimental wartime AT-42 and AT-45. The AT-T was based on the chassis and mechanical components of the short-lived T-44 medium tank and early T-54 MBT concurrently in production at Kharkov. The huge tractor was initially used in the early 1950s to tow medium and heavy artillery such as the tracked 152mm Br-2 gun and 203mm B-4 howitzer, and later the 130mm M-46, the 180mm S-23 and 130mm KS-30 anti-aircraft gun. It was also used for towing rockets such as the R-12 (8K63) MRBM. In addition to use as a tractor the chassis was used for several specialised engineer and radar vehicles. The AT-T was powered by a V-401 de-rated V-12 tank engine, developing 415hp. The tractor had a towed load capacity of 25,000kg and an ammunition load of 5,000kg in the cargo area, with a maximum speed of 45km/h and a range of 600km. The AT-T remained in series production until 1979. The AT-T was originally to have been replaced by the aborted "Izdeliye-429" (MT-T) tractor.

Support Vehicles

T-34T

IS-2T

TOP

A significant number of support vehicles have always been involved in Red Square parades, to provide emergency assistance should the unthinkable happen and a breakdown occur. Spare vehicles of each type on parade have always been historically parked near Red Square and recovery vehicles also located nearby. In the late 1930s the recovery vehicles were Komintern and Voroshilovets tractors. Post-war, turretless T-34T medium and IS-2T heavy ARVs performed the role for many years. From the late 1970s until 1995 TOP* ARVs were also introduced as emergency recovery vehicles. The TOP ARVs were rebuilt from the rarely encountered SU-122-54 self-propelled gun, disarmed and with the gun mantlet plated over. In an unusual twist, it was the appearance of the TOP vehicles near Red Square during parades that indicated the prior service of the SU-122-54 which throughout its short service life was never displayed in public, with only a single grainy photograph of an SU-122-54 stuck in a ditch indicating that the original tank destroyer had ever existed. TOP vehicles were replaced by the BREM from 2008.

T-34T

The T-34T was an ARV based on a standard T-34 with the turret removed and the turret race plated over, with a commander's cupola often added on the flat surface. The T-34T was used from the early 1950s until replaced by the TOP ARVs in the 1970s.

IS-2T ARV

The IS-2T, which constituted of a standard IS-2M heavy tank with the turret removed and the turret race plated was used as a parade heavy recovery vehicle, parked at the edges of Red Square from the 1950s until the 1970s.

TOP ARV

The TOP ARV is one of the most enigmatic vehicles to have ever been seen on Red Square, albeit not as a parade participant. The tracked ARV was built on the basis of the SU-122-54 (Obiekt-600) tank destroyer, with the armament removed and the hull reconfigured. The SU-122-54 was never seen in public during its entire service life with the Soviet Army, clues to its enigmatic service being latterly provided by the appearance of its ARV derivative on Red Square in the late 1970s and 1980s.

* TOP - Tyagach Obespecheniya Paradov (Tractor for Parade Support).

Data Tables

The data tables on the following pages show as accurately as a possible the tanks, vehicles and other military equipment paraded on Red Square from 1946 until the breakup of the Soviet Union in 1991. In most cases, the years during which any given equipment type was paraded are shown from initial parade debut appearance until removed from regular display on Red Square. It should be noted however that the parades and their content were far from sequential. Many equipment types, such as for example the 2S3 self-propelled howitzer and the BMD-1 airborne combat vehicle made a cameo parade debut appearance and then were not seen again for years. Some other systems such as the ZSU-23-4 self-propelled anti-aircraft gun although regularly paraded would drop out of certain years and then re-appear in modernised form in subsequent parades. Much of the film documentation, especially in early years and in foreign compilations, is conflated, and often the years cited are incorrect. In some years, again especially the early post-war parades, there is insufficient surviving evidence to exactly define the appearance or non-appearance of some less common vehicle or equipment types at any given parade. Where known and crosschecked against all available sources, the vehicles are recorded as being present in a given year. Where there are gaps, this is either because no exact confirmation is available, or if in the middle of a sequence of years, that the equipment type would appear not to have been shown in a particular year, as was a frequent occurrence. The overall "parade service" life of any given equipment type is however clear from the tables. The pattern of debut appearances by some equipment types without a subsequent appearance for some years continues to the present day.

1946-1949

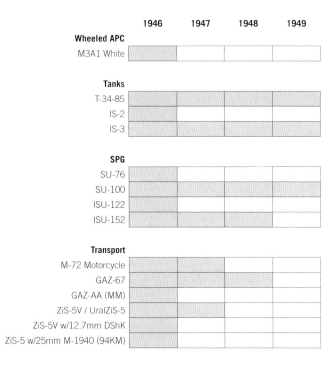

1946-1949

	1946	1947	1948	1949
ZiS-5V w/37mm M-1939 AAG	■			
ZiS-5V w/122mm M-1938 (M-30)	■			
ZiS-12 w/25mm 94KM AAG	■			
GAZ-51	■		■	■
GAZ-63	■			■
YaAZ-200		■	■	■
ZiS-150			■	■
ZiS-150 BM-13			■	■
ZiS-150 BM-31			■	■
YaAZ-210G w/152mm M-1943 (D-1)	■			
ZiS-151				■
Studebaker US6	■	■	■	
Studebaker US6 w/100mm M-1944 ATG	■			
Studebaker US6 w/85mm M-1939 AAG	■		■	
Studebaker US6 BM-8-48	■			
Studebaker US6 BM-13	■			
Studebaker US6 BM-31	■			
Ya-12 w/122mm M-1931 (A-19)	■	■		
Ya-12 w/152mm M-1937 (ML-20)	■	■		
M-2 w/152mm M-1937 (ML-20)	■			
Allis Chalmers w/trailers/non-indigenous guns	■			
Allis Chalmers w/152mm Br-2	■			
Allis Chalmers w/203mm B-4	■		■	
Allis Chalmers w/280mm Br-5	■			
Allis Chalmers w/210mm Br-17 / 305mm Br-18	■	■		
S-65			■	
AT-T				■

Artillery

	1946	1947	1948	1949
25mm M-1940 Anti-Aircraft Gun	■		■	
85mm M-1939 Anti-Aircraft Gun	■		■	
100mm M-1944 Anti-Tank Gun	■			
100mm KS-19 Anti-Aircraft Gun			■	
122mm M-1938 (M-30) Howitzer	■			
122mm M-1931/37 (A-19) Corps Gun	■			■
152mm M-1937 (ML-20) Corps Howitzer	■	■		
152mm Br-2 Heavy Howitzer	■			
152mm D-1 Howitzer	■	■		
160mm M-1943 Mortar	■			
203mm B-4 Heavy Howitzer	■		■	
210mm M-1939 (Br-17) / 305mm M-1939 (Br-18)	■	■		
280mm Br-5 Heavy Mortar		■		
BM-8-48 (Studebaker US6)	■			
BM-13N (Studebaker US6)	■			
BM-31 (Studebaker US6)	■			
BM-13 (ZiS-150)			■	
BM-31 (ZiS-150)			■	

SPADS

	1946	1947	1948	1949
ZSU-37	■			

1950-1959

	1950	1951	1952	1953	1954	1955	1956	1957	1958	1959
Wheeled APC										
BTR-152		■	■	■	■	■	■	■	■	
Tracked APC										
BTR-50P								■	■	■
Tanks										
T-34-85	■	■	■	■	■	■	■			
T-54								■	■	■
IS-3	■	■								
T-10								■		
SPG										
SU-76		■								
SU-100	■	■	■							
ISU-152	■	■								
SPAAG										
ZSU-57-2								■	■	■
Airborne AFVs										
ASU-57								■	■	■
Strategic Artillery										
2A3 (Ob.271) Kondensator								■	■	■
2B1 (Ob.273) Oka								■	■	■
OTR										
2P1 (2K1 Mars system)								■	■	■
2P4 (2K2 Filin system)*								■	■	■
SAMs										
S-75 Dvina								■	■	■
Transport										
M-72 motorcycle	■	■		■						
GAZ-67B										
GAZ-69				■	■	■	■	■	■	■
GAZ-51	■	■	■	■						
GAZ-63	■	■	■	■	■	■				
GAZ-63 w/85mm D-44					■					
YaAZ-200										
YaAZ-200 w/100mm M-1944 (BS-3)	■			■						
YaAZ-200 w/152mm M-1938 (M-30)	■									
YaAZ-214 (KrAZ-214) 2P5 Korshun								■	■	■
M-2	■									
M-2 w/100mm M-1944 (BS-3)	■			■						
M2 w/122mm M-1931/37 (A-19)	■									
M2 w/152mm M-1937 (ML-20)	■									
M2 w/240mm M-240 Mortar	■									
M2 w/100mm KS-19 AAG	■		■							

* The 2K2 "Filin" system is also seen designated 2K4; but the latter was the GRAU description for the "Drakan" ATGM system.

1950-1959

Vehicle/System	1950	1951	1952	1953	1954	1955	1956	1957	1958	1959
YaAZ-210G w/152mm M-1943 (D1)	■	■								
ZiS-150	■	■	■	■	■	■	■			
ZiS-151		■								
ZiS-151 w/122mm M-1938 (M-30)	■	■								
ZiS-151 w/152mm D-1				■						
ZiS-151 w/37mm M-1939 (61K)	■	■								
ZiS-151 w/85mm M-1939 (52K)	■	■								
ZiS-151 w/85mm D-44	■	■								
ZiS-151 (BM-13)	■	■								
ZiS-151 (BM-31)	■	■								
ZiS-151 (BM-14)			■	■	■	■	■	■	■	■
ZiS-151 BM-24					■	■	■	■	■	■
ZiS-151 (BMD-20)				■	■	■	■	■	■	■
ZiS-121B w/S-75 Dvina SAM								■	■	■
AT-P							■	■	■	■
AT-L (Izdeliye 5 / Izdeliye 5A)							■	■	■	■
AT-L w/57mm S-60							■	■	■	
AT-L w/160mm M-160 Mortar								■	■	■
AT-S					■	■	■	■	■	■
AT-S (BM-24T)								■	■	■
AT-T	■	■	■	■	■	■	■	■	■	■
AT-S w/130mm M-46					■	■	■	■	■	■
AT-T w/152mm Br-2	■	■	■	■						
AT-T w/180mm S-23							■	■	■	■
AT-T w/203mm B-4	■	■	■	■	■					
AT-T w/100mm M-1949 (KS-19)		■	■	■	■	■	■	■	■	■
AT-T w/130mm KS-30 AAG				■	■	■	■	■	■	■

MRS

System	1950	1951	1952	1953	1954	1955	1956	1957	1958	1959
BM-13 (ZiS-151)		■								
BM-31 (ZiS-151)		■								
BM-14 (ZiS-151)		■	■	■	■	■	■			
BMD-20 (ZiS-151)				■	■	■	■			
BM-24 (ZiS-151)					■	■	■	■		
BM-24T (AT-S)								■	■	■
2P5 Korshun (YaAZ-214)								■	■	■

Towed Artillery

Weapon	1950	1951	1952	1953	1954	1955	1956	1957	1958	1959
37mm M-1939 (61K) Anti-Aircraft Gun		■								
57mm ZiS-2 Anti-Tank Gun	■	■	■							
57mm S-60 Anti-Aircraft Gun				■	■	■	■	■	■	■
76.2mm M-1942 (ZiS-3) Dual Purpose Gun	■	■								
85mm D-44 Field Gun	■	■	■	■	■	■	■	■	■	■
85mm D-48 Anti-Tank Gun							■	■	■	■
85mm M-1939 (52-K) Anti-Aircraft Gun	■	■	■	■						
100mm BS-3 Anti-Tank Gun	■	■	■	■	■	■				
100mm KS-19 Anti-Aircraft Gun		■	■	■	■	■	■	■	■	■
122mm M-1938 (M-30) Howitzer	■	■	■	■	■	■	■			
122mm M-1931/37 (A-19) Corps Gun	■	■	■	■	■	■				
122mm D-74 Howitzer							■	■	■	■
130mm M-46 Gun-Howitzer					■	■	■	■	■	■
130mm KS-30 AAG								■	■	■

THE SOVIET ARMY ON PARADE 1946-91

1950-1959

	1950	1951	1952	1953	1954	1955	1956	1957	1958	1959
152mm M-1937 (ML-20) Howitzer	■	■		■	■					
152mm D-1 Howitzer	■			■	■					
160mm M-160 Mortar				■	■					
180mm S-23 Field Gun						■	■	■	■	
240mm M-240 Mortar	■	■	■	■	■	■	■	■	■	

Strategic Rockets

	1950	1951	1952	1953	1954	1955	1956	1957	1958	1959
R-5M (8K51) (NATO:SS-3 Shyster)							■	■	■	■

1960-1969

Armoured Cars

	1960	1961	1962	1963	1964	1965	1966	1967	1968	1969
BRDM		■	■	■	■	■				
BRDM 2P27 (2K16)				■	■					
BRDM 2P32 (2K8)			■	■	■	■	■	■	■	■
BRDM 9P110					■	■	■	■	■	■

Wheeled APC

	1960	1961	1962	1963	1964	1965	1966	1967	1968	1969
BTR-152	■	■								
BTR-60P		■	■	■	■	■				
BTR-60PA (PK)			■	■	■	■				
BTR-60PB						■	■	■	■	■

Tracked APC

	1960	1961	1962	1963	1964	1965	1966	1967	1968	1969
BTR-50P	■	■	■	■	■	■				
BTR-50PK	■	■	■	■	■	■	■	■	■	■

MICV

	1960	1961	1962	1963	1964	1965	1966	1967	1968	1969
BMP-1								■	■	■

Tanks

	1960	1961	1962	1963	1964	1965	1966	1967	1968	1969
T-54	■	■	■							
T-55			■	■	■	■				
T-62						■	■	■	■	■

Airborne AFVs

	1960	1961	1962	1963	1964	1965	1966	1967	1968	1969
ASU-57	■									
ASU-85		■	■	■	■	■	■	■	■	■

Self-Propelled Artillery (MRS)

	1960	1961	1962	1963	1964	1965	1966	1967	1968	1969
BMD-20 (BM-20-4) (ZiL-157)				■	■					
BM-24 (ZiL-157)					■					
YaAZ-214 (KrAZ-214) 2P5 Korshun	■	■	■	■	■	■				
9K51 (BM-21) (Ural-375D)						■	■	■	■	■

1960-1969

System	1960	1961	1962	1963	1964	1965	1966	1967	1968	1969
Strategic Artillery										
2A3 (Ob.271) Kondensator	■	■	■	■						
2B1 (Ob.273) Oka	■	■	■	■						
OTR										
2P4 (2K2 Filin system) (FROG-1)	■	■	■	■	■					
8U218 (8K11) (R-11M) (Scud A)	■	■	■	■	■	■	■	■		
2P16 (2K6) (ZR-9 rocket) (FROG-3)		■	■	■	■	■	■	■	■	■
2P16 (2K6) (ZR-10 rocket) (FROG-5)			■	■	■	■	■	■	■	■
2P19 (9K72) (R-17) Elbrus (Scud-B)		■	■	■	■	■	■	■	■	■
2P5 (2K5 Korshun)	■	■	■	■	■					
2P30 (2K17) (R-5 Cruise Missile)		■	■	■	■	■				
9P113 Luna-M (FROG-7)						■	■	■	■	■
9P117M Elbrus (Scud-B)									■	■
Front Level Rockets										
9P120 (9K76) (SS-12 Scaleboard)						■	■	■	■	■
SPADS										
ZSU-57-2	■	■	■	■	■	■	■	■	■	
ZSU-23-4						■	■	■	■	■
SAMs										
2P24 (2K11) Krug				■	■	■	■	■	■	■
2P25 (2K12) Kub						■	■	■	■	■
S-25 Berkut	■	■	■	■	■	■	■	■	■	■
S-75 Dvina	■	■	■	■	■	■	■	■	■	■
S-125 Neva					■	■	■	■	■	■
Izdeliye-400 (Dal)			■	■	■	■	■	■	■	■
Transport										
GAZ-69/GAZ-69A	■	■	■	■	■	■	■	■	■	■
GAZ-66B w/85mm SD-44						■	■	■	■	■
GAZ-66B w/RPU-14						■	■	■	■	■
YaAZ-214 2K5 Korshun	■	■	■	■	■					
AT-P w/85mm D-48	■	■	■	■	■	■	■		■	
AT-S w/130mm M-46	■	■	■	■	■					
ATS-59 w/130mm M-46						■	■	■	■	■
ATS-59 with M-1937 (ML-20)						■	■	■	■	■
AT-T w/130mm M-46	■	■	■	■	■					
AT-T w/180mm S-23	■	■	■	■	■	■	■	■	■	■
AT-T w/R-12 MRBM	■	■	■	■	■	■	■	■	■	■
AT-T w/RT-15 (4K22) MRBM									■	■
AT-T w/R-13 / R-29 SLBM		■	■	■	■	■	■	■	■	■
MAZ-502V w/Izd.400 Dal			■	■	■	■	■	■	■	■
ZiL-135K (2P30) (2K17)		■	■	■	■	■				

1960-1969

	1960	1961	1962	1963	1964	1965	1966	1967	1968	1969
ZiL-157V w/S-25	■	■	■	■	■	■	■	■	■	■
ZiL-157V w/S-75	■	■	■	■	■	■	■	■	■	■
ZiL-157 w/S-125 PR-14A TZM					■	■	■	■	■	
YaAZ (KrAZ)-214 2K5 Korshun					■	■				
MAZ-535A w/MRBM/ICBMs						■	■	■	■	■
MAZ-537V w/ MRBM/ICBMs						■	■	■	■	■
Ural-375S w/ Izd.400 Dal						■	■	■		
Ural-375D (BM-21)						■	■	■	■	■
ZiL-135K 2K17 / 4K95 (2P30)		■	■	■	■	■	■	■	■	■

Towed Artillery

	1960	1961	1962	1963	1964	1965	1966	1967	1968	1969
85mm D-44 Field Gun	■	■	■	■	■	■				
85mm D-48 Anti-Tank Gun	■	■	■	■	■	■				
85mm SD-44 Self-Propelled Field Gun	■	■	■	■	■	■	■	■		
130mm M-46 Gun-Howitzer	■	■	■	■	■	■	■	■	■	
140mm RPU-14 (8U38) MRS	■	■	■	■	■	■	■	■		
152mm M-1937 (ML-20) Corps Howitzer	■	■	■	■	■	■				
180mm S-23 Field Gun	■	■	■	■	■	■	■			

Strategic Rockets

	1960	1961	1962	1963	1964	1965	1966	1967	1968	1969
R-5M	■	■	■							
R-12	■	■	■	■	■	■				
R-14U (8K65U)					■	■	■	■	■	■
RT-2						■	■	■	■	■
RT-15 (Obiekt-815/8U253)						■	■	■	■	■
RT-15 (towed on trailer)						■	■	■	■	■
RT-20P (15U51) (Obiekt-820/821)						■	■	■	■	■
R-26 (8K66)				■	■	■				
R-36 (8K67) R-36M (15A14/15A18)						■	■	■	■	■
GR-1 (8K713)					■	■	■	■	■	■
Naval MRBMs (R-13, R-29)			■	■	■	■	■	■	■	■
A-35 A-350Zh (5V61) (ABM-1)					■	■	■	■	■	■

1970-1979

Armoured Cars

	1970	1971	1972	1973	1974	1975	1976	1977	1978	1979
BRDM 2P32 (2K8) (Swatter)			■							
BRDM 9P110 (Sagger)	■	■	■	■						
BRDM-2 9P122 (Sagger)				■	■	■	■			
BRDM-2 9P124 (2K8M) (Swatter)				■	■	■	■			
BRDM-2 9P148							■	■	■	■
BRDM-2 9A31 Strela-1 SAM					■	■	■			

1970-1979

	1970	1971	1972	1973	1974	1975	1976	1977	1978	1979
Wheeled APC										
BTR-60PA (PK)	■	■	■	■	■			■	■	■
BTR-60PB			■	■	■	■	■	■	■	■
Tracked APC										
BTR-50PK	■	■	■	■	■	■				
MT-LB W/100mm MT-12								■	■	■
MICV										
BMP-1	■	■	■	■	■	■	■			
Tanks										
T-62	■	■	■							
T-62 M-1972 (T-62A)				■	■	■	■	■	■	■
T-72A								■	■	■
Airborne AFVs										
BMD (BMD-1)				■	■			■	■	■
ASU-85	■	■	■							
ASU-85M				■	■	■	■	■	■	■
Self Propelled Artillery										
2S1 Gvozdika SPH						■	■	■	■	■
2S3 Akatsiya SPH								■	■	■
9K51 (BM-21) Grad (Ural-375D)			■	■	■	■	■	■	■	■
OTR										
2P16	■	■								
2P19	■	■								
9P113 Luna-M	■	■	■	■	■	■	■	■	■	■
9P117/9P117M Elbrus	■	■	■	■	■	■	■	■	■	■
Front Level Rockets										
9P120 (SS-12) (MAZ-543)		■	■	■	■	■	■	■		
SPADS & SAMs										
ZSU-23-4	■		■	■	■			■		
2P25 Kub (2K12)	■		■	■	■	■	■	■		
2P24 Krug (2K11)	■	■	■	■	■	■	■	■	■	■
9A31 Strela-1 (9K31)						■	■	■	■	■
9A33B Osa (9K33)								■	■	■
S-25 (ZiL-157V + PR-3 TZM trailer)	■	■								
S-75 (ZiL-157V + PR-11 TZM trailer)	■	■	■							
S-25 (ZiL-131V + PR-3M trailer)				■	■	■	■	■	■	■
S-75 (ZiL-131V + PR-11M trailer)				■	■	■	■	■	■	■
S-125 (ZiL-131) PR-14M TZM				■	■	■	■	■	■	■
Transport										
GAZ-69	■	■	■							
UAZ-469B				■	■	■	■	■	■	■
Ural-375D 9K51 (BM-21)			■	■	■	■	■	■	■	■
ATS-59G w/ 130mm M-46			■	■	■	■	■	■	■	■
AT-T w/180mm S-23	■	■								

1970-1979

	1970	1971	1972	1973	1974	1975	1976	1977	1978	1979
AT-T w/MRBM/ICBM	■	■	■	■	■					
MAZ-535A w/MRBM/ICBM	■	■	■	■	■					
MAZ-537V w/MRBM/ICBM	■	■	■	■	■					
MAZ-537V w/naval MRBM	■	■	■	■	■					
MAZ-537V (A-35/135) ABM-1	■	■	■	■	■					
MAZ-537V w/S-25	■	■	■	■						
ZiL-157V w/S-75	■	■	■							
ZiL-157 S-125 PR-14A TZM	■	■	■							
ZiL-131						■	■			
ZiL-131 w/122mm D-30				■	■	■		■	■	■
ZiL-131 w/100mm MT-12			■	■	■	■		■	■	■
ZiL-131V w/S-25			■	■	■	■	■	■	■	■
ZiL-131 w/S-75			■	■	■	■	■	■	■	■
ZiL-131 S-125 PR-14M TZM			■	■	■	■	■	■	■	■

Towed Artillery

	1970	1971	1972	1973	1974	1975	1976	1977	1978	1979
100mm MT-12 Anti-Tank Gun			■	■	■	■		■	■	■
122mm D-30 Howitzer			■		■	■		■	■	■
130mm M-46 Gun-Howitzer		■	■		■					
180mm S-23 Field Gun		■								

Strategic Rockets

	1970	1971	1972	1973	1974	1975	1976	1977	1978	1979
RT-2	■	■	■	■	■					
RT-15	■	■	■	■	■					
RT-20P	■	■	■	■	■					
UR-100	■	■		■	■					
R-36	■	■	■	■	■					
GR-1	■	■	■	■	■					
A-350Zh (A-35) (ABM-1)	■	■	■	■	■					
Naval MRBMs (R-13, R-29)		■	■	■	■					

1980-1989

	1980	1981	1982	1983	1984	1985	1986	1987	1988	1989
Armoured Cars										
BRDM-2 9P148	■	■	■	■	■	■	■	■	■	
Wheeled APC										
BTR-70	■	■	■	■	■	■	■			
BTR-80								■	■	■
Tracked APC										
MT-LB w/100mm MT-12	■	■	■	■	■					

1980-1989

Equipment	1980	1981	1982	1983	1984	1985	1986	1987	1988	1989
MICV										
BMP-1	■	■								
BMP-2			■	■	■	■	■	■	■	■
Tanks										
T-64B-1						■				
T-72/T-72A	■	■	■	■	■					
T-72B							■	■	■	■
T-34-85 (historic)						■				
SU-100 (historic)						■				
Airborne AFVs										
BMD-1	■	■	■							
BMD-1P				■	■	■	■	■	■	■
BTR-D						■	■	■		
2S9 Nona-S SPG						■	■	■	■	■
Self Propelled Artillery										
2S1 Gvozdika SPH	■	■		■	■	■	■	■	■	■
2S3M Akatsiya SPH		■		■	■	■	■	■	■	■
BM-21 (Ural-375D/4320)	■	■	■	■	■	■	■	■	■	■
BM-13 (ZiL-157) (historic)						■				
OTR										
9P113 (9K52) Luna-M	■	■	■	■	■	■	■	■	■	■
9P117M (9K72) Elbrus	■	■	■	■	■	■	■	■	■	■
9P129/9P129M Tochka						■	■	■	■	■
Front Level Rockets										
9P120 (9K76) (SS-12 Scaleboard)						■				
SAMs										
2P24 (2K11 Krug)	■									
2P25 (2K12 Kub)						■	■			
S-25 (ZiL-131V + PR-3 trailer)	■	■	■	■	■	■				
S-75 (ZiL-131V + PR-11 trailer)	■	■	■	■	■	■				
S-125 (V-600 rocket) (ZiL-131)	■	■		■	■	■				
9A33B Osa (9K33)	■	■		■	■	■				
9A33BM3 Osa-AKM (9K33M3)						■	■			
9A34/9A35 (9K35 Strela-10) (MT-LB)						■	■			
9P31 (9K31 Strela-1) (BRDM-2)						■	■			
Transport										
UAZ-469B	■	■	■	■	■	■	■	■	■	■
ZiL-157 (historic)						■				
ZiL-131V (S-25 SAM TZM)	■	■		■	■	■	■	■		

1980-1989

	1980	1981	1982	1983	1984	1985	1986	1987	1988	1989
ZiL-131V (S-75 SAM TZM)					■	■	■	■	■	
ZiL-131 (S-125 SAM TZM)	■	■			■	■	■	■	■	
ZiL-131 (w/122mm D-30)	■									
KrAZ-260 w/152mm 2A36						■	■	■	■	■
Ural-375D (BM-21 Grad)	■	■	■	■	■	■	■	■	■	
Ural-4320 (BM-21 Grad)										■
Ural-4320					■					■
MT-LB with 100mm MT-12	■	■	■		■					■

Artillery

	1980	1981	1982	1983	1984	1985	1986	1987	1988	1989
76.2mm ZiS-3 Dual-Purpose Gun						■				
100mm MT-12 Anti-Tank Gun	■	■	■	■	■					
122mm M-1938 (M-30) Howitzer						■				
122mm D-30 Howitzer	■	■								
152mm 2A36 Field Gun						■	■	■	■	

1990-1991

	1990	1991
Wheeled APC		
BTR-80	■	
MICV		
BMP-2	■	
BMP-3	■	
Tanks		
T-72B	■	
T-80 (T-80UD)	■	
T-34-85 (historic)	■	
Airborne AFVs		
BMD-2	■	
2S9 Nona-S SPG	■	
Self Propelled Artillery		
2S1	■	
2S3M	■	
9K51 MRS (BM-21) (Ural-4320)	■	
9K57 MRS (BM-27) (BAZ-135)	■	
BM-13 (historic)	■	
OTR		
9P113 (9K52) Luna-M	■	
9P129 (9K79) Tochka	■	
9P117M (9K72) Elbrus	■	

	1990	1991
SAMs		
9A33M3 Osa-AKM	■	
9P85S (S-300) (MAZ-543M)	■	
9A34/9A35 (9K35) Strela-10 (MT-LB)	■	
S-75 (PR-14M TZM)	■	
Transport		
UAZ-469B	■	
ZiL-157 BM-13 (historic)	■	
ZiL-157 w/ZiS-3 (historic)	■	
ZiL-131 w/122mm M-1938 (M-30) (historic)	■	
ZiL-131 w/37mm M-1939 AAG (historic)	■	
ZiL-131 w/S-75 TZM	■	
Ural-4320 w/85mm M-1939 AAG (historic)	■	
KrAZ-260 w/152mm 2A36	■	
Towed Artillery		
152mm 2A36	■	
Strategic Rockets		
RT-2PM Topol (MAZ-7917)	■	

Soviet & US/NATO reporting terms for Soviet missiles systems demonstrated on Red Square 1957- 1990

Surface to Surface Tactical (OTR) Rocket Systems

Soviet System Designation	SPU Vehicle	Chassis	GRAU Designation	US/NATO Designation
2K1 "Mars"	2P2	S-119A	2K1	FROG-1
2K2* "Filin"	2P4	Obiekt-804	2K2	FROG-2
2K5 "Korshun"	2P5	SM-44	2K5	BM-25
2K6 "Luna"	2P16	S-123A	2K6	FROG-3/5**
8K11 (R-11) (8A61)	8U218	Obiekt-803	8A61	SS-1 Scud-A
8K11 (R-11M)	8U218	Obiekt-803	8K11	SS-1 Scud-A
9K72 "Elbrus"	2P19	Obiekt-810	9K72	SS-1 Scud-B
9K52 "Luna-M"	9P113	BAZ-135LM	9K52	FROG-7
9K72 "Elbrus"	9P117/117M	MAZ-543A	9K72	SS-1 Scud-B
9K79 "Tochka"	9P129	BAZ-5921	9K79	SS-21 Scarab

Front Level Rocket Systems

9K76 "Temp-S"	9P120	9K76	MAZ-543A	SS-12 Scaleboard

Shore Defence Cruise Missiles

FKR-2 (S-5)	2P30	2K17	ZiL (BAZ) -135K	SSc-1a Shaddock/Sepal

Surface to Air Rocket Systems

Soviet System Designation	US / NATO Reporting Designation
Static Launch (PU) Systems	
S-25 "Berkut" (V-300 rocket)	SA-1 Guild
S-75 "Dvina/Desna/Volkhov" (V-750 rocket)	SA-2 Guideline
S-125 "Neva" (V-600/5V24 rocket)	SA-3 Goa
S-200 "Angara/Vega/Dubna" (V-860/5V21 rocket)	SA-5 Gammon (Often conflated with Izdeliye-400)
Izdeliye-400 "Dal" (V-400/5V11 rocket)	SA-5 Gammon/Griffon (Often conflated with S-200)
Mobile Launch (SPU) Systems	
2K11 "Krug"	SA-4 Ganef
2K12 "Kub"	SA-6 Gainful
9A33 "Osa"	SA-8A Gecko (early)
9A33M2/M3 "Osa-AK/AKM"	SA-8B Gecko (late)
9A31 ZRK "Strela-1"	SA-9 Gaskin
S-300	SA-10B Grumble
9A83, S-300	SA-12A Gladiator
9A82, S-300	SA-12B Giant
9A34/35 ZRK "Strela-10" (Strela-10SV)	SA-13 Gopher

---

* Often reported as the 2K4, but the Soviet GRAU index 2K4 is used for the "Drakon" anti-tank missile system.

** The 2P16 "Luna" SPU vehicle fired several rocket types. When mounting the ZR-9 or ZR-10 rockets it was designated FROG-3 and FROG-5 respectively by the US / NATO. The base chassis was the Obiekt-160 built at VgTZ (Volgograd).

Strategic Missile Systems (Pad/Silo Launched) (including early OTRs)

Soviet Designator	GRAU Designator	US / NATO Designation
R-1	8K11	SS-1A Scunner
R-5M	8K51	SS-3 Shyster
R-9/R-9A	8K75/76/77	SS-8 Sasin
R-11 (8A61)	8K11	SS-1 Scud-A
R-17	8K14	SS-1 Scud B
R-12/R-12U	8K63/8K63U	SS-4 Sandal
R-14/R-14U	8K65/8K65U	SS-5 Skean
R-16	8K64	SS-7 Sadler
R-17	9K72	SS-1 Scud B
R-26	8K66	SS-8 Sasin (often conflated with R-9/R-9A)
R-36	8K67	SS-9 Scarp
R-36M	15A14/15A18 (RS-20)	SS-18 Satan
RT-2	8K98	SS-13 Savage
GR-1	8K713	SS-X-10 Scrag
UR-100	8K84	SS-11 Sego

Submarine Launched Systems

Soviet Designation	GRAU/System	US / NATO Designation
R-13	4K50 (D-6)	SS-N-4 Sark
R-29	4K75 (RSM-40)	SS-N-8 Sawfly

Strategic Missile Systems (Land Mobile Platform Launched)

Soviet/Russian Designation	GRAU Index	US / NATO Designation	SPU vehicle
RT-15	8K96	SS-X-14 Scapegoat/Scamp	15U59* (Obiekt-815Sp1/Sp2/8U253)
RT-20P	8K99	SS-X-15 Scrooge	15U21/15U51 (Obiekt-820/821)
RT-21 (RSD-10) Pioner	15Zh45	SS-20 Saber	15U106 (MAZ-547A)
RT-2PM (RS-12M) Topol	15Zh58	SS-25 Sickle	15U168 (MAZ-7917)

Anti-Ballistic Missiles

Soviet Designator	GRAU/Other Soviet Designator	US DoD / NATO
A-35 Aldan, A-35M	5V61 (rocket) 5P81 (TPK)	ABM-1 Galosh

---

* The 15U59 "service" designation was latterly applied - in development the system was known as Obiekt-815Sp1, 8U253 (Obiekt-815Sp2) though the system was only deployed for trials purposes.

Bibliography

Journals, Magazines, Newspapers

Aerokosmichesky Vestnik, Armies & Weapons
Avtomobil Na Sluzhbe, Bastion, Bronya
Frontovaya Illustratsiya, Izvestia
Jane's Defence Weekly
Jane's Soviet Intelligence Review
Joint Services Recognition Journal (UK MoD)
Kommersant, Military History Monthly
Moskovsky Komsomolets, Nauka i Tekhnika
Nevsky Bastion, Ogonyok, Oruzhye
Poligon, Pravda, RIA Novosti
Soviet Military Review, Tekhnika-Molodezhi
Tekhnika i Vooruzhenye, Voenny Parad
WPT (Poland)

Books

Voennye Parady Na Krasnoy Ploshadi. Multiple authors. Voennoye Izdatelstvo MoD USSR, Moscow 1980

Arndt, Richard F. Weapons and Equipment of the Soviet Land Forces. Walhalla U Pretoria Verlag, Regensburg, 1971.

Baryatinsky, Mikhail. Boevie Mashini Desanta. Bronekollektsia №1 (9). Modelist Konstruktor, Moscow, 2006.

Baryatinsky, Mikhail. Otechestvennie Kolesnie Bronetransporteri BTR-60, BTR-70, BTR-80. Bronekollektsia №1 (x). Modelist Konstruktor, Moscow, 2007.

Baryatinsky, Mikhail, Kolomiets, Maksim. Broneavtomobili Russkoy Armii 1906-1917. Tekhnika-Molodezhy, Moscow, 2000.

Baryatinsky, Mikhail. Parady Stali i Motorov. Zheleznodorozhnoe Delo, Moscow, 2003.

Baryatinsky, Mikhail. Sredny Tank T-62. Bronekollektsia №2 (53). Modelist Konstruktor, Moscow, 2004.

Baryatinsky, Mikhail. T-54 i T-55. Yauza, Eksmo, Moscow, 2015.

Baryatinsky, Mikhail. Tank XXI Veka. Yauza, Eksmo, Moscow, 2012.

Baryatinsky, Mikhail and Kinnear, Jim. The Russian T-28 Medium Tank. Barbarossa, Tiptree, Great Britain, 2000.

Baryatinsky, Mikhail. T-54 i T-55 Tank-Soldat. Yauza, Moscow, 2015.

Baryatinsky, Mikhail. Tyazhely Tank IS. Yauza, Eksmo, Moscow, 2006.

Chubachin, Aleksander. SU-76. Yauza, BTV-Kniga, Moscow, 2009.

Chuprin, K.V. Vooruzhenye Sily Stran SNG i Baltii. Sovremennaya Shkola, Moscow, 2009.

Dashko, Dmitry. Transport Krasnoy Armii Velikoy Otechestvennoy Voiny. Avtomobilnogo Arkhivnogo Fonda, Moscow, 2015.

Drogovoz, Igor. Raketnie Voiska SSSR. Harvest, Minsk, 2007.

Drozdov, Georgy, Ryabko, Evgenny. Parad Pobedy. Planeta Publishing House, Moscow, 1985.

Dupouy, Alain. Les Dossiers Des Vehicules Sovietiques (multiple titles). Grenoble, France.

Evtifeev, M.D. Iz Istorii Sozdaniya Zenitno-Raketnogo Schita Rossii. Vyzovskaya Kniga, Moscow, 2000.

FM 30-40 Handbook on Soviet Ground Forces HQ Department of the (US) Army. 30.06.75.

Frankopan, Peter. The Silk Roads. Bloomsbury, London, 2015.

Kinnear, James. Russian Army on Parade. Tankograd. Erlangen, 2009.

Kirindas, Aleksander. Artilleriysky Tyagach "Komintern". Yauza, Moscow, 2017.

Kochnev, Evgeny. Avtomobili Krasnoy Armii 1918-1945. Yauza, Eksmo, Moscow, 2009.

Kochnev, Evgeny. Avtomobili Sovietskoy Armii 1946-1991. Yauza, Eksmo, Moscow, 2011.

Kochnev, Evgeny. Avtomobili Velikoy Otechestvennoy. Yauza, Eksmo, Moscow, 2010.

Kochnev, Evgeny. Entsiklopedia Voennykh Avtomobily 1769-2006. Za Roulem, Moscow, 2008.

Kochnev, Evgeny. Sekretnye Avtomobili Sovietskoy Armii. Voina Motorov, Yauza, Moscow, 2011.

Kolomiets, Maksim and Kinnear, Jim. The Russian T-35 Heavy Tank. Barbarossa, Tiptree, Great Britain. 2000.

Kolomiets, Maksim. Bronya Na Kolesakh. Yauza, Eksmo, Moscow, 2007.

Kolomiets, Maksim. Legkye Tanki BT. Yauza, Eksmo, Moscow, 2007.

Kolomiets, Maksim, Moshchansky, Ilya. Mnogobashennye Tanki RKKA. Frontovaya Illustratsiya, Moscow, 1999.

Kolomiets, Maksim. Russkie Broneviki v Boyu. Yauza, Eksmo, Moscow, 2013.

Kolomiets, Maksim. Sredny Tank T-28. Yauza, Eksmo, Moscow, 2007.

Kolomiets, Maksim. Sukhoputnye Linkory Stalina. Yauza, Eksmo, Moscow, 2009.

Kolomiets, Maksim. T-35 "Sukhoputnye Linkory" Stalina. Yauza, Eksmo, Moscow, 2014.

Kolomiets, Maksim, Fedoseev, Semeon. Tank №1 Reno-FT. Yauza, Eksmo, Moscow, 2010.

Kolomiets, Maksim. Legkye Tanki BT. Yauza, Eksmo, Moscow, 2007.

Kostenko, Yu. P. Nekotorye Voprosy Razvitiya Otechestvennoy Bronetekhniki v 1967-1987. Uniar-Print, Moscow, 2000.

Kostenko, Yu. P. Tanki Vospominaniya i Razmishleniya. Nizhny Tagil, 2008.

Luzhkov, Yury (Head of Council). Parad Paradov. Atlantida - XXI Vek, Moskovskie Uchebniki, Moscow, 2000.

Martyanov, Andrei. Losing Military Supremacy. Clarity Press Inc. Atlanta, USA, 2018.

Milsom, John. Russian Tanks 1900-1970, Arms & Armour Press, London, 1970.

Pavlov, Ivan. Pavlov, Mikhail. Osnovnoi Tank T-80. Yauza, Moscow, 2017.

Pavlov, I.V, Pavlov, M.V, Solyankin, A.G, Zheltov, I. G. Otechestvennye Bronirovannye Mashiny XX Vek. Volume 1 1905-1941. Eksprint, Moscow, 2002.

Pavlov, I.V, Pavlov, M.V, Solyankin, A.G, Zheltov, I. G. Otechestvennye Bronirovannye Mashiny XX Vek. Volume 2 1941-1945. Eksprint, Moscow, 2005.

Pavlov, Ivan. Pavlov, Mikhail. Osnovoil Tank T-80. Yauza. Moscow, 2017.

Prochko, E.I. Artilleriiskie Tyagachi Sovietskoi Armii. Bronekollektsia №5 (62). Modelist Konstruktor, Moscow, 2005.

Service, Robert. A History of Modern Russia From Nicholas II to Putin. Penguin Books, London, 2003.

Shirkorad, Aleksander V. Atomny Schit Rossii. OOO Veche, Moscow, 2017.

Shirkorad, Aleksander V. Entsiklopedya Otechestvennoi Artillerii. Harvest, Minsk, 2000.

Shunkov, Viktor N. Polnaya Entsiklopedya Sovremennogo Vooruzheniya Rossii. AST. Moscow, 2017.

Shunkov, V.N. Polnaya Entsiklopedya Vooruzheniy SSSR 1939-45. Harvest, Minsk, 2010.

Simakov, V.G. Sovremennoye Voennoye Oruzhie Rossii. Eksmo. Moscow, 2014.

Soviet Military Power (US DoD). Various years and editions.

Suvorov, Sergei. Tank T-72 Vchera, Segodnya, Zavtra. Tekhnika Molodezhi, Moscow, 2001

Suvorov, Sergei. Russky Tigr. Yauza, Eksmo, Moscow, 2016.

Svirin, Mikhail. Samokhodki Stalina. Yauza, Eksmo, Moscow, 2008.

Svirin, Mikhail. Stalnoy Kulak Stalina. Yauza, Eksmo, Moscow, 2006.

Ustyantsev, Sergei, Kolmakov, Dmitry. Boevie Mashini Uralvagonzavoda - Tank T-72. Nizhny Tagil, 2004

Voennye Parady Na Krasnoy Ploshadi. Multiple authors. Voennoye Izdatelstvo Soviet MoD Moscow 1980.

Zaloga, Steven J. T-80 Standard Tank. Osprey New Vanguard No152, Oxford, 2009.

Zheleznyakov, Aleksander. 100 Luchshikh Raket SSSR & Rossii. Yauza. Moscow, 2016.

Soviet & Russian Television and Newsreel Sources

RIA Novosti
RT (Russia Today)
Moskovskoye VOKU imeni Verkhovnogo Soveta RS-FSR - Uchilische Na Parade - parade documentaries, various years
Zvezda (Telekanal Zvedza)

Digital Sources

Istoriya Voennykh Paradov na Krasnoy Ploshadi. Krilya Rossii, Moscow, 2013.
Parad na Krasnoy Ploshchadi 1941-45 (DVD) Voenkino Rossii, Moscow, 2003.

Websites

Club.foto.ru
Defence.ru
Kap-yar.ru
Kolesa.ru
Kommersant.ru
Oruzhie.ru
Photosight.ru

Coldwar.org
Gruzovikpress.ru
Kbtomash.com
Kollektsia.ru
Lifeisphoto.ru
News.rambler.ru
Sputnik.by

Glossary

(Russian Terms)

ABTU (АБТУ)	Avtobronetankovoye Upravlenie (Auto-Tank Directorate)	
AMO (АМО)	Avtomobilnoye Moskovskoye Obshchestvo - Moscow Automobile Society - later ZiS, ZiL	
ANIOP (АНИОП)	ANIOP Artillery Proving Grounds (Gorokhovets)	
ArtKom (АртКом ГАУ КА)	Artillery Committee Main Artillery Directorate of the Red Army	
AT-L (АТ-Л)	Artilleriskie Tyagach - Lyegky (Artillery Tractor - Light)	
AT-P	Artilleriskie Tyagach - Polubronirovannye (Artillery Tractor - Semi-Armoured)	
AT-S	Artilleriskie Tyagach - Sredny (Artillery Tractor - Medium)	
AT-T	Artilleriskie Tyagach - Tyazhyely (Artillery Tractor - Heavy)	
BMD (БМД)	Boevaya Mashina Desanta - Airborne Combat Vehicle	
BMP (БМП)	Boevaya Mashina Pekhoty - Infantry combat vehicle	
BRDM (БРДМ)	Bronirovannaya Razvedyvatelnaya Mashina - Armoured Reconnaissance Vehicle	
BTR (БТР)	Bronetransporter - Armoured Personnel Carrier	
ChTZ (ЧТЗ)	Chelyabinsky Tractorny Zavod (Chelyabinsk Tractor - and from 1941-1958 Tank-Plant)	
CPSU	Communist Party of the Soviet Union	
DOSAAF (ДОСААФ)	Dobrovolnoe Obshestvo Sodeistviya Armii,Aviatsii i Floty - Volunteer Society for Cooperation with the Army,Aviation and Navy	
GABTU KA (ГАБТУ КА)	Glavnoye AvtoBronetankovoye Upravlenie KA - Main Auto-Tank Directorate of the Red Army. From 7th December 1942 renamed GBTU KA (ГБТУ КА)	
GBTU KA (ГБТУ КА)	Glavnoye Bronetankovoye Upravlenie KA - Main Armoured Directorate of the Red Army.	
GAU (ГАУ)	Glavnoye Artilleriiskoye Upravlenye - Main Artillery Directorate	
GAZ (ГАЗ)	Gorky Avtomobilny Zavod - GAZ plant (named after Molotov)	
GKO (ГКО)	Gosudarstnenny Komitet Oborony - State Defence Committee of the USSR	
GKOT	Gosudarstvennogo Komiteta Oboronoi Tekhnikie	
GRAU (ГРАУ)	Glavnoye Raketno-Artilleriyskoye Upravlenye - Main Rocket-Artillery Directorate	
GRU (ГРУ)	Glavnoye Razvedovatelnoye Upravlenye - Main Reconnaissance Directorate	
GVKhU (ГВХУ КА)	Glavnoe Voenno-Khimicheskoye Upravlenie Krasnoi Armii - Main Military - Chemical Forces Directorate (of the Red Army)	
KA (КА)	Krasnaya Armya - Red Army (also known as RKKA)	
KB (КБ)	Konstruktorskoye Bureau - Design Bureau	
KGB (КГБ)	Komitet Gosudarstvennoy Besopasnosti - Committee for State Security	
KhPZ (ХПЗ)	Kharkovsky Parovozostroitelny Zavod (Kharkov Steam Locomotive Plant) - Later Plant №183	
LKZ (ЛКЗ)	Leningradsky Kirovsky Zavod (Leningrad Kirov plant)	
LVO (ЛВО)	Leningradsky Voenny Okrug (Leningrad Military District)	
MO (МО)	Ministerstvo-Oborony - Soviet (latterly Russian) Defence Ministry	
MBR (МБР)	Mezhkontinentalnaya Ballisticheskaya Raketa (ICBM)	
MVD (МВД)	Ministerstvo Vnutrennikh Del - Ministry of Internal Affairs (1946-)	
MVO (МВО)	Moskovsky Voenny Okrug - Moscow Military District	
NATI (НАТИ)	Nauchny Avto-Traktorny Institut (Scientific Auto-Tractor Institute)	
NIBT (НИБТ)	Nauchno-Ispytatelny Bronetankovy (Scientific Tank Testing Institute). Kubinka, near Moscow. Evacuated to Kazan in autumn 1941, relocated back to Kubinka in the autumn-winter of 1942.	
NKAP (НКАП)	Narkomat Aviatsionnoy Promyshlennosti - Minsitry of Aviation Industry	
NKO (НКО)	Narodny Kommissariat Oborony - State Defence Committee (Narkomat as person - Kommissar)	
NKO (НКО)	Narkomat Oborony (Soviet/Russian Ministry of Defence)	

NKV (НКВ)	Narodny Kommissariat Vooruzhenya - People's Kommissariat of Armaments
NKVD (НКВД)	Narodny Kommissariat Vnutrennikh Del (People's Commissariat for Internal Affairs) 1934-46
OGPU (ОГПУ)	Obiedenennoye Gosudarstvennoye Politicheskoye Upravlenye (United State Political Directorate)
OKB (ОКБ)	Otdelnoye Konstruktorskoye Bureau - Independent Design Bureau
OTR (ОТР)	Operativno Takticheskaya Raketa (tactical rocket)
OTRK (ОТРК)	Operativno-Takticheskiy Raketny Kompleks (Ground-Ground Tactical Rocket)
PAZ (ПАЗ)	Protivoatomnaya Zaschita - Anti-Atomic (radiation) Protection
PPO (ППО)	Protivopozharnoe Oborudovannie - Anti-Fire Equipment
PU (РУ)	Puskovaya Ustanovka (launch vehicle)
PVO (ПВО)	Protivovozdushnaya Oborona - Air Defence
RGK (РГК)	Reserv Glavnogo Komandovanya (high command reserve)
RKKA (РККА)	Raboche-Krestyanskaya Krasnaya Armiya Workers and Peasants Red Army (Red Army)
RKKVF (РККВФ)	Raboche-Krestyansky Krasny Vozdushny Flot (Workers and Peasants Red Air Fleet)
RPU (РПУ)	Reaktivnaya Puskovaya Ustanovka (rocket launcher system)
RSFSR (РСФСР)	Russian Soviet Federative Socialist Republic (RSFSR)
RSZO (РСЗО)	Reaktivnaya (Raketnaya) Systema Zalpovogo Ognya - Multiple Rocket Launcher System
RVGK (РВГК)	Reserv Verkhovnogo Glavnogo Komandovanya (Supreme High Command Reserve)
RVS (РВС)	Revvoensovet - Revolutsionny Voenny Soviet (Revolutionary Military Council) - formed 1918
RVSN (РВСН)	Raketnye Voyska Strategicheskogo Naznacheniya - Strategic Rocket Forces - formed 1959
RYaN (РЯН)	Raketno Yadernoye Napadenya - Nuclear Rocket Attack
SAU (САУ)	Samokhodnaya Artilleryskaya Ustanovka - Self Propelled Artillery Unit (SAU or SU)
SU (СУ)	Samokhodnaya ArtUstanovka - Self Propelled Artillery Unit
SKB (СКБ)	Spetsialnoye Konstruktorskoe Bureau - Special Design Bureau
SM SSSR (СМ СССР)	Soviet Ministrov SSSR - Council of Ministers of the USSR
SNK (СНК СССР)	Soviet Narodnykh Kommissarov - Council of People's Commissars
SPU (СПУ)	Samokhodnaya Puskovaya Ustanovka (Self Propelled Launch Vehicle)
SSR (ССР)	Soviet Socialist Republic
STZ (СТЗ)	Stalingradsky Traktorny Zavod - Stalingrad Tractor Plant (later VTZ, VgTZ)
TsAGI (ЦАГИ)	Tsentralny Aerogidrodinamichesky Institut - Central Aerodynamic Institute (TsAGI)
TsAMO RF (ЦАМО РФ)	Tsentralny Arkhiv Ministerstva Oborony Rossiskoy Federatsii - Central Archives of the Ministry of Defence of the Russian Federation
TsIK (ЦИК)	Tsentralny Ispolnitelny Komitet - Central Executive Committee (of the USSR)
TsK KPSS i SM SSSR	Central Committee of the Communist Party and Council of Ministers of the Soviet Union
TsVKP(b) (ЦК ВКП(б))	Central Committee of the CPSU(b) - Communist Party (Bolshevik) of the USSR
TBr (ТБр)	Tankovaya Brigada - Tank Brigade
TIZ (ТIЗ)	Taganrog Instrumentalny Zavod (TIZ AM-600 motorcycle)
TOP (ТОП)	Tyagach Obespechenya Paradov - Tractor for Parade Support
TOS (ТОС)	Tyazhelaya Ognemetnaya Systema - heavy flamethrower system
TPK (ТПК)	Transportno-Puskovoy Konteyner (Transport-Launch Container)
TRK (ТРК)	Takticheskiy Raketny Kompleks (Tactical Rocket System)
TTT (ТТТ)	Taktiko-Tekhnicheskye Trebovanya - Tactical Technical Requirements
TU (ТУ)	Transportno-Ustanovochny Agregat - Transporter-Installation Vehicle
TZM (ТЗМ)	Transportno-Zaryazhayuschaya Mashina (transport-reload vehicle)
UMM RKKA (УММ РККА)	Upravlenye Mekhanizatsii i Motorizatsii - Mechanisation and Motorisation Directorate of the Red Army
VAMM (ВАММ)	Voennaya Akademya Mekhanizatsii i Motorizatsii (Military Academy of Mechanisation and Motorisation)
VgTZ (ВгТЗ)	Volgograd (Stalingrad) Tractor Plant - formerly STZ
Voenizdat	State Military Publisher NKO SSSR
VDV (ВДВ)	Vozdushno Desantnye Voiska - Airborne Forces
VKP(b) (ВКП(б))	The Communist Party of the Soviet Union (Bolshevik)
VKS (ВКС)	Vozdushno-Kosmicheskye Sily - Air Space Forces (formed 01.08.15)
VMF (ВМФ)	Voenno-Morskoy Flot (Soviet Navy)
VMS (ВМС)	Voenno-Morskye Sily - Naval Forces (Soviet Navy)
VTZ (ВТЗ)	Volgograd Tractor Plant (later VgTZ)
VVS KA (ВВС КА)	Voenno-Vozdushnye Sily Krasnoy Armii - Red Army Air Force
YaAZ (ЯАЗ)	Yaroslavl Avtomobilny Zavod - Yaroslavl Automobile Plant
ZRK (ЗРК)	Zenitno-Raketny Kompleks - Air Defence Rocket Complex
ZRPK (ЗРПК)	Zenitno-Raketno-Pushechny Kompleks - Air Defence Rocket-Gun Complex
ZRS (ЗРС)	Zenitno-Raketnaya Systema - Air Defence Rocket System
ZSU (ЗСУ)	Zenitnaya Samokhodnaya Ustanovka - Self Propelled Anti-Aircraft Gun

General Glossary

AAG	Anti-Aircraft Gun
APFSDS	Armour Piercing Fin Stabilised Discarding Sabot
ATGM	Anti-Tank Guided Missile
CEP	Circular Error Probability (rocket - generally nuclear weapon - accuracy)
DEFCON	Defence of the Continent (U.S. Government Alert status)
FROG	Free Rocket Over Ground (NATO term for early Soviet OTR tactical rockets)
GS	General Service
GSFG	Group of Soviet Forces Germany
ICBM	Inter-Continental Ballistic Missile
INF	Intermediate Nuclear Forces (treaty)
MAD	Mutually Assured Destruction
MBT	Main Battle Tank
MoD	Ministry of Defence
MRS	Multiple Rocket System
MRBM	Medium Range Ballistic Missile
MRD	Motorised Rifle Division
MRS	Multiple Rocket System
NBC	Nuclear, Biological, Chemical warfare
RAP	Rocket Assisted Projectile
SAM	Surface to Air Missile System
SLBM	Submarine Launched Ballistic Missile
SPAAG	Self Propelled Anti-Aircraft Gun
SPADS	Self Propelled Air Defence System
SPG	Self Propelled Gun
SPH	Self Propelled Howitzer
SPM	Self Propelled Mortar
SRBM	Short Range Ballistic Missile
SSM	Surface to Surface Missile
TEL	Transporter Erector Launcher
US DoD	United States Department of Defence

Soviet Ministries

Soviet ministries were abbreviated to NK (Narodny Kommissariat - People's Commissariat) followed by the responsibility, e.g. NKV (Vooruzhenye - armaments), NKSM (Srednye Mashinostroenye - medium machine building (actually tank production)) etc. The minister was known as the Narkom (Kommissar). Commissariat can be interpreted as Ministry, and Commissar as Minister

NKAP	People's Commissariat of Aviation Industry
NKGK	People's Commissariat of State Control
NKO	People's Commissariat of Defence
NKS	People's Commissariat of Machine Tool Building
NKSM	People's Commissariat of Medium Machine Building
NKSP	People's Commissariat of Steel Production
NKTM	People's Commissariat of Heavy Engineering
NKTP	People's Commissariat of Heavy Production
NKTP	People's Commissariat of Tank Production
NKV	People's Commissariat of Armaments
NKVD	People's Commissariat of Internal Affairs

Soviet Ministries - As written in the original Russian

НКАП Наркомат Авиационной промышленности - People's Commissariat of Aviation Industry - NKAP
НКГК Народный Комиссариат Государственного Контроля - People's Commissariat of State Control - NKGK
НКС Народный Комиссариат Станкостроения - People's Commissariat of Machine Tool Building - NKS
НКСМ Наркомат Среднего Машиностроения - People's Commissariat of Medium Machine Building - NKSM
НКТП Народный Комиссариат Танковой Промышленности - People's Commissariat of Tank Industry - NKTP
НКВ Народный Комиссариат Вооружения - People's Commissariat of Armaments - NKV
НКТМ Наркомат Тяжелого Машиностроения - People's Commissariat of Heavy Machine Building - NKTM
Наркомат (Ministry....)
Народный (People's....)

Russian Terms (in original language)

АБТУ	Автобронетанковое управление (Auto and Armour Directorate)
АНИОП	Артиллерийский научно-исследовательский опытный полигон - Artillery Scientific Experimental Test Range
БТР	Бронетранспортер (Armoured Personnel Carrier)
БТУ	Бронетанковое управление (Tank Directorate)
ГАБТУ	Главное автобронетанковое управление (Main Armoured Directorate)
ГАУ	Главное артиллерийское управление (Main Artillery Directorate)
ГКО	Государственный Комитет Обороны (State Defence Committee)
ГКОТ	Государственный комитет по оборонной технике (State Committee for Defence Equipment)
ГРАУ	Главное ракетно-артиллерийское управление (Main Rocket-Artillery Directorate)
ЗСУ	Зенитная самоходная установка (Self Propelled Anti-Aircraft System)
КА	Красная Армия, Краснознаменная армия (Red Army)
КБМ	Конструкторское бюро машиностроения (Machine Building Design Bureau)
ЛВО	Ленинградский военный округ (Leningrad Military District - LVO)
МВО	Московский военный округ (Moscow Military District - MVO)
МИТ	Московский институт теплотехники (Moscow Institute of Heating Technology) (i.e. rockets)
МО	Министерство обороны (Ministry of Defence)
НКВД	Народный комиссариат внутренних дел (NKVD and other internal security forces)
НКО	Народный комиссариат Обороны (State Defence Committee)
ПВО	Противовоздушная оборона (Air Defence Forces)
ПТУР	Противотанковая управляемая ракета (Anti-Tank Guided Rocket)
ПУ	Пусковая установка (Launch System)
ПУАЗО	Прибор Управления Артиллерийским Зенитным Огнём (Anti-Aircraft Gun Fire Control System)
РГК	Резерв Главного Командования (Main Command Reserve)
РВГК	Резерв Верховного Главного Командования (Main Higher Command Reserve)
РВСН	Ракетные войска стратегического назначения (Strategic Rocket Forces)
РККА	Рабоче-крестьянская Красная Армия (Workers and Peasants Red Army)
РККВФ	Рабоче-крестьянский красный воздушный флот (Workers & Peasants Red Air Fleet)
РСЗО	Реактивная система залпового огня (Reactive Rocket System - MRS)
САУ	Самоходная артиллерийская установка (Self Propelled Artillery Unit)
СВГК	Ставка Верховного Главного Командования (High Command)
СКБ	Специальное конструкторское бюро (Special Design Bureau)
СПУ	Самоходная пусковая установка (Self Propelled Launch System)
СТЗ	Сталинградский тракторный завод (Stalingrad Tractor Plant)
ТЗМ	Транспортно-заряжающая машина (Transport-Reload Vehicle)
ТТТ	Тактико-технические требования (Tactical Technical Requirements)
ТТХ	Тактико-технические характеристики (Tactical Technical Characteristics)
УММ	Управление механизации и моторизации РККА (Mechanisation and Motorisation Directorate)
УТТХ	Улучшенные тактико-технические характеристики (Improved Tactical-Technical Characteristics)

Acknowledgements

The Soviet Army on Parade 1946-1991, as with the first volume entitled The Red Army on Parade 1917-1945, could not have been written or adequately illustrated without the assistance of many individuals. The author would like to in particular thank Andrey Aksenov, Mikhail Baryatinsky, Aleksandr Koshavtsev, Yuri Pasholok, Vladimir Nikitin, Nikolai Polikarpov, Sergei Popsuevich, Mikhail Svirin, Steven J. Zaloga and Igor Zheltov for their assistance in compiling the material used in this book, and for the myriad corrections made relating to the Soviet and modern designations. The material for this volume was collected over a period of many years, and as is always the case with such publications, the enthusiasm of individuals willing to help is remembered long after the material has been located or an obscure question answered.

The author would also like to thank the Russian Ministry of Defence for releasing photographic material used in all three volumes of this book, without which the result would be far less complete. Thanks also go to Roger Waters for permission to use his song lyrics, which defined for many the era in which the author grew up in a world which was largely at peace without fear of major international conflict.

Photographic Archives and Credits

AA	Andrey Aksenov	NII-38 Institute Kubinka, Russian Federation
AK	Aleksandr Koshavtsev	RGAKFD -Rossisky Gosudarstvenny Arkhiv Kino-Foto Dokumentov (Russian State Archive of Cine and Film Documents)
AM	Aleksei Mikheev	Russian Ministry of Defence (MO)
IZ	Igor Zheltov	TsAMO RF - Central Archives of the Ministry of Defence of the Russian Federation
MB	Mikhail Baryatinsky	TsFFKA - Tsentralny Foto Fonodokumentov (Arkhiv) Krasny Armii (Central Cine and Photo Archive of the Red Army)
SP	Sergei Popsuevich	TsGAFF - Tsentralny Gosudarstvenny Arkhiv Foto Fonodokumentov (Central State Archive of Photographic Documents)
SZ	Steven Zaloga	Tank Museum, Bovington, UK (TM)
VK	Viktor Kulikov	TASS (ITAR-TASS), Russian Federation
YP	Yuri Pasholok	Tank Museum, Bovington, Dorset, Great Britain

Note on Russian State Archive records

The dates shown for specific vehicles illustrated in this book have generally been taken from the archival notes appended to the original photographs, where available. However, these original records are not always entirely accurate particularly with regard to the date. Original Russian archive photographs were often filed years after the parade concerned, and in some cases the date of the archive being raised is conflated with the date the photograph was taken, particularly in early years such as 1946 where the archives from 1st May and "Tankman's Day" on 9th September are conflated. Many original data cards were also removed from the archives during the 1990s and the original text accompanying negative archives lost. Available recorded film footage is also sometimes conflated, with the same background being shown in footage supposedly of different years, and is often only a snapshot of vehicles paraded on any given day. The author has cross-referenced the photograph material presented in this book as far as possible from the occasionally conflated original sources, but there will undoubtedly be some errors with regard to exact parade years as shown, for which the author bears full responsibility. The archives from some years are also more prolific than from others, and accordingly some photographs have been moved to balance the chapter content, which is noted in the text where appropriate.

Use of the term "Soviet Premier"

The use of the term "Soviet Premier" as leader of the Soviet Union is not entirely correct either historically or linguistically. Depending on the dateline, the "Premier" might for-instance officially be the Chairman of the Communist Party of the Soviet Union, but in that position also acting as leader of the country. Kruschchev, Brezhnev and Kosygin were all "Premiers" at varying times while having different and changing titles, with the triad that operated in the early Brezhnev years being particularly complex. The use of "Premier" rather than the often long-winded formal Soviet titles has been done to shorten the description for ease of reading for English speaking readers.

Grammar Nuances

Some minor liberties have been taken with grammar rules and Russian transliteration in the writing of this book. With regard to the constantly changing rules of capitalisation, the term "20th Century" has been written as a number and capitalised rather than being written out as "twentieth century" in order to minimise the text.

The Russian word ending "ogo" is pronounced "ovo" which is known to Russian speakers. It is translated in this book as formally written rather than as pronounced. Russian cannot always be directly translated into English and there are innumerable nuances such as whether for-instance the name Sergey is written in English as Sergey or Sergei, both of which are correct. Names have been translated as ending in "ey" rather than "ei" for consistency in the main text.

About the Author

James Kinnear was born in Aberdeen in Great Britain in 1959 and graduated with an MA (Hons) from Aberdeen University in 1982. He has researched the topic of Soviet and Russian military hardware since his first visit to the enigmatic and mysterious Soviet Union as a young teenager in 1973. James subsequently lived and worked in the post-Soviet Russian Federation and the other states of the former Soviet Union throughout the entire period of post-Soviet "stability" - the decades between the Soviet Union being considered a military threat and the Russian Federation finding itself again categorized as such for political purposes in recent history.

James has written hundreds of articles on Soviet and Russian military technology after having taken a more long-term interest than most in the subject matter of the blurry British and American sourced images of Soviet military equipment used for training purposes during British military service.

This series of books on Russian, Soviet, and now again Russian military parades on Moscow's Red Square is the culmination of many years of collecting material on a subject which, despite it being a primary source for foreign intelligence, and a relatively public one at that, has never been covered in depth as a dedicated subject either in the Russian Federation or abroad.

It is hoped that the reader will find the content of this second volume in a three volume series both an interesting and enlightening window on what is not only the 100 year anniversary of the start of military parades on Moscow's Red Square and in other former Soviet cities; but is also by association a window on 100 years of the military history of a state which always had at its centre what is today the Russian Federation.

James has published books on Soviet military technology with Barbarossa, Canfora, Darlington, Osprey and Tankograd. He is also a formal contributor to IHS Jane's defence yearbooks.

With special thanks to
The Russian Ministry of Defence
The Kommendatura of the Kremlin
The Russian Federal Security Service (FSB)

The author is indebted to the patience and assistance of his family with regard to his esoteric interests,
in particular Elizabeth and Katya for their proof reading and editing assistance.